Protecting Women

Recovering the rarely heard voices of immigrant soldiers, Indigenous women, and Mexican women alongside officer's narratives, this book richly portrays the US Army at war in Florida and Mexico. Its unique focus on interactions between the army and local women uncovers army culture's gendered foundations. Countering an almost exclusively officer-focused historiography, it amasses enlisted men's accounts to describe what life was like for ordinary soldiers, shows how enlisted men participated in and shaped army culture, and demonstrates how officers wrote their reports to achieve specific ends. By piecing together scattered mentions of women from personal writings, military and civilian newspapers, court-martial proceedings, and official records, it also shows the wide spectrum of Indigenous and Mexican women's wartime activities. Army authors erased or reframed evidence of women's combatancy to bolster their status as women's protectors, but undoing this process reveals that even in the most understudied conflicts, evidence exists to tell women's stories.

Justine Meberg received her PhD from Columbia University, where she won the Bancroft Dissertation Award.

Protecting Women

US Army Culture in the Second US–Seminole War and the US–Mexican War

JUSTINE MEBERG

Shaftesbury Road, Cambridge CB2 8EA, United Kingdom

One Liberty Plaza, 20th Floor, New York, NY 10006, USA

477 Williamstown Road, Port Melbourne, VIC 3207, Australia

314–321, 3rd Floor, Plot 3, Splendor Forum, Jasola District Centre,
New Delhi – 110025, India

103 Penang Road, #05–06/07, Visioncrest Commercial, Singapore 238467

Cambridge University Press is part of Cambridge University Press & Assessment,
a department of the University of Cambridge.

We share the University's mission to contribute to society through the pursuit of
education, learning and research at the highest international levels of excellence.

www.cambridge.org
Information on this title: www.cambridge.org/9781009647281
DOI: 10.1017/9781009647304

© Justine Meberg 2026

This publication is in copyright. Subject to statutory exception and to the provisions
of relevant collective licensing agreements, no reproduction of any part may take
place without the written permission of Cambridge University Press & Assessment.

When citing this work, please include a reference to the DOI 10.1017/9781009647304

First published 2026

A catalogue record for this publication is available from the British Library

*A Cataloging-in-Publication data record for this book is available from the
Library of Congress*

ISBN 978-1-009-64726-7 Hardback
ISBN 978-1-009-64728-1 Paperback

Cambridge University Press & Assessment has no responsibility for the persistence
or accuracy of URLs for external or third-party internet websites referred to in this
publication and does not guarantee that any content on such websites is, or will
remain, accurate or appropriate.

For EU product safety concerns, contact us at Calle de José Abascal, 56, 1°, 28003
Madrid, Spain, or email eugpsr@cambridge.org

For my soldiers

Contents

List of Figures	*page* ix
List of Maps	xi
Acknowledgments	xiii
Introduction: Army Paternalists, Enemy Women, and US Army Culture in Wartime Florida and Mexico, 1835–1848	1
PART I WAR IN FLORIDA	31
1 The Dilemma of Army Cohesion: West Point Officers, Immigrant Soldiers, and the Beginnings of an Army Culture, 1802–1842	34
2 Developing a Logic of Protection: Army Debates on the Treatment of Seminole Women in Florida, 1835–1842	70
3 "Find Where Their Women Are": The US Army's Pursuit of Seminole Women, 1835–1842	106
PART II WAR IN MEXICO	143
4 Rescuing the Enemy: Mexican Women and the US Army's Transformation in Northern Mexico, 1846–1847	147
5 A Perfect Sacrifice: The Unexplored Rape Case That Radically Expanded Military Justice, 1847	183
6 Buying Benevolence: Contested Legitimacy during the US Occupation of Mexico, 1847	217

7 "They Were Our Best Friends": Army Misunderstandings
   of Mexican Women's Wartime Activities, 1847–1848   256
  Conclusion: Beyond Men's Military History   294

Bibliography   303
Index   327

Figures

0.1 Portrait of Alexander Macomb, painting by Thomas Sully, 1829	*page* 18
0.2 Portrait of Winfield Scott, painting by Robert Weir, 1856	19
4.1 "Pimo Village with a group of Indians," watercolor by Samuel Chamberlain, circa 1861	160
4.2 "Comanches on the War Path," watercolor by Samuel Chamberlain, circa 1861	160
5.1 Photograph, detail from military commission, case number EE-363, 1847	184
6.1 "Major Sherman, trusses a Guard, and bastes a wounded patriot," watercolor by Samuel Chamberlain, circa 1861	243
6.2 "Massacre of the Cave," watercolor by Samuel Chamberlain, circa 1861	249
7.1 "Street fighting in the 'Calle del Iturbide,' 'Capella Santa Maria,' Monterey," watercolor by Samuel Chamberlain, circa 1861	260
7.2 "Grande Plaza of Monterey as seen from the top of the Post Office," watercolor by Samuel Chamberlain, circa 1861	261
7.3 "The Great Western as Landlady," watercolor by Samuel Chamberlain, circa 1861	265
7.4 "A Close Shave," watercolor by Samuel Chamberlain, circa 1861	284
7.5 "El Tuerto and His Peon Wife," watercolor by Samuel Chamberlain, circa 1861	285

7.6 "La Belle Carmeleita," watercolor by Samuel Chamberlain,
circa 1861 286
7.7 "Fiends and Fireworks, Saturnalian orgies in the Grand Plaza
of Saltillo to Commemorate Peace," watercolor by Samuel
Chamberlain, circa 1861 289

Maps

1 The New York of Officers and Enlisted Men — *page* 33
2 Florida and the Second US–Seminole War — 69
3 The War in Northern Mexico — 145
4 Greater Santa Fe — 146
5 The Case of Isaac Kirk in Veracruz — 182
6 The US Occupation of Mexico — 216
7 Mexico and the Treaty of Guadalupe Hidalgo — 293

Acknowledgments

If there is any brilliance in these pages, I credit my beloved advisor Stephanie McCurry with inspiring it. I will always be profoundly grateful for her intellect and mentorship. Karl Jacoby's insights and unflagging kindness made this project (and me) better. Drew Lipman gave his time and conversation and helped me to envision the historian I could become. Lou Roberts provided feedback that greatly improved the quality of my analysis. Sam Watson put his terrifyingly encyclopedic knowledge of the early army at my disposal, and enthusiastically encouraged me to challenge orthodoxy. Zach Fry and Benjamin Schneider read portions of this project and offered extremely useful comments.

In a full circle moment, Peter Guardino encouraged this project in its earliest form during my first year at grad school, and years later served as a reader for this manuscript. I thank him for his support and useful comments. I also thank the second reviewer and hope I did justice to their feedback. From Columbia, many brilliant peers sharpened my thinking. I especially thank Brooks Swett, Yoav Hamdani, and Emily Hawk. I thank Gregory Tomlin, who first helped me down this path, and Victoria Phillips, who commented on everything from my application essay to this manuscript. I thank Martin Walsh, who first set my heart beating for history. I thank two excellent administrators: Lawino Lurum at Columbia and Krista Hennen at West Point. I thank the West Point Department of History, West Point Museum, and the USMA Library and Archives & Special Collections. Curator of Art Marlana Cook provided expertise and high-resolution scans of Samuel Chamberlain's journal. Jeffrey Goldberg created wonderful maps.

I value the cadets I got to teach and thank them for engaging in interesting conversations. I am an appreciative recipient of the General Omar N. Bradley Fellowship in Military History, which funded much of my archival research. For inspiration, advice, and support, I thank Gail Yoshitani, Bryan Gibby, Seanegan Sculley, Ray and Mindy Kimball, David Frey, Rory McGovern, Brian Drohan, David Krueger, Devon Collins, Stephen Morillo, Denis and Kate Alfin, Kevin Malmquist, Louisa Koebrich, Eric and Annie Muirhead, Mak Campbell, Wes Moerbe, Maura Kohl, Joseph Babb, and Michael Diaz.

From my time in Korea, many encouraged me to finish this project and took great pride in my academic work, especially Kurt Connell. I appreciate Anja Zapla, Pedro Eitz Ferrer, Ari Quintana, Victoria Wadsworth, and Denise Nemeth, old friends, and current D&D players. Military life makes one itinerant. Though time brings us together or apart, I appreciate all the army buddies who made life shine over the years, especially Adrienne Rolle, Jen Million, Sam O'Rourke, Stephanie Lazo Kibbe, Sarah Naletelich, Nicola Rathbun, Jessica Borries, and Cecili Chadwick.

I thank the extended Rodgers, Latona, Meberg, Rodriguez, Garcia, and Serrano clans for decades of unwavering support, especially Desiree Dickey, Valerie Hankins, and Raul Serrano. My grandmother Roberta Stefanik is a keen researcher and intrepid traveler who inspires me more than she knows. My grandmother Patricia Simpson died during the pandemic. We sent each other many books over the years. I wish I could have sent her mine. My mother Gail Hillsgrove is the world's best grandmother and my finest teacher. My father James Rodgers shares my soul and has encouraged me in many ways. No one surpasses my stepmother Maria Alejandra Pérez in kindness or generosity of spirit.

When we moved to New York, my son Coulter and I shared a big first day of school, I at Columbia and he at preschool. He is now a kind and curious sixth-grader, an avid reader, a player of games, and a reluctant entertainer of his little sister. Alice is precisely the same age as this project. I began graduate school and her third trimester simultaneously, and she was born just as my concept for the book took shape. When I completed comps, I came home to make her first birthday cake. When she saw me reading volume after volume in the throes of research, she piled up baby books in her crib and slept on top of them, a dragon guarding her hoard. I hope this project contains some of her bold creativity.

Sean Meberg and I have been together our entire sentient lives. We wedded a respectable three days after graduating from West Point, aged twenty-two and twenty-one, clutching officer's commissions in one hand and marriage licenses in the other. We have seen each other from every possible angle – many irredeemably unglamorous – yet we have grown together. This is love. In writing this, my thoughts have often drifted to my soldiers. I have gained a deeper appreciation for the challenges of enlisted life and will carry that with me always. This book is for you.

Introduction

Army Paternalists, Enemy Women, and US Army Culture in Wartime Florida and Mexico, 1835–1848

In January of 1838, as the Second US–Seminole War dragged on in Florida, a Seminole woman led a mixed detachment of US soldiers, sailors, and marines into a devastating ambush. The troops had emerged from the Everglades near Jupiter inlet, the Loxahatchee River's coastal mouth on the southeastern coast of Florida, to find a "fresh trail" that led to her as she watched over a herd of livestock. She agreed to guide them to the Seminole groups camped several miles away and took them down a wide trail through the open country until they reached the edge of a cypress swamp, full of vegetation that offered ample cover and concealment for her waiting compatriots. From here, the Seminole party could attack from the relative safety of the trees, while the troops remained easy targets, unprotected in the open. Afterward, the Seminole fighters knew they could retreat into the swamp, where their enemy would be disinclined to follow. Here, at the border of field and forest, they sprang their ambush and inflicted heavy casualties. US Navy Lieutenant Levi Powell, the officer in command, reported that his losses amounted to twenty-seven, with twenty-two wounded and five killed, including most of the officers, out of the eighty or more men he brought. Yet none of these embarrassing details, least of all the woman's successful deception, appeared in the army's final report.[1]

---

[1] Niles, *Niles' National Register*, 1838, 53:388. Fifth Series, No. 25, Vol. III, February 17, 1838, "Florida – Official, Camp Pierce, on Indian River," report from Lieutenant Levi Powell to Commodore Dallas, dated January 17, 1838. Reprinted in Homans, *Army and Navy Chronicle*, 1838, 6:135. Vol. VI, No. 8, February 22, 1838. Historian of the Second Seminole War, John Mahon, reports that "the human cost [to Powell] was high: two soldiers, two sailors, and Naval Surgeon Dr. Frederick Leitner killed, and fifteen wounded."

In fact, the official report erased her from the historical record. General Thomas Jesup, the officer in command of US troops, submitted it to the Secretary of War, Joel R. Poinsett. In his letter, Jesup observed that Powell's detachment

> landed at the head of one of the branches of Jupiter River; fell in with and attacked a body of Indians, and after a most gallant effort, was overpowered by their numbers, and compelled to retreat with the loss of several officers and men killed and wounded. He killed three Indians and a negro [a Black Seminole] and made one prisoner.

Jesup had sent Powell to lead a special joint force consisting of eighty-five sailors, two artillery companies operating as infantry, and one company of volunteer infantry. Their mission was to penetrate the Everglades and expel the Seminole people.[2] Jesup's report cast Powell as the primary actor. It was Powell, according to Jesup, who found the Seminole warriors and initiated an attack. To conjure a battle out of an ambush, Jesup had to erase the woman.

When General Jesup wrote his report to the Secretary of War, he rewrote history – her victory became Powell's Battle.[3] Jesup penned his account from the perspective of a general seeking to prove that his campaign was a successful one. While he may not have convinced posterity of his military brilliance, he successfully removed the woman from history and the ambush from the war. Until now, no other account of this incident in the more than 180 years has characterized what happened to

---

Mahon, *History of the Second Seminole War*, 232. Mahon used the following sources: Motte, *Journey into Wilderness*, 168, 182–84; Powell to Jesup, Adjutant General Letters Received. For the early US Navy, see: Karsten, *The Naval Aristocracy*; Leeman, *The Long Road to Annapolis*. The Seminole people had long ago emerged from Muscogee society, an ethnic minority who spoke a Hichiti language and settled in Florida during the 1700s. Shire, *The Threshold of Manifest Destiny*, 6; Snyder, *Slavery in Indian Country*, 214; Wright, *Creeks & Seminoles*, 16.

[2] "Negro" is a derogatory term and appears only in quotation. Niles, *Niles' National Register*, 1839, 55:30, Report acknowledged as received by Poinsett on July 7, 1838. Also in: Sprague, *The Origin, Progress, and Conclusion of the Florida War*, 190. Mahon, *History of the Second Seminole War*, 219–20. Mahon's *History of the Second Seminole War*, initially published in 1967, was the first history of the war since army officer John Sprague, who served in Florida during the war and published *The Origin, Progress, and Conclusion of the Florida War* in 1848. The century-long gap between these monographs demonstrates how understudied the conflict remains. Ibid., Preface; Sprague, Brevet Captain, Eighth Regiment US Infantry, *The Origin, Progress, and Conclusion of the Florida War*. The most recent book argues that the US shrouded the war in a "legitimating illusion" to veil settler colonialism. Monaco, *The Second Seminole War and the Limits of American Aggression*, 7, 64.

[3] For example, see the following map: Motte, *Journey into Wilderness*, 179.

Powell's detachment on 15 January 1838 as a deliberate ambush. That is partly because it was one short moment in a long and chronically understudied war. But it is also true that military historians of the Jacksonian era have given short shrift to Indigenous women's wartime activities and have treated reports like Jesup's as accepted fact rather than constructed narratives framed by army culture's assumptions and intents.

Powell's initial report to his superior included more of the truth. While he noted the woman's presence, he failed to consider her motives or potential to act as an enemy. To Powell, she was a "guide," an asset. He wrote that after landing,

we found a fresh trail, which, in following, led us to a herd of cattle and horses; amongst these, we captured a squaw. The woman, on being questioned, told us of several parties of Indians camped in the neighborhood, we took her as a guide, and after a march of five miles struck a large beaten trail at the head of a cypress swamp; at the same instant we heard the war-whoop before us.

He later said, "the enemy was in greater force than we expected and outnumbered our party so much as to cover our flanks, the squaw whom we brought off says one hundred" and "the officers were all shot at the head of their divisions."[4]

The versions of the event published in early 1838, initially in the *Savannah Georgian* and quickly reprinted in publications like *Niles National Register* and the *Army and Navy Chronicle*, described how Powell

with about eighty men, including regulars, landed at Jupiter Inlet and took a squaw; she told them she would carry them where the Indians were encamped, which was about seven miles off. Lieutenant P. attacked them, the Indians returned the fire with a great deal of spirit, when the sailors ran, and had it not been for the artillery, they would all have been cut to pieces. All the officers were wounded.

A fellow officer noted that after the marines fled, the artillerymen covered their retreat. He concluded that the engagement "was a complete defeat" for Powell. In addition to taking heavy casualties, the troops left behind two boats, including one containing a keg of powder and a box of cartridges, giving the Seminole group valuable resources to continue the fight. Though Seminole warriors attacked in strength, struck down Powell's detachment in droves, and nearly surrounded the US servicemen,

---

[4] "Squaw" is a derogatory term and appears only in quotations. Niles, *Niles' National Register*, 1838, 53:388; Homans, *Army and Navy Chronicle*, 1838, 6:135.

these authors categorically insisted that the officers led a charge "across a deep swamp in a handsome manner," and gallantly "attacked" the enemy. Their writings reveal a "production of specific narratives" that shaped the making of history, a process that at once silenced women and amplified officers' pens.[5]

Methodologically, this book delineates the hazy outlines of women like this one, whom army officers only ever hastily sketched. Doing so begins to clarify not only the historical subject but also the writers themselves, the men who wrote army history. The ways officers and enlisted men wrote about women, understood or failed to understand women's combatancy, and described how they believed men and women should act, mattered because they gave form to army culture. In reading army records, one must find the author's hand. Army discourse about women did more than describe women. It gave form to military men.

The officers caught in the ambush had all the pieces of the story, but none could admit that they were a woman's enemy, or that a woman led them into harm. Authors of reports clung to the belief that she freely offered her services. They wanted to believe that Seminole women wanted to help. Historians of the war, like John Mahon, did caveat that she may not have done so willingly. He argued that she was "captured and forced to act as guide." Still, Mahon remained blind to her potential combatancy. Men who interpreted this event came, always, to one of two conclusions. Either the US forced her to guide them, or she "offered to guide [Powell] to the place where the Indians were."[6] But there was a third prospect: she led them into a trap. Why were neither the participants then nor the historians since able to recognize that possibility?

This project focuses on the US Army and enemy women's interactions in the Second US–Seminole War of 1835–1842 and the US–Mexican War of 1846–1848 to explore how men's beliefs about women in war shaped army culture. Military histories of this era and these conflicts that exclude source material about women give the impression that there

---

[5] Niles, *Niles' National Register*, 1838, 53:351, Fifth Series, No. 23, Vol. III, February 3, 1838, "From Florida"; Homans, *Army and Navy Chronicle*, 1838, 6:93–94, Vol. VI, No. 6, February 8, 1838; Michel-Rolph Trouillot, *Silencing the Past: Power and the Production of History* (Boston: Beacon Press, 1995), 25.

[6] Kirby, *Kirby Papers*, January 16, 1838; Niles, *Niles' National Register*, 1838, 53: Savannah Georgia, January 28, 1838, page 353; excerpted letter from an officer to the editors of the *Savannah Georgian*, dated near Indian River Inlet, January 18, 1838, 383; Camp Pierce, on Indian River, Lieutenant L. M. Powell to Commodore Dallas, January 17, 1838, page 388; Mahon, *History of the Second Seminole War*, 232.

exist insufficient primary sources to tell women's stories. This is not so. Although there are significant silences in the archive – evidence of Black women's experiences in these conflicts is exceedingly rare – and while Seminole women are certainly more challenging archival subjects than, for instance, officers' wives, there exists a substantial body of primary sources, especially material written by soldiers (often officers though sometimes enlisted men) that addresses them.[7] This approach seeks a nuanced portrayal of army culture by beginning with the assumption that what soldiers had to say about enemy women was important – not ornamental or sentimental, but elemental. This type of scholarly attention to discourse about women, the prototypical outsiders in histories of war, can help historians consider the discursive processes at work in army documents.

Even though soldiers often erased women from official narratives, such encounters prompted them to confront their beliefs about women and war. It was easy for them to label white US women on the home front as innocent and ignorant of war. But the women of a non-white, non-US enemy people encountered during wartime forced the army to reckon with the complex and contradictory category of enemy women. To understand that population, army officers first sought formal answers in the laws of war as written by eighteenth-century jurist Emerich de Vattel, whom the army regulations crafted by General Winfield Scott closely followed.[8] When applied to militaries and warfare, Euro-American jurists labeled these doctrines not as international law but as a specific subset, the laws of war. Rather than binding laws, the term referred to an evolving set of Euro-American conventions derived from a predominantly European body of writing. As historian Deborah Rosen shows, the US emerged from the First US–Seminole War of 1816–1818 with new ideas, asserting "a selectively applicable international law" that conferred rights to white people, while limiting those of Indigenous and Black persons. This "blatant legal line-drawing based on race and culture helped solidify an exclusionary vision" in the laws of war.[9] Within this climate of changing US norms, Scott's guidelines attempted to answer

---

[7] Marisa Fuentes shows how to work against "the machinations of archival power" through "a methodology that purposely subverts the overdetermining power of colonial discourses" to reveal how violent white supremacy limited what one can know about Black women in colonial Bridgetown, Barbados. Fuentes, *Dispossessed Lives*, 1, 4–5.
[8] Vattel, *Law of Nations*; Halleck, *International Law*, 1861; Scott, *General Regulations for the Army*, 1825.
[9] Rosen, *Border Law*, 6.

the thorny question of who could be made a prisoner of war, who was a combatant, whether (or when) an army could target civilians and civilian property, and when an army may pursue an exemption to the established laws of war.

Women's separation from war was foundational to all of these because of the embedded assumption that even if a woman was an enemy, she remained "the essential noncombatant."[10] Years before he wrote the massively influential Lieber's Code during the Civil War, Francis Lieber formulated perhaps the most straightforward explanation for why women's incapacity to make war must hold. During the Second US–Seminole War in 1838, he wrote that "the woman cannot defend the state: if she were physically able to do it, she would necessarily lose her peculiar character as woman, and thus a necessary element of civilization would be extinguished." For Lieber, women's innocence was a foundational aspect of society. He continued, "here, too, emergencies may make exceptions – exceptions of the noblest and proudest kind; but should they cease to form exceptions, a subversion of the whole moral order of things would be the consequence."[11] Lieber insisted on women's separation from war.

Much as the laws of war allowed arbiters of army culture in this era to claim that they were building their institution on the purportedly stable terrain of law, discourse about women provided "a reliable foundation of other hierarchies allegedly based on natural and bodily difference," especially hierarchies of military masculinity. Yet, as Elena Schneider reminds us, "neither empires nor imperial subjects were stable categories." Interactions with enemy women shaped imperialist policies crafted by US political leaders and wielded against Florida and Mexico. Such interactions also shaped a kind of internal imperialism within the army.

---

[10] McCurry, "Enemy Women and the Laws of War in the American Civil War," 669. Vattel writes, "women, children, feeble old men, and sick persons, come under the description of enemies," but they are "enemies who make no resistance; and consequently we have no right to maltreat their persons or use any violence against them, much less to take away their lives. This is so plain a maxim of justice and humanity that at present every nation in the least degree civilized acquiesces in it." Vattel, *Law of Nations*, 351. Book III, Chapter VIII, Paragraph 145.

[11] Lieber, *Manual of Political Ethics*, 2:125. If, in contrast, women sullied their innocence by taking up arms, Halleck (writing after his service in Mexico) echoed Vattel to describe how the attacking army could subject women to "the common fate of military men, and sometimes to a still harsher treatment" such that if women "so far forget" their sex "as to take up arms, or to incite others to do so, they are no longer exempted from the rights of war, although always within the rules of humanity, honor and chivalry." Halleck, *International Law*, 1878, 1:428. Vattel, *Law of Nations*, 351. Book III, Chapter VIII, Paragraph 145.

In the Jacksonian era, army discourse about, and interactions with, enemy women molded a paternalistic hierarchy that also affirmed officers' naturalized dominance over their soldiers. Studying the experiences of those whom the military deemed enemy women, including in the context of intimate relationships, can illuminate the "structures of domination" that produced and changed army culture.[12]

Paternalism, a system where those with power claimed to control and care for those without it, came to pervade army culture partly because of its broad utility. Eugene Genovese notes that there are different variants of paternalism in different "historical settings," each distinct even as each "defines relations of superordination and subordination," a "prevailing ethos" that "increases as the members of the community accept – or feel compelled to accept – these relations as legitimate." Army paternalism was not synonymous with Genovese's Old South variant, which primarily shaped relations between enslavers and the enslaved (rather than relations between free persons of different military ranks, as in the army), but it unfolded from within the same slaveholding republic. Like Southern paternalism, army paternalism "grew out of the necessity to discipline and morally justify a system of exploitation." While it encouraged "kindness and affection," it also "encouraged cruelty and hatred."[13] Moreover, most officers had some direct experience of commanding enslaved labor.

Leveraging a random sampling technique, Historian Yoav Hamdani's analysis of military pay records shows that between 1816 and 1861, over three-quarters of officers held enslaved servants at some point in their careers. The Military Peace Establishment Act of 1802 which created the military academy at West Point and institutionalized the presence of army laundresses also allotted one additional ration to officers for "one servant, not a soldier of the line." Then in 1816, major postwar reforms prohibited officers from using soldiers as servants, authorizing additional subsidies so that officers could hire civilian servants instead. Many officers chose to maximize their profits by hiring enslaved labor and keeping the additional funds. This bureaucratic process racialized servitude, carving out a distinct identity for soldiers as white men while also equating Black with servant, a term that became a euphemism for slavery. Within the US "slaveholding republic," the regular army was a "slaveholding institution" that incentivized officers to participate in slavery. Also,

---

[12] McCurry, *Women's War*, 13; Schneider, *The Occupation of Havana*, 3; Stoler, *Haunted by Empire*, 13.
[13] Genovese, *Roll, Jordan, Roll*, 4, 6.

US politicians who controlled the US Army consistently used it against Native groups. Army culture thus emerged from a uniquely Jacksonian context characterized by rapid territorial conquest, expelling Indigenous societies, and expanding slavery.[14]

Within the army, although soldiering was exclusively for white men, army officers used the tools of enslavers – including physical punishment and religious instruction – to control enlisted men. Officers appealed to Christianity to pacify soldiers and naturalize submission to patriarchal officers, as children obey fathers and enslaved people obey masters. More frequently, they punished. Enslavers, often through white overseers, imposed horrific violence on enslaved people. They whipped, beat, confined, chained, tortured, and hanged. Officers sentenced soldiers to punishments including lashes, imprisonment, extended periods in stressful positions, months of hard labor with a ball and chain, branding with the letter "D" for a deserter, and hanging. They often directed sergeants to administer this violence. It is difficult to imagine these punishments imposed on another group of white men in Jacksonian America.[15]

Punishment supported a hierarchical order that brought order to the complex realities of wartime Florida. Historian Stephanie McCurry notes that in the South Carolina Low Country, households were spatial and social units, "organizing the majority of the population – slaves of both sexes and all ages and free women and children – in relations of legal and customary dependency" to a male head.[16] Army officers, too, leveraged race and gender-based notions of dependency, not to define autonomous households but to assert power over their army family. An officer's army family encompassed all those they controlled. For a captain in Florida, that meant his wife and children, his lieutenants, his soldiers, his company's laundress, any other family members that accompanied his unit, his servants (free and enslaved), and any Indigenous guides or auxiliaries assigned to him. Each officer led his own army family as a father, and each member's position in the family shaped their obligations.

In an addition that complemented this US context, regular officers also sometimes understood themselves as inheritors of British and Continental

---

[14] Baptist, *The Half Has Never Been Told*, 362–63; "Military Peace Establishment Act of 1802"; Hamdani, "The Slaveholding Army," Abstract, 1–2, 6, 11, 27.

[15] Genovese, *Roll, Jordan, Roll*, 162–63; Johnson, *River of Dark Dreams: Slavery and Empire in the Cotton Kingdom*, 168–69, 174–75; "Court-Martial Case Files, 1809–1894," n.d.; McGrath, "An Army of Working-Men," 184.

[16] McCurry, *Masters of Small Worlds: Yeoman Households, Gender Relations, and the Antebellum South Carolina Low Country*, 6.

military traditions. General Winfield Scott, author of the army's *General Regulations* and its Commanding General from 1841 to 1861, maintained deep ties across the Atlantic. He toured Europe in 1815, arriving in England soon after Napoleon's defeat at Waterloo and hastening across the channel to see the great allied armies occupying France. Scott met many leading European military thinkers, and throughout this career drew on European precedents to shape the emerging US Army.[17]

In his study of English paternalism in the Victorian Era's early years, David Roberts characterizes an outlook that matched the worldview of officers like Scott. Roberts argues that "in any definition of the paternalist social outlook three aspects must be considered: paternalism's basic assumption about the framework of society; its doctrines concerning the duties of the wealthy, privileged, and powerful; and the many and various attitudes which, while not essential to the paternalist outlook, are often associated with it." Robert emphasizes that "at the heart of a paternalist's hierarchical outlook is a strong sense of the value of dependency, a sense that could not exist without those who are dependent having an unquestioned respect for their betters." Benevolence could be a prominent trapping of paternalism, but at its center stood the "obligation to rule firmly and to guide and superintend."[18]

Officers combined these elements – a preference for a rigid and almost aristocratic hierarchy of officers over enlisted men, alongside the notion that harsh paternalistic discipline was an expression of loving care. Indeed, paternalistic officers claimed an ethic of care to justify immense authority over the lives of enlisted men. Moreover, when it came to interactions with Native and Mexican women, paternalism offered a vocabulary through which all members of the army, officers or enlisted, could claim authority over local peoples. In this, paternalism offered both a measure of institutional cohesion to army culture and a way to stabilize the army's hierarchical power structure.

Most officers considered themselves – primarily native-born, middle-class Protestants – superior to enlisted men, often foreign-born, working-class, and Catholic. Where officers believed themselves to be collectively disciplined, intelligent, and authoritative, they cast themselves in relief against the purported tendencies of soldiers toward indiscipline,

---

[17] Scott, *Memoirs*, 157, 257–58.
[18] Roberts, *Paternalism in Early Victorian England*, 2–4, 6. This paternalistic outlook helped many to justify and underplay British imperial violence. Elkins, *Legacy of Violence*, 9–10.

vulgarity, and unbridled passions. Therefore, to ensure women's safety and US military honor, officers leveraged discourses about protecting women to control the perceived sexual threat posed by potentially dangerous enlisted men. The army as a whole protected enemy women from non-army men, like white settlers in Florida, Native men, and Mexican men. But army *officers* protected enemy women from enlisted men.

THE GENRE OF ARMY WRITING

A feminist approach to military history considers how army leaders constructed women's presence in, and absence from, military records in specific, deliberate ways. It does so through close readings of army documents and the excavation of source material related to discourse about women and women's war experiences. The field of postcolonial studies closely informs this approach. Both seek to decolonize the Indigenous and Mexican women who appear in army archives and contribute to the "sustained assault on the politics of knowledge" that "orients the postcolonial field."[19] Through the "study of imperialism and culture," as Edward Said argues, "we can better understand the persistence and durability of saturating hegemonic systems like culture when we realize that their internal constraints upon writers and thinkers were *productive*, not unilaterally inhibiting." Army officers shaped the archive by failing to see, or excluding, women's combatancy from official documents, and by adding narratives describing the army's protection of women. These "internal constraints" produced vital cultural elements. The field of military history has just begun to consider the Mexican War's imperial character and generally exists apart from postcolonial approaches.[20]

On balance, scholarship on the US Army in Florida and Mexico bolsters the "still resilient paradigm" that there is no American Empire. To deconstruct that paradigm, Amy Kaplan argues that one must connect culture to US imperialism.[21] Studying army culture at war in the aggressively expansionist climate of the 1830s and 1840s makes exactly that connection. Exploring the relationships between soldiers and colonized

---

[19] Stoler, *Haunted by Empire*, 2.
[20] Said, *Orientalism*, 14; McCaffrey, *Army of Manifest Destiny*. For mariners and US maritime empire, see: Rouleau, *With Sails Whitening Every Sea*.
[21] Amy Kaplan and Donald E. Pease, eds., *Cultures of United States Imperialism* (Durham: Duke University Press, 1993), 11; Stoler, *Haunted by Empire: Geographies of Intimacy in North American History*, 59; William Appleman Williams, *The Tragedy of American Diplomacy* (New York and London: W.W. Norton & Co., 1962), 53–56.

women makes it even more pointedly because US officers and enlisted men often treated women as subjects of military protection and thus sources of potential legitimacy for US occupation.

This book explores how gender shaped the army's cultural assumptions and therefore the army's policies and behaviors.[22] Isabel Hull's study of the wartime Imperial German military offers a model. Drawing on insights from anthropology and social science, Hull examines German military culture using Edgar Schein's three levels of organizational culture – visible behaviors and artifacts, professed beliefs and values, and the foundational but often unseen assumptions that motivate members to act. This study follows Hull's conclusion that "basic assumptions tend to coalesce into a pattern. The resulting constellation of mutually supporting assumptions lends stability and consistency to the whole."[23]

Hull emphasizes the importance of studying military cultures in times of conflict. In this, she shares a concern with military historian John Keegan's classic study, *The Face of Battle*. Keegan found that just as war "compromises the purity of doctrines, it damages the integrity of structures, upsets the balance of relationships, interrupts the network of communication which the institutional historian struggles to identity and, having identified, to crystallize." War is, rather, "the institutional military historian's irritant," causing such scholars to hold a "preference, paradoxically, for the study of the armed forces in *peacetime*."[24] It remains difficult to work out which peacetime assumptions an army adheres to in the crucible of war, and Keegan famously grappled with this question to reveal the battlefield experiences of ordinary soldiers. Even compared to the challenges of researching enlisted men, it is harder still to resurrect women's experiences, but it *is* possible. And it is no less necessary.

Hull describes how German military culture incentivized sexual violence as an expression of male dominance rooted in the right of the conquerors to dominate the conquered and enhanced by the myth of

---

[22] Ann Curthroys defines gender as a concept that "denotes the social, cultural, and historical distinctions between men and women." Where sex referred to biological difference, gender is "a social and cultural construction." Curthroys, drawing on Judith Butler, notes "gendered subjectivity is produced in a series of competing discourses," and so "gender relations are a process involving strategies and counter-strategies of power." That power-struggle shaped relationships between officers and enlisted men of the army through competing discourses concerning men's protection of women. Curthroys, "Gender." Butler, *Gender Trouble*, 24–25.
[23] Hull, *Absolute Destruction*, 95–96. Schein, *Organizational Culture and Leadership*.
[24] Hull, *Absolute Destruction*, 94. Keegan, *The Face of Battle*, 28.

hyper-sexualized women in "uncivilized" societies. Hull reminds us that military culture is a way to understand that which is "habitual and unquestioned," the norms and instincts that shape actions in war. In regulations and practice, norms operated on hidden assumptions, creating "systematic but unintentional results." In the case of the US Army, one such hidden assumption was an internal logic that they protected helpless women.[25]

It was a claim well fitted to the needs of army leaders who sought to accomplish their assigned expansionist missions. Shelley Streeby's work on "the production of popular culture" encapsulates an approach applied here to the production of army culture, whose development is easily oversimplified to a professionalizing officer corps. She argues, "an understanding of the U.S.–Mexican War (1846–1848) and mid-nineteenth-century empire building is required in order to understand the histories of race, nativism, labor, politics, and popular and mass culture in the United States." To go further, where the US war on Mexico "crucially shaped US politics and culture," mass cultures also shaped the US Army. Streeby contends that mass culture was "inextricable from scenes of empire-building" in Mexico and elsewhere. Her book, in turn, draws on classic works like Robert Johannsen's *To the Halls of Montezuma*. Both emphasize cultural experiences of the US–Mexican War, and this project builds on theirs.[26] It demonstrates how the war shaped US and army culture in a formative era, and argues that historians must understand army culture in Mexico in the context of wartime experience gained in Florida.

Earlier studies of army culture often focus on the army while in garrison – yet, as John Keegan would remind us, one cannot understand the development of a military culture without studying war. Edward Coffman's social history of the nineteenth-century army during peacetime emphasizes how officers' wives, romantic partners, and children experienced life in the frontier army. He situates the army as a part of US society. Coffman's regulars, with their social worlds full of officers, enlisted men, women, and children remains a model of scholarship, as does his call for further scholarship on the topic of army women and children, and his valuable insight into army wives' peacetime lives. There is much room to build on his work. *The Old Army* offers "a portrait of

---

[25] Hull, *Absolute Destruction*, 92–94, 97, 126, 151.
[26] Streeby, *American Sensations*, xi, 15; Johannsen, *To the Halls of Montezuma*. See also: Rodríguez, *The Literatures of the U.S.–Mexican War*.

Introduction: Army Paternalists 13

the American Army in peacetime," while interactions between regulars and women in times of war exist beyond its scope.²⁷

The field of postcolonial studies offers a way to extend such a study past the army's peacetime domestic space. The army participated in "the domesticating strategies of empire," and interactions between soldiers and enemy women shaped the contours of imperial domestication.²⁸ Taming Florida and later Mexico meant gaining local women's support and willing submission. Yet, when officers enforced norms regarding how enlisted men were to treat local women, they not only domesticated local populations to US rule – they also domesticated soldiers to officers' authority.

Like the nation, the regular army underwent a significant transformation in the years leading up to 1848. Thus, scholars of imperialism such as Shelley Streeby, Amy Greenberg, and Paul Foos have located the US–Mexican War as a formative moment where the US became an empire.²⁹ In *Cultures of United States Imperialism*, Amy Kaplan argues that the US nation and empire-building were "historically coterminous and mutually defining." She relates "internal categories of gender, race, and ethnicity to the global dynamics of empire-building" and, in doing so, challenges the opposition between men who perform public actions internationally and women whose experiences remain bounded by the domestic nation and private activities. Studying the unique subculture of the US state's most-used instrument of empire-building produces an improved understanding of the mutually constitutive and understudied relationships between empire, gender, and culture.³⁰

Accounts of the antebellum army of "the kind with the women still in it" enrich our historical understanding.³¹ Indeed, US military policy changed when Seminole women's resistance to forced removal met a US strategy increasingly premised on their capture. When Mexican women sold goods and services to the US, it produced an archetypal view in US minds of such women as affectionate allies. Those views matched stronger but narrower noncombatant protections in the Treaty of Guadalupe Hidalgo.

---

²⁷ Coffman, *The Old Army*, vii–viii, 500; Skelton, *An American Profession of Arms*, vii–viii. Those chapters are: "Officers and Enlisted Men," "Officers, Politicians, and Citizens," "Officers and Indians," "Officers, Foreign Affairs, and War," and "The Officer Corps and the Sectional Crisis."
²⁸ Stoler, *Carnal Knowledge and Imperial Power*, 18.
²⁹ Streeby, *American Sensations*; Foos, *A Short, Offhand, Killing Affair*; Greenberg, *Manifest Manhood and the Antebellum Empire*.
³⁰ Kaplan and Pease, *Cultures of United States Imperialism*, 14, 16–17.
³¹ McCurry, *Women's War*, 14.

Scholars have not recognized these effects of women's wartime activities on military and national policy. Ann Stoler writes in *Carnal Knowledge and Imperial Power* that much of the work "on gender and empire has tacked tentatively between a feminist concern that focuses on women, their daring and despair, and one that focuses on how a wider domain was shaped by gendered sensibilities and sexual politics." While the "first tends to stop at the threshold of women's direct agency and direct presence; the latter does not." Although "tacking back and forth is not a problem in itself," Stoler believes that "a broader gendered history may offer more than women's history tout court." In US military history, even traditional women's history remains underdeveloped. John Belohlavek's *Patriots, Prostitutes, and Spies* is the sole monograph by a US military historian about women and the War on Mexico.[32] He writes of women from different nationalities and backgrounds but narrates women's experiences without connecting them to military policy, imperialism, or army culture. Of the broader gendered approach that Stoler describes, there is still less. Amy Greenberg's *Manifest Manhood and the Antebellum Empire* and Laurel Clark Shire's *Threshold of Manifest Destiny* are exceptions, although neither focuses on the regular army, as is Peter Guardino's *The Dead March*, which draws on gender, race, and religion to tell the history of war between the US and Mexico.[33]

In this underdeveloped field, Stephanie McCurry's question remains emphatically relevant: "Why, given all the potent evidence of their significance, have women been rendered invisible in histories of war?" McCurry locates a process of erasure following the Civil War in a postwar need to return to the comforting fiction of women's innocence. She notes that after the war, "on matters of gender, Thermidor set in."[34] This study of army culture in Florida and Mexico demonstrates how that erasure can happen not just after war, but *during* it. As when General Jesup turned an ambush into a battle, from the first moment army officers touched pen to paper to make a report they transformed the present into recorded history. In doing so, they often eliminated records of women's participation. Instead of recording women's wartime activities,

---

[32] Kaplan and Pease, *Cultures of United States Imperialism*, 15; Stoler, *Carnal Knowledge and Imperial Power*, 212; Belohlavek, *Patriots, Prostitutes, and Spies*. See also: Salas, *Soldaderas in the Mexican Military*.

[33] Greenberg, *Manifest Manhood and the Antebellum Empire*; Shire, *The Threshold of Manifest Destiny*; Guardino, *The Dead March: A History of the Mexican-American War*, 2017, 22.

[34] McCurry, "Enemy Women and the Laws of War in the American Civil War," 13, 61.

report writers preserved a sentimental army fiction of female harmlessness and submission. It was Thermidor in Brumaire.

A point made by Susan Lee Johnson in her study of the California Gold Rush's Southern Mines offers a related way to understand women's historiographic disappearance. Johnson writes, "Our failure to consider such scenes and ask such questions is part of a larger problem of collective memory." Johnson argues that the Gold Rush came to be "remembered as the historical property of Anglo Americans" and men. Similarly, the antebellum US Army's military history remains a story populated almost entirely by white men, mostly high-ranking ones.[35] Much as the ideologies of conquest that produced Manifest Destiny have "masked the long history of Native peoples," the histories of Indigenous and Mexican women at war have been subject to a process of erasure that left them doubly concealed.[36]

Leaving these women out misses how paternalism shaped army culture; naturalized officers' authority over enlisted men; and provided a cultural foundation for military law, policy, and strategy. This project begins to expose the "circuits of knowledge production" that erased women from army records and military history.[37] Seeing army documents – like reports of battles, casualty lists, correspondence, journals, and drawings – as a genre shaped by army culture and individual (white male) authors allows one to uncover new perspectives and insights.

This project locates points of connection by drawing on material written by soldiers of all ranks. It traces how and why facts and interpretations changed as information moved up or down the chain of command. While this approach reveals points of difference, it also reveals specific areas of unity – those assumptions and beliefs held by most military men. The view that soldiers should protect women was one such potential source of agreement. It sometimes served as a common language between officers and enlisted men, sometimes as a path for enlisted men to challenge officers' claims to moral superiority, and sometimes as a justification for changes in military policy and strategy. By 1848, these workings cohered into an engine of army paternalism, a deep-seated logic whose machinations were sometimes overt, sometimes submerged, and underlay the army's choices. I call this the logic of protection.[38]

---

[35] Johnson, *Roaring Camp*, 11.
[36] Witgen, *An Infinity of Nations*, 369.
[37] Stoler, *Haunted by Empire*, 6.
[38] For related concepts from scholarship on the US wars in Iraq and Afghanistan, see: Judith Hicks Stiehm, "The Protected, The Protector, The Defender," *Special Issue*

This logic of protection stretched and adapted to accommodate use by the many groups of men within the army. For all that changeability, its core remained static – it was always about the soldiers, not the women the army claimed to protect. Like Edward Said's Orientalism, it "responded more to the culture that produced it," army culture, "than to its putative object," women.[39] It expressed individual and institutional male identities as protectors. It always needed a subject but did not require universal applicability. Instead, the logic attached to the best available subjects for protection. Typically, this was whatever group of women over whom the army held direct power and came the closest to white women.

In Florida, the army captured and thus had power over Seminole women, who became its subjects. In Mexico, under US occupation, Mexican women became the army's preferred subject population. Perceived proximity to "civilization" as opposed to "savagery" established a spectrum of preference, where the army leveraged the logic of protection in accordance with proximity to an idealized recipient of chivalric masculinity. The logic of protection was situational, never absolute, because it was always about upholding the military belief of the soldier-protector. Paternalism was a malleable ideology that the army could use in many ways. There remained the potential for tension, even dissonance, between a self-perception of protecting women and a reality of wartime violence.

THE ARMY CULTURE OF PATERNALISM

Army use of the logic of protection could be sincere or insincere, performative or personal, and reached freely across the boundaries between military and popular cultures. Although descriptions of a unique army culture often rest on officers' distance from civilian life, US society profoundly influenced the army. Army culture was, as historian Kristin Hoganson writes of late nineteenth-century US culture, a "framework from within

---

Women and Men's Wars 5, no. 3 (January 1, 1982): 367, 369–70, 374; Iris Marion Young, "The Logic of Masculinist Protection: Reflections on the Current Security State," *Signs* 29, no. 1 (2003): 2–4; Keally McBride and Annick T. R. Wibben, "The Gendering of Counterinsurgency in Afghanistan," *Humanity: An International Journal of Human Rights, Humanitarianism, and Development* 3, no. 2 (2012): 200–03, 206; Laleh Khalili, "Gendered Practices of Counterinsurgency," *Review of International Studies* 37, no. 4 (2011): 1473–74; Helen M. Kinsella, "Sex as the Secret: Counterinsurgency in Afghanistan," *International Theory* 11 (December 2018): 1, 3, 18–19. See also: Porter, *Military Orientalism*; Owens, "Torture, Sex and Military Orientalism"; Barkawi and Stanski, *Orientalism and War*.

[39] Said, *Orientalism*, 22.

which individuals perceived and responded to the wider world," and cultural borrowing strengthened that framework.[40] One popular source of importance to the army in the 1830s was American Romanticism. The Romantic movement – a collection of ideas, and creators, which produced various cultural products – began in the late eighteenth century in England. In the US, it took flight in the 1830s and 1840s, just as a professional US Army with a distinct culture developed. Romantics embraced the heady combination of a love for nature, commitment to nationalism, and interest in folklore to produce fiction, often focused on an Indigenous figure. Army Romantics embraced "Indian plays" and novels and added to this mix an interest in chivalry and heroism.

Army use of popular culture changed over time, but consistently located a particular place for itself within the broader cultural landscape, one that encircled and elevated it based on chivalric ideals of protecting the weak and doing one's duty. Mass culture in the 1830s offered powerful support for increasingly distinct racial and gendered hierarchies. In the army, that enabled stricter distinctions within and without its ranks. This included a ban on recruiting Black and Indigenous men, a prohibition that bolstered the otherwise questionable whiteness of recent immigrants. Much as a gendered logic of soldierly protection softened officers' power, so did an increasingly monolithic construction of race-based identity. Indeed, much of that logic's usefulness came from its potential to knit together a sense of institutional superiority based on shared whiteness. Naturalized differences helped officers draw a line around soldiers and all others *and* let them elevate the officer corps more rigidly above enlisted men. Protection amplified similarities, smoothed out differences, and domesticated enlisted responses to officers' authoritarian power.

No one embodied the logic of protection's cultural and literary roots quite like Alexander Macomb: playwright, author, and commanding general. He had been the army's senior leader before the Second US–Seminole War and remained so until he died in 1841. Winfield Scott replaced him. During his career, Macomb published, among other works, an "Indian play" entitled *Pontiac: The Siege of Detroit* and a popular guide called *The Practice of Courts Martial*. With his interest in writing "Indian plays" and regulating courts-martial, that is, with his commitment to sentiment and discipline, Macomb represented the warp and woof of regular army paternalism (Figures 0.1 and 0.2).

[40] Hoganson, *Fighting for American Manhood: How Gender Politics Provoked the Spanish–American and Philippine–American Wars*, 2.

FIGURE 0.1 Portrait of Alexander Macomb, painting by Thomas Sully, 1829.

Macomb's foray into theater involved high and low-ranking affiliates of the army, from Secretary of War Lewis Cass, the "faithful and affectionate friend" and former territorial governor of Michigan to whom he dedicated *Pontiac*, to the US Marines who starred in a staging of the play in 1838 Washington. His efforts reflected a lifelong embrace of the theater of war. While commanding Detroit's military garrison in 1816, "the officers under his command had organized and conducted the first known theatre activity in that city." Though sentimentality was a

FIGURE 0.2 Portrait of Winfield Scott, painting by Robert Weir, 1856.

"national project" in antebellum US society, scholars of the army have not previously applied such insights to analyses of military culture.[41] The wartime setting of these plays exemplified this entanglement. The best

---

[41] Dunlap, *A History of the American Theatre*, 151–52. Macomb's play probably benefitted from Edwin Forrest's famous performance in *Metamora*, which debuted at New York's Park Theater in December of 1829. Samuels, *The Culture of Sentiment*, 3.

known, *Metamora*, drew on the distant King Philip's War. *Pontiac* fictionalized the 1763 Pontiac's Rebellion. Military and civilian audiences alike found meaning from within these narratives.[42]

"Indian plays" did the cultural work of paternalism through an "emphasis on indigenous traditions, folk customs, and the glorification of the national past" that "dovetailed with the drive towards cultural nationalism in the newly independent nation."[43] That work dealt with the essential question of how, in a republican democracy, an authoritarian institution like the army could justify its control over citizens. In response to this question, officers and enlisted men used sentimental culture to give different answers.

Enlisted men used the era's rugged individualism to emphasize that they were men of action. One anonymous writer who published a collection of stories glorifying enlisted men and pillorying the officer corps asserted that he wrote while serving in the regular army. This veteran dedicated his book to "the rank and file" and endowed his soldier-heroes with "handsome forms" and "expressive features" showing they were "God's noblest works." This beauty betokened manly virtues. Corporal Mannerly was "a man of feeling" and "one of undaunted courage, firm resolution, and who would sooner lose his life than be dishonored." The author delivered harsh judgment on officers: "scorn and degradation has been heaped upon me by pitiful apologies for men," who were usually West Point graduates. Cruel and cowardly officers endowed with charactonyms such as "Lieutenant Hardcase" and "Captain Meanman" abused their power and "degraded" Mannerly.[44] The message was unequivocal – although soldiers were inferior to officers in rank, they were the superior men. They made a civilization out of the wilderness and killed those Indigenous people who resisted, all with their own hands. Officers, aristocratic and weak by comparison, just gave the orders.

Officers experienced mass culture in another way entirely. Macomb's *Pontiac* drew on the themes of "civilization" extinguishing "savagery" to imbue the US Army with purpose. Writing on the British army, Daniel Ussishkin argues in *Morale: A Modern British History* that "the notion of morale has been inherently linked to understandings

---

[42] Stone, *Metamora*; Cox, "The Characterization of the American Indian in American Indian Plays, 1800–1860," 2–3, v–xi.
[43] Berkhofer, *The White Man's Indian*, 86–87.
[44] An American Soldier, *Recollections of the United States Army*, 3–5, 8–9.

of, and expectations from, the exercise of power in modern mass-democracy." He describes how managing collective morale assumes that modern citizens cannot and should not "be brought to submission by coercive forces alone. In a liberal-democratic polity, coercion would be impractical, inefficient, and undesirable." To leverage morale to produce discipline requires the "harmonization of subjective freedom and collective goals (however defined)." Officers' dilemma was how to impose military discipline – conceived as absolute obedience to one's superiors – on white men, members of a democratizing and slaveholding society that increasingly rejected physical punishment as fit only for the enslaved. The question of how the US Army navigated this process of internalizing discipline and domesticating enlisted men has yet to be pursued, and this study of army culture makes a start. Part of the answer was the shared paternalistic, civilizational project that writers like Macomb described.[45]

While the army implemented Andrew Jackson's Indian Removal Act and fought Seminole groups in Florida, authors drew on "both the noble and the savage Indian" to evoke feeling in readers and audiences and connect them to the nation's contested frontiers. They used the "nostalgia and pity aroused" by the purportedly "dying race" of a monolithically constructed "Indian" to leave an "impression of the Indian as rapidly passing away before the onslaught of civilization."[46] Popular writers had a different impact a few years later in Mexico. Rather than emphasizing the "noble savage" they embraced depictions of the US Army as chivalric rescuers of Mexican women, the willing partners of superior US soldiers. Shifting modes of thought about enemy women marked cultural change. Unlike "Indian plays," the war stories from the US–Mexican War a decade later emphasized how US rescues of Mexican women underscored Anglo-American superiority, a narrative officers used to bolster their power and the regular army's institutional legitimacy.[47]

Beyond literature, another type of army writing – courts-martial records – marked the institution's development over the same period. In his study of antebellum soldiers, Dale Steinhauer demonstrates that "irregularities in courts-martial became so common during the years of the Seminole War" that at the behest of the Secretary of War, Macomb

---

[45] Ussishkin, *Morale*, 1–2.
[46] Berkhofer, *The White Man's Indian*, 86–88. This narrative existed in stark contrast to the violent, coercive, and unprecedented reality of how the US expelled Indigenous people in the 1830s. Saunt, *Unworthy Republic*, xiv–xv.
[47] Pearce, *Savagism and Civilization*, xii, 49.

published *The Practice of Courts-Martial* in 1840 to remedy the problem.[48] He sought "the introduction of a regular system of procedure in Courts-Martial" in response to wide discrepancies in how army officers assigned to courts-martial duty carried out their responsibilities.[49] Discrepancies often involved breaches of protocol concerning rank, the very stuff that formed officers' power.

Macomb wrote from personal experience. In 1837, he refused to approve the results of a court-martial in Fort Marks, Florida, for inattention to rank. The appointed officers had improperly convicted a soldier of mutiny, Macomb declared, because mutiny by its legal definition referred to violence against officers. The soldier had attempted to shoot a non-commissioned officer – a sergeant. Macomb vented his frustration, writing that "in every instance where the word officer is used in the Articles of War, without qualification, it means Commissioned Officer: a Non-Commissioned Officer is, technically, not considered an officer, the classification being officer, non-commissioned officer, and private." Because of this discrepancy, Macomb ruled that the prisoner must be released from confinement and would therefore escape "a just punishment for one of the most dangerous crimes of which a soldier can be guilty."[50] He sought to guard the legal gates around officership and systematize how officers disciplined enlisted men. Where officers like Macomb wanted during the Second US–Seminole War to give form to a limited concept of military justice, Macomb's successor Winfield Scott would drastically expand the scope of military justice in the Mexican War with the advent of military commissions. During these years, a changing army culture grew in tandem with a remarkable expansion and bureaucratization of military power.

Macomb's conception of discipline had much to do with what many scholars have termed an era of professionalization. Between 1835 and 1848, from the early years fighting the Seminole people in Florida to its final months in Mexico, the army gained considerable legitimacy in the US public's eyes thanks largely to its increasingly West Point educated, middling officer corps. During these years, it enacted the policy of Indian Removal, fought a seven-year war to forcibly relocate the Seminole from Florida, and later conquered and occupied much of Mexico at the behest

---

[48] Steinhauer, Dale Richard, "'Sogers': Enlisted Men in the U.S. Army, 1815–1860," 263.
[49] Macomb, *The Practice of Courts Martial*, x.
[50] *Orders, Headquarters of the Army, 1835–39*, 225A: General Orders 77, December 21, 1837.

of President James Polk – a long decade full of wartime crucibles. William Skelton's *An American Profession of Arms* defines professionalism as "a regular system of recruitment and professional education, a well-defined area of responsibility, a considerable degree of continuity in its membership, and permanent institutions to maintain internal cohesion and military expertise."[51] Skelton reveals those traits in the regular officer corps decades before the Civil War. In the 1830s, the army systematically recruited men through a consolidated recruitment service, educated its officers at the military academy, accepted civilian authority, and developed regulations to govern conduct.

For these reasons, recent histories have established the Jacksonian era as formative for the US Army. While historians have increasingly understood these years as necessary to a rapidly professionalizing institution, such scholarship has focused on army officers commissioned out of West Point and educated by a standardized curriculum for the "profession of arms." But this focus on the officer corps is just one (important) part of a significant demographic shift. While West Pointers came to dominate the officer corps, foreign-born recruits came to numerically dominate the enlisted force. Just as the 1840s saw an emergent middle-class, to include increasingly respectable army officers, within the same decade, immigration, especially from Ireland, remade the white working-class and thus the army's recruiting pool.[52] Irish recruits were not only different from native-born officers in terms of their birth country, but were often Catholic, religiously distinct from the overwhelmingly Protestant officer corps. It was yet another source of difference-making and thus of control even though officers and US politicians made little effort to develop official Protestantism in the army. Officers and enlisted men were strikingly dissimilar, but little scholarship considers what it meant for the army to be increasingly led by West Pointers *and* manned by foreign-born soldiers.

Simultaneously, the Jacksonian era's political climate featured a growing belief in the political equality of white men alongside a strain of sputtering nativism that ebbed and flowed with the nation's economic

---

[51] Samuel Huntington's work exemplifies this earlier view. Since Huntington, Military historians such as William Skelton and Samuel Watson have firmly established how army professionalism within the officer corps took shape in the antebellum era. Huntington, *The Soldier and the State*. For the professionalizing army before the Civil War, see: Watson, "How the Army Became Accepted"; Watson, *Peacekeepers and Conquerors*; Skelton, *An American Profession of Arms*.
[52] Streeby, *American Sensations*, 11.

fortunes and rates of immigration. Although officers and enlisted men were different in many ways, the Jacksonian period's dramatic shift to universal white male suffrage promised (or, for officers, threatened) a leveling sameness.[53] The complex interplay – of officer and enlisted, of middle-class Protestant academy graduates and poor, recent Catholic immigrants, of equality and exclusion – merits closer attention. Untangling these many dynamics suggests how officers were not just part of a cohort of middle-class men joining professions. They were leaders of the most authoritarian organization of their time within the United States.

An army-specific version of chivalry served as both a source of officers' power and a binding agent for a broader army culture. This iteration of chivalry was a smaller and shallower system of ideas than the medieval original – a sentimental copy. It focused on protecting innocent women from villainous men and fighting for women's love. Although such declarations seemed to belong to an imagined past of gallant knights, the army's use of chivalric discourse spoke clearly to the profession of arms. Gendered discourse about women channeled and narrowed the public service ideal that animated professionalization in US society. Where doctors' public service ethic bound them to help all and harm none, the army preferred a more particular set of ethical restraints: to help (in theory) those who were supposedly harmless – women and children – and to destroy male combatants as dictated by the civilian government.

In this fashion, professionalization bureaucratized the separation of supposedly harmless women from war and its histories. Women's absence from records of war and the chivalric positioning of women as outsiders, victims, and subjects of rescue emphasized masculine mastery of professional military knowledge because "the social role and status of professionals is legitimated by their esoteric expertise."[54] Military men's claims to the unique skills and abilities necessary to protect women (incapable, by definition, of defending themselves) elevated soldiers even as it submerged women's wartime activities.

One can begin to interrogate how claims to professionalization obscured relations of power between men and women, and among

---

[53] For suffrage in the 1830s and 1840s, see Keyssar, *The Right to Vote*; Howe, *What Hath God Wrought*; Sellers, *The Market Revolution*.

[54] Goldstein, "Foucault among the Sociologists," 184. See also: Haber, *The Quest for Authority and Honor in the American Professions, 1750–1900*.

soldiers with the paternalistic notion of the army family. Officers brought the disciplinary mechanisms of the state *and* the family to bear on enlisted men.[55] When scholars begin within an officer's army family of subordinates, and works outward to the army as an institution, paternalism displaces professionalism as the dominant paradigm. As paternalists, officers bolstered their authority with a father's naturalized power over his family, within which he disciplined his soldiers, servants, and enslaved people – his permanent children – and protected his women. In officers' estimations, some soldiers were good children, but most were prone to misbehavior and required a firm hand. The fact that most enlisted men were young and unmarried made it even easier for officers to sustain this outlook. Fatherly authority cloaked and naturalized power.

Officers smoothed out the rough edges of their authority in part by using the genre of army writing, with its reports, regulations, courts-martial, and correspondence, perpetuating officers as the army's "voice of authority." Mary Beard maintains that one must consider how such authority is constructed, and officers used discourse emphasizing the army's obligation toward women to bind enlisted men to their officers. Such language offered a potential point of agreement between the different cultures of middling officers and poor, immigrant soldiers of varying nationalities and ethnicities. Like other architects of professionalization, antebellum regular army officers became "if not exactly administrators of 'discipline,' certainly its handmaidens and accessories." If power produces truth, officers' power made officers' truths, and therefore officers' military histories.[56] Rather than simple repositories of information, army archives were artful constructions.

ENEMY WOMEN AND ARMY POLICY

When enemy women resisted the US Army, they forced soldiers to confront contradictions between an idealized female and the real threat such women posed.[57] It was paternalism in extremis. During the formative, institution-building years that followed West Point's rise to prominence,

---

[55] Goldstein, "Foucault among the Sociologists," 177.
[56] Beard, *Women and Power: A Manifesto*, 45; Goldstein, "Foucault among the Sociologists," 176; Garland, "What Is a 'History of the Present'?," 366.
[57] Adelman and Aron, "From Borderlands to Borders," 814–16; Baud and Van Schendel, "Toward a Comparative History of Borderlands," 212.

the regular army fought two wars – the Second US–Seminole War and the US–Mexican War. Cultural change, born of war, shaped military and foreign policy.

The same decades that witnessed the development of a coherent army culture also saw fierce competition between different ideals of manhood in US society. Skelton and Watson argue that army professionalization happened before the Civil War and not in the late nineteenth century. In those same decades, Amy Greenberg argues for the importance of competing masculinities that prefaced the late century rise of hegemonic "primitive" masculinity based on physical prowess. Her work encompasses sites of masculinity, from urban volunteer fire departments to the Mexican War-era army to filibustering expeditions.[58] Greenberg draws to an extent on Anthony Rotundo, whose work on northern middle-class manhood in the long nineteenth century argued for a shift from communal manhood, to self-made manhood, to passionate manhood defined in stark contrast to womanliness. In *Manifest Manhood*, Greenberg departs from Rotundo's progression to argue that antebellum debates over manhood debates coalesced by 1848 into "two preeminent and dueling mid-century masculinities: *restrained manhood* and *martial manhood*." The latter draws on McCurry's "martial manhood," which was "grounded in the household and in the prerogatives of masters." While other varieties of masculine identity remained available, these gained pre-eminence and "competed for hegemony" in different arenas, for instance, in the US–Mexican War, where martial men strongly supported "aggressive expansionism."[59]

Yet, the regular soldiers who were the actual instruments of this discourse – who performed aggressive expansion rather than expressed aggressive expansionism – straddled both schools of masculinity. The regulars and the society they served had an uneasy relationship. Although the US public generally accepted regular officers, they disdained poor, immigrant enlisted men. Moreover, many Jacksonians remained uncomfortable with the idea of a standing US Army. Popular society preferred the volunteers, citizen-soldiers who performed temporary military service and returned home. In contrast to "aggressive, violent" volunteers who adhered to martial masculinity and believed

---

[58] Greenberg, *Cause for Alarm*; Greenberg, *Manifest Manhood and the Antebellum Empire*; Greenberg, *A Wicked War*.

[59] Rotundo, *American Manhood*, 3, 5; Greenberg, *Manifest Manhood and the Antebellum Empire*, 9, 11–12, 14; McCurry, *Masters of Small Worlds: Yeoman Households, Gender Relations, and the Antebellum South Carolina Low Country*, 261.

that Indigenous and Mexican noncombatants were "racial inferiors" they could attack with impunity, regulars insisted they were professionals, more competent than undisciplined, ineffective volunteer soldiers.[60] Officers, like Greenberg's martial men, elided class both to support "territorial expansionism grounded in masculine privilege," and to create a sense of unity that included enlisted men. Yet, those officers also "grounded their identities" in their army families, "valued expertise," and endeavored to promote temperance among soldiers.[61] The US Army combined elements of the leading restrained and martial modes in a developing army culture.

After his Indian Removal Act passed in May 1830, Andrew Jackson's annual message to Congress in December of that year lauded his "benevolent policy" to affect the "speedy removal" of Indigenous tribes from the nation's southeastern slave states. He claimed that this "not only liberal, but generous" program would allow US settlements to grow, separating "the Indians from immediate contact" with white settlers so Native groups could be free "in their own way," causing "them gradually, under the protection of the Government and through the influence of good counsels, to cast off their savage habits" and form "civilized" communities.[62] The regulars reshaped this imperial message to fit their needs.

Their subset of the masculine ideal combined elements of the predominant restrained and martial modes into a self-conception of regulars as the arbiters of government protection. Moreover, because regulars considered themselves superior to volunteers and viewed white settler men with contempt, they often justified their participation in forcing Seminole people out of Florida much as Jackson did – by claiming that moving them away from white settlers would benefit Native peoples. This paternal strain in army culture continued to gain adherents in Mexico, where regulars expressed an institutional identity in contrast to the extreme kind of martial manhood (marked by atrocity) that regulars attributed to volunteers. As a result, even as the army patently invaded Mexican territory, its members claimed that they came to protect Mexicans. By 1848, the logic of protection animated and expressed an increasingly dominant army culture of paternalism.

---

[60] Guardino, "The Constant Recurrence of Such Atrocities: Guerrilla Warfare and Counterinsurgency during the Mexican–American War," 7, 19.
[61] Greenberg, *Manifest Manhood and the Antebellum Empire*, 11–12, Note 28.
[62] Jackson, "Annual Message to Congress."

The officer corps' claims to professionalization sped this process along. Simultaneously, officers rationalized their authoritarian power over subordinates by pointing to increased immigration, which justified parental control over supposedly child-like foreign-born soldiers. Officers also drew on mass cultural currents to naturalize hierarchies of difference and validate their efforts to position all soldiers, regardless of rank, *above* non-white men and *in front of* all women as their chivalric protectors. The logic of protection – the set of ideas related to the deeply held belief that the soldier as an individual and the regular army as an organization protected women (who in return remained thankful and sometimes helpful noncombatants) – enables one to map changes to army culture in its formative period. Based on shifting army experiences with enemy women – Seminole and Creek women in Florida, Mexican, and Indigenous women in Mexico – soldiers changed the logic of protection, altered how the army acted on that logic, and generated violent consequences for the women they claimed to protect.[63]

Taking seriously the available source material on women illuminates the gendered history of army culture. Feminist scholarship on the "interlocking of sexual, racial patterns of dominance that crisscross historical fields" has the potential to open new areas of research in the field of military history.[64] This approach provides a method to critically interpret army writing as a genre – one as formulaic and purposeful as any "Indian play" or penny press paper. Straightforward readings of army writing miss the discursive process that sought to resolve war's complex realities into the simple, bureaucratically digestible report formats. Grasping that process matters because it operated as an engine of legitimization for the

---

[63] Today, Creek women's descendants call themselves the "Muscogee (Creek) Nation." I reflect their choices and use Muscogee or Creek to describe group members. The Muscogee may have labeled earlier groups of Seminoles *isti Seminoli*, "wild men" because those people left behind Muscogee society to settle in Florida and represented an ethnic minority whose members spoke a Hichiti language. Three distinct waves of Creek migration to newly Seminole land occurred, first as Creeks escaped clashes with US settler colonialists in Georgia. Next, Red Sticks fled to Florida to gain distance from US encroachment and other Muscogee factions. A third wave occurred in the 1830s as some Muscogees escaped displacement to Indian Territory by joining forces with the Seminoles. The Seminoles separated from the Muscogees in the early 1700s, but by the 1830s, many Muscogees sought refuge in Seminole society. Still, there remained ethnic tensions between these groups, and with other refugees not absorbed by the Muscogees such as the Koasatis, Alabamas, Tuckabatchees, Yuchis, and Shawnees. Snyder, *Slavery in Indian Country*, 214. Wright, *Creeks & Seminoles*, 16. See also: Chaudhuri and Chaudhuri, *A Sacred Path*.

[64] Stoler, *Haunted by Empire*, 8, 30, 216–17.

profession of arms.⁶⁵ Army leaders from Alexander Macomb to Winfield Scott were part of a lineage of officers who produced army culture and who attempted throughout their careers to write their way into their desired future, using the specific cultural forms that comprised official army correspondence.

Moreover, the genre of army writing was not static, even if elements like authors' need to promote their bravery and successes remained. The army's wartime experiences in Florida from 1835 to 1842, compared to those in Mexico from 1846 to 1848, straddled massive changes to transportation and print technologies. These years, so formative for the army, also transformed the nation. Cities sprung up, the army conquered new territories and expelled more Indigenous communities, immigration changed the country's demographic character, slavery grew, and technology integrated "this vast and varied empire through dramatic and sudden improvements in communications." Popular culture responded to these multiple changes through new popular media, which Shelley Streeby calls the "culture of sensation."⁶⁶ Army culture also responded by changing. Before the Second US–Seminole War, commanding general Alexander Macomb authored a guide to courts-martial and a well-known "Indian play." After the Mexican War, Macomb's successor Winfield Scott issued a flurry of grand proclamations and courts-martial proceedings that immediately went into print by the many soldier-operated newspapers along the army's path. Soon after, his words reached national periodicals through the pens of US war correspondents. Like the nation, the army found itself remade by the print revolution.

This project is in part a story of what the early regular army, and generations of military historians, wanted to believe: that "civilized" norms of warfare protected noncombatants; that innocent women deserved military protection; and that US officers and enlisted men were willing and able to give that protection. Upon these beliefs, an army culture of paternalism grew, including a professionalizing officer corps and a bureaucratized system of discipline to control enlisted men. Breaking up the "policy fiction" that women existed separately from war allows one to see how army culture developed between 1835 and 1848.⁶⁷ It also illuminates how that culture ultimately shaped, rather than removed, violence against women.

---

⁶⁵ Goldstein, "Foucault among the Sociologists," 183.
⁶⁶ Howe, *What Hath God Wrought*, 4; Streeby, *American Sensations*, 27–28.
⁶⁷ McCurry, *Women's War*, 8.

PART I

WAR IN FLORIDA

At seven years long and 30 million dollars spent, the Second US–Seminole War of 1835–1842 was the longest, most costly "Indian War" the US ever fought and among the deadliest.[1] The army's mission was not simply to defeat Seminole warriors in battle but to forcibly gather and remove a whole society. Following orders from the War Department, Andrew Jackson invaded Florida in 1818 with thousands of volunteers, allowing the US to negotiate with Spain from a position of strength and retain the peninsula. The US soon pushed the Seminole people out of northern Florida and into a reservation farther south, but after the 1830 Indian Removal Act, it voided that agreement and declared all Seminole groups must remove to Indian Territory. The war began when a Seminole group seized the initiative by ambushing a regular army element and killing over 100 regulars.

The US Army was the nation's agent of empire, ordered by its leaders to expel Indigenous groups from Florida. Their work would make way for white settlement and a vast expansion in slavery-based agriculture. In December of 1837, General Thomas Jesup commanded the war's largest US Army contingent: 4,636 regular and 4,078 volunteer troops. It was an astonishing figure given that the total authorized size of the regular army was only 7,140. Their objective was to compel about 4,000 Seminole people to emigrate west to an allotted portion of Indian Territory in modern-day Oklahoma. Of that 4,000, there were between 900 and

---

[1] Missall, *The Seminole Wars*, xv; Weisman, *Unconquered People*, 58. 1,466 members of the US armed forces died in the war.

1,400 men, all of whom the army labeled warriors.² The US Army killed an undetermined number of Seminole people and shipped thousands of survivors west. Perhaps 300 remained, deep in the Everglades. They never surrendered and kept Seminole culture intact, the basis for the modern-day Seminole Tribe of Florida, the Miccosukee Tribe of Indians of Florida, and the Independent Seminoles.

In the years before the war, the regular US Army underwent dual transformations. While the officer corps filled with United States Military Academy graduates, more and more new enlistees were immigrants. Officers left the military academy at West Point with deeply held beliefs regarding what it meant to be a leader in the army family – a stern father to enlisted men, servants and enslaved people, and the Native peoples whom the army considered its wards, and a committed protector of supposedly harmless women. The officer corps sought a reputation as professionals, and to establish the regular army as a permanent, respected institution. To accomplish this, they imposed military discipline on their soldiers. Soldiers, however, strove to assert their privileges as white men, often resisting officers' efforts.

---

² Mahon, *History of the Second Seminole War*, 122, 225, 226.

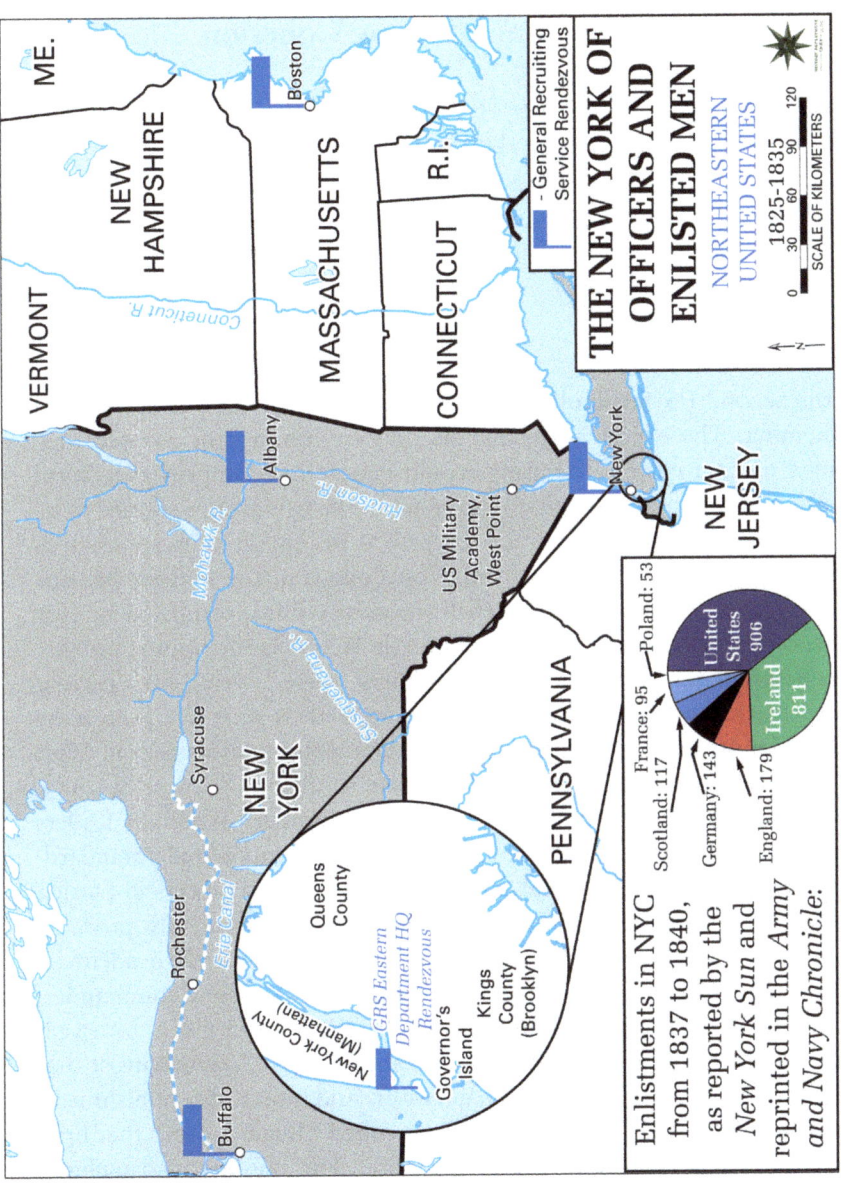

MAP 1 The New York of Officers and Enlisted Men
Map by Mr. Jeffrey Goldberg, Cartographer at the West Point Department of History.

I

The Dilemma of Army Cohesion

West Point Officers, Immigrant Soldiers, and the Beginnings of an Army Culture, 1802–1842

As the Second US–Seminole War began in 1835, US Army officers faced a dilemma. The officer corps and its majority-immigrant enlisted men formed distinct castes. The army would benefit from improved cultural cohesion to function and fight in Florida, but the two groups seemed to be growing farther apart. The officer corps was becoming more cohesive as its junior members graduated from West Point, but the soldiery became more diverse as foreign-born men from across Europe enlisted in ever greater numbers – the Second US–Seminole War was the tipping point.

Following the War of 1812, soldiers were twenty-five percent foreign-born, but that figure rocketed to more than sixty-five percent by 1860. The officer corps underwent a simultaneous transformation. West Point officers comprised over seventy percent of the officer corps by 1835, thus creating for the first time in US history a community of military leaders who had shared both the experiences of cadet socialization and a standardized curriculum of professional training. Senior ranking officers in Florida and Mexico were not West Point graduates – they generally predated the military academy – but they were decisive influences on the academy.

Colonel William Worth, the US–Seminole War's final commander, served as West Point's Commandant of Cadets from 1820 to 1828. Today's cadets still know "Worth's Battalion Orders," which insist that officers must impartially uphold regulations and administer punishment. His words are part of a required booklet called "Bugle Notes" that first-year cadets (called plebes) must memorize. The booklet also includes General Winfield Scott's "Fixed Opinion." It quotes Scott, who led the army in Florida and Mexico: "but for our graduated cadets, the war between the United States and Mexico might, and probably would have

1 The Dilemma of Army Cohesion: West Point Officers

lasted some four or five years, with, in its first half, more defeats than victories falling to our share," but with West Point graduates filling the officer corps, "in less than two campaigns, we conquered a great country and a peace without the loss of a single battle or skirmish." In his memoirs, Scott recorded that after a cadet's four years, he emerged "in most cases, polished, pointed, and sent to a regiment with a head upon his shoulders." Scott visited the academy many times, sometimes living there for extended periods with his family. On one occasion, he went as President of the 1824 Board of Tactics. He also served as President of the Board of Visitors, which supervised certain aspects of the military academy. Scott lived at West Point after retiring, and is buried there.[1]

In 1835, the soldiers in these two New Yorks – the officer stronghold of West Point and the poor neighborhoods of lower Manhattan from which enlisted men so often came – regarded one another with suspicion, across a chasm of class, ethnicity, culture, and religion. Although growing nativism challenged immigrant claims to whiteness, the US convulsed unevenly into an "ethnocultural democracy" for white men.[2] These major social shifts increased the urgency attached to the dilemma of army cohesion and underscored the potential utility of a common army culture.

Captain William Grier moved between these parallel worlds. After graduating from West Point with the class of 1835, Grier served as a recruiting officer in New York in 1838. He enlisted 114 men there, half of whom were foreign-born. Recruiters consistently disregarded the passage in the regulations that prohibited enlistments of foreigners without special permission. The army's need for manpower encouraged recruiters like Grier to be pragmatic and accept those white men who wanted to enlist. The city was the nation's most crucial arrival point for immigrants and its largest recruiting center. It thus housed the Eastern Department of the General Recruiting Service, an organization whose inception in 1825 had nationalized the earlier decentralized recruiting system.[3]

---

[1] Worth, "Worth's Battalion Orders"; Scott, "Scott's Fixed Opinion"; Scott, *Memoirs*, 36, 207.

[2] Steinhauer, Dale Richard, "'Sogers': Enlisted Men in the U.S. Army, 1815–1860," 71; Watson, "How the Army Became Accepted," 229; Watson, *Jackson's Sword: The Army Officer Corps on the American Frontier, 1810–1821*, 28.

[3] Steinhauer, Dale Richard, "'Sogers': Enlisted Men in the U.S. Army, 1815–1860," 28–29, 69–70, 75, 109, Registers of Enlistments in the U.S. Army; Scott, *General Regulations for the Army*, 1825, 354, Paragraph 1287. The western department sometimes supplemented eastern department recruits. Before the Civil War, it operated from 1825 to 1829, then from 1833 to 1837, and finally from 1846 to 1849. Eastern recruits vastly outnumbered westerners.

Much like West Point formalized the process of officer education, the new system brought standardized control to recruitment. The General Recruiting Service and the military academy came of age in the same decade of the 1830s and the same region of New York. Together, they marked the development of an army bureaucracy that streamlined the procurement system for both officers and soldiers. The various regimental recruiting services, and the Mounted Recruiting Service, supplemented general recruitment to lesser degrees. In addition to the administrative role of the New York recruitment offices, the city housed the most successful of the five eastern recruiting rendezvous. Between 1825 and 1860, a quarter of all General Recruiting Service recruits enlisted in New York City.[4]

Recruiters also maintained rendezvous in Albany and Buffalo, cities at the ends of the Erie Canal. These locations opened in 1825 just as workers completed the construction of Clinton's Ditch, and the army quickly enlisted many newly unemployed laborers. Many of these traveled to New York City by river – sailing past West Point on the way – to join their regiments. Other cities brought in recruits, but New York remained the army's most concentrated source of labor.... The *Army and Navy Chronicle* reprinted an article from the popular *New York Sun* in 1840 on enlistments in New York City. It found sixty-one percent of enlisted men were immigrants.[5] Likewise, Grier's experiences recruiting in New York City reflected the broader reality of an army where half of enlisted men were foreign-born.

Recruits came from across Great Britain and Europe for the entire period from 1835 to 1848. The army accepted "all free white male persons" between ages eighteen to thirty-five who met physical and medical requirements. The army did not take Black or Indigenous recruits, and these rules generally held even as recruiters violated the regulations

---

[4] Steinhauer, Dale Richard, "'Sogers': Enlisted Men in the U.S. Army, 1815–1860," 30–31. Within those years, it provided 19.5% in 1825–1837, 24.2% during 1838–1845, and 21.1% in 1846–1848.

[5] Homans, *Army and Navy Chronicle*, 1840, 11:75. Reprinted from the *New York Sun*. The article reported that 906 US citizens, 811 Irishmen, 179 Englishmen, 143 Germans, 117 Scotchmen, 95 Frenchmen, and 53 Poles enlisted. Immigrants represented 60.7% of the total. These men came from many professions, but the most common was laborer at 653 men. Over 100 men came from the professions of farmer, carpenter, and soldier. The *Sun*, with its smaller newssheet, nonpartisan approach, and one cent price, was the first successful penny newspaper. It reached a mass audience of New Yorkers, across lines of class, ethnicity, and religion, and launched a penny press revolution in print journalism. Huntzicker, *The Popular Press, 1833–1865*, 1, 2, 8, 15. For the Erie Canal and its impact, see: Howe, *What Hath God Wrought*, 117–20. For canals in the context of the Transportation Revolution, see: Taylor, *The Transportation Revolution*, IV:32–55.

1 The Dilemma of Army Cohesion: West Point Officers 37

prohibiting foreign recruits – a judgment on the value of whiteness over national origin. Still, immigrant soldiers made the soldiery an ethnically diverse group. Lieutenant Henry Prince described marching to the Withlacoochee River in Florida, in December of 1835, with a remarkable "medley" of men, including Irish, German, French, Scottish, British, Spanish, Minorcan, Polish, Swedish, Canadian, Nova Scotian, and "South American" soldiers. When Grier returned to New York City as a recruiting officer a few years later, in 1852, he found that the proportion of immigrants in his pool of potential recruits had risen precipitously, from fifty percent in 1838 to seventy-nine percent in 1852–1853. Of the 303 men he enlisted, 240 were immigrants. Most were Irish, a trend across the entire army.[6]

Nativism directed against groups like the Irish worked to the officer corps' advantage because anti-immigrant sentiments legitimized greater authority over enlisted men and hastened the development of army paternalism. As Dale Knobel argues, stereotypes of the Irish grew more negative and less assimilable leading up to the Civil War. Simultaneously, in the army, Irishmen as soldiers and Irishwomen as laundresses carved out gradually surer – but more surely subordinated – places for themselves. Native-born soldiers noticed and resented this shift. One wrote that there was not "a sufficient number of *American citizens*" to fill the ranks, and "hence, as if to render the 'service' still more odious and anti-American, foreigners have been freely received." He believed that "*Certainly half*, and possibly two-thirds of the present rank and file are aliens," noting with disdain the many "intemperate and worthless" soldiers from England, Ireland, Scotland, Wales, Denmark, Sweden, Prussia, Poland, Austria, France, and Italy. He concluded, "is it surprising, then, that young men, entertaining a manly self-respect, and an elevated tone of mind, shun our military service as a moral degradation?"[7] Nativism could work to the advantage of officers who enlisted immigrant men because the officer corps sought to establish itself as a professional cohort, rigidly elevated over a permanently subordinated working class of enlisted men.

---

[6] Skelton, *An American Profession of Arms*, 262; Scott, *General Regulations for the Army*, 1825, 354, Paragraph 1287. The same paragraph contains: "No foreigner shall be enlisted in the army without special permission from general head-quarters. This restriction will not extend to re-enlistments, nor to the enlisting of musicians." In contrast, the army hewed more closely to the prohibition on Black and Indian recruits, though exceptions remained. Prince, *Amidst a Storm of Bullets*, 42; Steinhauer, Dale Richard, "'Sogers': Enlisted Men in the U.S. Army, 1815–1860," 74.

[7] Knobel, *Paddy and the Republic*, 12–13; An American Soldier, *Recollections of the United States Army*, viii.

Officers also sought to retain enlisted men despite a system of military justice that degraded ordinary soldiers and stripped them of many freedoms. William Skelton, a leading historian of the Jacksonian officer corps, poses this very quandary. Skelton notes that the officer corps' central but rarely acknowledged problem was maintaining strict military discipline in an increasingly democratic, individualistic society.[8] Officers continued to employ punishment in the name of military discipline. Yet, rising norms of white male supremacy generated conflict as some enlisted men made claims to equality that contradicted officers' claims to superiority. Army officers managed the growing divide between dual imperatives – the need to impose discipline versus the rising prerogatives of universal white male citizenship.

At West Point, cadet socialization contributed to a nascent culture of paternalism that officers imposed on enlisted men. Working-class enlisted men, in turn, challenged many of the gendered assumptions of their middle-class officers. Officers often subscribed to the rising cult of domesticity and the view of the true woman as a moral leader, a "dignified Christian woman" who "demanded respect and esteem for her sex." Yet, among the working class, the "image of the vain, foolish, sexually duplicitous woman" persisted.[9]

The immense authority of officers, rather than any consensus between officers and enlisted men, enabled officers to push a culture of paternalism onto the rank and file. Still, cultural change was more than mere coercion, and a shaky bridge emerged between New York's ramshackle tenements and Fortress West Point from a somewhat unexpected quarter – the Bowery. The vibrant culture of the Bowery b'hoy had by the 1830s produced a "working-class paternalism" that "stressed the protective rather than the antagonistic elements" of men's involvement with women.[10] For all the differences between officers and enlisted men, the shared notion that men should protect women contained a potential answer to the dilemma of army cohesion.

---

[8] Skelton, *An American Profession of Arms*, xvi, 53, 206.
[9] Stansell, *City of Women*, 68, 96. Barbara Welter argues that "the attributes of True Womanhood, by which a woman judged herself and was judged by her husband, her neighbors and society could be divided into four cardinal virtues – piety, purity, submissiveness and domesticity. Put them all together and they spelled mother, daughter, sister, wife – woman. Without them, no matter whether there was fame, achievement or wealth, all was ashes. With them she was promised happiness and power." Welter, "The Cult of True Womanhood," 152.
[10] Stansell, *City of Women*, 68, 96.

1 The Dilemma of Army Cohesion: West Point Officers 39

Greenberg notes the temptation to map her martial masculinity, embodied by conquering sexualized women, and restrained masculinity, centered around companionate marriage and paternal care for women, onto class. In this simplification, one might label middle-class officers as restrained and working-class enlisted men as martial. But she warns that "although social and economic transformations shaped these two masculinities, they did not determine them."[11] More broadly, while officers and enlisted men often possessed different understandings of manhood, men from across the army shared the belief that women should be subordinate to men. All ranks could share the assumption of women's helplessness.

Cultural formation was just beginning in the late 1830s, when an increasingly West Point-trained officer corps had to fight alongside its increasingly foreign-born, multi-ethnic soldiery in Florida. Nonetheless, by that point, the regular army as an institution had considerably changed. West Point officers led a more structured US Army, a distinct point of departure from the early republic's fledgling force that had participated in the War of 1812 or the First US–Seminole War. As opposed to earlier, more sporadic conflicts with Indigenous peoples, a substantial majority of the officers and soldiers in the regular army served in the Second US–Seminole War, making it the first time since the Revolution that most of the army had waged the same war.[12] The Second US–Seminole War was the regular US Army's first collective, organizational experience. Historian John K. Mahon estimated that 10,169 individuals served in Florida as part of the regular services, mainly from the regular army, with far fewer coming from the regular navy and small marine units.[13] Unlike the War of 1812, where elements of the military dispersed to various locations in North America, the Second US–Seminole War took place entirely in Florida. It was a uniquely complicated place where the army confronted the peninsula's challenging terrain, weather, and disease environment.

Regulars also encountered a landscape of Indigenous groups dating back to Mississippian cultures, the legacies of Spanish and British colonialism, and the effects of US slavery, including through the presence of Black Seminoles, many of whom were, or descended from, people

---

[11] Greenberg, *Manifest Manhood and the Antebellum Empire*, 13.
[12] Skelton, *An American Profession of Arms*, xvi, 53, 206.
[13] Mahon, *History of the Second Seminole War*, 325. In addition to the regulars, about 30,000 volunteers served during the war, often for short periods of time.

who freed themselves from enslavement on US plantations.[14] As the war progressed, army campaigns reached farther south and inland. Fighting a single "Indian War" together, in a single territory, for many years, caused officers' and soldiers' ideas about what it meant to serve to collide amid the complex realities of what many called the Florida War.

Scholars of the Jacksonian army argue for the importance of the 1830s and 1840s as a time of institution building, but there are few scholarly conversations on the search for army cohesion and strategies to achieve or resist it.[15] Historian Lorien Foote offers an exception and takes the need for army unity as a central concern of the Union Army, primarily composed of volunteer soldiers, during the Civil War. Foote notes that "for the army to fight effectively, it had to overcome tensions in the ranks born out of the many cleavages within northern society."[16] Foote's approach to military unity offers a model for earlier periods of army history, although the majority US-born and volunteer-based Union Army's power dynamics were distinct from officer-enlisted relations among the regulars in Florida.

The army that fought the Second US–Seminole War was not a mass of citizen-soldiers, but a small organization dominated by career officers and manned by poor immigrants. Although Union officers could use a rhetoric of equality to persuade volunteers, officers in the 1830s rarely, if ever, spoke of enlisted men as equals. Officers were the paternalistic fathers of the army family, and enlisted men the permanent children, at best elevated to the rank of sergeant and the status of an empowered son. Foreign-born enlisted men served the officer corps well. The portrayals of such men, especially the Irish, as passionate and reckless though good-natured children justified and naturalized officers' authoritarian control over soldiers. If "Paddy was born, not made," that suited officers fine and stabilized their supposed superiority over ethnic inferiors.[17] Within the army family, cadets and recruits walked very different paths and arrived at very different destinations: an officer's commission versus a private soldier's term of enlistment.

---

[14] Porter, *The Black Seminoles*, 5–7.
[15] Edward Coffman's classic *The Old Army* offers a useful example of an army history that uses this organizational device. It separates the experiences of officers from those enlisted men, and from army families. In it, he offers a chapter on officers, another on women and children, and a third on enlisted men, for the period 1815–1860. Coffman, *The Old Army*.
[16] Foote, *The Gentlemen and the Roughs*, 1.
[17] Knobel, *Paddy and the Republic*, 27–28.

THE ARMY FAMILY

As cadets graduated from West Point and became officers, they carried a preference for hierarchy, an assurance that as officers, they would occupy that hierarchy's upper rungs. They believed their authority over enlisted men was proper and natural. Samuel Watson notes that these officers "reacted to individualism, egalitarianism, and anti-institutionalism with a strong distaste for disorder and an emphasis on structured advancement through a bureaucratic hierarchy." While Watson argues that "career officers do not seem to have attempted to replicate military hierarchy in their families" and instead "spoke a temperate language of duty and affection," it is essential to recognize that families *were* hierarchical.[18]

Indeed, the family was the first school of naturalized hierarchy. Its distinct pattern of subordination legitimized men's authority over women and parents' authority over children. Middle-class officers emerged first from the paternalistic domain of the family and then from the paternalistic environment of the military academy, prepared to impose those beliefs on soldiers. Rather than bringing military hierarchies to their families, officers brought a *family hierarchy to the military* and, with it, infused the developing army with a culture of paternalism. Military history has yet to explore how middle-class family structures – newly remade in the Market Revolution – impacted army development.

The years leading up to the war in Florida were seminal ones for West Point. Founded in 1802, the military academy remained a small institution until the 1820s, a decade in which the newly arrived Sylvanus Thayer expanded on the work of earlier Superintendents and took advantage of increasing support for the United States Military Academy following the War of 1812. Thayer departed from the position of Superintendent under political pressure from President Andrew Jackson in 1833 and left behind an enduring institution and a sixteen-year legacy of reform. By 1835, Thayer and others shaped the military academy into a form still familiar to cadets today. Officer Ethan Allen Hitchcock felt that the academy "owed to Major Thayer nearly all of its reputation." Thayer's was an enduring legacy, in part because the Academic Board that he helped render powerful and autonomous remained the military academy's governing body. The 1833 Academic Board members continued in their positions unchanged until 1848, when board member Claudius Berard's death created an opening.[19]

---

[18] Watson, "Flexible Gender Roles during the Market Revolution," 83, 85–86.
[19] Denton III, "The Formative Years of the United States Military Academy, 1775–1833," 282–85; Hitchcock, *Fifty Years in Camp and Field*, 49.

Institutional continuity ensured that cadets throughout the Second US–Seminole War received similar educations. New lieutenants left West Point with deep beliefs in a military hierarchy that invoked officers' supposed moral and cultural superiority to enlisted men and presumed the subordination of women to men. West Pointers had clear-cut ideas about how enlisted men should treat officers. Still, in practice, this hierarchy's complexities based on rank, class, race, and gender revealed the shifting politics and uneven negotiations of power that characterized officer-enlisted relations.

In the 1820s and 1830s, the Secretary of War informally allotted a cadet appointment to each congressional district. This system, ratified by Congress in 1843 during J. R. Poinsett's term as Secretary of War, ensured that every Congressman had a stake in the military academy's success.[20] Although this selection process provided geographical dispersion, as historian William Skelton points out, Congressional nominations "virtually guaranteed" cadets would come from "politically influential, if not necessarily affluent, families, known personally to the representatives of their districts." Cadets came overwhelmingly from middling families, and eighty-six percent of cadets in the antebellum era listed their economic circumstances as "moderate." Unlike most young men in a nation where the majority lived on farms, cadets were far more likely to come from the emerging professional class – merchants, lawyers, physicians, officers, and officeholders.[21] This appointment process, gradually formalized during the Second US–Seminole War as West Point grew in prominence, produced a corps of cadets with heterogenous geographic origins that was nonetheless homogenous by other measures. Most were white, Protestant, native-born, middle-class young men raised in towns and cities.

West Point and the army were homosocial environments that were overwhelmingly, though never entirely, male. In her study of the California Gold Rush's Southern Mines, Susan Lee Johnson demonstrates how gender ordered a majority-male social world. She illustrates how a gendered hierarchy nonetheless interacted with perceived differences in race, ethnicity, social status, and class to shape domestic life. Like Johnson's California, cadet life unfolded in a largely homosocial milieu. Cadets fit into a gendered set of relations – often based on differences in

---

[20] Skelton, *An American Profession of Arms*, 139.
[21] Ibid., 41; Morrison Jr., *"The Best School in the World" West Point, the Pre-Civil War Years, 1833–1866*, 61–62.

rank – that produced domination within the army family. Johnson argues that "skewed sex ratios meant drastically altered divisions of labor in which men took on tasks that their womenfolk would have performed at home."[22] Cadets performed feminine work in proportion to their cadet rank, which advanced as they moved through their years at the academy.

New underclassmen, known as plebes, were the most feminized. They cleaned and followed more senior cadets' instructions. More intimately, among all cadet classes, a longstanding (and against the regulations) tradition of cooking for peers in the barracks emerged and encouraged bonding.[23] But cadets cooked, cleaned, and performed tasks for upperclassmen temporarily – a time scale contingent on rank. The young men passed through such labor as they might pass through a gate. Upon graduation, they became men with the power to compel and feminize their inferiors. When a cadet became an officer, he became more than a man – he became a patriarch.

As future patriarchs – that is, men who generate "interdependence and solidarity" among junior men (their soldiers) partly based on subordinating women – cadets had an abiding interest in shaping how women fit into army families and US society. The cadet Dialectic Society – a group where members met to debate topics from philosophy to politics – addressed such topics. It decided "Ought females to receive a first-rate education?" in the affirmative yet concluded "Ought females to reign over nations?" in the negative.[24] By admitting the importance of education for future mothers yet emphasizing that women should not use education to shape politics, these cadets reflected the Jacksonian era's

---

[22] Johnson, *Roaring Camp*, 100.
[23] Perhaps the most entertaining example of this tradition occurred in October of 1841 when five cadets wrote Secretary of War John Spencer to protest the Superintendent's investigation into two missing ducks. Cadets allegedly stole the ducks from the Superintendent's property and cooked them in the barracks. Cadet Selden explained this miscarriage of justice in indignant (and incriminating) language: "It is generally understood by the members of the Corps, that on, or about the night of the 14th instant two ducks were taken from the vicinity of the Superintendent's quarters, and from the fact that the head and feathers of one were found near the barracks the crime was laid to the charge of the Corps." Selden, "Letter to the Secretary of War," 118–23, Selden to Spencer, October 24, 1841; Meberg, "Murder Most Fowl."
[24] Dialectic Society Cadets, "USMA Dialectic Society Journal 1840–44." Heidi Hartmann writes, "we can usefully define patriarchy as a set of social relations between men, which have a material base, and which, though hierarchical, establish or create interdependence and solidarity among men that enable them to dominate women." Hartmann, "The Unhappy Marriage of Marxism and Feminism: Towards a More Progressive Union," 14. Eve Sedgwick incorporates this definition in her classic study of homosocial desire: Sedgwick, *Between Men*, 3.

broader norms, including new ideas of domesticity born of an increasingly market-oriented society.

Moreover, like other debating clubs and literary societies of the period, the Dialectic Society shaped manhood in a system where "youthful members socialized each other" in the absence of women and older men. Like other young men in similar groups, cadets "trained each other in the harnessing of passions and the habits of self-command," a process heightened by internal hierarchies of rank and seniority within the corps of cadets. Debating and literary clubs were the oldest officially sanctioned cadet extracurricular organizations, beginning with the Amosophic Society of 1816. Several groups combined into the Dialectic Society in 1837. It met on Saturdays, and its invitation-only membership consisted exclusively of "upper-class" cadets who had completed freshman year.[25] The group was an important outlet for members, whom it provided with camaraderie, intellectual challenge, entertainment, and a sanctioned space away from academy officials.

The Superintendent had varying and sometimes contradictory responses to the Dialectic Society. Major Richard Delafield helped the cadets to secure Benjamin Butler, Martin Van Buren's former law partner and Andrew Jackson's recent Attorney General, as a speaker and wrote that he had "taken pains to raise the standing of this society, and stimulate it to increased exertions." Mr. Butler gave an address at the academy in 1839 that stressed how the foundations of good character for the military profession were "*subordination* and *courtesy*," a position obviously in line with West Point's intent to produce officers who accepted the supervision of civil authorities. Yet, in 1842 Delafield disbanded the society for being too divisive. The next Superintendent, Henry Brewerton, reinstated a watered-down version in 1845.[26]

As the Dialectic Society grew, cadets described West Point's emergence from "youth" and into a more mature "Empire of Reason." The institution had conquered ignorance and now yielded voluntarily "to all acknowledged authorities and to the law of nations." The cadet experience supported this concept, as they advanced from the "school of the

---

[25] Rotundo, *American Manhood*, 21; Morrison Jr., *"The Best School in the World" West Point, the Pre-Civil War Years, 1833–1866*, 75–76.

[26] *Superintendent's Letter Book*, 1:164, Major Delafield to BF Butler, April 28, 1839; Butler, *The Military Profession in the United States*, 16; Crackel, *West Point: A Bicentennial History*, 123–24. The file of the Dialectic Society ends in 1843. Dialectic Society Cadets, "USMA Dialectic Society Journal 1840–44" (West Point, New York, 44, and membership roll 1839–42).

1 The Dilemma of Army Cohesion: West Point Officers 45

soldier" in their first (plebe) year at the academy, to the "school of the corporal," then cadet sergeant, then cadet lieutenant, before graduating and commissioning as second lieutenants.[27] When cadets envisioned the empire of reason, they saw themselves walking coolly forward along its carefully laid paths. Theirs was an orderly advancement through the ranks of cadet life, culminating in an officer's privileges upon graduation. They believed that more rank did, and should, confer greater respectability. This regular system led young men to understand that if they met all requirements and continued moving down the road set out for them, they would commission – a model for their expected careers of gradual but probable promotion in the army.

In many ways, this depiction of West Point confirms Ethan Rafuse's characterization of Enlightenment values as a hierarchy with reason and conscience at its peak, competing with the more vigorous base faculties of passions and appetites. Surely officers saw their control over supposedly base and passionate enlisted men in such terms. Rafuse notes that West Point's focus on rationalism reflected the "cultural milieu in which most cadets spent their pre-academy lives." That is, cadets did not learn rationalism *de novo* after arriving at West Point. Instead, they brought notions of hierarchy, reason, and conscience with them from their middle-class households, especially from their fathers. It was a simple transition. As middling US families came to label mothers as the primary parents and caregivers, fathers became heads of household, financial providers, supervisors of son's educations, and chief disciplinarians – the same functions military academy officers performed for cadets.[28]

Notions of family and domesticity illuminated a straightforward route from good son to good cadet, such that cadet conceptions of the "Empire of Reason" had as much to do with Catherine Beecher's domesticity as with John Locke's Enlightenment. Or Locke's *Thoughts Concerning Education* more than his insights into civil government.[29] The father who led his middle-class family was to control himself and offer paternalistic

---

[27] The Rover (Anonymous Cadet Authors, Members of Dialectic Society), *The Empire of Reason*, 15.
[28] Rafuse, "'To Check the Very Worst and Meanest of Our Passions,'" 408; Rotundo, *American Manhood*, 26–28.
[29] Catherine E. Beecher, *A Treatise on Domestic Economy: For the Use of Young Ladies at Home and at School*, Third Edition (New York: Harper & Brothers, Publishers, 1856); John Locke, *An Essay Concerning the True Original Extent and End of Civil Government* (Edes and Gill, in Queen-Street, 1773); John Locke, *Some Thoughts Concerning Education* (University Press, 1892).

guidance to subordinates: his wife and children. Although she could never overcome the sentimental emotions of a woman's nature, the wife and mother embodied conscience, and extended love and care to the children. The children would learn to overcome their base passions, becoming self-controlled adults.

Cadets graduated from child to father when they graduated from West Point, having become men able to lead soldiers, like fathers leading their sons, in "moderation, and Enlightenment rationalism." Their middle-class ethos meant providing leadership, whether in business, government, or the military, and sought progress through institutions.[30] Once cadets reached maturity, they would make the army an "Empire of Reason" where proper subordination reigned. But while at West Point, cadets remained junior members of the army family.

The cadet experience unfolded as advances in transportation and the market economy wrought tremendous change. Like many towns along the newly completed trade route (made possible by the Erie Canal) that stretched from the Great Lakes to Albany and down the Hudson River to New York City, economic reorientation transformed West Point. It went from an isolated outpost to an easily accessible place along an important waterway. The canal system also brought the military academy into the orbit of massive evangelical revivals in the upstate Burned-Over district during the Second Great Awakening. A broader domestic shift accompanied these shifts, marking a transformation from an older household model ruled by an authoritarian man to the new ideal of a home managed by a loving mother and led by a paternalistic father who worked outside the home for wages.[31]

Even as men's work moved out of the household, middle-class norms of domesticity and women-run households moved in at West Point. Mrs. Amelia Thompson, the widow of Captain Alexander Thompson, gained permission to operate a boarding house on West Point after her husband died in 1809. Using her widowhood to claim military protection, she entered the business emblematic of middle-class women's work during the market revolution: monetizing the newly domesticated home. She did so with the labor of both her daughter and a woman of color, Souverine, who ran the Thompson dining room. Souverine was originally from Haiti and spoke French to cadets. One described her as the *maîtresse d'hôtel* and related how cadets enjoyed the "relaxed atmosphere" so much that

---

[30] Rafuse, "To Check the Very Worst and Meanest of Our Passions," 409–10.
[31] Ryan, *Cradle of the Middle Class*, xi.

1 The Dilemma of Army Cohesion: West Point Officers 47

the "cherished privilege was passed on by each graduating boarder to a successor of his choice," with the Superintendent retaining veto power. Another pensioner, like Mrs. Thompson, operated a "soda shop" in the basement of the barracks where cadets could spend one dollar per month on small items such as cakes and candy.[32]

These women were part of the academy's maturation into a developed institution, a process that in turn lent cohesion to the officer corps and its ideas. Socialization into the army's class system continued after graduation. Just as cadets lived in a society literally divided by class – cadet privates formed the "lower-class," then advanced to the "upper-class" ranks of sergeants and officers – cadets emerged as new second lieutenants and took their prescribed places. The *General Regulations* sought to formalize a preference for eating by rank, writing that "it is very desirable that officers of the same regiment, particularly the unmarried officers, should form themselves into a mess, and live together" though "undue familiarity" tends to "disturb the harmony of the mess." Not only with whom one ate, but how one behaved while eating mattered. Regulations stressed that class-based markers remained critical and emphasized "the rules of good breeding." The regulations went on to state that soldiers should form subsequent messes organized by "class" and that it was "highly desirable for the maintenance of the respect and authority due the non-commissioned officers, that a separate mess for this class should be organized." Finally, for soldiers' messes, privates should take turns preparing food, with an emphasis on healthy preparation rather than respectability.[33]

In 1834, Military Affairs committee member Congressman Richard Mentor Johnson argued in defense of the military academy during the latest effort to abolish it. In doing so, he illuminated what it meant for cadets to join the army family. He believed that "the discipline to which the cadets are subject is a judicious combination of military and paternal rule." The academy sought to act as a parent to mold young cadets into officers with the "capacity for command." Johnson believed the academy succeeded, such that "the implied contract with parents to provide moral instruction for their children is fulfilled." To this end, West Point required cadets to maintain clean rooms and persons because they needed

---

[32] Cullum, *The Early History of the United States Military Academy*, III:616–17 from the "Recollections of the Cadet Life of George D. Ramsay"; Morrison Jr., *"The Best School in the World" West Point, the Pre-Civil War Years, 1833–1866*, 78.
[33] War Department, *General Regulations for the Army of the United States*, 91, 94.

to develop a sense of responsibility and set an example for their future soldiers. The "personal comfort and health" of soldiers would "depend materially, if not entirely, upon" the officer.[34]

Johnson's ideas about paternal discipline emerged from his experiences as an "Indian fighter" and slaveowner. He grew up on his family's Kentucky plantation and used enslaved labor to run it as an adult; he fought in the War of 1812, where he led the charge that killed Indigenous leader Tecumseh; supported the Indian Removal Act and the Second US–Seminole War, to include as Martin Van Buren's Vice President; and ran an "Indian School" also called the "Choctaw School," the group whose annuities partly funded it. Such arrangements were part of a broader "discourse of adoption" that brought Indigenous children into white homes to assimilate them into a "white national family," making them "permanent youth whose social, political, and intellectual maturity was constantly deferred." Men like Johnson saw cadets as future managers in this national family. Once commissioned, new officers would care for and discipline immigrant soldiers – permanent sons who would never rise to equality. Still, as white men, soldiers stood above Native peoples, who in turn remained higher than the enslaved population. It was, as Laurel Clark Shire notes, "the same paternalism that justified slavery and Indian Removal."[35]

Johnson's whole life embodied an imperialistic idea of paternalism rooted in taming Indigenous subject populations. He applied these hierarchical standards to cadets, expecting them to develop into men capable of imposing discipline on inferiors. Johnson gave voice to a powerful set of obligations and dependencies. West Point assumed a parent's role to dependent cadets, whom the academy's officers expected to return obedience. Yet, officers at the academy only enacted this program to prepare cadets to assume the role of parent. Even the most newly minted lieutenant from West Point was a provider to his subordinates.

To become an officer, then, was to become not only a man but a father to one's soldiers. Under the watchful gaze of a patriarch in the

---

[34] *Twenty Third Congress, First Session*, 347–51, Richard Johnson, May 17, 1834.
[35] To illuminate how gender fit into Johnson's thinking, it is worth noting that he treated Julia Chinn, an enslaved mixed-race woman, as his common-law spouse, but never emancipated her – a choice in keeping with his paternalistic idea of hierarchy. Among other duties, she helped administer the Choctaw School. "Something About Col. Dick Johnson's Indian School," 39; Peterson, *Indians in the Family: Adoption and the Politics of Antebellum Expansion*, 2–3, 234, 245, 246–47, 259–62; Shire, "Sentimental Racism and Sympathetic Paternalism," 113.

form of the Superintendent, the military academy of the 1830s pursued its mission of producing morally grounded and well-educated citizens who understood their subordinate place to civil authority. West Point's ethic of care – in which officers were responsible for cadets' moral, physical, and intellectual development and disciplined those who broke the rules to rehabilitate the rulebreaker's character – was distinctly paternal. Understanding West Point as a paternal institution helps make sense of how young men shifted from childlike obedience and dependence as cadets to manly authority and independence as officers and demonstrates the importance of officers' parental approach toward their soldiers.

This approach also reveals an internal civilizing mission, where officers sought to impose their values onto enlisted men. Discourse on civilizing missions most frequently refers to US efforts to pacify, remove, or destroy Indigenous peoples from the midst of encroaching white settlements. Officers also enacted this process within the army to excise "savage" elements of soldiers' behaviors and emphasize officers' civility. The Second US–Seminole War era army was only just beginning to be an accepted institution in US life. Its leaders saw that to enhance their respectability, they needed to raise the army's perceived morality. So, they engaged in repeated efforts to encode moral influence into the institution itself. It was no benign process.

Officers' internal civilizing mission aimed to subordinate young officers to army authority and unruly enlisted men to officers' authority. Balancing punishment with caretaking enhanced the institution's respectability – officers had to discipline *and* support soldiers. Yet, the superiority necessary to this paternalistic conception of officership could also contribute to general "disaffection...between privates and their officers." Army regulations required that officers' authority "shall be even, mild, and paternal." Officers should treat enlisted men "with particular kindness and humanity." The regulations conceded that although punishment is "sometimes unavoidable" because "the government requires that the superior shall always find in the inferior a passive obedience," they also enjoined the officer "not to injure those under him," and to create a "spirit of goodwill, and even of brotherhood." Officers should dispense advice and admonishment as a father might.[36]

The reality of a soldier's life fell short of these gentle ideals, and punishment remained part of the enlisted experience's very fabric.

---

[36] *Twenty Fourth Congress, Second Session*, March 1, 1837; Scott, *General Regulations for the Army*, 1825, 13–15, 31–32.

Regular army officer Lieutenant John Phelps described a mild example of an informal reprimand in a letter to his sister. He wrote that the army in Florida was "something like an excerpt of feudal times, the law you know is arbitrary. Which fact a recruit I think learned today since he was obliged to walk to and fro briskly for a long time with a gag in his mouth, and merely because he did not feel inclined to work!" Phelps concluded of this Dutch immigrant soldier that "he is a youngster yet and has a great deal to learn," presumably about obeying his superiors in rank.[37]

The military justice system's most formal tool to construct submission was the court-martial. Officers who ran the court-martial process used it to destroy challenges to their authority. Most cases in Florida dealt with some combination of guard duty, alcohol, disobedience to superiors, and desertion. These offenses reflected the limited scope of early military justice, which focused on regulating internal relationships between officers, non-commissioned officers, and junior enlisted men rather than regulating external interactions between members of the army and other groups. Later courts-martial during the US–Mexican War greatly expanded in scope to encompass crimes committed against civilians. Yet, in Florida, the courts-martial process reflected the army's early stage of development. They were an administrator's tool to create order, discipline, and subordination.

In service of this goal, the officers called to serve on courts and the senior officers who approved punishments handed down various penalties in Florida. A soldier found asleep at his post was sentenced to "three months hard labor by day and close confinement by night and to forfeit one month's pay." A soldier who drew a knife on a lieutenant and refused to obey an order was sentenced to "three months hard labor by day and close confinement by night, chained by the leg to an iron ball until the expiration of his term of service" and forfeiture of pay. Several soldiers found guilty of desertion were sentenced to "fifty lashes with a cat-o'-nine-tails on his bare back, and to be drummed out of service."[38] Physical punishments like these were common, and they were applied exclusively to soldiers (and slaves) – officers could not receive sentences of corporal punishment.

[37] John W. Phelps, "Letters from J. W. Phelps to Sisters, Miss Helen M. Phelps," 1837–1838, December 17, 1838, Library of Congress Manuscript Division, Manuscript Collection. John Phelps to sister, Helen.
[38] "Court-Martial Case Files, 1809–1894," RG153, Case numbers 150 (April 8, 1836), 151 (April 11, 1836), and 215 (October 30, 1836), National Archives, Washington DC.

1 The Dilemma of Army Cohesion: West Point Officers

Cases dealing with alcohol offer valuable examples of the parallel standards applied to officers compared to enlisted men. Regulations stated that "any commissioned officer who shall be found drunk on his guard, party, or other duty, shall be cashiered," meaning expelled from the army. "Any non-commissioned officer or soldier so offending, shall suffer such corporeal punishment as shall be inflicted by the sentence of a court-martial."[39] The essential differences between those who could be beaten and those who could not exemplified how army officers imagined their institution in the family's image and used the rules of fatherly discipline: fathers did not receive physical punishment. They administered it.

Samuel Watson argues that "The concept of family had potent ideological value for officers. Commanders frequently used familial and patriarchal metaphors to describe their relationships with enlisted men." Officers' letters in *Military and Naval Magazine* and the *Army and Navy Chronicle* "stressed the family's role in moral and patriotic education, and officials at West Point, like those in civilian colleges during the period, considered themselves in loco parentis to their charges." One Lieutenant in Florida, writing of a brother officer's death, noted the man's final words: "He addressed his men in that familiar but decisive manner, (which made them always love and obey him)." He said, "Boys, *stand* your ground, and don't give way an *inch*." None questioned that the officer was the father in his army family and the enlisted men the sons. Officers said as much. One wrote that "what the child is to the parent, the private is to the General, or least officer commanding; and from him, he expects justice and kind treatment, as a member of the same family."[40] Of course, this exchange of total obedience and loyalty for just and fatherly treatment lived more fully in officers' fantasies than in reality, where the paternal ideal gave way to a climate marked by mistrust and misunderstanding.

IMMIGRANT TO SOLDIER

Toward the end of the Second US–Seminole War, a mixed navy and army force undertook a canoe expedition deep into the Everglades to root out remaining Seminole families. In the official report, the expedition

---

[39] War Department, *General Regulations for the Army of the United States*, 10, Article 45, Appendix.
[40] Watson, "Flexible Gender Roles during the Market Revolution," 85; Homans, *Army and Navy Chronicle*, 1839, 8:281, C. E. Woodruff to H. P. Russell, dated March 3, 1839; Rapp, "The Soldier."

commander US Navy Lieutenant John Rodgers noted that he and his men had "less rest, fewer luxuries, and harder work than fall to the lot of that estimable class of citizens who dig our canals." Rodgers may not have known how apt his comparison was. He intended to underscore how arduous the expedition had been in comparison to despised canal work, typical for immigrant laborers in the 1830s. Yet many sailors, like many soldiers, *had* dug canals before enlisting. Soldiering meant manual labor far more than firing a weapon.[41] Rodgers sought to compliment his men by noting how hard they worked and how well they performed in thankless conditions. Still, he demonstrated a failure to grasp the enlisted world. The group he sardonically termed the "estimable class of citizens" of canal workers was, in fact, the provenance of many soldiers.

One poor enlistee was New Yorker James Bennett, who joined the army in Rochester to alleviate his mother's poverty. Bennett traveled down the Hudson to New York City, where in his barracks at Governor's Island the room "contained from 60 to 70 persons from all quarters of the globe. Ethiopia excepted." That night, he watched and listened to his fellow soldiers and recorded their diverse origins in a litany of tropes. He first "Heard a Dutch song by a group of German representatives. In another place is heard the 'Sacre, Mon Dieu!' which emanates from a dark, curly-headed French man. We next hear a witty story, from a son of Erin's Isle, interrupted of course by long whiffs of smoke from his stump of a pipe." In addition to the major demographic groups of German and Irish recruits, Bennett noted that

> In another portion of the room is seen in earnest converse a party of Poles and Hungarians, perhaps sympathizing with each other upon their countries' recent annexation by Austria. We also see an Englishman complaining of the bill of fare while at one corner of the fireplace sitting "solitary and alone" whittling and whistling is a Yankee right out of Vermont.[42]

Officers accepted that Bennett's observations would be true of most units and that many soldiers would be immigrants, because most native-born men would not enlist.

Many enlisted men were also Catholics, and regular army attitudes toward religion changed in the 1830s and 1840s. Several years after the

---

[41] Preble, The Late Rear Admiral, U.S.N., "The Diary of a Canoe Expedition," March 29, March 30, April 11. Autumn Hope McGrath demonstrates that US military labor relied on a "partially-unfree labor force essential to the advance of U.S. imperialism." McGrath, "An Army of Working-Men," vii.

[42] Bennett, *Forts and Forays*, 1, 4–5.

1 The Dilemma of Army Cohesion: West Point Officers

War of 1812, the only regular army chaplain was the one overburdened soul who held that position at West Point and was responsible both for teaching the humanities and ensuring cadets' spiritual development. As the US waged war against the Catholic nation of Mexico a few years later, the army gained twenty chaplains, mostly attached to volunteer units, including two Catholic chaplains without official appointments who served as de facto brigade chaplains – a pragmatic decision in Catholic Mexico rather than an embrace of religious freedom or an attempt to serve Catholic enlisted men.

Despite the Second Great Awakening's religiosity and the anti-Catholicism that Protestant zeal sometimes supported, the US Army demonstrated a marked disinterest in officializing religion. Although US politicians passed a law in 1838 authorizing commanders to hire civilian chaplains to serve army posts and another in 1847 authorizing brigade chaplains, the Secretary of War never ordered the clergy to leave their garrisons and accompany troops into Mexico. Of the twenty Mexican War chaplains, only one served with the regulars. The rest belonged in volunteer units. Regular army officers *employed* civilian chaplains – usually to advance officers' efforts to civilize enlisted men – but they rarely *commissioned* chaplains into their officer corps.[43] In the army of the 1830s and 1840s, where officers strove to establish themselves as respectable professionals, clergy were a tool for officers in a crusade against enlisted intemperance and disobedience.

Building on religion's supposed connection to improved discipline, some officers began to lobby for a chaplain program. First Lieutenant J. S. Gallagher wrote to Senator Benjamin Swift in 1836 "on the want of religious and moral instruction in the army" and argued that the army was uniquely denied "religious privileges" in contrast to the rest of society. He continued, "Nowhere more than in the army are the fruits of religion needed: fidelity, temperance, and cheerful obedience are the sinews of its efficiency." Gallagher argued that chaplains would improve the performance of enlisted men by rendering them sober and hard-working. They would also help make soldiers' influence on Indigenous groups "one of unmixed good." As a result of this internal civilizing mission, the army went from having a single chaplain at West Point to appointing Protestant chaplains in 1838.[44] As in Florida, the army needed to civilize

---

[43] Budd, *Serving Two Masters* Chapter Two, "American Military Chaplaincy, 1607–1860."
[44] *Twenty Fourth Congress, First Session*, 119–20, February 17, 1836. Gallagher to Swift; *Twenty Fifth Congress, Second Session*, 259, July 5, 1838. "An act to increase the present military establishment of the United States, and for other purposes."

itself before civilizing other peoples and places. Officers hoped increased religiosity among soldiers would lessen the need for corporal punishment.

Army chaplains provided more than religious instruction – they offered practical schooling. An 1832 proposal suggested that young soldiers receive an education "after the manner of the cadets at West Point, only beginning at the very rudiments of instruction in everything to be taught." This policy would require the army to establish schools on army posts "for the purpose of teaching such branches of education as will fit and prepare the soldiers for situations of usefulness in life." The proposal further claimed that boys, when they enlist, should be far younger than the minors now allowed to enlist at sixteen or seventeen. Instead, enlistees would ideally be twelve or thirteen – a proposal that emphasized how officers considered good soldiers to be boys, not men – so that they could learn English reading and writing, mathematics, and "the various handicrafts" useful to soldiers. While this plan from Army Headquarters did not come to fruition, the army successfully developed its chaplain program to include schooling. General Orders published in 1838 confirmed the employment of chaplains at military posts. As at West Point, it required chaplains to serve as schoolmasters, and in this capacity, chaplains taught the children of both officers and enlisted men. The army's use of chaplains for religious and secular instruction, an outgrowth of West Point policy, underscored the academy's importance as a primary site of institutional development.[45]

In the Governor's Island barracks, James Bennett and the Yankee were two US-born men in a barracks room full of immigrants. Rather than attempting to change this, officers created a place for foreign-born soldiers in their units in exchange for submission enforced by punishment. In his extensive study of antebellum soldiers, Dale Steinhauer notes that "while Americans declined to step forward to fill the ranks, the Irish and others of foreign birth performed the despised and necessary task of defending the nation." An immigrant army had its benefits, and foreign-born soldiers were less likely to desert. Measured by desertion rates, the most reliable soldiers were non-native English speakers, many of whom were German.[46] Yet, if necessity ensured immigrants had a place in the army, that place was permanently subordinate.

---

[45] *Twenty Fifth Congress, Second Session*, 121, from Army Headquarters, February 1832, received by House of Representatives December 17, 1832; *Orders, Headquarters of the Army, 1835–1839*, 225A:198–99, General Orders 29, War Dept, Adjutant General Officer, August 1838, order conforms to Act of July 5, 1838 Section 18.

[46] Steinhauer, Dale Richard, "'Sogers': Enlisted Men in the U.S. Army, 1815–1860," 211, 114.

1 The Dilemma of Army Cohesion: West Point Officers

Officers' treatment of soldiers may have brought enlisted men together. Many built relationships with peers, as did enlisted soldier and Scottish immigrant George Ballentine, who recalled his company's debating society while stationed in Tampa. Ballentine's New York orderly sergeant (first sergeant) Sergeant Beebe formed the society and found a room to hold debates. A dozen soldiers joined from 120 or so stationed there, and they held meetings on Friday evenings. Ballentine believed that his society was a source of some knowledge and much amusement and found it reflective of similar societies in civilian life. The men who joined had been in debating societies before the army. After about three months, their society ended. They believed it was because the commanding officer heard about the most recent debate topic, "whether does the civil or military life offer the highest rewards and incentives to an honorable ambition?" and found it dangerous. One can see why the commander may have thought so in an army that, like many armies, suppressed dissent. Thus disbanded, they voted to use their excess funds on "as much whiskey as the money would procure" and spent "an exceedingly convivial evening."[47] Ironically, this officer reinforced the need for unquestioning subordination in these soldiers at the cost of magnifying intemperance. Officers may have wanted soldiers to be virtuous, but this one wanted obedience more.

Drunkenness among soldiers could help officers consolidate control by demonstrating the need for paternal guidance. Complaints of intemperance often came coupled with remarks on efforts to reform soldiers, as when Colonel William Worth wrote that "It appears that drunkenness prevails amongst the troops stationed at Fort Micanopy, notwithstanding the efforts of the officers to the contrary, to the great injury of their health and efficiency."[48] Officers sought to improve soldiers, either inwardly through moral suasion or outwardly by punishment, and thus increase discipline. Temperance offered one form of "improvement," but many officers found temperance policies – like the 1832 proposal to eliminate the soldier's daily ration of whiskey – insufficient. In response, they sought greater control over enlisted morality.

---

[47] Ballentine, *Autobiography of an English Soldier*, 115–20. While the Second US–Seminole War ended in 1842, and Ballentine wrote of his debating society in the summer of 1846, it is likely such societies proliferated in wartime and across the army. In 1842, Cadets of the West Point Dialectic Society debated a similar question: "Has our government derived more glory from her military men than from her statesmen?" They decided it in the negative. Dialectic Society Cadets, "USMA Dialectic Society Journal 1840–44."

[48] *9th Military Department, Letters Sent*, 123–24, June 26, 1841. Worth to Lieutenant Colonel Riley.

Officers invoked both religious and secular arguments to enhance their power, claiming they knew best. An article in *Military and Naval Magazine* that argued in favor of Sunday inspections claimed the practice mirrored the preparations "a well-constituted and cultivated man daily undergoes to preserve his health and comfort...a privilege which consists in the ability to be cleanly and decently clad." They continued, "its mere enjoyment constitutes in itself a moral duty." Soldiers would not, officers argued, make the right choices. Instead, officers had to impose mandatory time "devoted to moral or mental culture." Much as this supervision was like that of a stern father holding sons to a high standard, the act of inspecting soldiers was "analogous to that of the fond mother who scrubs and decently arrays her heedless and wayward urchins ere she leads them forth to the house of worship." Were the army to cancel this beneficial practice, the author continued, and enlisted men left to their own devices, only moral and mental degradation would result: "Thus released from the supervision of their officers on the day of rest, how does the philanthropist imagine the soldier is employed, without intellectual cultivation enough to relish a book, and not furnished with the means of religious instruction?"[49]

One imagines that highly literate enlisted men like George Ballentine, who once silenced a civilian disparaging Ballentine and his fellow soldiers with an apt Shakespeare quotation, could have found many responses to such a question. Yet to the author, the answer was vice: "Speaking of a body, as a mass, let one who has some experience tell him; in sleep or supine sloth, in plotting the means of procuring, or in using vicious indulgences, in drinking and gambling. These are the recreations of uncultivated men, abandoned to themselves and released from the control of their Inspectors." Officers had to lead (regulate and discipline) their soldiers, who would otherwise be "heedless and wayward wretches" and "uncultivated men." When army policy moved inspections from Sunday, a similar article invoked the prerogatives of a patriarch, writing that the Sunday inspections were a "custom which prevails throughout Christendom, where every head of a family sees that all under his charge are, on this day, neatly and cleanly clad, becoming the day and befitting its services."[50] Officers did not want anyone interfering with the running of their army families.

[49] Vent, "Sunday Inspections."
[50] Ibid. Ballentine related the following anecdote, which occurred as he and other recruits traveled by steamboat from the Battery in New York City to join his unit in Rhode Island. The majority of the boat's passengers "seemed to look upon us in the light of

1 The Dilemma of Army Cohesion: West Point Officers

Despite these disadvantages, enlistment offered employment, education, and a measure of job security to immigrant men. Though military service came with strict discipline and plentiful discomfort, "coming into American society at or near the bottom, the Catholic Irish sorely needed allies, even protectors." David Roediger explains, "They quickly found them in two institutions that did not question their whiteness: the Catholic Church and the Democratic party." To this list, one should add the enlisted ranks of the US Army. The regulars heavily recruited Irishmen, whom it considered "free white male persons," and imposed no religious qualifications on enlistment.[51] Even if Irish soldiers became sergeants less easily than English and US-born men, the army promoted Irishmen as non-commissioned officers (the equivalent of foremen in civilian life).

Although the officer corps made it nearly impossible for enlisted men to earn a commission, becoming a soldier offered some social benefits. Regulations prohibited Black or Native recruits, so those the army took gained a measure of whiteness by implication. Many Whiggish members of the middle-class considered Irish Catholics wild or partly "savage," but officers had few qualms about using such men as soldiers. They simply responded to concerns over Irish "savagery" by excluding enlisted men from the officer corps, exercising rigid and violent discipline, and deploying those soldiers against Native peoples that the US public considered more "savage" than the Irish.

---

a degraded caste, and seemed to think that there was contamination in the touch of a soldier; for it is a singular fact that though Jonathan [a Yankee, an American] is so vain of his military prowess, and a little too apt to boast of the wonderful exploits of those armies of his that can whip all creation so easily, it is only in the collective term, or as an abstract idea; he is exceedingly shy of the individuals who compose it. In reply to some casual observation made by a fellow passenger upon our appearance on board, I chanced to overhear an old fellow of most vinegar-looking aspect drily remark, 'Ay, ay! They are a fine set of candidates for the States prison.' I was standing partly concealed by some boxes that stood upon the deck, and to do the old fellow justice, I believe he did not intend that his remark should reach a soldier's ears: however, I could not resist the impulse of the moment which prompted me to repeat for his edification Sir John's reply to Prince Hal, when criticizing his soldiers rather too curiously, 'Tut, tut, good enough to toss, food for powder, food for powder; they'll fill a pit as well as better: tush, man, mortal men, mortal men.' My quotation, while it rather took the old fellow by surprise, and raised a smile among a few of the surrounding passengers, had the more substantial effect of being the means of procuring me a good bed that night." Ballentine, *Autobiography of an English Soldier*, 30–32; Vent, "Sunday Inspections."

[51] Roediger, *The Wages of Whiteness*, 140; Scott, *General Regulations for the Army*, 1825, 354, Paragraph 1287.

The Democratic Party of the 1830s "appreciated the ways in which the idea that all Blacks were unfit for civic participation could be transmuted into the notion that all whites were so fit," and so too did the army. Although other work for recent immigrants, like digging canals, could also be performed by free or enslaved Black men, this was not true of soldiering, which was racially exclusive. As a soldier, Irish-Americans could distinguish their labor as a job fit for white men. However slight, soldiering conferred a racial benefit on immigrant men who might otherwise perform unskilled manual labor alongside enslaved people.[52]

While enlistment offered economic and racial opportunities, officers ensured a strict separation from the rank and file. Although cadets moved predictably from cadet private to cadet officer to commissioned officer, significant barriers prevented enlisted men from commissioning. It was exceedingly rare for soldiers to become officers, whether directly or through an appointment to attend the military academy. Dale Steinhauer's study of enlisted men from 1826 to 1860 showed that less than 0.3% of soldiers did so. This small number of enlisted men included nine commissioned as second lieutenants in 1837 and 1838, after a sixth of the officer corps resigned in 1835 and 1836, and were the last such promotions until the Mexican War. West Point strengthened this barrier between soldier and officer. One veteran wrote that because of West Point, "young men of character and enterprise rarely enlist, because they well know, that on a peace establishment, no higher rank than a *Sergeantcy can be obtained.*" As West Point cadets came to receive an increasing majority of commissions, fewer non-military academy officers could gain them.[53]

Those few who made or attempted the leap from soldier to officer often hid their past to avoid the perceived stigma of enlisted service. When Edgar Allen Poe arrived as a cadet in 1830, he concealed two years of enlisted service from 1827 to 1829. Poe was so successful it was not until years after his death that a biographer uncovered his time in the First Artillery Regiment. Poe's experience illuminates a second barrier.

---

[52] Roediger, *The Wages of Whiteness*, 141. See Seth Rockman's description of laborers at work on the Chesapeake & Delaware Canal in 1826: Rockman, *Scraping By*, 71.

[53] Steinhauer, Dale Richard, "'Sogers': Enlisted Men in the U.S. Army, 1815–1860," 281–82, 305–6; An American Soldier, *Recollections of the United States Army*, vii; Homans, *Army and Navy Chronicle*, 1837, 5:378. The 1850s saw two more such promotions though most (16) occurred during the Civil War. In total, from 1815 to 1860, only about 100 officers had a history of service as enlisted men, many only for the duration of the Mexican War.

1 The Dilemma of Army Cohesion: West Point Officers

Where most immigrants remained private soldiers, many native-born enlisted men quickly ascended to non-commissioned officer. In just two years' service, the native-born Poe attained the high rank of Sergeant Major.[54] Officers limited enlisted men's access to the officer corps *and* promoted native-born and English soldiers to sergeant at higher rates, thus limiting immigrant men's influence.

Limiting access was a central value of officer paternalism. It carried over to how officers incorporated working-class women, usually the wives of enlisted men, into the army as laundresses. Although camp followers had served in the military since the Revolution's early days, the officially sanctioned army laundress was born a twin to the military academy at West Point. The same Military Peace Establishment Act of 1802 brought both into the world, and of the two, the laundress was the elder. Section 5 established that "the women who may be allocated to the particular corps" should not exceed four to a company and would receive one ration each, the same as a non-commissioned officer, private, musician, or officer's servant. Matrons and nurses employed in army hospitals would also receive one ration per woman. This policy worked out to a ratio of about one woman per seventeen men. Section 27 directed that the garrison at West Point "shall constitute a military academy."[55] From these shared beginnings grew a complicated relationship wherein officers led large army families populated by men and women of many ranks, races, and statuses.

The presence of female workers in most army units "violated some of the dearest held genteel precepts" of women's domestic nature that middle-class officers cherished. Simultaneously, laundresses offered concrete subjects for officer paternalism – a way to improve men's values. This reformist impulse meant that an officer who walked among his soldiers and soldiers' families in garrison had much in common with his middle-class counterparts who walked through the tenements of New York – both saw a need for uplift. The parallel processes of class formation and the "thorough-going transformation of the gender system" in New York described by historian Christine Stansell produced not only

---

[54] Steinhauer, Dale Richard, "'Sogers': Enlisted Men in the U.S. Army, 1815–1860," 2, 291, 341. Poe left the academy after only a few months. He was one of only three former soldiers known to have attended West Point from 1815 to 1860. It is possible that there are others, whose histories of enlisted service remain undiscovered.

[55] "Military Peace Establishment Act of 1802"; US Army Military History Institute, "Army Laundresses: A Working Bibliography of MHI Sources." For camp followers during the American Revolution, see: Mayer, *Belonging to the Army*.

a "domestic ideology as part of a vision of a reformed city, purged of the supposed perfidies of working-class life," but a vision of a reformed army.⁵⁶ Officers hoped they would rule temperate, dutiful, and obedient enlisted men, purged of the vices – drinking, violence, disobedience – they believed marred the soldiery. Relationships within the army between reform-minded officers and the poor men and women they controlled thus fostered paternalism.

Being a laundress meant hard labor but offered much in return. She received cash at standardized rates set by the officers who comprised a unit or post's Council of Administration. What a soldier owed to a laundress would by army regulation be deducted from his pay before he received it, like his debts to the sutler, with "the Laundress having the preference." Many a court-martial ended with a soldier's pay stopped, except for the "just claims of the laundress."⁵⁷ Compared to the starvation wages poor women received in New York City and the many hours of unwaged labor that poor women performed, the guarantee of army payments – hard cash for hard work plus a measure of economic independence – must have felt like a breath of freedom.

Unlike women in the working-class neighborhoods of lower Manhattan, extreme poverty did not menace the laundress who lost a male provider. In fact, laundresses could easily out-earn a husband who served as a private and could earn more by hiring out her services to cook and clean for an officer or a group of officers organized into a mess. One lieutenant described an arrangement where a laundress in the Seventh Infantry Regiment, Mrs. Lindsay, would cook and do laundry for three officers for fifteen dollars per month. Assuming she earned a typical eight dollars over the same period for doing her company's laundry, Mrs. Lindsay would have made about twenty-three dollars a month, nearly the same as monthly twenty-five dollar pay drawn by a second lieutenant and far more than an infantryman's seven dollars or a sergeant's thirteen. Together, a couple could combine their earnings to achieve a level of comfort beyond subsistence and provide for the children many either brought along upon enlistment or had while in service.⁵⁸

---

⁵⁶ Stansell, *City of Women*, xi–xii.
⁵⁷ War Department, *General Regulations for the Army of the United States*, 37, Article XL, Paragraphs 201 and 202. "Court-Martial Case Files, 1809–1894," RG153, National Archives, Washington DC. Case File EE338, March 23, 1847, Tampico. *9th Military Department, Letters Sent.* April 1, 1841, Order Book No. 4, Orders No. 13, Tampa.
⁵⁸ Stansell, *City of Women*, 45. Dana, *Monterrey Is Ours!*, 8. War Department, *General Regulations for the Army of the United States*, 347. By comparison, a cadet under the

1 The Dilemma of Army Cohesion: West Point Officers

Still, laundresses labored under many disadvantages. Most were married women, who had no legal control over their wages, and officers could arbitrarily expel laundresses for purportedly bad behavior. Plus, units could only have a handful of official laundresses, so wives of non-commissioned officers were more likely than those of newly enlisted men to claim the limited and lucrative positions.[59] Also, though living in New York City for recently emigrated families was hard, when a husband enlisted and brought along his wife to be a laundress, she lost the support network of women in her urban neighborhood and entered a homosocial space.

An urban community could generate collective female power that "counterposed itself to men's privileges," but the handful of working women at an army camp had no such power. In an army camp or frontier post, a few fellow laundresses might be her only immediate source of communal support. The other women consistently present, officer's wives, belonged to a distinctly different social world. Though they held junior positions, laundresses who labored in the army were, as military historian Robert Wetteman argues, "part of the extended family of the regular soldier." More than that, working women were a part of the army family that officers sought to manage as patriarchs.[60]

CADET TO OFFICER

Second Lieutenant William Warren Chapman of Springfield, Massachusetts, graduated from West Point with the Class of 1837. He was at war in Florida only months later, arriving in October of that year. During the few months between West Point and Fort Brooke, he wrote to his fiancée: "our duties are pretty hard at present as we are fitting the troops for Florida. I have command of a company of 65 men. I am allowed an orderly who keeps with me all the time ready to obey my slightest wishes: besides him, I keep a valet." His valet was probably a civilian servant, free or enslaved, though servants in Florida were more likely than elsewhere to be enslaved. Like Chapman, many newly minted

---

same "Artillery and Infantry" pay table rated sixteen dollars per month, a second lieutenant twenty-five, and a first lieutenant thirty. Robert P. Wettemann, "The Girl I Left behind Me? United States Army Laundresses and the Mexican War," *Army History* PB-20-99-1, no. 26 (Fall to Winter 1999 1998): 2–3.

[59] Steinhauer, Dale Richard, "Sogers," 52.
[60] Stansell, *City of Women*, 83. Wettemann, "The Girl I Left behind Me?," 6.

second lieutenants began fighting in the Second US–Seminole War only months after graduating from West Point. They arrived with deeply held ideas about social "relations of difference and domination," ideas that warranted using soldiers and (free or enslaved) servants to cater to one's "slightest wishes." Chapman's attitude closely matched not so much his New England origins but a regular officer's perspective – a testament to army paternalism's malleability. Having always expected to lead his army family, he found command over soldiers *and* servants natural.[61]

The West Point's Dialectic Society reflected this insistence on hierarchy. It twice debated whether universal suffrage should be allowed and twice decided it should not. In a third debate soon after, the young men concluded that "the right of suffrage in our Government [was] generally too extended at present."[62] While cadets chafed against the academy's many restrictions and regulations, most believed that they deserved more privileges than the lower sort of men. Cadets simultaneously resisted control from superiors and expected that they would soon control subordinates, mediating a Jacksonian outlook for their rights as members of a broad class of white men with aristocratic expectations of commanding others.

The most recent revision of army regulations before the war in Florida, published in 1825, emphasized this difference. While they limited the type of corporal punishment that the army could legally use, they permitted confinement and various sanctioned forms of corporal punishment for noncommissioned officers and soldiers. In contrast, regulations prohibited such penalties for cadets and officers except under extreme circumstances. For cadets, that required Presidential approval. In this social hierarchy, cadets assumed they would occupy the upper echelons. They would remain subordinate to US civil authorities and superior officers as befitted a standing army that still existed somewhat awkwardly in the US republic. In return, they expected entrance into respectable society.

Cadets also assumed they would rule over subordinates. Accordingly, the Dialectic Society believed the US should permit foreign (probably meaning European) immigration. At a time when most enlisted men were immigrants, cadets recognized the need for this recruiting pool. They believed that such men, deemed admissible but inferior, would fit naturally into their spheres of command. Dialectic Society cadets also

---

[61] Johnson, *Roaring Camp*, 12; Chapman, "A West Point Graduate in the Second Seminole War: William Warren Chapman and the View from Fort Foster," 447, 453–54; Hamdani, "The Slaveholding Army," 256.

[62] Dialectic Society Cadets, "USMA Dialectic Society Journal 1840–44," February 6, 1841, May 1, 1841, February 12, 1842.

found phrenology consistent with nature and believed the feudal system benefited society. They cherished republican ideals over democratic ones and believed government should not always legislate according to the people's will. They claimed that the US government derived more glory from her statesman than from her military men, marking the essential subordination of army to state, mirroring the submission of soldiers to officers.[63]

Clubs were one outlet for a cadet's limited free time. The library was another. Cadets supplemented required reading with more exciting books on heroes, war, conquest, and chivalry. Cadets could check out one book at a time, on Saturdays only. In the years leading up to the Second US–Seminole War, they read epic histories of the US, England, and the ancient world. They devoured works on George Washington, studied Napoleon's Peninsular War, read philosophy, and learned of the crusades. They followed popular newspapers such as *Niles' Register* and the *American Quarterly Review*. In addition, the Dialectic Society maintained a small, separate library that included numerous periodicals and several dozen books. Like the West Point library, the society's contained works on ethics and chivalry, notably *On Chivalry and the Crusades* and G. P. R. James's *History of Chivalry*, which promoted a romanticized view of war in keeping with 1830s popular literature.[64]

Although the officer corps, like the military academy, often tried to insulate itself from the civilian world, complete cultural separation was impossible. When cadets read *History of Chivalry*, published in 1830, they found similarities to the cadet experience. James understood chivalry as "a military institution" that was "sanctioned by religion," whose purpose was to "protect the weak...and to defend the right."[65] West Point was, of course, a military institution, sanctioned by religion via

---

[63] Dialectic Society Cadets, "USMA Dialectic Society Journal 1840–44."
[64] *USMA Library Records* (West Point, New York, 1831). Records for books checked out begin in December of 1831 and end in January of 1836. Subsequent records are missing, and resume on March 7, 1849. *Dialectic Society Library Catalogue* (West Point, New York, 1855). In 1855, the library consisted of 750 bound volumes, 185 pamphlets, and 44 books. Fire destroyed the society's library in 1871.
[65] Watson, "Flexible Gender Roles during the Market Revolution," 83. James, *The History of Chivalry*, 18. An 1838 speech to the Dialectic Society closely mirrored James's approach, emphasizing the chivalric imperative to protect the weak from oppression, and insisting that chivalry "served to elevate, honor and protect, that gentler sex, whose milder graces have ever inspired gentleness of manner and genuine courtesy, and have ever given encouragement to every thing that can adorn and dignify the human character." Alvord, *Address before the Dialectic Society of the Corps of Cadets*, 7–8.

mandatory (Protestant) religious services and instruction from an army chaplain, and depicted protecting the weak as a core value.

Chivalry and its nature were topics of public conversation beyond James's monograph. Francis Lieber, who would famously write Lieber's Code during the Civil War, asserted in his *Manual for Political Ethics* that in chivalry, "religious ardor, desire of adventure, and devotion to woman were romantically blended." James's definition was similarly tripartite. He laid out a three-fold vision of the "Spirit of Chivalry" that included the utility of chivalry in civilizing "savage" places, the protection of women, and the preservation of limited access to the privileges of chivalry. James argued that "Chivalry, more than any other institution (except religion) aided to work out the civilization of Europe." It first taught "devotion and reverence to those weak, fair beings, who but in their beauty and their gentleness have no defense." Because chivalry elevated women, James argued that it then civilized Europe. James extended this claim, writing that chivalric protection of women animated the laws of war tradition, that it "smoothed even the rugged brow of war."[66] Positioning women as the essential expression of innocence in war remained a foundational belief behind US officers' paternalist rhetoric.

The symbiotic impulses of civilizing "savage" people and protecting women, the essential agents of civilization, would collide in Florida when officers had to hunt, capture, and remove Seminole women. This collision would produce an emerging logic of protecting women specific to the US Army. That logic would draw on James's chivalry, the laws of war, first-hand experience in Florida, and the political requirements of Indian Removal. Further confrontations would occur when officers, as James said regarding the chivalry of old, sought to ensure that "the lower race…could not be invested with the honors of Chivalry." When cadets, and later officers, admired chivalry, they admired the skill required to achieve it, the glory of conquest that came with it, and its moral and religious requirements. And they saw its exclusivity reflected in their army, where the barrier between officer and enlisted soldier remained solid. Just as only knights possessed the right to make other knights, to better guard the knighthood "against the intrusion of unworthy or disgraceful members," army officers were the ones who made new officers – through West Point. They did not draw replacements from the soldiery.[67]

[66] Lieber, *Manual of Political Ethics*, 2:134. James, *The History of Chivalry*, 19, 31.
[67] James, *The History of Chivalry*, 27–28.

1 The Dilemma of Army Cohesion: West Point Officers

Officers who embraced the internal civilizing mission felt that although enlisted men ought never to gain a commission, they could evolve toward respectable (obedient) behavior. White people in the US tended to agree by distinguishing between foreign white men who could be civilized, and Native men condemned to "savagery" in perpetuity. The best-known cultural touchstone of the "Indian play" era, which neatly matched the period of hostilities in Florida, was *Metamora*. It debuted in New York City as Indian Removal became national policy, and the play gained popularity as the Second US–Seminole War continued. It transformed the bloodshed of King Philip's War into a racialized, tragic romance that complemented the rising nationalism of the 1830s. In it, Metamora seeks friendship and peace with white settlements and rescues a white woman, until settlers betray him. He attacks. More white treachery leads to Metamora's capture. He escapes, only for settlers to later defeat him. Metamora kills his wife so white settlers cannot enslave her, just before the white men kill him – he curses them with his last words.[68] Jill Lepore describes how King Philip's War was "not only the most fatal war in all of American history but also one of the most merciless." Both *Metamora* and the Second US–Seminole War unfolded just as mythmaking about the early US frontier reached new heights. Jill Lepore argues that plays like *Metamora* allowed white people in the US to "define themselves in relation to an imagined Indian past." For the public, this required "that there be no Indians in the present, or at least not anywhere nearby."[69] Yet, for the army this was no distant past. Soldiers in Florida defined themselves against an Indigenous present.

The army faced both sides of the myth, the "two faces of savagery – brutality and nobility" that supposedly explained the "disappearance of the Native peoples of North America, and the triumphant rise of the United States."[70] Among the Seminole people, the army found both the "brutal savages who haunted the backcountry" and men like Osceola, whom many soldiers judged "a good Indian," one whose goodness

---

[68] Stone, *Metamora*. The play was so popular that it inspired satires, such as: Brougham, *Metamora*.
[69] Lepore, *The Name of War: King Phillip's War and the Origins of American Identity*, 193.
[70] Ibid., xiii, 193. Witgen, *An Infinity of Nations*, 9. Witgen describes how William Wadsworth Longfellow's Hiawatha, came to serve a purpose similar to Edwin Forrest's Metamora and Osceola's legacy. Witgen shows how the 1855 poem *The Song of Hiawatha* provided an "ideological justification for the dispossession of the Native peoples of North America." Ibid., 10.

stemmed from his respect for innocence and who "constantly urged the war-parties to spare women and children."[71] The *Metamora* version of King Philip in the 1830s traced its roots to the earliest white portrayals of King Philip and reached from Increase Mather to Washington Irvine. While *Metamora*, according to Lepore, "flowered in the nineteenth century," it was "nonetheless rooted in the rich soil of myth, memory, and history." During the Indian Removal Act era, that foundation led to a profusion of "Indian plays" that expressed Jacksonian desires for a national literature. Such plays offered a way to justify dispossessing Indigenous communities, and provided others a vocabulary to challenge injustice.[72] Where male protection rested on a dualistic belief of male strength and female weakness, the plays assumed white superiority and Native inferiority.

Moreover, *Metamora* and especially its star actor Edwin Forrest had a powerful appeal to some enlisted men. Working-class people in New York City – the army's largest source of recruits – embraced Forrest, who was enormously popular in the Bowery, that "lower-class world of rough amusement" of the 1830s. The Bowery's audience of working men praised the Manhattan-born Forrest, whom historian Sean Wilentz terms "the hero of the Bowery Theatre."[73] Forrest's appeal as a native-born son, a US Shakespearean who challenged the dominance of Englishmen in New York theaters, resonated with US-born soldiers. His appeal to workingmen and disdain for British actors like William Macready probably also found a broad audience among Irish-born soldiers. In 1848, Forrest's supporters snuck into the sophisticated Astor Place Opera House – a very different venue than the Bowery Theater – and drove Macready off the stage. When wealthy New Yorkers staged a second performance protected by police and militiamen, Forrest's supporters protested. The night ended with militiamen firing into the crowd, killing nearly two dozen people. Perhaps there were several would-have-been soldiers among the dead.

---

[71] Sprague, *The Origin, Progress, and Conclusion of the Florida War*, 316. Army officer John Sprague, a soldier in the war and its first historian, attributed this quote to a Black interpreter named Sampson. Colonel Gad Humphreys enslaved Sampson, who was purportedly captured by Seminoles – or perhaps had fled enslavement – in 1837 but eventually returned to the army. Thus, Sprague could use this phrase as proof of two tropes: "noble savage" and "loyal slave." For more on Osceola, see Wickman, *Osceola's Legacy*.

[72] Lepore, *The Name of War*, 198; Anderson, "The Image of the Indian in American Drama during the Jacksonian Era, 1829–1845," 800.

[73] Wilentz, *Chants Democratic*, 257, 358. For more on the Bowery Theatre, see: Shank, "The Bowery Theatre, 1826–1836."

Part of Forrest's appeal to potential recruits was his performance of workingmen's masculinity. He was a man of action. Forrest kept his word even if it cost him. He hissed at rivals. He publicly beat the man he believed seduced his wife. He played warriors such as King Philip, Othello, and Spartacus.[74] West Point paternalism best served the officers who created it, but popular culture, populated by men like Forrest and Native archetypes like Metamora, offered glorification to enlisted men.

Yet, the appeal of "Indian plays" went deeper than the personal appeal of individuals like Forrest or the national fascination with tragic Native archetypes. Commanding General Alexander Macomb's play *Pontiac* shows how such works characterized Native women as allies of the US civilizing mission. It "emphasized the typical Romantic concept of the noble savage in a natural, innocent state." Macomb's Pontiac pursued war against all reason, and for his stubbornness, a "faithful Indian" killed him. Macomb believed that European interference had turned the "savage native of this blessed land" into a "revengeful, cruel" man: "When first we saw him in his pristine state, The native knew not what it was to hate." Pontiac, and by extension most Native men, would commit themselves to an "eternal war." They would, in this story, skillfully wage that conflict, yet eventually lose: "He stakes his life his country to defend, and in that noble duty finds his end." In the play, a somewhat reluctant Anglo-American army watches as Indigenous resistance dies a natural death.[75]

The play also features an argument for US military professionalism and an Indigenous maiden who recognizes and affirms Anglo superiority. Macomb notes that tensions between royal and colonial troops arose "partly from the assumed superiority of the former over the latter, but mostly from the uncourteous manner in which the latter were treated, both by the British commanders and their subordinate officers, who pretended to regard the Americans as their inferiors." The US officers "although naturally unassuming, could not tamely submit to such arrogance." Of the assimilating Indigenous maiden trope, Ultina, an "Indian woman," recognizes white men's virtues. She loves and admires

---

[74] For more on Forrest, see: Rees, *The Life of Edwin Forrest*.
[75] Cox, "The Characterization of the American Indian in American Indian Plays, 1800–1860," 153; Macomb, *Pontiac, or, the Siege of Detroit*, 7, 9–10. For more on ways that New Englanders erased and then memorialized Indigenous nations to produce an enduring myth of extinction, see: O'Brien, *Firsting and Lasting*.

the British "good white Chief" and says her "woman's heart leads her to save, not to destroy. Pontiac's secret schemes I cannot withhold." Ultina tells the British commander, to whom she feels drawn, that Pontiac plans to attack. This intelligence allows British troops to defeat the attempt. Her universalized "woman's heart" closely matches Angelique's, another character described as a "Canadian lady," who also safeguards a white man from Native attackers. After performing this rescue, Angelique says that she is "amply repaid...in having had it in my power to obey my father's directions, and in the success which has attended my efforts." She immediately falls in love with the young soldier.[76]

Yet Angelique married her white soldier. Ultina refused. British officer Gladwin tries to reward Ultina's efforts with a relationship, asking, "Shall I take you home with me across the great waters? or shall I provide for you here, in your own country?" But Ultina declines, saying, "To your country? Across the wide waters? Among strangers? where I shall know no one, and where I must perish among a cold-hearted people, who will despise me because I am less fair than they?" She concludes that she "will return to the woods, and die under the weeping elm, or in some unknown cave."[77] After serving the army, she would erase herself because she accepted her inferiority.

Officers in Florida would face each element of James's chivalric trinity: civilizing a "savage" land by removing the Seminole, upholding the imperative to protect (even Seminole) women, and maintaining the officer corps' privileges over enlisted soldiers. The first of these, taming the land, was non-negotiable. The army had to meet the mission of Indian Removal meted out by US political leaders to survive as an institution. The last of these, maintaining officership's exclusivity, was both a priority and a serious problem for the officer corps. They had to hold the army together to fight a war, but could not do so by punishment alone. They needed enough enlisted cooperation to make it through the miserable conditions of active service in Florida. Much as officers sought to tame Florida's wilderness and Seminole people, they sought to gentle their soldiers. The second of James's objectives, the imperative to protect women, offered a compelling vocabulary that officers would deploy during the war to accustom enlisted men to officers' authority.

---

[76] Macomb, *Pontiac, or, the Siege of Detroit*, 8, 38–40.
[77] Ibid., 57–58.

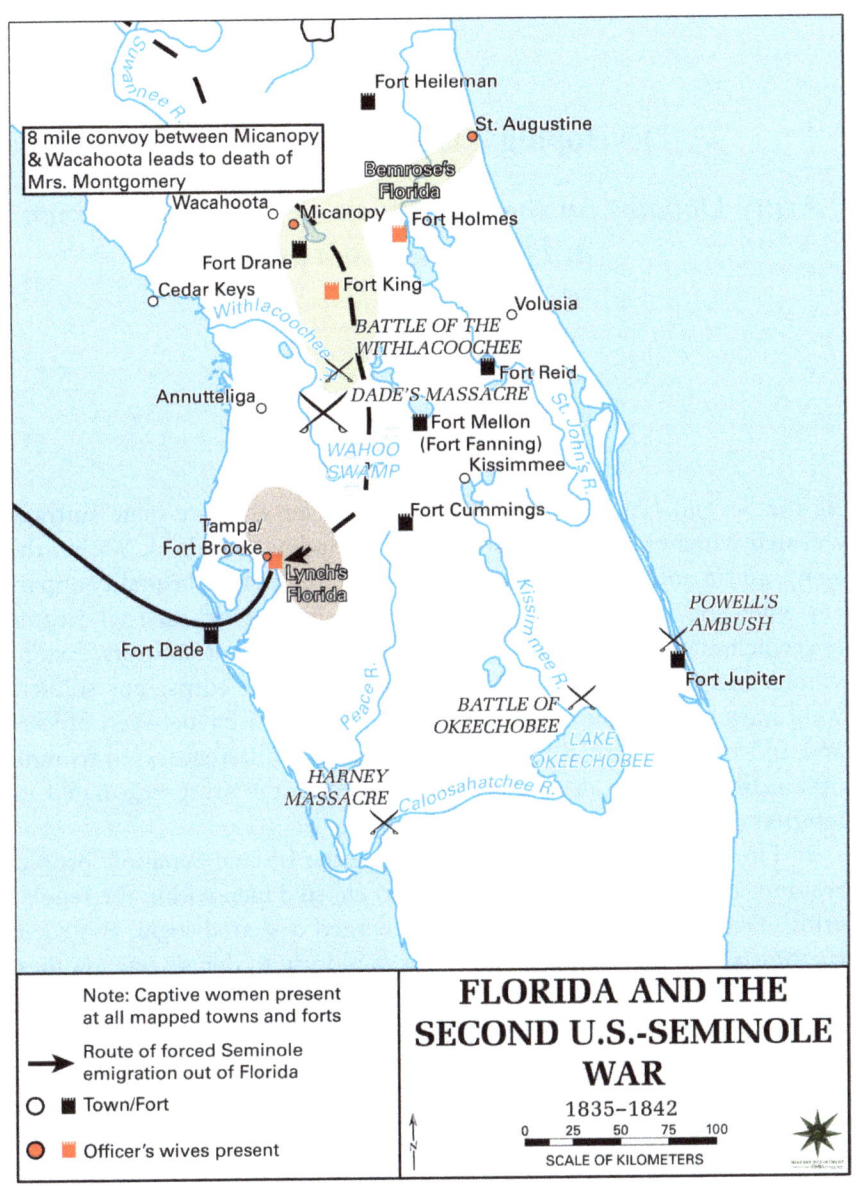

MAP 2 Florida and the Second US–Seminole War. Map by Mr. Jeffrey Goldberg, Cartographer at the West Point Department of History.

2

Developing a Logic of Protection

Army Debates on the Treatment of Seminole Women in Florida, 1835–1842

As the Second US–Seminole War raged, universal white male suffrage elevated white men to citizenship while excluding all others. Within the army, an elite officer class made the limits of that political equality apparent when they imposed harsh punishments on enlisted men who came overwhelmingly from a population of poor immigrant laborers. Extant scholarship focuses overwhelmingly on the officer corps, but soldiers were more than officers' subordinates. Class disparity between officers and enlisted, heightened by ethnic and cultural differences, led to multiple claims of army manhood that collided as the army negotiated its internal tensions.

In Florida, there were conflicts between the US and Seminole people, regulars and volunteers, and officers and enlisted men within the regular army. From these many battlefields emerged a shared logic, rooted in rhetoric about women, that all groups could use to debate one another. Because Jacksonian manhood involved concepts like competition, personal reputation, and assertions of self-worth that contradicted military hierarchy and subordination, defining *army* manhood more specifically around the idea of protecting women took advantage of the shared elements of Jacksonian masculinity while avoiding dangerous emphasis on social equality.

An Indigenous name for the several US wars against the Seminole is the "White Wars."[1] Indeed, hierarchical white male unity – based on a concept of the army family where all men protected and subordinated all women – helped the army function cohesively despite the pressures

---

[1] Shire, *The Threshold of Manifest Destiny*, 102.

2 Developing a Logic of Protection: Army Debates

contained in its authoritarian hierarchy. This framework appealed to paternalistic officers because it nonetheless allowed for intense distinctions (of rank) between white men. In this bargain, officers claimed to care for and control their soldiers as patriarchs and expected soldiers' submission in return. Junior officers incurred the additional obligation of obeying senior officers. All officers obeyed the nation's political leaders.

Within this family, Colonel William Worth was a patriarch of patriarchs, a senior leader of other officers. He described the accepted beau ideal of what it meant to be an officer – a fatherly figure, in contrast to the childlike position of soldiers, when he wrote to the Army Adjutant General during the war in praise of his men. The officers demonstrated "activity, intelligence, and untiring zeal." The soldiers showed "good conduct and patient endurance." Army leaders required both groups to be uncomplaining, and there was a measure of shared suffering. Still, officers were supposed to be active and intelligent. In contrast, leaders wanted enlisted men to obey quietly. A few months later, Worth wrote that "the troops suffered almost incredible hardship and privations without a murmur, both officers and men, evincing their habitual energy and constancy." A participant described a similar experience: "We have been in the field actively engaged since the date of my last [letter], wading thro' mud and water."[2] While discomfort was also a part of officership, officers required a double submission from their soldiers, first to their officers and then to the pains of war.

Likewise, when General Macomb praised soldiers in Florida, he wrote that their "sacrifices and suffering" conferred "honor on the character of the American army, and entitles them to the approbation and regard of their government and country." Still, compliance, especially "submission to disciplines," was a virtue he expected of enlisted men.[3] Rather than courage or patriotism, zeal or intelligence, Macomb's telling phrase clarified that good soldiers, like good sons, submitted to their fathers.

The war in Florida offered a training ground for the submission so prized by officers. In the Florida borderlands, officers sought to bring soldiers under their control *while also placing* Florida under US hegemony

---

[2] *9th Military Department, Letters Sent*, 106, Worth to Adjutant General, undated, circa 16 July 1841; 483, Worth to Adjutant General, December 15, 1841; Phelps, "Letters from J.W. Phelps to Sisters, Miss Helen M. Phelps," January 16, 1837. Worth made similar statements while stationed on the Canadian border. Watson, *Peacekeepers and Conquerors*, 296.

[3] *Orders, Headquarters of the Army, 1835–39*, vol. 225A, 93, Macomb, General Orders 61, September 16, 1836.

in a complex landscape of Native and American interests.[4] These goals operated sometimes in consonance and sometimes in dissonance. At their most harmonious, men of the regular army in Florida acted in concert – officers giving orders and soldiers following them – and proved their manhood to themselves. Regulars viewed themselves favorably to other white men in Florida. They claimed settler men were incapable of protecting settler women, and volunteers were too undisciplined to be effective. They contrasted themselves to Seminole men, who supposedly attacked white women. In all cases, the regulars' rhetorical emphasis on women generated a point of unity across ranks.

Historian Laurel Clark Shire shows how US political and military leaders used gendered rhetoric about protecting white settler homes to displace Seminole people and make white settlement in Florida permanent. Ideas about white women, and white women themselves, produced an "expansionist domesticity" that aided US settler colonialism, expelled Native communities, and grew US slavery. Shire argues that gender "shaped how the military executed this policy." Yet, "military" is a broad category. Interrogating how its many components – officers, enlisted men, servants, laundresses, regulars, volunteers, captives, guides, the several branches of service – interacted with one another builds on Shire's work to show how regular army paternalism's cultural power aided the US conquest of Florida.[5]

Regulars leveraged white claims to "presumed superiority and dominance over nonwhite others" and women in specific ways. Enlisted men used rhetoric about protecting women to challenge officers' claims to authority, moral or military, over soldiers. In Ann Stoler's famous essay, "Tense and Tender Ties," she demonstrates how state efforts to educate the consent of the colonized had first to school their desires. Yet, enlisted men in Florida were subordinators (colonizers) and subordinates. They were both part of the army's efforts to remove Seminole people and the target audience for officers' efforts to school soldiers on their desires and relative social places. US political leaders used the army to remove purportedly childlike "savages" to Indian Territory, a new home that would better raise them in the school of US civilization. Officers feared the corrupting influence of white settlers on Seminole people and used that risk to justify Indian Removal. Simultaneously, army officers imposed

---

[4] Watson, *Jackson's Sword: The Army Officer Corps on the American Frontier, 1810–1821*, 29.
[5] Shire, *The Threshold of Manifest Destiny*, 138, 148, 194.

2 Developing a Logic of Protection: Army Debates 73

"strict surveillance" on enlisted men, the army family's permanent children, and the underlings responsible for expelling Seminole communities from Florida.[6]

For its members, the regular army's self-described virtues contrasted with its nearest relatives – volunteer army units. Where the regulars believed themselves disciplined, volunteers were "wasteful of human life." In the estimation of its members, the regular army possessed "true humanity."[7] Regulars extended this critique to white settler men, deemed cowardly. Colonel Worth wrote amid the army's two-month-long pursuit of a Seminole group that attacked white settlers that the group remained "unobstructed and unresisted by the male population of that settlement." Because local white men failed to protect, the Seminole group "murdered <u>four persons and burned two dwellings</u>, remained about the burning buildings till morning, and then leisurely, for a time, retreated with their plunder" before the army heard of it and took up the chase. Ironically, less than a year earlier Worth hoped to encourage white families to resettle the region, believing "sturdy frontier settlers" would discourage Seminole attacks.[8] Experiences like this one encouraged the career army officer to conclude that only regulars were man enough to offer protection.

Officers demonstrated similar distaste toward volunteer army units whom they felt applauded unmanly behavior, as when a Florida newspaper celebrated an attack on a Seminole camp where a volunteer unit indiscriminately fired into a settlement and killed women. The paper wrote, "we are happy to learn that a detachment of Capt. Rowel's company of Florida militia...surprised Tiger Tail's camp, and fired into it." As a result, "two squaws [were] taken prisoners, both mortally wounded, and died soon after."[9] Regular army records did not categorize women's deaths as accomplishments.

Rather than publicly praising the killing of Seminole women, as did some of the volunteers and many local civilians, army officers carefully

---

[6] Ibid., 200; Stoler, *Haunted by Empire*, 43.
[7] Homans, *Army and Navy Chronicle*, 1837, 5:56, January 1837. From the *Ontario Repository and Freeman*.
[8] *9th Military Department, Letters Sent*, 80, Worth to Army Adjutant General, March 16, 1842, of an attack on the settlement of Mandarin by a Native group including the leader Short Grass and his family. For army critiques of settlers, and vice versa, see: Denham, "Some Prefer the Seminoles." Worth to Wilcox, June 24, 1841, quoted in: Shire, *The Threshold of Manifest Destiny*, 155.
[9] Niles, *Niles' National Register*, 1839, 55:49, September 15, 1838. Reprinted from the *Tallahassee Floridian*.

labeled such deaths as accidental. Selectively acknowledging Seminole women's deaths helped emphasize that ethically, the regulars believed killing women was wrong and their deaths unintentional and infrequent. It was a rhetorical performance sometimes belied by troops firing into Seminole villages. A regular officer of the Second Infantry Regiment, Major Joseph Plympton, described one such attack. He wrote that his unit "came close upon their camp, first smelling and then seeing the smoke arising from a thick cabbage hammock." Plympton ordered a halt, prepared, and then charged: "we passed through their camp where they had left most of their comforts in great confusion." He continued, "no doubt many of the enemy were wounded as the track of blood in various places was seen and followed up till they were lost in the saw grass and water." From these actions, Plympton concluded that "on this occasion every man was a soldier and in my opinion has a righteous or just claim upon the favorable acknowledgment of his government."[10] But Plympton had no idea whether their weapons had struck enemy fighters or noncombatants. For all the regular army's rhetorical emphasis on protecting innocent women, it remained practical to measure success by destroying Seminole supplies, settlements, and lives – those of a faceless enemy who left a "track of blood" rather than an individual man, woman, or child.

More than practical, doing so remained a military necessity. Regulars' views toward Seminole people hardened as the war continued, and Seminole resistance persisted despite massive US investments of military resources. To officers and enlisted men, it seemed Seminole groups continued to inhabit the dense hammocks and waterways of Florida no matter how many villages the soldiers burned, supplies they destroyed, or people they captured or killed. This strategy meant that without fully acknowledging it, the army waged its war against the power of Seminole women.

In Creek society, an important cultural progenitor of Seminole people, women often controlled household property, managed food stores, and raised crops. As Christina Snyder demonstrates, "Seminoles reckoned descent matrilineally and maintained a clan system." Patricia Wickman notes that women "embodied the continuity of the clan, passing membership to the children of their wombs and sustaining its bounds with their very lives." In this system of gender complementarity,

---

[10] Mahon, "Letters from the Second Seminole War," April 1958, 349–51, refers to an attack made on January 25, 1842.

2 Developing a Logic of Protection: Army Debates

male children "reinforced the clan and, as husbands, broadened the clans genetically and implemented their deferential orderings."[11] Army metrics of success – camps burned, food and property destroyed, women captured – seemed to be the only alternative when the army found its most crucial metric, the number of Seminole people forced onto boats, to be lacking.

In the chaos of the Florida War, the army had to deal with its internal problem of disunity even as frustration with the war grew. In this climate, although rhetoric rooted in the need to protect women could bolster army cohesion, it was also a weapon. Soldiers used such language to rebut officers' claims to superiority. By identifying where officers failed to protect women, enlisted men served up strong proof that they, the honest and hard-working soldiers, were superior to hypocritical officers. Still, even when the soldierly responsibility to protect women produced challenges to officers' power, such arguments provided a contained arena for dissent. To wield the logic of protection against their officers, enlisted men first accepted the language itself as legitimate. Because all parties took this language as valid, even as they deployed it against each other, officer-enlisted debates over women's protection produced an emerging logic of protection by the war's end.

THE OFFICER'S LANGUAGE OF COHESION

Regular army culture included a set of norms embodied by West Point-educated officers. These men were an increasingly dominant proportion of the officer corps by 1835 when the Second US–Seminole War began with the stunning Seminole victory known today as Dade's Massacre. Seminole warriors ambushed a unit under Major Francis Dade's command and killed over one hundred regulars – eight officers and ninety-seven enlisted men, forty-three of whom were foreign-born. Three soldiers escaped, arriving seriously wounded at Fort Brooke. Again and again, Private Ransome Clark of the Second Artillery, the only survivor to witness the entire battle, told the story, which soon reached West Point.[12]

---

[11] Snyder highlights how the influence of Black Seminoles impacted matrilineality. She writes that although Seminole families traced descent through mothers, "Black Seminoles traced their bloodlines through both parents and lacked clans." Snyder, *Slavery in Indian Country*, 234; Wickman, *The Tree That Bends*, 213.

[12] Mahon, *History of the Second Seminole War*, 119; Roberts, "The Dade Massacre," 124–26. Dade was not a West Point graduate, yet West Point erected a memorial to Dade and his command in 1845.

Lieutenant Benjamin Alvord addressed cadets on the subject. He told them that "it is the true effect of your education to draw out, and elevate, and confirm all those admirable traits which make up the true American character," a character amplified in the US officer, marked by his devotion to duty and love of country. To meet these requirements, West Point cadets required "much moral, as well as mental cultivation" for the "root of all true military virtue, is to be sought in morality." War, he explained, was necessary to chastise Seminole people for faithlessness, contumacy, and rapine. In contrast, the "American character," and more specifically the military one, gleamed with mental and moral superiority. Alvord highlighted Seminole "savagery" to claim "the God of Nature" never intended "that this beautiful and magnificent continent should sleep on in benighted barbarism under perpetual vassalage to hordes of ignorant savages." He continued, "warfare appears to have been an inseparable concomitant of the advance of the whites into this country." In contrast, army officers behaved like civilized gentlemen: "the Seminole nation could not have experienced more kind and considerate treatment than they ever received from those military officers who were stationed among them."[13]

Alvord claimed that Dade's Massacre was no massacre at all. The enemy had not trapped the regulars. Instead, the troops chose to stay to protect their wounded comrades. The survivors could not "as in civilized warfare, leave their bleeding and wounded comrades upon the field in the hands of a humane and generous enemy." They could not trust Seminole groups to care for prisoners or casualties, so "They gather their wounded and the dying within a temporary breastwork, hastily constructed upon the spot, and there they determine to defend their unfortunate comrades until the last drop of blood shall be shed upon that consecrated ground, and until the last breath of life shall depart from their bodies." Alvord refused to see the army as the victim of a successful ambush, insisting that Dade's command "*did* meet the foe and it *was* a most brilliant though unsuccessful engagement" that "deserves the name of a *battle*, a *hard-fought battle*" where "*they conquered! They conquered!*" And perhaps they did conquer their fears, if not their enemies. The Seminole fighters overwhelmed them.[14]

Alvord offered a memory of uprightness to the fallen, but chivalrous valor in battle was only part of the equation. The other was the chivalrous

---

[13] Alvord, *Address before the Dialectic Society of the Corps of Cadets*, 33, 50–52.
[14] Ibid., 21, 24, 35–39. Five of the eight officers who died in Dade's Massacre were West Point graduates.

treatment of women. He emphasized that "the gallant Dade volunteered to command the expedition in the place of an officer whose lady was very ill and desired his presence. That chivalrous officer (Capt. Gardiner,) at first complied, but was soon afterward enabled to join the detachment, and thus gratify his earnest desire not to be absent from the post of duty and of danger." Dade and Gardiner perfectly manifested "the chivalry of our day [that] has assumed the broader and lovelier name of Patriotism." The army's creed of patriotic chivalry also perpetuated the "respect and devotion which is ever due the fair sex" even as it grew into a model of republican rather than aristocratic gallantry. For army officers, these twin concepts of bravery and protection of women were implicitly entangled. "Valor in the field and chivalrous devotion to the [fair] sex must ever go hand in hand." Henry Halleck, who would become a prominent army intellectual, was then a cadet, one of the young men who invited Alvord to speak at West Point. He later echoed Alvord's assessment to conclude that killing noncombatants was the very antithesis of "civilization" because "a savage enemy might kill alike old men, women, and children, but no civilized power would resort to similar measures of cruelty and barbarism."[15]

Halleck graduated in 1839, and during his cadet years the West Point Board of Visitors remarked on the unfortunate absence of schooling in international law. In 1837, it noted that while examining cadets was an "entirely satisfactory" process that "afforded great pleasure," cadet understanding of the laws of war was "not so great" as "might have been expected" because of the meager time allotment for the topic. The board hoped that respect for the laws of war would advance the US Army's respectability by governing officers' conduct.

The board also believed that officers who were well educated on the laws of war – a mostly European set of written works that shaped norms but lacked the force of law – would better regulate soldiers' behavior and contribute to the internal civilizing mission. Moreover, although scholarly works did not bind military men, army regulations based on the laws of war did. Educating officers would "protect the soldier from any unauthorized acts of violence and oppression" that might have been perpetrated by ignorant leaders. The corps of cadets that Alvord encountered, and to which Halleck belonged, was still metamorphosizing into

---

[15] Ibid., 11–13, 15, 40; Halleck, *International Law*, 1878, 2:445. The book, written in the 1850s and published in 1861, included verbatim passages of Vattel's 1758 *Law of Nations*.

a well-defined institution whose members embraced a common understanding of the rules. To foster an ethic of legal conduct, the board urged West Point to increase instruction. Cadets needed to know "the fundamental doctrines of international law, which, having been adopted as the rules of action by all civilized nations, regulate their mode of warfare, and distinguish it from the cruel butcheries of the savage."[16]

Both army regulations and Halleck's later published works hewed closely to Swiss jurist Emerich de Vattel, who published his landmark *Law of Nations* in the mid-eighteenth century. Due to growing demands on cadets as West Point introduced more topics to the curriculum, the academy only assigned Vattel to cadets from 1821 to 1825, though the (presumably) more widely read *General Regulations* followed Vattel. Otherwise, cadets received instruction through the works of William Paley on ethics and James Kent on US constitutional law. From 1820 to 1843, cadets used William Paley's *The Principles of Moral and Political Philosophy* as a textbook in the overtaxed and woefully understaffed "Department of Geography, History, and Ethics," whose membership consisted mainly of West Point's lone chaplain.[17]

Napoleon's legacy loomed large in the 1830s and 1840s. It reached cadets through translations by US officers such as J. M. O'Connor and Dennis Mahan, who read Antoine-Henri, Baron de Jomini, the best-known interpreter of Napoleonic warfare. Yet cadets only began reading Jomini's *Summary of the Art of War* in 1859 and then only briefly, as part of an experimental five-year curriculum from the late 1850s. Where the academy's approach to the practice of war was distinctly Jominian, on the laws of war Vattel and his seventeenth-century predecessor Hugo Grotius remained the most cited authorities. The two sought to make warfare more humane and less destructive to noncombatants.[18] A strange puzzle of West Point's curriculum in 1837, then, was the sharp

---

[16] Homans, *Army and Navy Chronicle*, 1837, 4: June 1837. West Point Board of Visitors report, signed by Chairman, Ellis Lewis.
[17] Paley, *The Principles of Moral and Political Philosophy*, 1831; Paley, *The Principles of Moral and Political Philosophy*, 1839.
[18] Weigley, *The American Way of War*, 82–84; *The Centennial of the United States Military Academy*, 1, Addresses and Histories:440–41, 464; Homans, *Army and Navy Chronicle*, 1839, 8:123; Grotius, *De Jure Belli Ac Pacis*. In a demonstration of Jomini's importance, Halleck later translated Jomini's *La Vie de Napoleon* into English. Jomini, *Life of Napoleon*. For more on the West Point curriculum and chaplain-taught courses, see Crackel, *West Point: A Bicentennial History*. Sam Watson notes that "chaplains often had little time to attend to their spiritual work, and the Academy periodically came under fire for failing to encourage religion," Watson, "Bicentennial History Pamphlet."

disconnect between theory and reality. Although cadets were nearly sure to fight "Indian Wars" after graduation, probably in Florida, their cursory laws of war training (and more copious instruction on the practice of war) focused on conflict against European nations.

Ironically, given the weak introduction to the laws of war cadets received, a common complaint of the curriculum was that "at West Point, too much attention is given to *theory*, far too little to *practice*," but there was neither theory nor practice when it came to fighting "Indian Wars." William Skelton describes how "at no time in the four-year program did cadets receive in-depth instruction in the task that would likely occupy the greater part of their careers." The only theory formally offered to cadets came via the briefest glimpse, in legendary West Point instructor Dennis Hart Mahan's class, when he urged cadets to overawe Indigenous foes through massive force.[19] Non-European warfare rarely entered the curriculum, and when it did, it was only to reinforce the importance of European-style conflict.

When Henry Wheaton published his *Elements of International Law* in 1836, West Point assigned it. It marked a departure from the classic laws of war tradition. Rather than the universalism of Vattel, Deborah Rosen argues that Wheaton "described international law as applying only to civilized, Christian nations." He explicitly carved out exceptions for the US Army when it fought Indigenous enemies and thus addressed what it meant to fight Native groups in a way that no other aspect of the academy's curriculum did. Wheaton legitimized suspending "the normal rules of war in conflicts with Indians." *Elements* said what an army fighting a long and brutal conflict against Indigenous groups wanted to hear: the army could destroy property to secure the national frontier and kill civilians and prisoners if necessary. Yet, the academy abandoned Wheaton in 1839.[20]

Instead, West Point added James Kent's *Commentaries on American Law*, "the most widely read law book of the century," published a decade earlier than Wheaton in 1826. Kent's *Commentaries* was a US work that represented a synthesis of English (especially William Blackstone's

---

[19] Homans, *Army and Navy Chronicle*, 1839, 8:123; Skelton, *An American Profession of Arms*, 306, 319. Mahan founded the Napoleon Seminar, which brought cadets and officers together to admire Napoleonic warfare.

[20] Rosen, *Border Law*, 150; Wheaton and Phillipson, *Wheaton's Elements of International Law*; *The Centennial of the United States Military Academy*, 1, Addresses and Histories: 367, 439–41. Vattel's *Law of Nations* was the first law textbook used at West Point, but only from 1821–1825.

Commentaries) and Continental thinking. Kent, to some extent, anticipated Wheaton's later conclusions. He wrote that Native peoples, who were examples of the "appetite of man in a savage state," gave proof to the "extravagant theory of Hobbes, who maintains, that the natural state of man is a state of war of all against all."[21]

The US would bring "civilization" to "savage" lands. It would be an indispensable gift, for "the peculiar character and habits of the Indian nations, rendered them incapable of sustaining any other relation with the whites than that of dependence and pupilage." Under US tutelage, Indigenous peoples would be "separate, subordinate, and dependent, with a guardian care thrown around them for their protection." Because they were likely to resist, Kent concluded in the Romantic mode: "the Indians of this continent appear to be destined, at no very distant period of time, to disappear with those vast forests which once covered the country."[22]

The military academy retained Kent in the curriculum for decades, from 1839 to 1875. This choice only added to the disconnect between the Europe-facing education cadets received at West Point and the realities of fighting Seminole groups. In Florida, Wheaton's "exclusionary vision" of the laws of war was closer to reality as army policy increasingly sought to remove Seminole people from Florida by any means necessary. It was also closer to the political norms in the US following the First US–Seminole War of 1816–1818. After that, US leaders crafted policies that excluded Indigenous groups from universalist ideas of international law, and instead subjected them to US designs.[23]

Although these developments shaped how the US deployed its army, they did not penetrate the West Point curriculum. Despite a past and present full of conflicts with Native groups and every indication that such disputes would characterize the future, West Point imagined itself as an institution focused on civilized and rational (European) warfare. There were real threats from Great Britain, Spain, and France, to be sure, but more than that, there was a frightening ideological gap between the kind of institution the army *was* and the type of institution it *wanted* to be.

Thus, West Pointers got a scattered and shallow education in the laws of war and arrived in Florida with little practical or theoretical

---

[21] Witt, *Lincoln's Code*, 83; Kent, James, *Commentaries on American Law*, 1:86, 53; Blackstone, *Blackstone's Commentaries*.
[22] Kent, *Commentaries on American Law*, 3:310, 318.
[23] Rosen, *Border Law*, 7, 149.

2 Developing a Logic of Protection: Army Debates 81

knowledge. In contrast, they spent a full four years learning their place in the army family. Instead of approaching the war in Florida with ideas drawn from the laws of war, officers approached it with cultural norms about hierarchy that radiated outward from the paternalistic family. The academy thoroughly socialized cadets in how they should behave after graduation, and in this context, cadets did learn something about Native peoples. They found that in the army family, Indigenous people were wards.

While officers characterized Indigenous peoples as inferior, "the army had an obligation to protect their rights as defined by the government and supply the guidance a stern father would show his children."[24] Officers could use paternalistic conceptions to guide their conduct. Indeed, how one treated a wayward ward would differ from dealing with an honorable and equal enemy. West Point socialization soon merged into personal experience as officers fought in the Second US–Seminole War, the most extended vehicle for this type of learning.

In his speech to the cadets, Alvord called upon that same family ethic to underscore army heroism, especially officers' heroism, during Dade's Massacre. Alvord described how the officers embodied a chivalric ethos antithetical to "savagery" and how "The men were inspired with the spirit of their officers." Officers led by personal example, and soldiers followed. Officers' bravery and soldiers' obedient emulation produced the most profound proof of army cohesion for Dade's command – they chose (Alvord insisted there was a choice) to stay together, fight, and die as a unit. While the men more likely had made a brave final stand because they could neither escape nor defeat their foe, the result was the same: "when their bodies were counted upon that field, the number answered officer for officer, man for man, name for name, with the regular muster-roll with which they were compared."[25] It was proof – grim and precise – of regular army cohesion.

At Dade's Massacre,

Officers and men have fought it out where they were told to fight: they have been killed in the tracks where they were told to stand. In no one of our Indian wars have our troops so stood together, and conquered together, and died together, as they have done in this one, and this standing together is the test of the soldier's character.[26]

---

[24] Skelton, *An American Profession of Arms*, 312–13.
[25] Alvord, *Address before the Dialectic Society of the Corps of Cadets*, 38.
[26] Ibid., 49. Alvord attributed this quote to an unnamed senator.

In earlier conflicts, the regular army had been underdeveloped and less subordinate to civilian authority. By December of 1835, the deaths of Dade's command showed how far the army had come. Alvord had crafted an image of army cohesion from the wreckage of Dade's command.

Officers' shared deaths alongside enlisted men offered a portrait in extremis, indeed a masterpiece, of army paternalism. Still, in the rough sketches of daily life, it was much simpler to enhance one's reputation by highlighting merciful treatment of women. Captain Seth Thornton of the Second Dragoons did so in a report to his superior following an attempted attack on a Seminole camp.[27] It eventually reached the commander in Florida, Colonel Worth, who sent it to the Army Adjutant General in Washington. At each level, officers capitalized on claims to gallantry and gentlemanly restraint – qualities shown to their best advantage when played opposite innocents.

Worth's letter claimed Thornton had decided that "to have opened a fire on the instant of coming upon the camp would have assured the destruction of the women and children; consulting a noble spirit of humanity the gallant officer hoped to secure the men without such a result." Thornton decided to surround the camp, and then take the inhabitants prisoner, rather than to shoot into it blindly. But "in the effort to throw his men around the camp, the alarm was taken, and the warriors sprang for the ever convenient hammock, two of them being shot in the flight." Worth concluded by listing the spoils: "the women, children, packs, utensils, three rifles and the bloody plunder from Tillis' house secured – possession of these women and children will secure the ultimate surrender of the warriors of that party."[28] Worth emphasized the value of capturing Seminole women and children, who were both enemy property and living bait to catch Seminole men. Worth, like other officers, clearly recognized the tactical utility of capture. Yet, he created

---

[27] Heitman, *Historical Register*, 641.
[28] *9th Military Department, Letters Sent*, 83, Worth to Army Adjutant General, March 19, 1842. Officers later spoke of these surprise attacks with romantic ambivalence. One account described how "one could but feel a kind of sympathy for them in this their terrible hour. The tall, brave warrior at that midnight moment dreaming of the manly, stand-up fight, and we stealing like serpents into his quiet bower to 'crunch' him; and the dark-eyed mothers and maidens, dreaming of chasing bright butterflies in the dewy morning, and of the succulent green-corn and exhilarating 'softkey' for breakfast – oh! it was too much. But let us not dwell upon the painful subject." Rodenbough, *From Everglade to Cañon with the Second Dragoons*, 60. The author borrowed this passage from Colonel A. T. Lee's "History of the Eighth Infantry."

a rhetorical victory to compliment the military one by insisting upon Thornton's gallantry in preventing harm to women and children.

When officers told the story, that sense of a shared commitment to protection extended to enlisted men. For instance, when army officers recounted how the wife of Lieutenant Alexander Montgomery died during a Seminole attack, they crafted a parable of perfect enlisted virtue and discipline in the service of women's protection. Although her death marked a unique incident, Mrs. Montgomery's presence in Florida was less singular.

Officers' wives were less common in wartime Florida than on other parts of the frontier, but wives sometimes lived there alongside husbands. One captain's wife and child arrived with him after returning from sick leave in New York.[29] Lieutenant Joseph Smith's wife Juliet joined him in Florida in 1840, where they had, and soon buried, an infant.[30] Officer's wives lived at numerous posts, including Fort Russell, Fort Holmes, and Fort King. Others lived in St. Augustine, as did "the beautiful Mrs. Lieutenant Thomas," who lived near several other officers' wives in the city. Others came to Tampa for visits or to nurse a sick husband back to health. Zachary Taylor's wife Margaret (Peggy) did this when he fell ill. She took him home to recover.[31] On December 28 of 1840, a Seminole war party attacked an element from the Seventh Infantry and killed the wife of Lieutenant Montgomery (her given name does not appear). She had been traveling – along with two lieutenants, a sergeant major, and ten privates – from Micanopy to Wacahoota, eight miles away, when Seminole fighters launched an ambush.[32]

Lieutenant Walter Sherwood requested that Mrs. Montgomery dismount her horse and get into a wagon for safety. That was when a

---

[29] McGaughy Jr., "The Squaw Kissing War," 197, May 5, 1839, Captain Henry Fowler. This source is a typewritten transcription of Lynch's journal, submitted by Felix McGaughy as a Master's Thesis in 1965.

[30] Mahon, "Letters from the Second Seminole War," April 1958, 347–48. Smith's papers included a poem about this dead child, titled "The Burial of an Infant in Florida." Penciled on the back of the poem is a note: "Mrs. Smith accompanied her husband through one campaign in the Florida Seminole Indian War but she always took the side of the Indians."

[31] Denham and Huneycutt, "Historic Notes and Documents: 'Everything Is Hubbub Here,'" 325, 334–36, 344; Chapman, "A West Point Graduate in the Second Seminole War: William Warren Chapman and the View from Fort Foster," 467–70; Bauer, *Zachary Taylor*, 94. Peggy took her husband out of Florida to recover his health on 1 May, 1840. Map 2 depicts locations where evidence confirms the presence of officers' wives, including the locations mentioned on this page.

[32] Sprague, *The Origin, Progress, and Conclusion of the Florida War*, 249.

Seminole shot her. She died quickly. So did Sherwood, who fell fighting, "the sergeant-major by his side," loyal to the end. The fight continued, and Private Lansing Burlingham of C Company, Seventh Infantry, supposedly kept fighting until "alone, and mortally wounded, he protected the body of Mrs. Montgomery from the merciless barbarities of the savages." When Lieutenant Montgomery arrived, having been told of the attack in progress and rushing to defend his wife, Burlingham said, "Lieutenant, I fought for her as long as I could; but they were too strong for me" pausing, then uttering his last words, "but I did my duty."[33] Much like the soldiers at Dade's Massacre (at least in Alvord's telling), Private Burlingham followed his lieutenant to a heroic death.

The best men died to shield those who could not help themselves – whether the wounded men of Dade's command or an officer's helpless wife. It was the ultimate expression of regular army manhood. Other versions of the story omit Lieutenant Montgomery's arrival and emphasize mutilated and scalped corpses. For the army, in either telling, this was a prime example of "atrocious scenes enacted by these Indians, disregarding the innocent and unoffending." Yet, a Second Dragoon officer who compiled the unit's history later wrote of "the massacre of Mrs. Montgomery and her escort of eleven men" and noted that "not one was left to narrate the simple tale of their heroism in laying down their lives in defense of a comrade's wife."[34] If all died before help arrived, regular officers probably created a narrative that suited then. Army casualty reports and the monument erected in honor of dead officers and soldiers at the end of the war do designate Private Burlingham and Lieutenant Sherwood as "Killed by Indians." After the attack, a Court of Inquiry confirmed that Sherwood was killed in action.[35]

Officer John Sprague, the Second US–Seminole War's first historian, was then serving in Florida and reflected the general military opinion that Mrs. Montgomery's death represented a "cold-blooded atrocity."[36] He thought so although she traveled with a detachment of armed officers and soldiers, a military convoy passing through disputed territory during a war. She was the sole noncombatant. Uniformed enemy soldiers were fair targets during wartime according to the laws of war. Because the

---

[33] Ibid., 249, 484.
[34] Rodenbough, *From Everglade to Cañon with the Second Dragoons*, 54.
[35] Sprague, *The Origin, Progress, and Conclusion of the Florida War*, 249–51, 274–75. Niles, *Niles' National Register*, 1841, 59:307. 9th Military Department, Letters Sent, February 26, 1841, Bliss to Commanders.
[36] Sprague, *The Origin, Progress, and Conclusion of the Florida War*, 250.

Seminole group attacked a military convoy in a rural area free of civilian habitations, an objective observer would probably admit that the attackers minimized harm to civilians.

Although Mrs. Montgomery's death was an outlier, the only known instance in records of the war when Seminole warriors killed a regular army officer's wife, the army widely interpreted her death as both a tragedy and an atrocity representative of indiscriminate warfare. While Sprague described Lieutenant Sherwood's "death" following an "attack," he labeled Mrs. Montgomery's death as a "brutal murder." In this, the regulars reflected an important strain of rhetoric in the broader white population, which "used white women's presence in Florida to justify violence against Seminole peoples and to rationalize generous social policies for white settler families, many of them slaveholders."[37] Even as the regulars depicted themselves as Florida's best men – superior to volunteers, settlers, the Indigenous, and the enslaved – they incorporated elements of settler thought into regular army paternalism. Mrs. Montgomery's death outraged officers who contrasted their narrative of Seminole actions with the army's civilized behavior. By comparison, when army officers reported that soldiers killed Seminole women, they took pains to record those deaths as accidental, never murders. A discordant note marked claims that the killing of an officer's wife in a Seminole attack on a US Army element was an atrocity while the army deliberately destroyed Seminole camps and captured Seminole women.

At the same time, regulars skewered settler men's aggrandized claims of Seminole violence against white women. One officer wrote to Colonel Worth, "I heard that Mrs. Often had been killed by Indians." When he arrived at a nearby settlement, "I learned that she was not killed, but it was generally supposed that she might have been shot at." When he arrived at her house, he learned "she had not even been fired on."[38] The army put little stock in white settler tales of Seminole depredations.

Seminole men like those who attacked the convoy were a common rhetorical target. Even before the war began, officers like General Duncan Lamont Clinch – a regular who did not attend West Point and received a commission from civilian life – described Seminole men as inferior and himself as "beset and surrounded, by a set of bad and designing [Seminole] men." Officers told how Seminole men purportedly mistreated Seminole

---

[37] Ibid., 249; Shire, "Sentimental Racism and Sympathetic Paternalism," 121.
[38] Sprague, *The Origin, Progress, and Conclusion of the Florida War*, 418–19, Letter from L B Branch to Colonel Worth, March 23, 1842.

women, which officers considered to be damning evidence. Lieutenant Henry Prince described witnessing a Seminole marriage, writing that Seminole custom doomed the bride to slavery in her husband's home.[39]

Prince, guided by civilizing discourse that characterized the US Army as protectors of women, seriously misunderstood Seminole society and marriage. While he believed a Seminole bride would leave her home and family and become trapped, in fact, Seminole husbands often moved into their new wife's matrilocal living arrangements and took on responsibilities toward her family upon marriage. In contrast, US society – reliant on a system of coverture that robbed married women of their legal identity – generally did require that women exit leave childhood homes, families, property, and surname to keep their husband's house.[40]

Officers also blamed evidence of female impoverishment on Seminole men, who supposedly could not provide despite woods allegedly full of deer, turkeys, fish, and the Seminole staple "coontie" root, a bounty that rendered Seminole raids on white settlements as laziness and aggression. Army surgeon Jacob Motte commented on the famished appearance of captured Seminole women in derogatory language, calling them "miserable, blackened, haggard, shriveled devils." These views conveniently ignored that the army systematically destroyed Seminole food supplies and limited Seminole men's access to weapons and ammunition for hunting after surrender.[41]

Army critiques of Seminole men also failed to understand that a wartime shift of resources like food to warriors rather than women was not a function of male selfishness but a defensive measure. Seminole clans hoped that strong, well-fed warriors would better protect the community – to ensure survival, security came first. Writing about nearby Muscogee-speaking peoples, Patricia Wickman describes an approach also used by Seminole groups: "When especially dangerous conditions existed,

---

[39] Clinch, *General Clinch Letter Book 1834–1835*, December 29, 1834; Prince, *Amidst a Storm of Bullets*, 23.
[40] Weisman, *Like Beads on a String*, 83. Kent's *Commentaries*, introduced earlier as a cadet textbook, also describes the legal doctrine of coverture, which the US inherited from British tradition: Kent, James, *Commentaries on American Law*, 1:442–45. For US marriage practices, see: Isenberg, *Sex and Citizenship in Antebellum America*.
[41] McCall, *Letters from the Frontiers*, 60–62; Motte, *Journey into Wilderness*, 120. Coontie is also called Arrowroot. Lieutenant Sprague, then Acting Adjutant General, wrote to Captain Gwynn on limiting weapons and ammunition to designated hunters, requiring that Gwynn must prevent "the issue of ammunition or firearms to any person except the hunters for your camp," and account for "the number of charges" given. *9th Military Department, Letters Sent*, August 28, 1841.

women, children, and noncombatants slept in the center of the town, and the warriors camped around them, to shield them physically." If warriors had prioritized access to food, it was so they could be effective shields.[42] These were productive misunderstandings for officers and enlisted men, interpretations that granted regulars moral superiority.

Private Bartholomew Lynch's casual dismissal of Seminole men expressed a common sentiment – Indigenous inferiority – when he claimed he had seen "a big Indian" who was "cruelly beating his squaw." In contrast, Motte conceded that Seminole men were at times capable of appropriate respect to women, as when he watched a dance and noted that the men were "not entirely void of gallantry, or deference to the softer sex, for…they always yielded to the ladies the place of honor." Like Motte, army officer Ethan Allen Hitchcock used women's protection to determine which Seminole men were honorable. He rendered a favorable verdict on Osceola, a figure increasingly embraced by the US press because he had supposedly directed Seminole chiefs not to harm white women or children, "for this fight is between men."[43] Captain John Sprague recorded how a Black Seminole had called Osceola "a good Indian, and constantly urged the war-parties to spare women and children."[44] Although officers deemed certain men, like Osceola, to be heroic, they condemned Seminole men in the collective. The idea that Native men mistreated women and therefore possessed less humanity was a powerful motif. Army authors were invested in women's helplessness, and fit these anecdotes into a matrix of belief where only they stood between violent men and passive women.

Focusing on Seminole men's "savagery" also emphasized the army's difficult mission in Florida. Officers like General Jesup noted that in measuring the army's success, "it should be remembered that more than peace has been sought to be obtained – that we are attempting for the first time the solution of the difficult problem of transferring a savage and warlike people from one widespread wilderness to another." He argued that US

---

[42] Wickman, *The Tree That Bends*, 99.
[43] McGaughy Jr., "The Squaw Kissing War," 154, written in Tampa, September 19, 1838; Motte, *Journey into Wilderness*, 214, 217; Hitchcock, *Fifty Years in Camp and Field*, 85.
[44] Sprague, *The Origin, Progress, and Conclusion of the Florida War*, 316. The Black interpreter's name was Sampson. For more on Black Seminoles, see: Porter, *The Black Seminoles*; Snyder, *Slavery in Indian Country*; Frank and Crothers, *Borderland Narratives*. For more on army relationships with Black Seminoles, see the Florida portion of: Hagstrom, "Learning Asymmetric War." For shifting memory about Osceola, see: Wickman, *Osceola's Legacy*.

soldiers had done well, such that "the pen of history, guided by the hand of justice, will not fail to assign to the officers and troops of his command a high place among the champions of their country's rights and honor."[45]

Seminole groups strategically conserved resources, only fighting when necessary or advantageous. They sought to outlast the US. Consequently, Seminole men denied officers a chance to prove themselves in open battle, leaving officers to wring glory from burnt cornfields and captured females. When Lieutenant Colonel William Whistler returned empty-handed from an expedition to capture Seminole people for forced removal, Colonel Worth could muster few compliments. Instead, he offered consolation: "You have discerned at least where the enemy is not; operations simultaneous in many points have been attended with the like results generally – the high praise of zeal and admirable energy is nevertheless, due to the officers and men."[46]

Officers emphasized the contrast between themselves as opposed to Native men and volunteers to unite the regular army's members in a shared identity. Private Bartholomew Lynch, often a critic of the regulars, nonetheless believed they were better than Seminole people and volunteers and wrote that "discharged vols. in Fla. are worse than the Indians themselves." Lieutenant Henry Prince believed that the Tennessee Volunteers were "the meanest rabble I ever beheld."[47] Officers emphasized that discipline lent the regular army a moral superiority over volunteers who engaged in vigilantism.

Florida volunteer James Ormond described the type of crimes regular officers often attributed to volunteers. He privately recorded the day his fellow soldiers murdered a Seminole woman walking into a white settlement and "mutilated her shamefully."[48] Volunteers gratified impulses; regulars controlled theirs. While the regular army regularly used violence against Seminole women by attacking their villages, food, and shelter – a topic explored in Chapter 3 – officers claimed their acts fell within the legitimate boundaries of the laws of war, in contrast to extralegal volunteer violence.

---

[45] Niles, *Niles' National Register*, 1838, 53:165, by order of Major General Jesup (J. A. Chambers, Aid-de-Camp and Acting Adjutant General), Orders, No. 203, Headquarters, Army of the South, St. Augustine, October 24, 1837.
[46] *9th Military Department, Letters Sent*, 40, February 18, 1842, Worth to Lieutenant Colonel Whistler.
[47] McGaughy Jr., "The Squaw Kissing War," 172, November 13, 1838; Prince, *Amidst a Storm of Bullets*, 63.
[48] Scallet, "This Inglorious War," 166, quote from James Ormond papers.

Officers used their sense of superiority to preach unity to soldiers whom officers hoped would join them on the moral high ground. This language found its most precise expression in protecting women, a vocabulary that could unite officers and enlisted soldiers as male protectors. Some soldiers heard this and agreed with it. Others, dissatisfied with their officers, used the same logic to challenge officers' claims to protector status.

THE SOLDIER'S LANGUAGE OF REBUTTAL

Soldiers took up their officers' logic of protection, but while some accepted it, others weaponized it, crafting a language of rebuttal. The most ardent critic of officer claims to superiority and protection of women was Private Bartholomew Lynch of the Second Dragoons, a regiment newly created during the war in 1836 and notorious for its poor treatment of enlisted men. Military historians often view Lynch as an outlier because he offers such a critical view and because he served in the Second Dragoons, which the army sent straight to Florida after its establishment. With inexperienced officers and soldiers thrown directly into a war, it produced more disciplinary problems than older units.[49] Also, its officers often came from civilian life – many of them partisan Democratic appointees rather than West Pointers. This emphasis on Lynch as an exception is helpful to historians of the army in that the Second Dragoons was unlike other regiments.

Still, *only* considering Lynch as an exception misses the ways he was typical – like a large portion of his fellow enlisted men, Lynch was an Irish immigrant who enlisted in New York City. He enlisted twice in the army with thirteen months between enlistments and served in the Second Dragoons from 1836 to 1839. When Lynch reenlisted in 1840, he did not disclose his past enlistment, and each time he gave his occupation as "Laborer." He also chose to enter a different regiment, the First Infantry (not uncommon when soldiers reenlisted after a period of civilian life).[50]

Lynch was an ordinary recruit in his national origin and place of enlistment, but unusual as a highly literate soldier whose written accounts survived the ravages of time.[51] Middle-class officers' families were far more likely to preserve and later memorialize their papers via donations

---

[49] Steinhauer, Dale Richard, "Sogers," 215.
[50] Ibid., 15, 34, 129, Captain W. W. Tompkins. Tompkins was a recruiting officer for the regimental recruiting service that managed enlistments for the Dragoons and recruited Lynch in New York City during September of 1836.
[51] Another is John Bemrose: Bemrose, *Reminiscences of the Second Seminole War*.

to archival institutions. Also, army record keepers prioritized officers' voices in published personal accounts and correspondence. Officers wrote reports of battles, recorded courts-martial, and promulgated orders. Because of this, archives often lack enlisted voices.

The diary is also an outlier in that it renders visible officers' exploitation of Seminole women. Officers' need for an aura of respectability, the very thing Lynch critiqued, generally rendered Seminole victims of sexual assault invisible because officers sought to protect both their reputations and that of the officer corps. Listening to soldiers like Lynch fills in the sanitized portrait of war officers crafted in their reports. In fact, outside of Lynch's journal, primary sources that address white men raping Seminole women are almost nonexistent, but historian Laurel Clark Shire uses Seminole oral histories to depict a wartime climate where such rapes were common. In matrilineal Seminole culture, this was not only an attack on individual women, but on Seminole women's power as clan mothers "to decide whose children would share membership in their clan."[52]

Lynch pointedly described being assigned to security details to escort officers to go "a hunting or a w---ng" almost daily. In another entry, he wrote that he had "gone hunting out in the bay with Capts. [illegible] an Indian squaw each for his own use. They had plenty brandy did very little shooting." Lynch bitterly wrote that "if the officers in Tampa would be half as mad to Buck Indians as they are to buck Indian Squaws, they would unquestionably be the bravest and gallantest officers in the world. The way they pitch into the squaws is a sin."[53] Lynch meant to communicate the depths of officers' hypocrisy, not hold them accountable for sexual violence. As an enlisted soldier, the army had unmanned Lynch, making him a permanent son to his officers. Focusing attention on officer mistreatment of women perhaps rehabilitated his damaged sense of masculinity. Lynch cared little about Seminole victims of rape, but cared very much about pointing out the difference between what officers said and what officers did.

Lynch believed that officers felt "no interest in the welfare of the poor devils under their command." So, he pilloried the Second US–Seminole War as the "squaw-kissing war." Officers who abused rather than protected women embodied his most potent argument on immorality.[54]

[52] Shire, *The Threshold of Manifest Destiny*, 108, 111, 113, 119, 121, 131.
[53] McGaughy Jr., "The Squaw Kissing War," 163, 169, 192. The word "squaw" is derogatory, and it appears only within the context of direct quotations.
[54] Ibid., 148, August 14, 1838 and 192, March 9, 1839. The full poem in Lynch's journal is as follows: "The squaw kissing war/The deer hunting war/The turtle soup and stewed

Lynch's diary must be understood not only as an exposé of his officers' misbehavior and criminality but as a language of rebuttal to officers' attempts to claim the moral high ground – an assault on undeserved privilege. When officers used the logic of protection to foster army unity, they assumed other officers were already behaving morally; their goal was to uplift enlisted men.

When Lynch cited examples of officers' moral failures, he meant to brand them hypocrites who claimed to protect women and encouraged enlisted men to do the same, yet declined to actually protect women or care for soldiers. Lynch followed his final diary entry by emphasizing that "the most scrupulous regard to truth is observed throughout the whole...that aught in malice is not set down here and that a great many atrocious incidents that have come under the author's observation have been suppressed." He concluded, "if any of this journal should ever be published the author would furnish any notes or explanations required by publishers."[55]

In one instance, Lynch described how two soldiers from his company had, "in the dead of night," stolen a trunk from a Mrs. Downs. The thieves broke into the trunk and left it by the post hospital when they found no money. Lynch was quick to condemn, claiming that "the thieves could be easily found out in fact they don't deny doing it, if a poor devil happened to meet a West Pt. puppy tied to a sword and not perform a [kowtow] he would be confined for disrespect to his superior officer." In contrast, "this capital crime of midnight robbery, lock breaking, is taken no notice of." He believed officers paid far more attention to submission than to the virtues or vices of their men. Lynch continued, "so the officers' notions or ideas of honesty can't be very nice. The affair of Mrs. Downs's robbery can give the reader an idea of the morals of the US Army. There is no sinecure in the world more pleasant with less trouble attached to it than a Captaincy in the US Army."[56] While officers might have justified an emphasis on obedience as an essential to military discipline, for Lynch, this selective use of authority amounted to shameful dishonesty.

After another theft, Lynch wrote that it again went unnoticed and made a compelling connection between theft and assault: "Such is the state of

---

oyster war/The war of snug places without clashing sabers/The joy of speculators – Sweet Florida War." Laurel Clark Shire uses the journal to uncover "how central sex was to the culture of privilege among white officers." Shire, *The Threshold of Manifest Destiny*, 122.

[55] McGaughy Jr., "The Squaw Kissing War," 208, July 1, 1839, Fort Columbus.
[56] Ibid., 143, 146, August 1838.

morals in the US Army that every crime is overlooked except passing your officer without saluting him and any other contempt is punished with great severity." He continued, "Or if you take liberties with any squaw, soldier's wife, or negro girl who is under the protection of an officer, you are fiercely fixed for it." In this context, for the women mentioned, an officer's protection ensured little more than his exclusive sexual access to her – her consent notwithstanding. Lynch concluded, "Rob, steal, curse, swear, fight, steal from your comrade, swindle their rations, break boxes, trunks, cut knapsacks, all are overlooked by the officer. He would not be bothered with the investigation of such damn stuff."[57] Officers' protection of women, then, encompassed many situations. There were supposedly benevolent actions, like declining to shoot into a village or capturing rather than killing Seminole women. Yet Lynch describes another arena, where protection meant merely protecting officers' property in women.

His attack on officers, through women, was also motivated by officers' failure to recognize good soldiers, among whom Lynch (censoriously, with great condescension) placed himself. Lynch believed that subpar soldiers who were drunk sycophants were nonetheless "a great deal more respected by the officers than the few manly and noble spirits who are always ready and fit for duty.... The spirited and brave honest soldier carries himself with a haughty democratic step" and looks on officers with contempt.[58] Making a similar point but in a more careful manner, in 1837 a group of noncommissioned officers advocated for enlisted men. The letter's signatories, most of whom were at war in Florida, wrote that "while commissioned officers of the army and navy have been petitioning" for pay increases, "the soldiers have remained perfectly quiet." They now courteously requested that noncommissioned officers be allowed to compete for a spot at West Point or a direct commission.

Like Lynch, they emphasized valor (not obedience) to claim that

When the patriotic soldier seriously reflects that being enlisted excludes him from preferment and that not one of his grade can ever obtain promotion, either by acts of bravery or otherwise, and that most of his officers are men who know not the soldier's wants by actual experience, he naturally loses his ambition, and either becomes a miserable outcast, deserts, or quits the army in disgust.[59]

---

[57] Ibid., 132, August, Fort Brooke; 163, October 6–7, 1838; 169, November 8, 1838; 186 Tampa Bay, March 3, 1838, 192, March 9, 1839.

[58] Ibid., 187, March 1839.

[59] *Twenty Fourth Congress, Second Session*, 988, January 16, 1837. "Memorial of certain non-commissioned officers of the army that persons of their grades be promoted to commissions for faithful and meritorious service."

Despite this stinging critique, the sergeants did none of those things. They remained in service and sent their letter to print – an example of how a gendered language of dissent, premised on a need for respect as brave men, both allowed critiques and contained them.

Where enlisted men wished to prove themselves and advance according to their abilities, officers wanted soldiers who quietly obeyed. In a statement that emphasized the utility of nativism to their argument, the group of presumably native-born sergeants continued, "In fact, very few Americans will ever enter the service under such circumstances; and we attribute, in a great measure, the present abandoned and degraded condition of the American soldiery to no other cause." They were "consequently led to believe that were a portion of officers promoted from sergeants, the ranks of the army would in a few years be greatly improved, and a meritorious and faithful class of officers added." As it stood, the non-com was "doomed to serve out a servitude of years, despised and degraded by all his countrymen, notwithstanding his qualifications and merits may be of a superior kind."[60] In other words, enlisting in the army meant being treated like an immigrant, bound to the service of one's superiors, and locked into a permanent inequality.

While officers defended their sexual privileges over local women and the special rights of rank, officers did not monopolize access to all women. When Lynch reported a group of prostitutes to the commander, Lieutenant Colonel Cummings told him not to bother his "head about the whores of Fla." Cummings suggested instead that Lynch should "call to them in a more business-like manner and take a sample to myself." Lynch noted that times were good in Tampa partly because there were "plenty women in the market absolutely at the disposal of the highest bidder." He concluded this anecdote by emphasizing how much work remained for the internal civilizing mission to mend "morals and manners" in the army: "What a field for missionaries does the US Army present, the finest in the world."[61]

Beyond rape, there were other forms of sex between Seminole women and US men that probably existed along a spectrum of coercion and consent. For example, Lynch refers to his Lieutenant, Croghan Ker, as "the darling among the squaws." Notably, Lynch applied this label to emphasize that Ker "seems to be an excellent officer." While evidence of sexual

---

[60] Ibid.
[61] McGaughy Jr., "The Squaw Kissing War," 136; 138, August 1838 Fort Brooke; 158, October 2, 1838; 161; 166, October 26, 1838; 189–91, March 5, 1839.

partnerships with Native women is scant for the Second US–Seminole War, much evidence from other army posts on US borderlands proves army officers habitually sought them out. This practice was widespread. A missionary's wife at Fort Snelling, on the Minnesota frontier, wrote in 1837 that all but two officers at the post had Native mistresses.[62]

Soldiers noticed these relationships, and, like Lynch, some critiqued their officers for failing to live up to refined ideals. James Elderkin was a young, recently enlisted soldier in 1839, when he arrived at Fort Gibson in Indian Territory, the destination for many Creek and Seminole people forced from Florida. Elderkin wrote that the lieutenant who served as their adjutant in the Fourth Infantry Regiment was "a very fine appearing man, but not well-liked by the men" because he mistreated a Creek woman known for her "perfect ladyship" and beloved by many. Elderkin explained, "the chief of the Creek nation was the father of the noblest and most beautiful maiden I ever saw. She was half white and every inch a lady." After "Adjt. – – – – fell in love with and married her, and lived with her two years," it was then "reported that he cruelly abandoned her." Elderkin felt the officer soon got his just deserts when "he paid the penalty with his life, as he was shot through the heart at the battle of Monterey, Mexico." The lieutenant's "dastardly act" of abandoning a woman he was duty-bound to love and protect earned him the lasting enmity of his soldiers, who understood the distance between his "fine appearance" and his ugly behavior.[63]

Casual references to local women as fruits of conquest represent another kind of evidence for coercion. One lieutenant described a soldier carrying off two pumpkins by saying, "he could not have been better pleased had he made a foray into some Indian wigwam, and gallantly borne off two round-cheeked squaws instead." While in nearby Pensacola, a jumping-off point for many troops entering the war, army officer George McCall characterized local women as typical recreation for officers. In Pensacola's more restful locale, officers put their soldiers on work details while courting the town's Spanish-descended women. Because of enlisted labor, men like him could be "gentlemen of leisure; cards, hunting, or making love to the pretty Creoles of the town, being their almost sole occupation," saying with a wink that the women's "morality" was "not always of the strictest character."

---

[62] Ibid., 163, October 7, 1838; Skelton, *An American Profession of Arms*, 189.

[63] Elderkin, *Biographical Sketches and Anecdotes*, 6–10. The modern spelling is "Monterrey" rather than "Monterey." Most US primary sources use the latter.

2 Developing a Logic of Protection: Army Debates 95

This sexual freedom was excellent news to McCall, who praised the women as "affectionate and friendly."[64] A climate that equated officers' pleasure and sex with admiring locals laid the groundwork for the sexual conquest of captured Seminole women.

Second Dragoon officer William Harney's brutal treatment of women deservedly earned him criticism from Lynch and others. Like many officers of the new regiment, Harney came to his commission from civilian life, not West Point. Mexican War diarist Samuel Chamberlain, a regular army enlisted soldier in that war, served under Harney and quotes an unattributed source as saying that Harney had, during the Second US–Seminole War, "ravished young Indian girls at night and had them strung up to the limb of a live oak in the morning."[65] No evidence directly supports this probably apocryphal claim. More likely, it was a composite sketch that combined several true elements – sex, murder, hangings – from Harney's life.

Before coming to Florida, Harney had a relationship with a mixed-race Winnebago woman, Ke-sho-ko, at Fort Winnebago, and she bore him a daughter in 1829 or 1830. In 1834 St. Louis, Harney murdered Hannah, a woman his family enslaved. He beat her to death with a rawhide strip and fled Missouri to avoid arrest, shocking other whites in St. Louis. Although many were themselves enslavers, they wanted *Harney's* blood after he murdered Hannah. A friend and relative, James Clemens Jr., wrote to Harney that "if you had remained one day longer I feel confident they would not have given you the benefit of a trial." It remains an enduring testament to Harney's viciousness that a white mob wanted to lynch a white man for killing an enslaved woman. A county grand jury indicted Harney for murder on July 28, 1834, and Clemens warned, "do not come back to this place – depend on it if you were here now it would go hard with you."[66] Harney never faced justice, and the rage quickly faded.

Harney also incited controversy when he hanged captive Seminole men – killing prisoners was a crime. After a group attacked his camp in July of 1839 (later termed the Harney Massacre) he chased down those responsible. Harney tracked this group not only to prosecute the US war against Seminole but for revenge. In the popular press, his tactics in the

---

[64] By a Lieutenant of the Left Wing, *Sketch of the Seminole War*, 156; McCall, *Letters from the Frontiers*, 13–14. McCall refers here not to Seminole women but to women of Spanish, or potentially mixed Spanish and Native, descent.
[65] Watson, "How the Army Became Accepted," 236.
[66] Adams, *General William S. Harney: Prince of Dragoons*, 35, 66.

last years of the war were commonly known as "War to the Rope," as in a *St. Augustine News* headline. In December of 1840, Harney and his men captured two Seminole families and hanged the men while women and children watched, then found Seminole leader Chakaika's camp and destroyed it. An officer described how Harney "caused twelve Indians to be executed and left hanging, ghastly pendants to the moss-covered pines" and brought back captured women and children, "striking consternation to the hearts of the savages, who had hitherto believed themselves safe from molestation" in the Everglades.[67] Although executing prisoners of war was a clear violation within the laws of war tradition, many described Harney's "war to the rope" with approbation. Floridians felt Harney did what was necessary.

Harney later gained the nickname "squaw killer" from his 1855 massacre of Sioux women and children at Blue Water Creek, also called Ash Hollow. Enlisted soldier James Elderkin suggested Harney could have achieved this epithet earlier, perhaps during the Second US–Seminole War, writing that the name came from his "killing a squaw who attacked him, and his ordering the men to fire on the squaws as well as the men." Susan Bettelyoun, the métis daughter of a French-American fur trader and a Brulé Lakota woman, was raised near Ash Hollow and later wrote that "it was for many years after this that the western people called Harney 'Squaw Killer Harney.'" American studies scholar Nick Estes notes that in Lakota tradition, the name was "Woman Killer," and Harney's biographer George Adams described the massacre as marking Harney "more than most officers as a killer of women and children."[68]

Because Harney commissioned out of civilian life and not West Point, his brutality is often harnessed to the argument that Harney was the exception that proved the rule. This line of thinking leads some to claim that the rise of West Point-educated officers marked the ascendancy of a more gentlemanly and increasingly professional army. In this sense, one can interpret the evidence of sexual coercion in the Second Dragoons as unusual. Yet, while other officers disdained Harney's cruelty, they openly admired his ability to get results. Stephen Watts Kearny, an officer whose outlook skewed toward paternalism and who generally considered

---

[67] Ibid., 76–77, December 6 and 10, 1840; Rodenbough, *From Everglade to Cañon with the Second Dragoons*, 46.
[68] Elderkin, *Biographical Sketches and Anecdotes*, 66; Bettelyoun, *With My Own Eyes*, 57; Adams, *General William S. Harney: Prince of Dragoons*, 17, 35, 47, 48, 133, 140; Estes, *Our History Is the Future*, 99.

2 Developing a Logic of Protection: Army Debates 97

Harney an inferior – he prefaced the compliment related here by saying that Harney had "no more brains than a Grey hound" – nonetheless appreciated Harney's achievements. In that letter, addressed to another officer, Kearny wrote that Harney "has done more to impress the Indians with a fear of us and the desperate state of their cause" than anyone else.[69]

According to his biographer, Harney "held a heroic view of officership that emphasized physical courage and achievement in battle," a true example of martial manhood. He believed in a system of honor that valued violence and aggression, where "men may take pride in attacking fellow men, whether they use this force to protect women or for other reasons." Harney's behavior fit an earlier model of gendered violence predicated on class, one where knights could assault peasant women, or women won from other men in combat, at will without damaging their reputations as protectors of aristocratic women. Harney's approach to honor, chivalry, and women's protection seems strikingly different from the paternalist views of his peer, regular officer and West Point graduate Ethan Allen Hitchcock. Historians sometimes cast the two as "a study of opposites."[70] Yet, Hitchcock understood they were pursuing different means to the same end – removing Seminole people from Florida.

Hitchcock believed his diplomatic approach to be more effective than "Harney's method of dealing with the Indians – to hang them wherever they were found," but recognized that they shared the same goal of Indian Removal, the mission the US government assigned to the army.[71] The desire to end the war encouraged soldiers to treat Seminole people like "savage" enemies and pursue all ways to remove them, thus creating tolerance for extreme measures. Superiors allowed Harney to use whatever tactics he chose. Many colleagues approved of the results.

Harney's ruthlessness may have been exceptional – we have little evidence of other officers acting so brutally – but his successful career demonstrated the disparate impulses of paternalism. While army leaders repeatedly sanctioned Harney on charges related to insubordination and indiscipline throughout his career, he never faced military justice

---

[69] Adams, *General William S. Harney: Prince of Dragoons*, 79. In the Mexican War, Kearny's conquest of New Mexico and Proclamation to the people of Santa Fe exemplified the logic of protection. For more on Kearny, see: Clarke, *Stephen Watts Kearny*.
[70] Adams, *General William S. Harney: Prince of Dragoons*, 74; Spierenburg, "Introduction," 2; Brownmiller, *Against Our Will*, 290–91; Monaco, *The Second Seminole War and the Limits of American Aggression*, 158.
[71] Hitchcock, *Fifty Years in Camp and Field*, 175.

for extralegal violence.⁷² Military justice remained a limited thing, and Harney emerged unscathed. The logic of protection that officers used to emphasize morality and communicate with enlisted men was only just emerging, and army culture like army law remained inchoate. Moreover, Army claims to protecting women situated it within the laws of war tradition. Yet, efforts to uphold this image and bolster the rising social status of the officer corps ultimately provided an incentive to remain silent when faced with evidence of other officers' abuses of women. Ultimately, when officers in Florida claimed to protect women, they made a cultural rather than a legal claim.

Army regulations and military justice were rarely concerned with women and instead focused on discipline, especially officer-enlisted relations. The still-developing army had not yet fashioned specific policies for dealing with enemy civilians. It would begin to do so a few years later in Mexico when the scale at which the army encountered the Mexican people, and the pressures of military occupation, demanded it. Courts-martial from the Second US–Seminole War focused on internal army issues: disrespect to officers and indiscipline.⁷³

Just as soldiers used the logic of protection to speak truth to officers' power, officers themselves sometimes used it to critique their superiors. Lieutenant John Phelps, a future abolitionist and handy antithesis to Harney, questioned the sincerity of his seniors' chivalric feelings during a scouting expedition. He wrote that General Hernandez (a Florida militia commander) left "animated with that same chivalric feeling that led De Soto through these wilds three hundred years ago. Fortune smiled upon him; he surrounded and captured between 30 and 40 hostiles." The people of St. Augustine feted this accomplishment with balls. After "the captured property," probably Black Seminoles or other refugees from US slavery, "was disposed of at a high rate," Phelps sardonically remarked

---

[72] Harney received a general order of reprimand in 1844 after pressuring a soldier to fight an enslaved man, a punishment that ultimately had little impact on his career. Harney retired as a Brevet Major General in 1865. Watson, *Peacekeepers and Conquerors*, 522.

[73] Officers did sometimes send offenders to civilian courts in serious cases that could involve women. For example, Lieutenant Colonel William Whistler wrote in a letter dated January 19, 1842 that "Private James Steck of C Compy 7th Infty murdered his wife [perhaps a laundress] on the 11th Inst. for which crime he has been turned over to the civil authority." Whistler requested Steck's discharge from the army. Letters Received by the Office of the Adjutant General (Main Series) 1822–1860. Roll 260, Record Group 94. National Archives Microcopy No. 567. Quoted in: Knetsch, "The Hardships and Inconveniences."

that "the officers concerned were astonished at their own chivalry, and there was such rejoicing as was perhaps never surpassed."[74]

Nathaniel Wyche Hunter, another young West Point graduate, critiqued Zachary Taylor's rumored 1840 order to "take no more Indians alive" as a severe violation of duty that amounted to murder. As the war continued and army attitudes toward unconquered Seminole groups hardened, Taylor expressed an increasingly common frustration. Hunter resisted this slide toward atrocity and wrote that to follow such an order would be to repeat "the hackneyed phraseology of the day merely – that I have no right to discuss the propriety of my order; that it is the duty of a soldier to obey; that government is but enforcing a treaty; that our enemies are barbarous murderers of women and children; and last, that I am paid for acting not thinking." Hunter concluded that he would refuse to follow any order that amounted to "wringing [his] hands in innocent blood."[75] Hunter rebutted such tactics and explored principled disobedience.

Soldiers such as Lynch and Elderkin and officers such as Phelps and Hunter used protection to refute superiors' claims to morality or condemn the hardening of army attitudes toward Seminole people. Yet others accepted those claims as fact. English immigrant John Bemrose enlisted as a hospital steward thanks to his experience as a druggist and served in Florida. As an educated, literate hospital orderly, Bemrose, like Lynch, was not an ordinary private. As a British immigrant who used rather than hid his education (as did the Irish-born Lynch), Bemrose was well positioned to receive better treatment from officers.

And he did. Where Lynch found his officers hypocritical, Bemrose found his sincere. Bemrose liked his supervisor, the post surgeon Dr. Weightman, who was "extremely kind" and promised that if Bemrose

---

[74] Phelps, "Letters of Lieutenant John W. Phelps," 79, letter to father, Fort Heileman, July 10, 1837, and 81–82, letter to sister Fort Heileman September 19, 1837. Seminole society incorporated Black men and women into the social body. Where the Muscogee (Creek), along with the Cherokee, Choctaw, and Chickasaw nations, came to label Black men and women as enslaved people, Seminole society "demonstrated a willingness to embrace people of African descent." Although Seminole people bought and sold African-descended enslaved people, they also welcomed runaways to form a pluralistic society "composed of allied but unequal groups." More so than free Black Americans who faced numerous restrictions on their freedom, Black Seminoles "enjoyed almost complete autonomy in fashioning separate communities." Snyder, *Slavery in Indian Country*, 212, 217, 228.

[75] Wik, "Captain Nathaniel Wyche Hunter and the Florida Indian Campaigns," 73–74. Hunter described Taylor's demand as an "order," but no corroborating record exists. It could have been a more informal written statement, or an unsubstantiated rumor.

suited as a hospital steward "and was anxious to do my duty, I should find he would not only aid me in my studies but that he would be a father to me."[76] Paternalism took root in army culture partly because, when sincere, it offered valuable support to soldiers.

Bemrose continued to believe in officers' self-presentations as kind paternalists. Even alongside his horrified commentary on witnessing slavery in St. Augustine and at General Duncan Clinch's Florida plantation, he was pleased to be chosen as a scribe for Clinch. Bemrose reflected with pride, "so now behold me two or three hours daily sitting at a rickety table opposite our kind old general." He praised Clinch and recorded the general's daily visits to a severely wounded soldier: "beaming with kindness, sitting upon the earthen floor," the general gave "comfort to a poor dying private soldier," saying, "My poor man! Bear your sufferings as a soldier, and you must now become a soldier of Christ." He described wounded officers under his care as "chivalric and brave" or "gentlemanly and brave" or "fearlessly brave."[77] In Bemrose's army officers and enlisted men worked well together.

Paternalism was beneficial in the opinion of believers like Bemrose. To him, army unity was not merely an officers' claim but a reality. Expecting contact with the enemy as the Battle of the Withlacoochee was fought nearby, his "little band" of soldiers scrupulously stayed on guard through a cold night. The lieutenant was, according to Bemrose, "one whom I loved and respected." Further expressing this regulars' sense of unity, Bemrose faithfully recorded the "cowardliness of the militia" during that battle. And he insisted Seminole warriors "seemed filled with a ravenous thirst for blood which must be satisfied upon all, whether men, women, or children."[78] Bemrose defined the army and its officers as virtuous in contrast to crude volunteers and bloodthirsty Seminole warriors who targeted, rather than protected, noncombatants.

Both soldiers like Bemrose, who believed in regular army virtue, and soldiers like Lynch, who saw hypocrisy in officers' moral claims, nonetheless responded directly to and thus accepted their officers' rhetoric. In this sense, whether officers *were* paternalists was beside the point: officers *articulated* paternalism, and soldiers responded to those claims. Enlisted

---

[76] Bemrose, *Reminiscences of the Second Seminole War*, 9. This may have been Dr. Richard Weightman. Heitman, *Historical Register*, 680.

[77] Bemrose, *Reminiscences of the Second Seminole War*, 38, December 14, 1835, 59, 61. Of note, Bemrose assembled his *Reminiscences* later in life to support his pension request.

[78] Ibid., 46–47, January 1, 1836, 51, 56.

men could only advocate for or critique that logic by using it. Favorable or not, usage rooted the ideal of army paternalism ever more securely in army culture. As Eugene Genovese asserts, "Wherever paternalism exists, it undermines solidarity among the oppressed by linking them as individuals to their oppressor."[79] Soldiers claimed that their individual officers were good or bad. Yet, when expressed in the logic of protection, both praise and condemnation bound soldiers to their officers.

THE EMERGING LOGIC OF PROTECTION

Although Bemrose and Lynch came to opposite conclusions about the sincerity of officers' claims to morality, both accepted that the logic of protection was legitimate. In part, this was because officers wielded great power over subordinates. Officers mediated soldiers' access to food, clothing, shelter, military justice, promotion, awards – even to marriage, through recruiting practices and laundress appointments. In an army that stripped soldiers of many, perhaps most, of their rights as free white men, they retained manhood if they could subordinate women. Transforming women into dependents, soldiers' protected subjects, asserted strength. The army subordinated captured Seminole women as men over women, soldiers over civilians, and white over Native peoples.

As army regulations and bureaucracy developed, paternalism's earlier ad hoc variant developed into a more formalized system – a process reflected in officers' efforts to enlist unmarried men, more easily treated as sons than married soldiers. Recruiting officers before 1841 sometimes tried not enlisting married men with children or were told to avoid doing so. The adjutant for the Sixth Infantry Regiment wrote to a recruiting officer in 1832 that "The number of laundresses already attached to companies is as many as is allowed by regulations," and any laundresses sent "in addition to this number the commanding officers conceives would not hold advantages to the service." Instead, additional women "would, on the contrary, greatly diminish the comfort of those authorized and operate as a serious burden to the companies: He, therefore, desires that you will not enlist men with wives and families." The adjutant concluded, "and when you can avoid it, you will refrain from sending laundresses with the detachments of recruits destined for this post."[80]

---

[79] Genovese, *Roll, Jordan, Roll*, 5.
[80] *6th Infantry, Letters Sent*, 1: February 11, 1832, Lieutenant Albert J. Johnston, Adjutant, Jefferson Barracks, to Lieutenant A. W. Bateman, Newport, KY.

By 1841, the revised *General Regulations* officialized the practice of enlisting only single men, stating that "No man having a wife or children shall be enlisted in time of peace, without special authority obtained from General Headquarters, through the superintendent. This rule is not to apply to soldiers who 'reenlist.'" This critical change reflected an army that increasingly formalized the culture of an army family. By 1841, officers' position as parents to dependent son-soldiers had become a normative standard. Yet, although soldiers' subordination relative to officers would be permanent, young soldiers could transition from child to adult sons who married and controlled dependents of their own – but only if they had the support of their officers. Lieutenant Henry Prince noted one such instance in his diary in 1836, writing that he gave written permission for a private "to be 'married' to Miss Dixon, Fort Brooke."[81] Prince, like other officers, mediated soldiers' access to women.

Just as enlisted men and marriage regulations developed during the Second US–Seminole War, so did other aspects of army bureaucracy. Army reports became less arbitrary and dependent on the individual author and more regulated. A month before the war started, the army introduced a standardized form as a cover sheet for all official letters. It divided the cover sheet into four sections, beginning with basic information, a concise analysis of the document's contents, numbered additional papers included, and the appropriate chain of command's added remarks. Whether officers followed these painstaking procedures is another question, but by regulation, an officer would fold the sheet and the accompanying letter with three folds parallel to the writing. He was to make each fold in a specified order, with the commander's endorsement placed carefully into a prescribed area. The neat creases on surviving documents in today's archives are a testament to this waxing uniformity. Courts-martial records, for instance, contain lines of precise handwriting using standardized indentations for different categories of information, inscribed on off-white or light-blue paper, with small cuts where the author threaded a ribbon to bind and seal the trifolded final product.[82]

---

[81] War Department, *General Regulations for the Army of the United States*, 121, Article 690; Prince, *Amidst a Storm of Bullets*, 58, September 20, 1836. This reflects Dale Steinhauer's statistical analysis of antebellum enlisted men. Seventy-five percent of soldiers in his sample eventually married. Steinhauer, Dale Richard, "Sogers," 53.

[82] *Orders, Headquarters of the Army, 1835–1839*, 225A: November 21, 1835, Revised Regulations for Adjutant General Department; "Court-Martial Case Files, 1809–1894," RG153, National Archives, Washington DC.

2 Developing a Logic of Protection: Army Debates

Because a professional army demanded an improved administrative system, the Second US–Seminole War marked the emerging genre of standardized reporting. This development occurred in tandem with an emerging logic of protection because both elements regulated a maturing institution. The army needed a measure of cultural unity and a more uniform organization. These informal and formal aspects of agreement were entangled and intermixed so that as a logic of protection developed, it affected and was affected by bureaucratization. This bureaucratization, in turn, shaped national conversations. Army correspondence regularly appeared in newspapers at all levels, from local papers to military-specific outlets like the *Army and Navy Chronicle* to popular publications like *Niles National Register*. Scholars should understand official army documents during the Second US–Seminole War as a developing genre of writing and as a source base that shaped and was shaped by national politics.

Army reporting, after all, had a point of view. Authors – invariably officers – sought to aggrandize their accomplishments and minimize their failures. Private Lynch cynically referred to this relationship between author and document when he wrote that the truth was "a thing never known through official reports," which contained officers' embellished accounts of bravery. Dale Steinhauer argues that "for performing his duty in combat, the officer earned praise, honor, and fame." In contrast, "Officers merely gave the credit for doing his duty to the enlisted man who exposed himself to the same danger. The officer who gave his life in military action became a hero, while the slain enlisted man immediately slipped into a forgotten past."[83]

Officers occasionally mentioned a specific enlisted man in their reports. Colonel Worth wrote to the Adjutant General that a Sergeant from the Second Dragoons had set up an ambush and captured four Seminole warriors and eight women and children. Worth praised Sergeant Stanger's "zeal and intelligence" and remarked that "the affair was managed very cleverly."[84] But such recognition of enlisted men was rare compared to the glory meted out to officers, and sergeants had little to gain in any case. Officers, however, hoped to turn almost any engagement with Seminole groups into brevet rank. It was possible with a sympathetic chain of

---

[83] McGaughy Jr., "The Squaw Kissing War," 140; Steinhauer, Dale Richard, "Sogers," 361.
[84] *9th Military Department, Letters Sent*, 127, July 29, 1841, Worth to Army Adjutant General, drawn from Captain Seawell's report.

command and a bit of luck. After an engagement in June of 1836, the army made Major Julius Heileman a Brevet Lieutenant Colonel for his meritorious conduct and "defeat" of a "very superior force."[85] On a list of officers recommended for brevet at the end of the war, Colonel Worth included Major Joseph Plympton based on his longstanding service as "a battle officer in the war of 1812" and because he rendered "zealous and efficient service during the past winter…and twice met the enemy in battle."[86]

Such reports helped members of the regular army define themselves in contrast to supposedly inferior groups, considering regulars in opposition to Indigenous men and volunteers. Bemrose provided an example when he wrote that there was "something so cruel in the sound of the war-whoop, something that tells of murder and bloody deeds in the melancholy wails or song that precedes the blood-curdling whoops!" He believed that the army protected innocents from Seminole men. Similarly, Army Surgeon Jacob Motte claimed that the "blood-thirsty Indian" was "a stranger to every feeling of humanity and compassion" who killed even as their victims "pierced the air with agonizing cries for mercy."[87]

He described the regular army's superiority, writing that "all the regular troops behaved as they always do, with the most consummate daring and courage." He continued, "it is to be regretted that the same cannot be said of the volunteers" who were "entirely devoid of discipline" and no more than "useless and unwieldy hordes." Motte thought only regulars had "those habits of subordination, implicit obedience, and perfect method."[88] As the army developed, the logic of protection gave fuller meaning to those habits. Obedience was a consequence of military discipline and the hallmark of a what many regulars claimed was morally disciplined force that exercised restraint, protected innocents, and fought only (male) enemies.

In the Second US–Seminole War, regular officers cultivated a culture based on a shared logic of protecting women to structure their relations with enlisted men, from whom officers demanded obedience. Their immense authority enabled officers to push the beginnings of an army culture grounded in paternalism down to the rank and file. A

---

[85] *Orders, Headquarters of the Army, 1835–39*, 225A:69, June 25, 1836, General Orders 42. The President of the US conferred brevets, and the commanding general, in this case Alexander Macomb, signed them.

[86] 27th Congress, 2nd Session, 7:24, Worth to Adjutant General, May 6, 1842.

[87] Bemrose, *Reminiscences of the Second Seminole War*, 22; Motte, *Journey into Wilderness*, 175.

[88] Motte, *Journey into Wilderness*, 195–96.

soldierly responsibility to protect women rooted in officers' notions of moral behavior and paternalism contributed to army cohesion even as it revealed the depths of army disunity.

Officers spoke the logic of protection in the context of the army family's officer-led military hierarchy. For them, a shared belief in protecting women was not a leveling force. It enhanced rather than erased the distinction between officer-fathers and enlisted men, who remained sons in the army family. Officers' efforts to engage soldiers in a shared sense of army unity called into being a soldier's language of rebuttal where enlisted men asserted their manhood by challenging officers' claims to the chivalric treatment of women. Soldiers articulated critiques based on officers' poor treatment of subordinates, women, and enlisted men alike.

Still, even these challenges to authority followed the logic of protection, debating only the relative adherence of enlisted men and officers to the ideal of the soldier as women's protector. This struggle over the logic of protection strengthened it even as members of the army deployed it against each other. Such rhetoric became widely accepted. Ironically, even as soldiers followed the logic of protection, they wielded it against Seminole women. And although a logic of protection emerged in Florida, profound distance remained between officers and enlisted men. Yet, officers' efforts to create a more unified (and more hierarchical) army *had* reaped a common language that allowed for dissent within acceptable boundaries and ultimately provided a basis for greater cohesion.

3

"Find Where Their Women Are"

The US Army's Pursuit of Seminole Women, 1835–1842

In the third year of the Second US–Seminole War, newly ex-President Andrew Jackson wrote to the Secretary of War in frustration. In a private letter to J. R. Poinsett dated October 1, 1837, he declared, "the Commanding Genl. ought to find where their women are...and capture them – this done, they will at once surrender." With remarkable clarity, Jackson revealed what the war would become: a war on Seminole women. In fact, Jackson had advocated this strategy since before the war began, ordering General Duncan Clinch on December 16, 1835 to "seize the women & children" to "inflict merited chastisement," retaliation for alleged Seminole attacks on white settlers. A consistent advocate for capturing women to end the war, Jackson now critiqued General Winfield Scott's efforts. In April 1837, he wrote a four-page memo on Scott's Florida campaign, beginning with a damning analysis. He argued that Scott's strategy was fundamentally flawed because to move troops into the Florida interior "without knowing where the Indian women were, was like a combined operation to encompass a wolf in the hammocks without knowing first where her den and whelps were."[1] To bring his national policy of Indian Removal to fruition, Jackson correctly understood that military success meant deliberate, wholesale targeting of

---

[1] Bassett, *Correspondence of Andrew Jackson*, V, 1835–1838:468, 512; Andrew Jackson to Duncan Clinch, "'Memorandum." quoted in: Shire, *The Threshold of Manifest Destiny*, 101. Jackson wrote three letters around late 1837 that dealt with the Second US–Seminole War. Two of the three focused on Seminole women. Interestingly, in Jackson's wolf analogy, Seminole men are the mother wolves, and Seminole women are the whelps. He displaced gender, but retained the subordination of women (as young) to men (as parents).

3 "Find Where Their Women Are": Pursuing Seminole Women

Seminole women. Slowly, and while refusing to openly acknowledge it, Scott's regular army came to agree.

The Second US–Seminole War was not merely fought against Seminole warriors, but against women. The logic of protection helped the army resolve the problem of waging war on women while upholding female noncombatancy. While characterizing Seminole women as subjects of protection and hunting Seminole women to affect Indian Removal appear to be conflicting goals, the army used a common set of ideas to resolve these apparent contradictions. Instead of simply seizing women as combatants and thus proper prisoners, the army framed Seminole women's captures and the destruction of their resources as a humanitarian policy that would bring women under military protection and relocate them to safe homes. Protection became a foundational assumption upon which army culture rested because it solved the paradox of making war on women while maintaining that the army was a force for good.

The army did not make war on Seminole women *despite* an army-specific logic of protecting women, but *because* of it. Attributing Seminole men's attacks to a "savage" nature allowed army leaders to frame their actions as necessary to uphold the march of civilization. In this, they drew on Jacksonian political practices that valued dispossessing Indigenous groups to expand national boundaries, extending white settlements and slavery. Regulars took what they needed from this framework – namely, a mandate to accomplish their mission of expelling Seminole people by whatever means. Yet, officers drew on their knowledge of a more universal view of the laws of war, mining it for evidence that they were a moral institution.

Army officer George McCall called this the "ameliorating influence of the *stars and stripes*." Army Surgeon Jacob Motte went further, writing that the army's feats in Florida were unsurpassed in the annals of history and motivated by "no other incentive than moral courage."[2] The army's purported commitment to women's safety paradoxically enabled violence. It became easy to argue that they protected Seminole women as soldiers marched into new territories and assaulted some civilians to achieve US control of an area because it ostensibly conferred US protection on all women.

Changes to army culture in Florida generated changes to the army's relationship with the laws of war. While the laws of war would have allowed violence against women who took up arms and therefore

---

[2] McCall, *Letters from the Frontiers*, 14; Motte, *Journey into Wilderness*, 141–46.

forfeited the protection supposedly conferred to noncombatants, the army did not make much use of this exemption. Even when Seminole women behaved as combatants, soldiers maintained that such women remained harmless. Instead, officers and enlisted men acted according to the deeply held belief within army culture that women needed them, and interpreted Seminole women's participation in war through a gendered lens that upheld female innocence and left men unable to comprehend women's wartime activities.

Following the dictates of US politicians, Army officers institutionalized a way to ignore violence done to Seminole women by only counting Seminole men as warriors and thus as casualties in military reports. This record-keeping practice reified a categorization of all Seminole adults as warriors or women and severed Seminole women from the army's official memory of the war. Soldiers emphasized their moral superiority, rooted in their ability to protect Seminole women, alongside claims that Seminole men were a "savage" foe. Together, these distinct approaches to Seminole men and women justified changes to military regulations that gave the army more freedom to take prisoners and violate flags of truce.

Moreover, throughout the war, even as army strategy morphed into a war on women, officers and enlisted men alike consistently interpreted Seminole women's actions in such a way as to uphold female innocence, even in the face of evidence that those women directly participated in war. Stephanie McCurry demonstrates how Confederate women's fierce resistance forced the US, specifically Henry Halleck and Francis Lieber, to change the laws of war as written into Lieber's Code to account for women's "identity as dangerous enemies."[3] But when the army fought Seminole groups in Florida two decades earlier, neither Lieber nor Halleck

---

[3] Deborah Rosen's *Border Law* is the sole monograph on the laws of war in Florida – a study of US military power in the First US–Seminole War. Geoffrey Best's *Humanity in Warfare* uses the turn of the century Hague Regulations and the Geneva Conventions as anchor points for the twentieth century. John Witt's *Lincoln's Code* bestrides US history, yet like Best, Witt emphasizes Euro-American interactions as that history's pivotal moments. Witt spends a portion of Chapter 3 on "Indian Wars" and concludes the chapter with several paragraphs on the Second US–Seminole War, resulting in generalizations. For instance, after describing the Gnadenhutten massacre, Witt writes, "By the 1830s such violence had become standard operating procedure in the regular army." Helen Kinsella's *The Image and the Weapon* traces the genealogy of the principle of distinction – the difference between combatant and civilian. Kinsella argues that understanding women as prototypical civilians is essential to comprehending the laws of war. Rosen, *Border Law: The First Seminole War and American Nationhood*; Best, *Humanity in Warfare*; Witt, *Lincoln's Code*, 92, 107–8; Kinsella, *The Image before the Weapon*; McCurry, *Women's War*, 25.

3 "Find Where Their Women Are": Pursuing Seminole Women 109

had thought that women could ever be such a thing. Even as Seminole women took active and varied parts in resisting removal, Lieber wrote that "the woman cannot defend the state."[4] Interactions between the regulars and Seminole women demonstrate how soldiers filtered their experiences through fervently held beliefs of female helplessness and harmlessness, exposing how ideas of protecting women filtered into the army's distinct milieu.

Women's perceived innocence prevented military men from understanding female leadership and participation in the war. Even as they captured Seminole women, destroyed their homes, and burned their food stores, soldiers considered Seminole women willing instruments who would persuade Seminole men to leave Florida. Politicians required that the US Army fulfill the civilizing mission of forcibly removing Seminole people from Florida. By reframing female captivity as the protection of innocent women and rewriting the laws of war, the army could civilize Florida and develop a reputation for good behavior. That is, the army could be both civilized and civilizers.

SEMINOLE WOMEN'S WAR

Although the laws of war only obligated militaries to safeguard women who took no part in the war – clearly offering a potential loophole to anyone claiming that Seminole women lost their innocence through combatant actions – army leaders refused that particular bait. Instead, their desire to preserve women's innocence and emphasize Seminole women's willingness to help the army overwrote women's participation in the war. Soldiers sometimes recorded how Seminole women "gave a most hearty co-operation" in the war effort and "supplied provisions indiscriminately to the warriors." In addition to cooking, women spent time "running bullets."[5] But even those soldiers who acknowledged women's wartime activities misinterpreted them according to the idea that a Seminole woman would possess "the modesty and quiet submission of the Indian female." They assumed women remained engrossed in activities like the "dutiful task" of mending a moccasin for a husband, with a child nearby "amusing itself and mother with the music of a rattle."[6] Pretty Seminole maidens and loving Seminole mothers

---

[4] Lieber, *Manual of Political Ethics*, 2:125.
[5] Sprague, Brevet Captain, Eighth Regiment US Infantry, *The Origin, Progress, and Conclusion of the Florida War*, 94, 113.
[6] Ibid., 464–68; McCall, *Letters from the Frontiers*, 56–59.

flattered the army's self-image as protectors. Recognizing women's fierce refusals did not.

Captain John Sprague, who fought in and wrote the first history of the war, described the imprisonment of Seminole leader Coacoochee's daughter. She was "an interesting girl about twelve years of age" captured near Fort Mellon and held at Fort Cummings. Coacoochee, known to the US public as Wild Cat, came to the fort and met with Colonel William Worth. His daughter, confined in a nearby tent, "escaped from it and joined him so soon as she heard his voice, and with the instinct peculiar to her race, brought him musket-balls and powder, pieces of cartridges which she has found about the camp and secreted, anticipating her father's arrival." Sprague did not see this as a capable young woman escaping from military custody with war materiel.

Instead, Sprague wrote that Coacoochee glowed with "manly gratitude" and wept, finding the "enemy of his race the protector of his child." As a result, he agreed to assemble his band for emigration. The army's ability to capture and, more importantly, protect Coacoochee's daughter established a hierarchy that placed members of the army – who could save not only their own but their enemy's women – over Seminole men, who could not. Sprague concluded this anecdote with, "who can but admire the stern dictates of human nature – the love of home?"[7] Female innocence remained intact despite the girl's actions because it helped Sprague identify the army as protectors fulfilling a civilizing mission.

Seminole women escaped from US custody and helped their people flee. Seminole leader Tiger Tail escaped from Fort Brooke with his baggage through the help of captured women and children, whom the officer in charge had noticed "were passing in and out with small bundles" later revealed to be Tiger Tail's belongings "smuggled out by those who participated in the plot, in such a manner as not to excite suspicion."[8] Other Seminole women themselves escaped. Lieutenant Prince described one captured Seminole woman as "intelligent" and wrote that "the squaw Sally finely dressed & on horseback…was set at liberty by Col. Foster who expects that [she and a male companion] will negotiate for him."

---

[7] Sprague, Brevet Captain, Eighth Regiment US Infantry, *The Origin, Progress, and Conclusion of the Florida War*, 258–60, March 5, 1840. Fort Cummings is approximately 70 miles away from Fort Mellon.

[8] Ibid., 432. This suggests that captive women and children had significantly more mobility than captured men. Where the army needed to restrain independent Seminole men from escaping, dependent Seminole women and children were perhaps expected to stay with their men, or with their captors, without restraints.

3 "Find Where Their Women Are": Pursuing Seminole Women

Prince noted a few days later that they "ought to have returned last night" as the pair "agreed to come back in four days," but they never did.[9]

In a similar incident, a writer described how "one of the squaws, taken on the Withlacoochee, conveyed a message to her tribe, that if the hostile Indians surrendered or came in, they would be received, and sent west of the Mississippi, agreeable to the treaty." He noted that

> She promised to return, if she could, three days since but has not as yet returned. She was provided with a good horse for her journey. After she had left, her course was trailed, and it appears that instead of going to the Withlacoochee, she turned off to the Ochle-wa-ha, where a very considerable number of Indian force are embodied.[10]

While the language "has not as yet returned" suggested some hope that she yet would, it seems clear that she made good her escape after obtaining a horse and evading the men who followed her. It appears she understood US assumptions and used them to her advantage.

In contrast, officers immediately grasped escape attempts made by enslaved people. One enslaved man "who was sent on an express last winter with the promise of a large reward if he did as told; but he never returned." The writer, Lieutenant John Phelps, concluded that "he is obstinate and surly – no information can be obtained from him."[11] Although the logic of protection inhibited soldiers' willingness and ability to comprehend Seminole women's combatancy, they understood it when Black men and women fled. Officers sometimes, if infrequently, mentioned Black Seminole men or referred in gender neutral ways to the enslaved population (that according to US Census results, accounted for forty-seven percent of people in Florida from 1830 to 1860), but they never referred to Black women as subjects of protection.

Protection's blind spots had definite racial limits. Regular officers purposefully constructed the genre of army writing to enhance their reputation as protectors. Including groups of women that the army did not protect was counterproductive. Where officers like Phelps imbued people of African descent with characteristics like surliness and called

---

[9] Prince, *Amidst a Storm of Bullets*, 72, 74, 75, 78, 79, entries for January 17, 1837, February 7, 1837, and February 11, 1837.
[10] Homans, *Army and Navy Chronicle*, 1836, 3:318, Charleston Courier, November 10, 1836, correspondent communication dated October 31, 1836, Garey's Ferry. Of note, this was a US Navy detachment, not an army unit.
[11] John W. Phelps, "Letters from J. W. Phelps to Sisters, Miss Helen M. Phelps," 1837–1838, January 16, 1837, Library of Congress Manuscript Division, Manuscript Collection; Shire, *The Threshold of Manifest Destiny*, 124, 203.

Indigenous men "savage," Seminole women inhabited a more liminal corner of the army mind. Perceived racial, cultural, and ethnic differences did not strip them of their womanhood – to the army, they were to some degree "Indians" *and* women.

Apart from engineering escapes, Seminole women used their bodies and voices to resist the army, sometimes violently, as when a Seminole woman "attempted to wrest a butcher knife from a soldier to kill him." Others raised the alarm to allow their communities to flee oncoming soldiers. When one US scouting party discovered a Seminole camp, the soldiers approached "with every possibility of surprising the camp" until the "alarm was given by an old squaw," and the group escaped.[12] Notably, when soldiers specified that a Seminole woman was old, they often did so when that woman challenged army authority. For example, in this chapter men used "old" to describe when a Seminole woman gave the alarm and villagers escaped, when another sowed misinformation, and when another prepared a white prisoner for torture.

Seminole women may also have participated in ritual violence. A civilian escapee from an attack on Harney's camp claimed in the *St. Augustine Herald* that Seminole people tied him to a tree and then "an old squaw brought a quantity of wood, placed it round the prisoner, set fire to it, and went away" though he supposedly escaped with the help of a rain shower. This example may be apocryphal, but it fits women's traditional responsibility to participate in prisoners' punishment and decide their fates. Another battlefield role of women may have been to carry away the dead. Following an engagement in a small hammock two miles from Fort King, Lieutenant Colonel William Whistler reported to General Zachary Taylor that "fifteen squaws" were seen "bearing off the dead (four)."[13] Seminole women fought, punished, and mourned.

Women also spread misinformation when questioned by the army. An army officer wrote, "the fight expected by Colonel Fanning, when I last wrote to you, seems to have turned out to be nothing but the fabrication of an old squaw." Rather than treating this as deliberate misdirection, the officer concluded the woman was like "old" women everywhere and simply "fond of hearing herself talk." Seminole women sometimes used interrogations as an opportunity to ridicule their captors. Lieutenant

---

[12] Guild, *Old Times in Tennessee*, 131; Homans, *Army and Navy Chronicle*, 1839, 8:299, Floridian, April 20, 1839.

[13] Niles, *Niles' National Register*, 1840, 57:57, 44, and extract of letter Fort Lauderdale October 5, 1839 on page 168; Wickman, *The Tree That Bends*, 102; Homans, *Army and Navy Chronicle*, 1840, 10:348, May 1, 1840.

3 "Find Where Their Women Are": Pursuing Seminole Women

Prince wrote, "the squaws laughed at us for not having succeeded against our foe." And women, working alongside men, rejoiced in Seminole victories, as seen in a letter that described how two Seminole men and two women in canoes remained nearby after a battle, having seen a Black interpreter for the US fall into the water.

> The squaws were chatting and laughing, George [the Black interpreter] trembled for his fate, the canoe approached him, he felt its ripple – its paddle passed an inch or two from his nose. One of the laughing squaws remarked as she was passing, "I think that interpreter is dead – for he fell sideways into the river as if he was wounded;" and appeared to be delighted at his fate – "he was so swongo" (proud) said she.[14]

Women sowed misinformation and dissent among their enemies and reveled in victory.

Officers sometimes described events that demonstrated female power in Seminole society and their involvement in war but without grasping these events' significance. A peace conference with General Jesup opened with the eldest woman present saying of the warriors that

> they were all her children; that she was tired of war; that her warriors were slain; her villages burnt; her little ones perishing by the roadside; that the great spirit frowned on his red children; that the star of her nation had set in blood. She desired that the hatchet should be buried forever, between her children and her white brethren.

The perplexed Jesup responded by emphasizing the "maternal" affections of the US president, surely a phrase never used before or since to describe Martin Van Buren. The officers do not mention her again, and there is no indication of how Jesup thought or felt about her presence. This woman's leadership in the peace process reflected a Seminole tradition of female participation in war as arbitrators and diplomats, which many other Native peoples shared across North America.[15]

Seminole women could also take the lead in bringing their families under US control, sometimes as part of a survival strategy when faced with starvation. Surrendering to an army camp would provide access to food, and escape would probably remain an option. Lieutenant Asheton wrote from his base in the Wahoo swamp that a Seminole woman "with her child, came in, and leaving the child, she went out again promising

---

[14] Prince, *Amidst a Storm of Bullets*, 39; Niles, *Niles' National Register*, 1840, 57:57, 44, and extract of letter from Fort Lauderdale, October 5, 1839 on page 168.

[15] Motte, *Journey into Wilderness*, 209, February 24, 1838; Wickman, *The Tree That Bends*, 102.

to return. The next day she brought in two warriors, who informed Lieut. Asheton that they would bring in 31 warriors and their families." Some women may have taken this action as an extension of their leadership responsibilities as clan mothers. After the army destroyed at least 100 acres of one Seminole group's "best corn," the officer in command wrote that "the prisoner woman...communicated that some of the bands on the Withlacoochee will come in. I shall adopt such measures as may induce them to do so, and anticipate the pleasure of informing the Dept. by next dispatch, that from 30 to 50 warriors have assembled in the camp."[16] When faced with the destruction of her food resources, she may have decided that surrender was the best way to ensure her community's survival.

In one case, a Seminole woman arbitrated, shared information, shaped the conditions of surrender, and secured needed supplies. Colonel Worth wrote to a subordinate commander that "the Indian woman brings important intelligence from Halleck Tustenuggee, and the Commanding General has dispatched her again to the camp of that chief to inform him that it will not be in his power to meet him at Fort King" and that the chief should come to the General instead. "Worth believed Tustenuggee would readily consent to this, as the woman affirms that her people are almost in a starving condition." To the army, her report of starvation demonstrated their success in destroying Seminole food supplies. As a result of this woman's work, Worth declared to all of his commanding officers that "no active operations of a hostile nature, be carried on for the remainder of this month" while they worked on securing the group's surrender.[17] While this woman wielded apparent power that produced a halt in US military operations – a significant achievement – the army did not grasp her importance beyond that of a willing go-between, a way for men to communicate.

Much as regulars remained ignorant of women's diplomatic and political influence, they also failed to see women's spiritual power. Instead, they saw feminine virtues imported from the US: beauty and modesty. US soldier James Simmons described a "war dance" that reached its peak:

[16] Homans, *Army and Navy Chronicle*, 1840, 10:41, St. Augustine, June 26, 1840; *9th Military Department, Letters Sent*, 35, June 9, 1840, Armistead to R Jones Adjutant General, Fort King.
[17] *9th Military Department, Letters Sent*, 127–28, October 5, 1840, Bliss, Acting Adjutant General, to Major Dearborn, First Infantry; October 7, 1840, Bliss, Acting Adjutant General, Commanding Officers.

When the Queen of the evening, a very graceful, pretty looking Squaw (wife of one of the chiefs) decorated in all her finery – with a production (some dozen sets) of beads around her neck, and a world of tinkling shells (the small terrapin shell perforated, and filled with shot) glided from under a tree where she had been making her [toilette] – and with her head modestly down – and the tips of her fingers employed in spreading out her dress on either side broad as the turkey's tail! – glided into the now fiery and impetuous circle, that carried her round as the wind would the gossamer![18]

Simmons may have witnessed a late-in-the-year iteration of the busk ceremony's fourth and final day, which climaxed in women joining men in the dance circle, with terrapin shell rattles on their legs. But it could have been many other things, perhaps part of a Hunting Dance or Snake Dance, both ceremonies where female dancers had essential roles. The Seminole busk ceremony required community-wide participation in dance grounds that were the spiritual center of life, complementing the matrilineal clan camp's position as the domestic center. Though usually taking place in July or August, the busk could start later and the war may have caused delays.[19]

Simmons could only view these ceremonies through his experiences, shaped by mediums like "Indian plays" that depicted Native women as archetypal "Indian princesses" who were assimilable and obliging. His description fits the modest yet sexualized characterization of a submissive Indigenous woman that many white men believed true. Theodore Irving (nephew of Washington Irving) published *The Conquest of Florida by Hernando de Soto* in 1835. The widely read book helped establish a basis for army interactions with Seminole women, especially female leaders. Irving's book featured several "Indian princesses" who recognized Spaniards' superiority. The wives and daughters of a chief were "touched with compassion" on seeing the youth of eighteen-year-old captive Spaniard Juan Ortiz and "interceded in his favor." They later rescued him from torture, and one of the daughters, "a kind-hearted maiden," masterminded his successful escape to the nearby camp of one of her suitors. Another Native woman – referred to as a female Cacique named Cofachiqui – welcomed De Soto as a friend. She supposedly invited his party to carry off baskets of pearls they pried from her people's mausoleums, just to soothe his dismay in not finding silver or gold, and she

---

[18] Simmons, "Recollections of the Late Campaign in East Florida," 5, November 1836, No. 11 edition, American Periodicals.
[19] Weisman, *Unconquered People*, 92, 93, 105; Weisman, *Like Beads on a String*, 151–52; Wright, *Creeks & Seminoles*, 27.

remained friendly even as the Spanish captured and enslaved her people. Though increasingly "cold in her conduct," she remained an ally until De Soto took her captive as a precaution against treachery. His strategy of keeping her hostage worked, validated by "the good treatment which De Sotos' army experienced during its subsequent march through the territories of his royal captive."[20] The trope of willing Native women lived on in Simmons's "graceful, pretty looking Squaw" gliding around a dance circle like gossamer in the wind.

Paternalistic officers actively embraced Seminole women as natural allies. Regular army officer Lieutenant George McCall wrote to his future wife Elizabeth that Seminole men had "become wilder and more vigilant than the beasts of the forest, and show more caution and sagacity in moving and concealing their wives and children than does the wild deer towards her fawn." Yet, he knew that the women, whom he portrayed as braver than the men – a common way to unman Seminole males – were on the side of civilization. He continued, "the women, who throughout the war have displayed more than Spartan heroism, now wept and implored their husbands to yield to the entreaties of the envoys." Then, "Three days and sleepless nights were passed in combating the resolution never to leave Florida. But the ladies at length (as is always the case) prevailed, and Assinoah, the chief, consented to come in."[21]

Like many paternalists, McCall believed that the real heroes of Seminole society were the women, whose hearts naturally inclined toward civilization and, therefore, toward army officers. Army Surgeon Motte's description of a quiet clan camp represents another kind of obliviousness. The US search and destroy strategy had fundamentally reshaped the clan camp into a place of silence, where women taught children to play noiselessly to avoid capture. He noted the silence but did not reflect on its meaning or the war's impact on Seminole mothers and children. Instead, Motte exclaimed, "How many reeking scalps have dried in the fires of their wigwams!"[22] While he acknowledged that women had at least an indirect role in the war, he remained disconnected from the consequences of military policy.

---

[20] Irving, *The Conquest of Florida, by Hernando de Soto*, 62–67, 274–95. Lieutenant Alvord's speech to cadets in 1838 referenced Irving's book, offering an example of its influence. Alvord compared de Soto's "romantic adventures" with the troubles faced by the officers and soldiers who died in Dade's Massacre. Alvord, *Address before the Dialectic Society of the Corps of Cadets*, 41.

[21] McCall, *Letters from the Frontiers*, 396, Fort Brooke, 27 February 1842, George McCall to Elizabeth McMurtrie.

[22] Motte, *Journey into Wilderness*, 213.

Likewise, Motte witnessed a women-only dance with fifty or sixty participants singing, stamping, and moving leg rattles with "their position and motion being that of a company of soldiers marking time in solid square."[23] Its meaning, like that of the quiet settlement, eluded him. While Motte wrote of his experience romantically, of women with their "sparkling dark eyes and classic cast of features" dancing in the firelight, he glimpsed the reality behind his obliviousness to women's wartime participation. Seminole women *were* like "a company of soldiers" because they fed and clothed warriors like a quartermaster corps. They gathered elements for ammunition and perhaps helped fabricate cartridges as an ordnance sergeant might. They collected and shared information, spread misinformation, and lured enemies into attacks, like army scouts and spies. Women provided advice, leadership, and diplomatic expertise, abilities needed in military officers.

Yet officers and enlisted men did not see Seminole women as combatants. Even though accepting Seminole women as such would have made it simpler to attack and capture them, soldiers insisted women were innocent. Misinterpretation of Seminole women's actions to uphold women's innocence helped preserve the army's self-image as an organization dedicated to protecting and defending women.

In addition to a strategy of hunting and capturing Seminole women to win the war, the US Army often used captive women as guides. Volunteer Lieutenant Colonel Josephus Guild gave an example drawn from his experiences in 1836. After attacking a Seminole camp located by the brigade's spies, "in which seven Indians were killed and eleven squaws and children were taken prisoner," an interpreter interrogated a Seminole woman, learning of a forthcoming council to be held nearby. He wrote, "I have in after life reflected upon the fact that the captured squaw was mounted on a horse and compelled to lead the enemy of her people along the by-paths to their places of retreat for the purpose of having them slaughtered." In an unpublished diary, Guild also mentions a fact he omitted from his memoir. The woman had a small child with her, and the volunteers forced her to leave the child behind with the other captives while she guided the troops.[24] He likely felt this detail was too shameful to publish. Guild's writing represented a rare thing – a US combatant

---

[23] Ibid., 214, 217.
[24] Guild, *Old Times in Tennessee*, 131–33, October 10, 1836; Scallet, "This Inglorious War," 166–67, interior quote from October 13, 1836, Josephus Conn Guild Diary, Tennessee State Library and Archives.

who understood the harm he caused and felt real shame at holding a child hostage to coerce a mother into betraying her community.

Guild was a volunteer officer, but the regular army's need for guides was just as desperate. In 1837, General Winfield Scott cited "Want of Guides" as a critical issue. This shortage persisted throughout the conflict. In 1842 Colonel Worth wrote, "I have not a solitary male Indian in hand who ever saw Okeechobee or south of this" and thus could not provide a guide to the requesting officer.[25] In the absence of suitable Seminole men, Worth could meet this need with Seminole women. A month later, he wrote to a subordinate officer that "the Indian woman to be ordered to you from Cedar Keys will be used as a guide, or sent out with a message to her people, as circumstances on the spot may determine most expedient. Instruct her to promise good treatment and protection to such as may come in." He also wrote to the commanding officer at Cedar Keys: "You will without any delay send one of the captured squaws, the eldest but one, recently sent to your post and also the lame Indian, to Fort Fanning. If you have an interpreter, make her understand that she is to be sent to look after her people."[26]

From his position as leader of the war effort, Worth possessed detailed knowledge of captured women. He did all in his power to use his female prisoners to accomplish his mission. Worth, like McCall, assumed women could not be party to Seminole resistance. Although officers used naked force and direct threats to ensure the loyalty of male guides, they believed women would inevitably return to the children kept in US custody.

The same day Worth wrote another letter to locate, from within a group of prisoners, the wife of Halleck Tustenuggee "from whom it is believed the chiefs may get important information." In addition to serving as guides, the army sometimes pushed Seminole women to provide information, as when an officer wrote that "we have learned from the squaws captured a few days before, that the Indians had made no corn the past summer." When the army attacked the Seminole leader Abiaka's camp in 1838, they destroyed all provisions and supplies. They took one prisoner, a woman, whom the soldiers questioned as to where the others

---

[25] Clinch, *General Duncan Lamont Clinch Collection*, January 38, 1837, from the National Intelligencer; *9th Military Department, Letters Sent*, 25, February 9, 1842, Worth to Capt. McLaughlin (US Navy), from Tampa.
[26] This desperation also caused the army to employ Black Seminoles (and Seminole women) as guides out of desperation after white volunteers and Creek guides failed to meet army needs. For more on Black Seminole service with the army, see: Hagstrom, "Learning Asymmetric War," 68–69.

3 "Find Where Their Women Are": Pursuing Seminole Women

fled. When the army captured the mother of Wild Cat, a Seminole warrior, she, alongside a Black captive named Sam, confirmed that enslaved people in St. Augustine supplied Seminole bands with powder and information "that has proved fatal to many travelers on the Picolata road" that connected St. Augustine to the Florida interior.[27]

Although her interrogators took her statement as proof that they had successfully extracted answers, she may have intended her words as taunts. Wild Cat's mother emphasized her people's continued resistance and resourcefulness and the army's powerlessness to stop exchanges between enslaved and Seminole people. Her resistance echoed another woman's claim earlier in the war that despite US efforts to starve and dislodge Seminole groups, they had planted and "would have a better crop than they ever had."[28] Whether based on women's abilities to produce food or strengthen alliances, each defiant claim emphasized female power.

Still, US men rarely questioned the intent behind women's answers. They wanted to think that Seminole women wanted to help. A letter to the *Florida Herald* editor expressed this commonly held view and described attacking a Miccosukee camp, "the most hostile and warlike of all tribes." The soldiers killed thirteen Miccosukee men, "who did not fire a shot," (a massacre) and took four women and eight children prisoner. They interrogated the women to learn of other camp locations, and the author noted, "we have found willing and able guides in the prisoner squaws, and derived much valuable information from them."[29] Regulars preferred to interpret Seminole women's actions as voluntary – decisions made by friends, not coerced from enemies.

---

[27] 9th Military Department, Letters Sent, 85–86, March 19, 1842, Worth to Lieutenant Colonel Whistler, Cooper, Acting Adjutant General, to Lieutenant Colonel Garland, Worth to Commanding Officer, Cedar Keys; Homans, *Army and Navy Chronicle*, 1837, 4:62, 215; Motte, *Journey into Wilderness*, 235; 9th Military Department, Letters Sent, 59, July 9, 1840, Lieutenant Newton Acting Adjutant General to Colonel Twiggs.

[28] Homans, *Army and Navy Chronicle*, 1837, 4:62, 215. Colonel Worth ordered the capturing officer to go to St. Augustine "with one or two of the Indian women captured by him, and samples of all the goods taken from Wild Cat's party" and report to the commanding officer at St. Augustine. Somehow, this plan went awry, and another officer informed Worth that "the Indian prisoners from St. Augustine (Wild Cat's mother and child and two women captured by Lieutenant Sibley) have been sent to Fort Reid instead of being detained." *9th Military Department, Letters Sent*, 141, November 9, 1840, Bliss, Acting Adjutant General to Commanding Officer, Fort Brooke; 157, August 22, 1840, Bliss, Acting Adjutant General, to Major Fauntleroy. Also see 66, August 17, 1840, Bliss Acting Adjutant General to Lieutenant Colonel Harney.

[29] Homans, *Army and Navy Chronicle*, 1836, 3:287, October 21, 1836.

ENEMY OR WOMAN?

Rather than making Seminole women into enemies, army reports institutionalized the idea that women remained outside of war by creating a binary between Seminole men, termed "warriors" in reports, and Seminole women. These reports assumed a systematic opposition of the gendered categories of "woman" and "warrior." One memo recorded how a "lame Indian who delivered himself up" was part of a Seminole group consisting of nineteen warriors "including himself," demonstrating the total overlap of the categories of "man" and "warrior" even when a man's physical abilities limited his capacity to fight.[30]

The need to separate male combatants from female civilians reflected the broader principle of distinction. Helen Kinsella notes that combatant status created a fundamental separation between "who fights and kills (and thus who may be killed) and who does not fight (and, thus should not be killed)." Army leaders believed that they could sort all Seminole adults into the mutually exclusive categories of warrior or woman, as in a report describing the escape of sixteen warriors and two women, or another listing captives as "14 warriors, 15 women."[31] The US separation of men categorically considered warriors, and women and children who were never warriors, persisted throughout the war. In the final estimate of the few Seminoles remaining in Florida in 1842, used by army commander Colonel Worth to justify claiming victory and ending the war, Worth emphasized that only 112 warriors remained, alongside 189 women and children.[32]

The army's interest in tracking the deaths and relocations of Seminole "warriors" came in part from requirements US political leaders imposed. A Senate resolution decreed the military must distinguish how many warriors were in Florida when the war started and how many warriors had been killed, imprisoned, surrendered, emigrated, and remained. It also required the army to report the number of "other classes" who emigrated or stayed in Florida. Notably, this ignores the possibility that soldiers would kill anyone other than male warriors – Seminole women would

---

[30] *9th Military Department, Letters Sent*, 571, December 1841, memo sent to Colonel Vose. The memo also notes that the band included 30 women and children.

[31] Kinsella, *The Image before the Weapon*, 31; Wickman, *Osceola's Legacy*, 103–4; Sprague, Brevet Captain, Eighth Regiment US Infantry, *The Origin, Progress, and Conclusion of the Florida War*, 393–94, November 13, 1841, Captain R.D.A. Wade Third Artillery, 441.

[32] *27th Congress, 2nd Session*, 7:10, 11, 30, February 14, 1842, Worth to Scott.

only enter official records if they left Florida. Though the Senate passed this resolution to affect the brutal policy of Indian Removal in Florida, Senators only wanted to hear about warriors' deaths.[33] They had no appetite to face the sorts of consequences measured in women's bodies.

Because the army did not consider Seminole women as warriors, and it only measured killed and wounded warriors, official reporting erased women's deaths and rendered female casualties irrelevant or unintentional. In reports, officers framed women's deaths as inadvertent or caused by volunteers. Even Lieutenant Colonel William Harney (the notoriously brutal officer) wrote that "it is a source of much regret that I have to report one squaw among the killed. She was taken for a warrior by one of the volunteers in the advance, and fired upon by him, as she was endeavoring to make her escape." Lieutenant James Willoughby Anderson made a similar claim. After attacking a Seminole camp, he wrote that "one Squaw was accidentally killed – having been taken for a warrior as she was running" away.[34] This type of casualty reporting proves the considerable irony of women's purported innocence. The laws of war claimed to protect innocent women, and the army sought to track its success in fighting male enemies. Because women were not enemies, the military did not need to count women's deaths. These deaths might appear in informal acknowledgments, but not in the formal tallies of enemies killed, which only accounted for dead warriors. Gender did not protect these women – it rendered them officially invisible.

The army struggled to implement the Senate's onerous reporting process. So, Army Adjutant General Roger Jones compiled what information he could and sent it to Commanding General Alexander Macomb. He maintained that any tracking of Seminole casualties, whether warriors or not, was impossible. Jones noted that the number of warriors killed and taken prisoner "cannot be correctly furnished." He continued that from December of 1835 to November of 1836, "the number of Indians reported to have been killed is 131; the number of Indians, women, children, and negroes, taken prisoners within the same period, 15." It was a shockingly disparate tally, with nearly ten times more killed than captured.

---

[33] *Senate, 25th Congress, 2nd Session*, 7:992, Senate resolution dated December 29, 1837. The category "emigrate" falsely implies a voluntary choice. Forcibly expelled would be more accurate.
[34] Niles, *Niles' National Register*, 1840, 58:260–61, Fort King, June 5, 1840 and Headquarters, Second Infantry, Fort King, June 9, 1840, from Lieutenant Colonel B. Riley to Colonel Twiggs; Denham and Huneycutt, "Historic Notes and Documents: 'Everything Is Hubbub Here,'" 355, Fort King, August 25, 1841.

Jones's use of the generic "Indians" to describe the 131 people killed demonstrates both a recognition of noncombatant deaths and discomfort when identifying women and children killed by the army. In contrast, Jones believed it appropriate to describe those captured as partly comprised of women and children. Jones told of the inevitability of civilian casualties among the Seminole: "The number of warriors cannot be separated from the mass, and of course cannot, with any accuracy, be specified."[35] The army could mention or disregard gender in reports as befit its purpose.

Ignoring the numbers of women and children killed helped the army and politicians legitimize the war and avoid blame for killing civilians. Conversely, actively counting women and children as captives helped the military emphasize its success in affecting Indian Removal. Thus, General Thomas Jesup congratulated volunteer Brigadier General Joseph Hernandez – a wealthy planter formerly of Spanish Florida who became a prominent man in US Florida – and his command for their "gallantly carried out" capture of "fifty-three Indians and negroes." While most of this group was likely women and children, as were most captured bands, Jesup's racialized (though gender and age neutral) language emphasized the total number alongside the "gallantry" of the capturing troops. In contrast, other sources, like newspaper accounts, might be more specific, as in "Lieut. May's company charged, and Philip, with another Indian and a number of women and children, were immediately captured."[36]

Seminole leaders were aware of the warrior-or-woman binary and sometimes used it to challenge US tactics. When the Seminole warrior and leader Coacoochee (Wild Cat) met with officer Thomas Childs of the Third Artillery, he saw an iron pot that belonged – like most property – to the women in his family. He offered a strong indictment of a war effort focused on capturing Seminole women and destroying clan camps rather than defeating warriors in battle. He told Childs, "you call yourself a warrior, and yet you took that pot from an old woman. If it had been a man; and taken in a fair fight, it would have been your pot, but you frightened the squaw and captured the pot. That was not a warrior's act." Coacoochee continued, "I would as soon taken baby linen from a picaninny, as a pot from a squaw. But I am a warrior, and I want my

---

[35] *Senate, 25th Congress, 2nd Session*, 7:993–94, R. Jones Adjutant General to Major General Macomb, Commanding General, January 27, 1838.

[36] Motte, *Journey into Wilderness*, xv, xxii, xxv, xxvi, 129, 135, Head Quarters, Army of the South, St. Augustine, September 27, 1837, Order No. 187; Niles, *Niles' National Register*, 1838, 53:66, "Florida War," St. Augustine, September 13, 1837.

3 *"Find Where Their Women Are"*: Pursuing Seminole Women   123

pot." According to this anecdote, Childs returned it.[37] Gender complementarity was a critical aspect of Seminole society, but the army's categorization of Seminole adults as warriors or women simplistically reduced it to suit army needs. Rather than distinguishing between Seminole men who were warriors and Seminole men who were not, the army labeled all men as warriors and thus legitimate subjects of attack.

The separation of women from men could also reveal, rather than conceal, the disproportionate effects of the war on women. In a report to the Army Adjutant General, Colonel Worth noted that since the last shipment of Seminole people west, three warriors had died, in addition to twelve warriors killed by the army. Worth also reported that eighteen Seminole women and children died in Tampa, awaiting emigration. This note followed Worth's description of sending a group of primarily women and children to the west, in which out of 230 people, he deemed sixty-eight warriors. Worth added, he retained eighty-six Seminole people, only forty-two of which were warriors, as leverage "in furtherance of future operations."[38] The numbers exposed the war for what it was, an attack on all members of Seminole society.

To conclude the policy of Indian Removal in Florida, the army would need to do more than distinguish between women and warriors. Naming Seminole people "savage" meant that "civilized" war's conventions did not bind the army. Instead, it could use any means necessary. As the war continued, the army availed itself of this potentiality more and more.

---

[37] Niles, *Niles' National Register*, 1841, 60:72, April 3, 1841; 211, June 5, 1841. Articles reprinted from the *Charleston Courier* and the *St. Augustine Gazette*. Because the words "squaw" and "picaninny" are derogatory, they appear only within quotations. Childs, West Point class of 1814, had been a Brevet Major since August of 1836, but was actually a Brevet Lieutenant Colonel as of February 1, 1841, before the Florida newspapers published this story. Cullum, *Biographical Register*, 1:135. For Wild Cat's later life in Texas and Mexico, see Cora Montgomery's (Jane McManus Storms) account of life in Eagle Pass. She also served as a war correspondent in Mexico. Montgomery, *Eagle Pass*.

[38] *9th Military Department, Letters Sent*, February 5, 1842, HQ Army Florida, Worth to Army Adjutant General. These Seminole women remained nameless, but records named some formerly enslaved Black women living among the Seminole. Enslavers regularly employed attorneys to recoup women they claimed to own. There are records of enslaved black women like Hannah, removed from Florida by General Armistead's authority in March of 1841, and her son Joe, who surrendered to General Zachary Taylor on the promise of his freedom, and whom Taylor removed to Indian Territory in 1839. Hannah left Florida with her daughter Maria Gracia, named Mary in army reports, 25 years of age, and Maria's 2-year-old child. The same document notes that Colonel Worth approved the emigration of another enslaved woman, Rosa. Ibid., 407, July 31, 1842, HQ 9th Military Department, Cedar Keys. The government asserted that the claimants did not offer sufficient proof of ownership.

Colonel Worth ordered a captain that if he should "fall in with portions of the enemy and deem <u>summary measures</u> of severity politic and necessary to ultimate success, you will not hesitate in adopting that course."[39] Those summary measures could encompass seizing prisoners under flags of truce, executions, and any form of action that would promote mission accomplishment.

Fighting an "uncivilized" foe also implied that victory should be easy or at least inevitable, but the war dragged on. At the beginning of the war, Lieutenant Henry Prince justified General Winfield Scott's inability to engage Seminoles warriors in battle by writing, "the Indians were always attacking and harassing the skirts of his army, and he was not the man to descend to their low cunning and unchivalrous system of warfare." Scott sought to fight honorably, but according to him the "savage" way of war meant hiding in the woods and attacking the innocent, warfare in which "none are spared."[40]

To the army's frustration, the public quickly grew angry with a war they deemed too costly and too long. As early as 1836, just a year into the fighting, this outrage exerted public pressure on the army to remove Seminole people by any means. One army officer who resigned claimed he did so because of his indignation that the US public scorned their military and denied its achievements. The officer desired to speak openly now that he no longer owed his "silent submission" to the public, proclaiming, "the history of the army and the frontier is a history of benefits conferred upon the country by the intelligence of the officers and the activity and discipline of the men." He continued, "it is God's truth I do not expect to find in any profession in civil life the same or as high code of honor" and "where is the instance in which the army has not acquitted itself with credit when in contact with savages?"[41] The writer argued that the army, far from being overpriced, was a great deal, an institution of extraordinary value to the nation.

Among letters presented to Congress in debates on overspending in Florida, an army surgeon lamented seeing "the army insulted by the taunts and stale jibes of every newspaper witling." A pseudonymous Army officer writing under the pen name Omicron defended the army, writing that its esprit de corps was "lighted at the altar of chivalry, and

---

[39] 9th Military Department, *Letters Sent*, 273, September 23, 1841, Worth to Captain Burk.
[40] Prince, *Amidst a Storm of Bullets*, 56, 60, 91, 95.
[41] Homans, *Army and Navy Chronicle*, 1836, 3:333–34, N.Y. Journal of Commerce.

3 *"Find Where Their Women Are"*: Pursuing Seminole Women   125

consecrated in defense of the country."[42] Passive strategy, though it would mean minimizing harm to Seminole civilians, was unchivalrous. For Omicron, active campaigning and hunting down Seminole people *was* chivalry. Despite his emphasis on the attack, Omicron presented the army as civilization's defenders.

Seminole fighters wisely avoided battle for much of the war to preserve finite numbers and limited resources. General Jesup expressed the frustration this strategy caused among army officers, writing that "the Seminole will fight only where he plans, and he is to be caught or captured only by surprise." Others also commented on the dilemma of waging war on an enemy who avoided conflict. The *Army and Navy Chronicle* republished a poem on the "unending Florida War" that bemoaned how the war had already "been 'ended' forty times, in twenty months or so" and would probably go on forever.[43]

As the army pursued Seminole bands more aggressively, the supposedly accidental or unofficial deaths of Seminole women came to exist alongside explicit acknowledgments that the military had to target women. Florida Governor Robert Reid's message to the Legislative Council of Florida in 1840 carried a similar message. According to Reid, the US must "penetrate the recesses where [Seminole] women and children are hidden." Writing to his sister, another officer believed the army would "have to exterminate them before we can rid the country of them."[44] Increasingly, many regulars agreed.

In 1839, a letter to the editor of the *Army and Navy Chronicle* suggested the US should "set a price on every Indian – pay any man who shall bring an Indian, dead or alive, or shall produce any undoubted evidence that an Indian has been disposed of." By 1840, the *Chronicle* reprinted a set of suggestions from the *Jacksonville Advocate*: "it has always appeared to us that, could the homes of the women and children be found, the war would very soon close" for Seminole men would surrender to avoid that "their women and children should become the victims of want and destitution." Another argued that a thorough search and destroy policy of all Indigenous "plantations, habitations or towns"

---

[42] Homans, *Army and Navy Chronicle*, 1837, 4:233, 248, 363, Steubenville, Ohio, October 1, 1837; Omicron, "Vindication of the Army," in response to the Globe's criticism of the army in Florida on June 25, 1836.

[43] *Thomas Sidney Jesup Papers*, Box 17, Loose Items: Undated, Jesup to the Editor of the Herald, likely the Florida Herald; Homans, *Army and Navy Chronicle*, 1839, 8:231–32.

[44] Van Swearingen, "Second Seminole War Correspondence," 1834–1837, Van Swearingen to sister, Elizabeth, June 19, 1837.

would be successful because "the women and children would be likely to fall into the hands of the troops, which would have a powerful agency in subduing the men" and because the family ties of "father to son, and husband to wife" are "much stronger in the savage than in the more civilized races." Furthermore, the *Advocate* emphasized that their overarching desire was to "be rid of [Seminole people], we care not by what means, as their treacherous, blood-thirsty character calls for no other treatment than that of speedy extermination."[45]

The official policy reflected these suggestions and required capturing Seminole women. Even in the war's early days, General Winfield Scott understood his orders as stated to President Jackson to mean "reduce the enemy to unconditional submission" and not say even that "kind treatment might be expected." In the same letter, Scott rued the difficulty of tracking Seminole women, writing, "no Indian woman, child, or negro, nor the trace of one, has been seen in that time. Those, noncombatants, it has been evident to us all, have been removed beyond the theatre of our operations."[46]

Army officers claimed "savage" enemies to justify increasingly unrestrained warfare. In the war's final year, Seminole leader Holartochee met with Colonel Worth to "plead for the lives of women and children in the approaching conflict." The army countered that Seminole actions forced soldiers to hunt noncombatants to end Seminole resistance. Soldiers in Florida resigned themselves to this inglorious strategy and believed it impossible "to make a brilliant campaign."[47]

Although it could not make a brilliant campaign, the army hoped to make a shorter one by any means necessary. Members of the military wrote the *Army and Navy Chronicle* about "the arduous, irksome, and thankless nature of Florida service." They bemoaned "the silly wailings of the public over the wrongs done the Seminoles" and insisted that the army has "unceasingly extended towards the Indians kindness." They believed the Seminole people "must no longer be recognized as a nation; but as so many hordes of banditti, which is their real character." They "must be declared outlaws, and a price set upon their heads, in the same manner as other desperate criminals." In the most explicit expression of this opinion, one argued "it is high time to give up the idea that Florida is

---

[45] Homans, *Army and Navy Chronicle*, 1840, 10:76, 268, signed W, 269, 299, article signed Wayne, 300.
[46] Sprague, Brevet Captain, Eighth Regiment US Infantry, *The Origin, Progress, and Conclusion of the Florida War*, 115, 131.
[47] Ibid., 456, Spring of 1842; Guild, *Old Times in Tennessee*, 127.

a field for military operations" and urged readers to "let the main object of every expedition be to secure the women, children, and slaves."[48] References to "woman" and "negro" or "women" and "slaves" implies that Black captives had no gender. The army situated Black women outside protection.

These writers indicated that while military operations should follow the laws of war, Indigenous groups did not merit special protections. The army, they felt, should not treat Seminole society as a nation, but as criminals to kill or imprison. Governor Richard Call (Reid's predecessor and successor) wrote a message to the Legislative Council of Florida that took even more humanity from Seminole people: "We are waging a war with beasts of prey – the tactics that belong to civilized nations are but shackles and fetters in its prosecution." Instead of foolishly adhering to the laws of war, Call thought the US must "penetrate the recesses where his women and children are hidden." Others in the papers, probably Florida settlers, merely debated what tactic would most effectively wipe Seminole people off the map. One pseudonymous correspondent emphasized that even a thorough search and destroy strategy might not be enough because they must not only be "driven out of their dens and hiding places, but must be kept out."[49] This radical approach represented a settler's view on how to conclude the war – total removal or eradication.

In contrast, top army officers regularly sought to end the war by allowing remaining Seminole people to stay in Florida, but each time, political leaders denied those requests. Political pressure, not innate bloodthirstiness, forced the army to seek the complete removal of Seminole groups from Florida. Still, the exterminatory point of view gained support over time among Florida politicians, white settlers, and sometimes army leaders who saw no alternative that the army's masters – the US government – would accept.

Zachary Taylor, writing from within these changing currents of opinion, wrote to Jesup that "it might also be well to consider the Florida Indians in the light of Banditti, which they are and of the worst description, and treat them as such by offering for each warrior who may be killed a handsome reward, and half as much for capturing a woman or

---

[48] Homans, *Army and Navy Chronicle*, 1839, 9:131, pen name Sam Jones, 132, name An Officer of the Line, 139, army officer's letter dated August 1, 1839, 201, "Florida War with Hints for Its Management," signed Pike, September 1839.

[49] Homans, *Army and Navy Chronicle*, 1840, 10:76, 268, signed W, 269, 299, article signed Wayne, 300.

child." Taylor hoped or perhaps expected Jesup to agree, and asked that if Jesup was "for my views in whole or in part and feel at liberty to do so, I will thank you to communicate with the Hon. Secretary of War on those subjects, as far as you deem it advisable and proper to do so, as well as with your friends in Congress at the coming session."⁵⁰ In 1841, Colonel Worth sent orders to all the commanders of districts in Florida to implement such a policy.

The orders, marked "Strictly Confidential," offered rewards to captors of Seminole men, women, and children:

I desire you to make known to the troops <u>as from yourself</u> that any soldier or detachment shall receive the gratuity of <u>fifty dollars</u> for each male over 14 years, <u>twenty-five</u> dollars for each female over 14 years, <u>twenty</u> dollars for each male under 14, and <u>ten</u> for each female under 14 years of age captured and delivered at any post and the like sums on <u>sufficient</u> evidence for such as may be killed in action.

Worth continued, "there are weighty reasons which will probably be obvious, why I enjoin the strictest confidence and desire the proffer to be made by yourself, and <u>this you, in the same confidence</u>, to the commanders of posts. I shall see that all your pledges in this respect are faithfully realized."⁵¹ Worth's clandestine offer of bounties revealed an army at once increasingly at war with all Seminole people regardless of age or sex, and sufficiently self-aware of that change's implications to make the offer as secretively as possible. Even after six long years of war, army leaders could only privately offer bounties for captured women or proof of dead Seminole people.

Because soldiers considered women innocent, they claimed to care for and protect captives as dependents. Army leaders intended women's systematic captures to hasten removal by encouraging families to join captives. Within this framework, access to food had symbolic value. While Seminole groups resisted removal, the army destroyed food supplies. Once they surrendered and accepted army protection, they became dependent. Then, the army family would extend food and care to its newest members. Army captures of Seminole women would ultimately reaffirm women's innocence and the army's self-image as a civilized institution because those captures became evidence that the army provided for dependents.

⁵⁰ *Thomas Sidney Jesup Papers*, Box 17, Loose Items: October 7, 1839, Zachary Taylor, Florida to Thomas Jesup, Washington.
⁵¹ *9th Military Department, Letters Sent*, August 19, 1841, Worth to the Commanders of Districts, FL.

3 *"Find Where Their Women Are"*: Pursuing Seminole Women 129

Despite considerable evidence of Seminole women's wide-ranging and vital involvement in the war, soldiers held to the idea of female harmlessness. Instead, they justified the distasteful mission of expelling Seminole people from Florida with the "savagery" of Seminole men. The army employed an emergent logic of protection to assert that soldiers could protect Seminole women (by capture) where Seminole men could not. These claims justified regular army beliefs in the institution's superiority and rendered women's captures a supposedly positive good.

CAPTURE TO PROTECT

The US Army explained capturing Seminole women as a measure in keeping with the imperative to protect women even though the reality of army policy meant that Seminole women suffered disproportionately from starvation and displacement. Nonetheless, officers insisted that compelling Seminole groups to leave Florida was humanitarian. In March of 1835, before the war began, General Clinch wrote that "the wise and benevolent course" of Indian Removal, which had been "adopted by the Government, is the only one that can save [Seminole people] from utter destruction; and when all other plans fail, then it is humanity to compel the refractory to conform to the measures that have been wisely adopted, for the general good of the whole Nation." It would be better, according to Clinch, for Seminole groups to submit to the army and depart Florida because they would then "be under the watchful care of their faithful and efficient [Indian] agent," supplied by the military to protect them.[52]

Inflicting pain to guarantee purported salvation in Indian Territory meant that burning Seminole camps was common. Lieutenant Henry Prince made casual mentions of burnings in his journal, writing "17th burnt an Indian Village – took the corn & hogs & rice," then ten days later, "arrived at midday at a large town on the Withlacoochee. 16 houses – burnt it." Destroying Seminole dwellings and property meant a war on women because matrilineal clans organized Seminole society. Clan camps were the basis of Seminole life, and burning settlements meant removing women's abilities to provide food and shelter for their families. Some soldiers saved war trophies. One officer noted that he burned "two bushels of garden seeds" but also that he took "a war dress of the great Tallahassee chief, Tiger Tail...[and] some of Mrs. Tiger

---

[52] Clinch, *General Clinch Letter Book 1835–1836*, March 16, 1835, Clinch to Brigadier General Jones Adjutant General.

Tail's dress, beads, etc." noting that it was "the second camp I have surprised and taken property from."[53] There was some plunder among the destruction.

Colonel Worth noted in a report that his troops found a "favorite retreat and planting ground" that hosted the green corn festival and "had never been penetrated by our troops." An expedition of 100 men went to the site and found two villages, the first "numbering about 25 huts." Worth reported about a month later expeditions led the army to "numerous villages, and very extensive fields, and island planting grounds, covered with food crops...as also extensive magazines of jerked beef and coontie." Worth reported to the Army Adjutant General that villages and food supplies "have been discovered and destroyed" for a summer campaign.[54]

A month later, a fifty-man canoe expedition under Lieutenant Gates discovered "a town of some 50 huts, several extensive planting grounds, all of which destroyed, securing some canoes, cattle, and hogs. Several Indians have been captured who will be useful as guides." The expedition found another of the "enemy's island planting ground, and destroyed extensive crops, covering almost the entire surface of three of their largest" islands. Later that summer, Colonel Worth gave a subordinate officer a standard order to find a Seminole band's last remaining planting ground and "destroy every vestige of it."[55] Without grasping women's power in Seminole society, the army nevertheless waged a successful war against matrilineal life.

It did so ever more intensely. Earlier in the conflict, troops generally spent summers in Florida's various forts, avoiding the brutal summer climate and hoping to evade the shocking levels of illness created by summer campaigns. By June and July of 1841, Worth described the year-round destruction of Seminole dwellings and food supplies. The army realized that summer campaigns were necessary because, without them, women replanted and harvested crops all summer, giving their people the resources needed to continue fighting for another year.

---

[53] Prince, *Amidst a Storm of Bullets*, 11, 15; Weisman, *Like Beads on a String*, 152; Mahon, "Letters from the Second Seminole War," April 1958, 344–45, February 29, 1840, Camp on the Wacasassa Near Ft. Jennings; and 346, March 17, 1840, Camp near Fort Fanning.

[54] *9th Military Department, Letters Sent*, 11, June 13, 1841, Worth to Army Adjutant General Jones.

[55] Ibid., 53, 55, July 5, 1841, Worth to Army Adjutant General Jones; 139, August 2, 1841, Worth (Sprague, Acting Adjutant General) to Captain Gwynn. Gates graduated from West Point in 1836. Cullum, *Biographical Register*, 1:515.

3 "Find Where Their Women Are": Pursuing Seminole Women

This summer pause was common in earlier years. One army officer noted in 1837 that a Seminole group came into a US camp and agreed to emigration, but one morning in early June, the officer found they had "all disappeared men women and children and took to the swamps" because they knew the army could not "pursue them during the summer to their hiding places."[56] Officers noted they would continue to resist as long as women grew food and men had ammunition. One observed that "the hammock in which [Seminole people] are has several large fields well planted with corn, beans, potatoes, pumpkins, melons, squash, etc., they are determined not to give up but to fight as long as their ammunition holds."[57]

Eventually, the army decided to destroy Seminole resources year-round. By 1841 Worth reported active expeditions throughout the "inauspicious season" of summer. He believed this would allow the army to "capture some [Seminole people], destroying their fields and produce an excellent effect by such as evidence that we can and will penetrate their most hidden recesses at all seasons." Worth's typical orders to subordinate commanders were to exhaust "every effort to find and destroy the enemy's planting grounds, etc." Subordinates responded with the hoped-for news that they destroyed an enemy group's ability to resist. One officer reported back to Worth that he successfully rendered a Seminole band destitute of "everything they had," promising they would have to surrender soon.[58] US strategy caused Seminole starvation.

Soldiers were sometimes uncomfortable with the human – and conspicuously female – cost of famine. Army Surgeon Jacob Motte wrote that Seminole leader Halleck Hadjo told General Jesup that "wives and children were dying from the hardship of being chased about so much." Motte told of Seminole women collecting corn left on the ground after soldiers fed their horses. In contrast to the healthy-looking men, the women

---

[56] Van Swearingen, "Second Seminole War Correspondence," Van Swearingen to sister Elizabeth, June 5, 1837 and June 19, 1837. Van Swearingen was from Frederick, Maryland and an 1824 graduate of West Point. He brought an enslaved man, Dennis, with him to Florida. Van Swearingen died at the Battle of Okeechobee on December 25, 1837.

[57] William Davenport, *Colonel William Davenport Papers*, 1835–1842, January 30, 1839, Lieutenant James Belger Sixth Infantry to Lieutenant Colonel John Green, Fort Andrews.

[58] *9th Military Department, Letters Sent*, 11, June 13, 1841, Fort King, Worth to Army Adjutant General R. Jones; 53, 55, July 10, 1841 Fort Brooke, Worth to Jones; 79, Worth to Florida Governor R. K. Call; 82, July 12, 1841, Worth to Jones; 95, Cooper, Acting Adjutant General to Commanding Officer of Fort Wacassassa; McCall, *Letters from the Frontiers*, 404.

"presented a most squalid appearance; being destitute of even the necessary clothing to cover their nakedness." Motte believed "the burden of war to have principally fallen upon the female portion of the natives."[59] He was right. But where he blamed Seminole men, it was the army strategy of destroying Seminole clan camps and crops that warred on women.

Even as officers worked to bring Seminole leaders in for talks, they remained under specific orders not to help Seminole groups until they surrendered for emigration. To that effect, in 1840, Colonel Worth issued the following directives: "the white flag will be raised at all posts east of the Suwannee, and all Indians coming in will be directed to repair to these Head Quarters, where presents will be distributed, and a talk held with them. The commanders of posts will not furnish them with rations or clothing." Officers were to demonstrate US power and wealth with presents and military displays but must not provide goods to help Seminole groups survive. In 1841, the commander's adjutant reminded officers that "it would be impolitic to make any issues of clothing to Indians who may come into your camp other than such as positive humanity may dictate, particularly such articles as may afford comfort to an enemy, in this however every thing is left to your discretion in which implicit confidence is placed."[60] Yet, once Seminole groups acquiesced to forced emigration, the army became responsible.

The army had a duty to provide for those who surrendered to it, an "obligation to furnish rations to such as may remove."[61] It set about issuing food to the same people whose food it so recently destroyed. One emigrating party late in the war departed with subsistence stores of 210 barrels of corn, alongside thousands of pounds of bacon, hard bread, rice, soap, salt, coffee, and sugar. After spending much effort burning corn, the army then purchased large quantities to give to the same people. The military even protected friendly Seminole women by guarding their crops. To cultivate friendship with Tiger Tail's band, the commander in Florida sent orders to three subordinate officers to ensure the group's fields were not damaged: "It is understood that they have some small

---

[59] Motte, *Journey into Wilderness*, 205, 207.
[60] *General Orders, August 1838 to January 1843*, 1, May 30, 1840, Orders No. 18, Lieutenant Newton, Assistant Acting Adjutant General, Fort King; *9th Military Department, Letters Sent*, August 28, 1841, Lieutenant Sprague Acting Adjutant General, Tampa, to Captain Gwynn, Camp Hospitaka.
[61] War Office, "Office of the Judge Advocate General: Opinions of the Attorney General, 1821–1870, No. 3" (Book, Washington), 32, RG 153, Box 3, National Archives, Washington DC. April 8, 1845, Adjutant General Office, Opinion of John Y. Mason.

corn and pumpkin patches somewhere about Annuteliga which it would be a good policy to leave undisturbed."[62]

This connection between food and protection even applied to Seminoles who remained in Florida at war's end. The army deemed them "defeated," even though they never stopped resisting forced emigration. In 1842, Worth ordered that within specified boundaries, "the few remaining Indians in the southern portion of Florida...are permitted for a while to plant and hunt on the land."[63] Destroying women's crops and homes was warfare, and before surrender, Seminole people were "savage" enemies. After surrender, they became the army's wards and gained its blessing to grow food again. Ideas about women and protection gave shape to war and peace alike.

The army often burned the homes and food stores of the matrilineal clans that structured Seminole life even as army leaders bemoaned Seminole women's impoverishment. Yet, soldiers reconciled these acts with their identity as protectors. Per Vattel's maxim that "when we are at war with a savage nation, who observe no rules, and never give quarter, we may punish them in the persons of any of their people whom we take, (these belonging to the number of the guilty) and endeavor, by this rigorous proceeding, to force them to respect the laws of humanity."[64] Though women had to remain noncombatants to uphold the very basis for moral order, militaries could still imprison women and destroy women's means of subsistence. Vattel wrote that an army "may lawfully secure and make prisoners" any person exempted from fighting, including women "either with a view to prevent them from taking up arms again, or for the purpose of weakening the enemy, or, finally, in hopes that, by getting into his power some woman or child for whom the sovereign has an affection, he may induce him to accede to equitable conditions of peace." He caveated, these expedients must be rare.[65]

However, General Scott's 1825 regulations imposed stricter standards. By regulation, militaries could only imprison combatants and must provide good treatment. Scott wrote,

---

[62] *9th Military Department, Letters Sent*, May 5, 1841, Special Orders 24, Armistead (Bliss Acting Adjutant General) to Worth; 416, August 4, 1842. Subsistence stores for the emigrating party included: 25 barrels pork, 1283 lbs bacon, 9025 lbs hard bread, 804 lbs rice, 210 barrels corn, 106 lbs soap, 2 barrels salt, 721 lbs coffee, and 2078 lbs sugar.

[63] *General Orders, August 1838 to January 1843*, 1, August 11, 1842, Cooper, Acting Adjutant General, Orders No 27.

[64] Vattel, *Law of Nations*, 348.

[65] Ibid., 352.

the persons to be considered as prisoners of war, and those to be released as noncombatants, together with the exchange of the former, will depend on the conventions, or cartels agreed upon by the belligerents; or, in the absence of such agreements, on the usages of war, the example of the enemy, and the particular instruction given by the government.[66]

Scott's formulation of prisoners of war and noncombatants as opposing categories reflected the foundational separation between women and soldiers in the laws of war.

The US Army published an updated set of General Regulations in 1841 that entirely dropped the prisoner of war provisions. This meant that by regulation, the army could imprison anyone, as did Jesup when he seized several hundred Seminoles under a white flag as prisoners of war. He justified this by terming the captured Seminoles – men, women, and children – as "all prisoners of war or hostages who had violated their parole." Though he attempted no explanation of how children could "violate their parole," a phrase generally applied to enemy military officers, Jesup emphasized his mercy. He continued, "notwithstanding their character as prisoners and hostages who had violated their parole, and who, according to the laws of war, as recognized by civilized nations, had forfeited their lives," a dubious claim that lost validity centuries ago when executing prisoners ceased to be within the laws of war tradition, "I directed that they should be treated with every kindness, and have every accommodation consistent with their security." Jesup argued that his stratagem led to significant victory at minimal cost. It produced "the peaceable surrender of between eleven and twelve hundred Indians and negroes, three hundred and nineteen of whom are warriors, or men capable of bearing arms."[67] By this math, Jesup made over 800 women and children into prisoners of war.

It is ironic that taking female and child prisoners evoked little public outcry, while the national press widely condemned Jesup's capture of specific male leaders, notably Osceola, under a flag of truce. Violating flags of truce carried such a uniquely dark stain that a few decades later during the Civil War, it was one of four acts unequivocally forbidden in Lieber's Code. The others were torture, assassination, and poison. The outrage over Osceola's capture echoes into historiography. C. S. Monaco concludes that the capture "while under a flag of truce betrayed the code of honor that was so deeply instilled at the military academy at West

---

[66] Scott, *General Regulations for the Army*, 1825, 63, 140.
[67] Jesup, "Report from Major General Jesup," 5, 10.

3 "Find Where Their Women Are": Pursuing Seminole Women

Point and contradicted Euro-American cultural mores of gallantry and fair play." The army captured Osceola alongside members of his family, including two wives, two children, a sister, and possibly Osceola's mother.[68] However, these women did not figure in a controversy centered on men betraying other men's trust.

Capturing women was, after all, an accepted practice. It produced the dependency of captive to captor, and soldiers believed dependency on men to be women's proper state. Soldiers' beliefs in their superiority to Seminole men only heightened this naturalized self-image as ideal male protectors. Upon taking possession of a Seminole band that had declared itself friendly to the US, Zachary Taylor wrote that "although I placed but little confidence in their professions of friendship, or their intentions of coming in, yet I had no time to look to their women and children, who had fled and concealed themselves in the swamp, or to have encumbered myself with them." Because Taylor was marching into battle, he chose not to pursue the women and instead sent a captive old man to "collect all the women and children and take them into Captain Munroe, at the Kissimmee, the next day."[69] Seminole men's promises of friendship meant little to Taylor, while possession of Seminole women guaranteed success. Although capturing women seemed to contradict the supposedly natural female innocence essential to the laws of war, an even more powerful belief – that of women's dependency on men – naturalized it.

The systematic, officially sanctioned hunting of Seminole women throughout seven years of war prompted this critical change to regulations, bringing theory in line with practice. It was, after all, a military necessity to capture women. Just a few months into the war in April 1836, Lieutenant Henry Prince wrote that he apprehended a Spanish smuggler who promised: "to guide us to the women & children if for his life." Even at that early stage, Prince articulated an understanding that the key to winning in Florida was capturing noncombatants. In August, Prince noted some progress in the army's search for families, reporting

---

[68] Witt, *Lincoln's Code*, 4; Lieber, *Instructions for the Government of Armies of the United States, in the Field*, Paragraphs 16, 117, 148; Monaco, *The Second Seminole War and the Limits of American Aggression*, 1; Wickman, *Osceola's Legacy*, 59, 103–4, 135. Of note, Jesup was not a West Point graduate. Many of these women appear to have been related, but kinship ties are difficult to confirm. Still, it is indisputable that Jesup captured Osceola along with several women.

[69] *Senate, 25th Congress, 2nd Session*, 7:987, December 25, 1837, Zachary Taylor, report of the battle of Lake Okeechobee.

that "the Indians at Tampa Bay told the situation of the three bodies of hostile women & children."[70]

Seminole leader Halleck Tustenuggee told Colonel Worth toward the end of the war in 1842 that of the remaining Seminoles, many would say, "our wives and children are gone – let us go with them."[71] In this sentiment, the army saw evidence that capturing women paid off. Its mission in Florida was to carry out the political policy of forced removal. Revised regulations enabled this convergence of policy and practice, adding a necessary legal tool for soldiers to pursue Native women in all the "Indian Wars" its leaders expected to fight in coming decades.

A year after General Thomas Jesup began capturing Seminoles under flags of truce, Francis Lieber wrote in his textbook on political ethics that "flags of truce must be honored; heralds were sacred in most ancient times; indeed, with them begins, we may say, international law."[72] But the 1841 General Regulations reflected the army's experiences in the Second US–Seminole War rather than Lieber's ideals. In Florida, army leaders learned it was much easier to imprison Seminole people who came in for peace talks than to find and capture Seminole families in the wilderness. Capturing Seminole groups under flags of truce might be unsavory, but new regulations justified it.

Officers stripped the flag of truce of its universal protection. Henceforth, whether to honor them would depend on an enemy's perceived integrity. Regulations stated, "persons bearing a flag of truce from the enemy, are to be treated with attention and civility; but, as communications of that nature are frequently designed to gain intelligence, and for reconnaissance, the most strict and efficacious means must be adopted to frustrate such consequences." When dealing with Native peoples, "whenever they evince a disposition to act treacherously, or assume a hostile attitude, it is better to anticipate their designs than allow them the advantage of attack."[73] Preemptively capturing Seminoles, before the men could reveal their "hostile" and "treacherous" natures, allowed the army to expand the protective net of civilization.

Even critics of Jesup's actions admitted that violating the laws of war when fighting an Indigenous enemy mattered little. One wrote

---

[70] Prince, *Amidst a Storm of Bullets*, 39, April 6, 1836, August 1836.
[71] Sprague, Brevet Captain, Eighth Regiment US Infantry, *The Origin, Progress, and Conclusion of the Florida War*, 464–68.
[72] Lieber, *Manual of Political Ethics*, 2:455.
[73] By Authority of the War Department, *General Regulations for the Army of the United States*, 264, 307.

that Jesup's capture of Osceola was counterproductive, but not exactly wrong: "if practiced towards a civilized foe" Jesup's actions "would be characterized as a violation of all that is noble and generous in war." Others supported Jesup wholeheartedly, as did a "gentleman" of St. Augustine who described the mass imprisonment of Seminoles as "a glorious haul" that has "drawn the fangs from the reptile, so that he can no longer bite."[74] If Jesup had done the unseemly by capturing Seminoles under a white flag, it was only to contain dehumanized Seminole men's violence.

While the army leaned heavily on the European laws of war tradition, it also sought to revise that tradition to better conform to US territorial expansion. This approach legitimized Seminole women's captures and clarified the strategic value of capturing women: taking women weakened the Seminole war effort and induced men to surrender. Therefore, a US agent to the Seminole argued the army should charge a Seminole camp in Withlacoochee cove because while "the men might have fled," the "capture of their families would have soon induced them to surrender." Officers wrote of following "fresh signs of women's and children's tracks" to capture them.

In one instance, US soldiers captured "a negro man" with his wife and child and imprisoned both to coerce the man to find Seminoles and convince them to surrender. A newspaper article reported the army's success "in capturing two squaws, a negro, and three children," noting that "these prisoners, by the last accounts, were conducting the troops to the strongholds and hiding places of the Indians."[75] A lieutenant reported that he and his men had surrounded a camp of "two wigwams" and made a "vigorous assault, capturing five rifles, six squaws, and three children." They "destroyed everything useful to the Indians," including large amounts of prepared coontie root, deer skins, clothing, and cooking implements. The *Army and Navy Chronicle* praised West Point officer General Walker Armistead (the war's penultimate commander) for reports of "cornfields destroyed, women and children captured, camps broken up, and new trails found and followed." Another article reported approvingly that "five Indian women and seven children were taken"

---

[74] Niles, *Niles' National Register*, 1838, 53:145, 148, 165, by order of Major General Jesup (J.A. Chambers Acting Adjutant General), Orders, No. 203, Headquarters, Army of the South, St. Augustine, October 24, 1837.

[75] Homans, *Army and Navy Chronicle*, 1842, 13:59, 155. March 12, 1842, *St. Augustine News*.

by a Lieutenant in the Second Dragoons.[76] Captured Seminole women brought victory closer.

For Seminole women, being hunted and captured meant a waking nightmare. An army officer described a chase that extended over several days. The soldiers chased four canoes, with a Seminole family and their possessions in each, carrying a total of five men, five women, and two children. Of these, the soldiers claimed to have shot three men and captured three women and one child. The officer claimed a Seminole mother killed the other child to avoid capture and that a man and two women escaped into the darkness. The army continued its pursuit, finally catching one of the women and then her husband, named Chia. The soldiers imprisoned the woman and then forced her husband to be a guide, threatened "with a gallows in perspective, should he prove false."[77] The remaining woman may have escaped, having lost all her belongings and seen her family killed or captured.

Many US observers recorded a romanticized version of capture. Army Surgeon Jacob Motte described his time in a camp of 500 Seminoles, who had gathered to await a decision on whether the US would permit them to stay in Florida. When Washington's answer came back no, Jesup had his soldiers surround the camp and imprisoned everyone. While awaiting this forced emigration, Motte observed men and women playing a single-pole ball game, noting "the women were always the winners at this game, but whether owing to their superior skill and agility, or the gallantry of the men in allowing them to be victorious, I could not positively decide." After witnessing this game, and a dance later that day, Motte felt that a spirit of play and happiness reigned. He concluded "that their captivity did not produce a very depressing effect upon them."[78] Sentimental notions of Seminoles

---

[76] Sprague, Brevet Captain, Eighth Regiment US Infantry, *The Origin, Progress, and Conclusion of the Florida War*, 166, 174, Colonel Henderson's Report, January 28, 1837, 176, 313, 383, March 23, 1842, Lieutenant Commanding J. B. Marchand. Seminole Agent G. Humphreys to Florida Governor William Duval; Homans, *Army and Navy Chronicle*, 1840, 11:62, July 7, 1840, Jacksonville, FL, 331, November 9, 1840. One way to periodize the war is by commanders – John K. Mahon took this approach. They were Winfield Scott, Richard K. Call, Thomas Jesup, Zachary Taylor, Walker Armistead, and William Worth. All except Call, a politician and a Governor of Florida, were career army officers.

[77] Niles, *Niles' National Register*, 1841, 60:72, Charleston Courier, 211, St. Augustine Gazette, June 5, 1841. The letter described Colonel Harney's expedition in the everglades, written by an officer who participated, and dated January 6, 1841.

[78] Motte, *Journey into Wilderness*, 219.

going west to a better future in Indian Territory reflected the army's desire to transcend the war's sordid realities, to see themselves as agents of progress.

Popular culture, exemplified by *Metamora's* success and the national interest in Osceola, helped naturalize Indigenous expulsion. This cultural current nudged US observers toward conclusions that overlooked Seminole suffering. An observer in Arkansas noted that an emigration party of 260 with a "good portion" of women and children arrived "all fat and good-humored, and look as if they had been living a life of indolent ease, instead of being hunted like wild beasts from fastness to fastness."[79] Army leadership could claim their protection was real by transforming captured Seminoles from starving to well-fed.

Similarly, army paternalists like regular officer Ethan Allen Hitchcock believed Indian Removal would preserve Seminole women's virtue. He thought that "where Indians and whites were neighbors," Indigenous women would resort to prostitution to survive. He took pride in advancing the supposed civilizing mission because it guarded Native women from the degradation that accompanied white settler encroachment in Florida.[80] He cast government policy as a gift.

Hitchcock described his success in convincing Creek leader Pascofa's band to leave Florida. He issued blankets, shirts, and turbans to the men and "a calico dress and handkerchief to each woman" along with food. When the group approached the boats waiting to take them away from Florida, the "women were nearly all in tears." One "woman stood near with a little child in her arms," and Hitchcock "told her that they had been living more like wild animals than like human creatures, and she could now bring up her children in peace and safety. At this she dropped her head and burst into tears."[81] Hitchcock interpreted these as tears of relief. Much like Hitchcock thought the crying Creek women were grateful to him, other officers similarly interpreted women's behavior to the army's advantage. Many believed capturing Seminoles under a flag of

---

[79] Lepore, *The Name of War: King Phillip's War and the Origins of American Identity*, 194; Niles, *Niles' National Register*, 1839, 56:131, reprinted from the Arkansas Gazette of Little Rock, April 3, 1839. Lepore notes that *Metamora*, written in 1829, rose to great popularity and was ubiquitous by 1846.

[80] Hitchcock, *Fifty Years in Camp and Field*, 127. Hitchcock's unease at proximity between Seminole women and white settler men reflects Roy Pearce's observation that "civilized, Christian life did not raise up all savages as it should have. Rather it lowered some savages and destroyed others." Pearce, *Savagism and Civilization*, 66.

[81] Hitchcock, *Fifty Years in Camp and Field*, 172.

truce was humanitarian because it prevented "the loss of a single drop of blood on either side."[82]

Some officers grasped that army enforcement of Indian Removal forced people to live "like wild animals" in the first place and would now tear them from their homes. On the death of a friend and fellow officer from typhus at Fort Dade, Lieutenant Robert Buchanan wrote, "thus is there added one more to the list of those noble souls sacrificed to the outrageous and scandalous policy pursued by our Government towards the Seminoles."[83] While Buchanan condemned US policy as immoral, he saw US soldiers as the victims rather than the Seminoles.

While Buchanan expressed doubt, Hitchcock believed in the army as protectors of women. At a banquet following the end of the war in 1843, hosted by Florida Governor Richard Call for army officers, the governor made a toast: "Beauty and Chivalry – the pride and glory of our country." Hitchcock responded, "Beauty – its defense and protection the noble privilege of Chivalry, whether with or without the button."[84] The button referred to regular army insignia. Hitchcock's meaning was that both regulars like himself and volunteers like Call behaved admirably. Interestingly, Hitchcock replaced pride and glory with defense and protection. In the multicultural social world of wartime Florida, where the army often loathed white settlers, both respected and suspected Seminole warriors, and begrudgingly valued Black Seminole guides and interpreters – the army's gendered rhetoric of protecting women provided a language accessible to both officers and enlisted men, to regulars and volunteers. Moreover, Hitchcock offered these words to other men, which exhorts one to remember that chivalry was foremost a performance for "fellow knights, not for the lady herself."[85] Hitchcock's display of chivalry had a logic of protection at its foundation and located its clearest expression in congratulations exchanged with other men.

[82] Niles, *Niles' National Register*, 1838, 54:113, Order No. 77, Headquarters, Army of the South, Fort Jupiter, Florida, 23 March 1838, by order of Major General Jesup (J.A. Chambers Acting Adjutant General).
[83] Buchanan, "A Journal of Lt. Robert C. Buchanan during the Seminole War," 142, December 19, 1837.
[84] Hitchcock, *Fifty Years in Camp and Field*, 175. Regular army and volunteer troops had very different relations to the army. Regular soldiers enlisted for a term of years, usually five, frequently for multiple terms. Regular officers commonly spent decades in military service. In contrast, volunteers came from civilian life and served only during wartime, sometimes for as little as three months, often with no prior training. These two groups frequently clashed. This sense of hostility is what Hitchcock's toast aims to obviate.
[85] Kinsella, *The Image before the Weapon*, 49.

3 "Find Where Their Women Are": Pursuing Seminole Women 141

To assert US control over Florida, enable white settlement, and expand slavery, the US Army fought the Second US–Seminole War not merely against Seminole warriors, but against women. The logic of protection helped the army resolve the problem of waging war on women while upholding female noncombatancy. While characterizing Seminole women as subjects of protection and hunting them appear to be conflicting goals, the army used a common set of ideas about "civilization" versus "savagery" rooted in women's protection to resolve these apparent contradictions. Instead of simply seizing women as combatants and thus proper prisoners, the army framed women's captures and the destruction of their resources as a humanitarian policy to bring women under military protection and relocate them to safe homes. Protection became a foundational assumption upon which army culture rested because it solved the paradox of making war on women yet maintaining that the army was a force for good.

Changes to army culture in Florida generated changes to the army's relationship with the laws of war. While the laws of war would have allowed violence against women who took up arms and therefore forfeited the protection supposedly conferred to noncombatants, the army did not make much use of this exemption. Even when Seminole women behaved as combatants, soldiers maintained that such women remained harmless. Instead, officers and enlisted men acted according to a deeply held belief that women needed military protection. They, therefore, interpreted Seminole women's participation in war through a gendered lens that upheld female innocence and left men unable to comprehend women's wartime activities.

Following the dictates of politicians, Army officers institutionalized a way to ignore violence done to Seminole women by only counting Seminole men as warriors and thus as casualties in military reports. This record-keeping practice reified a categorization of adult Seminoles as warriors or women and severed Seminole women from the army's official memory. Soldiers emphasized their moral superiority, rooted in an ability to protect Seminole women, alongside claims that Seminole men were a "savage" foe. The army's logic of protection produced two levels of harm. First, women's protection became justification for many forms of military action. Second, this motivated a kind of archival violence that erased women's actions and deaths from official records.

Distinct approaches to Seminole men and women justified changes to military regulations that gave the army more freedom to take prisoners and violate flags of truce. Though many officers and enlisted men expressed concerns over the injustice of expelling the Seminoles, they dutifully followed orders while referring to the necessity of protecting Seminoles by moving them away from white settlers. The army would revisit this approach in Mexico as the US appetite for territorial expansion only grew.

PART II

WAR IN MEXICO

The war began when the United States invaded Mexico. President James K. Polk's war emerged after the Texas Revolution, where white settlers fought to control territory and expand slavery. It was a conflict many in the US saw as "a race war between brown Mexicans and white Texians," and they supported the latter.[1] After the US annexed Texas in 1845, Polk saw his opportunity to both expand borders and extend US control over much of northern Mexico. He ordered General Zachary Taylor, only a few years distant from fighting the Seminoles in Florida, to advance south through disputed territory. All involved knew it would provoke a war.

Both sides acknowledged a fight had begun after the Battles of Palo Alto and Resaca de la Palma in May of 1846. The US Army, regulars and volunteers, commenced several lines of advance. Generals Taylor and Wool continued to push south from the contested border toward Monterrey. In the latter half of 1846, General Stephen Watts Kearny marched on Santa Fe and continued west to San Diego. Colonel Alexander Doniphan, of the volunteers, remained with Kearny until Santa Fe, then moved south through El Paso toward Taylor's forces.

As the war continued and Mexico remained defiant, Winfield Scott – the army's Commanding General following Alexander Macomb's death in 1841 – prepared another campaign designed to strike the Mexican capital and force a favorable peace. Scott's 1847 march took him from the port of Veracruz to Mexico City, the country's densely populated heart. In contrast, US efforts in Northern Mexico thrust the army into

---

[1] Greenberg, *A Wicked War*, 8.

a vast, arid landscape of dispersed settlements, where Mexican towns existed alongside centuries-old Pueblo Indian communities and where large regions remained firmly under the control of Native power brokers who extracted tributes and captives from Mexicans and Pueblo Indians alike.

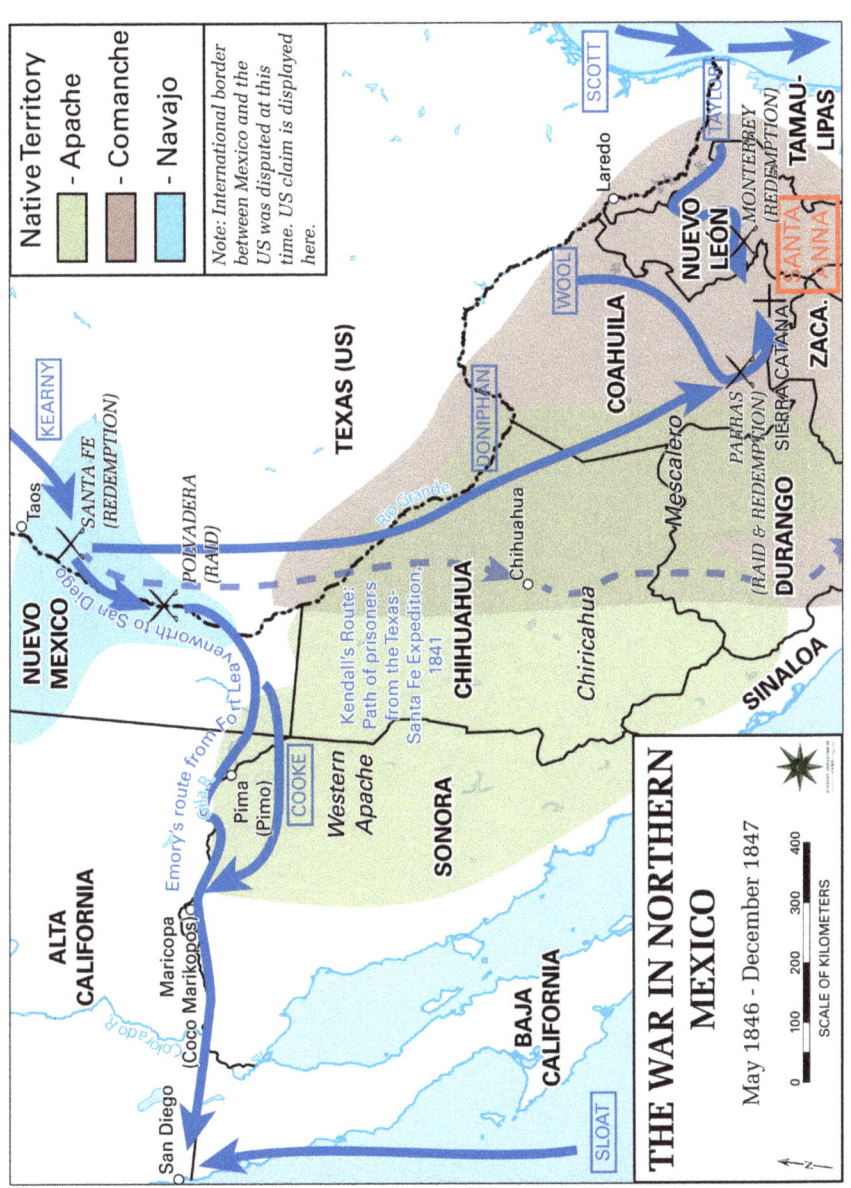

MAP 3 The War in Northern Mexico.
Map by Mr. Jeffrey Goldberg, Cartographer at the West Point Department of History.

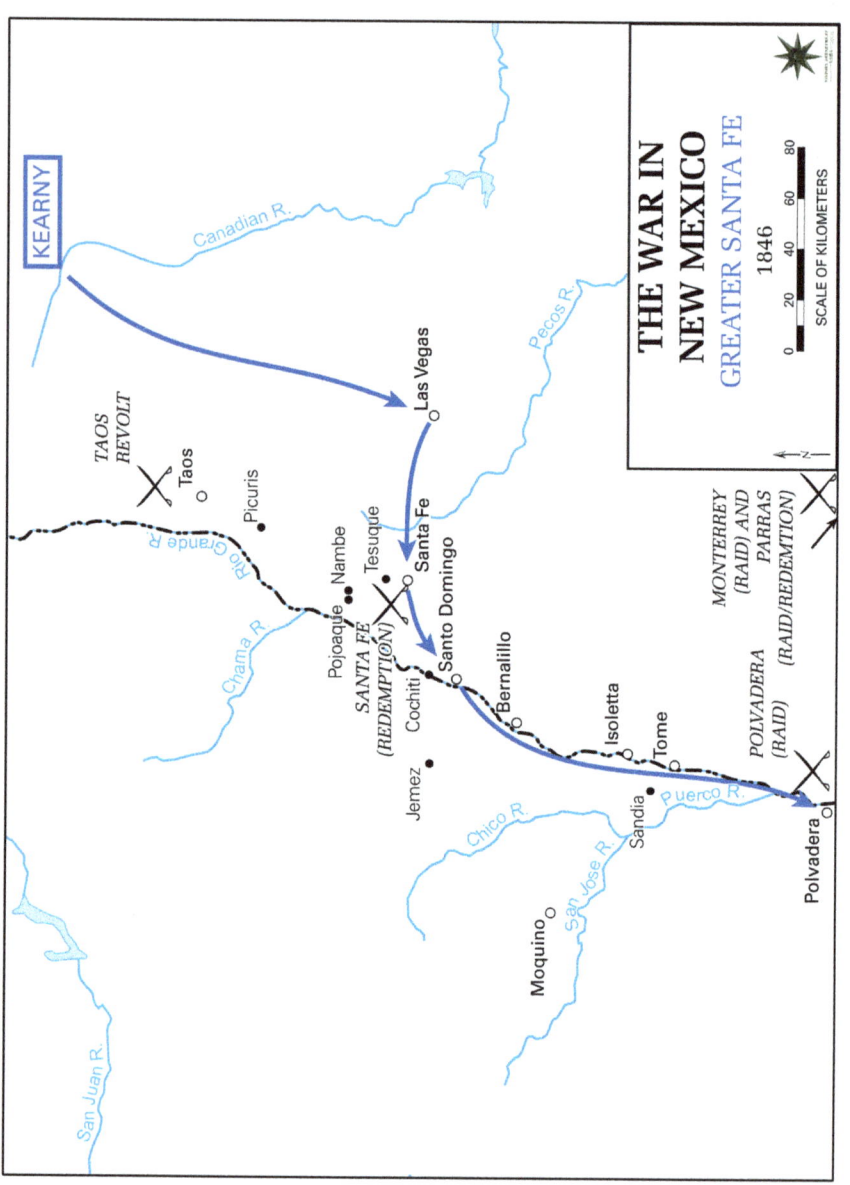

MAP 4 Greater Santa Fe.
Map by Mr. Jeffrey Goldberg, Cartographer at the West Point Department of History.

4

Rescuing the Enemy

Mexican Women and the US Army's Transformation in Northern Mexico, 1846–1847

In August of 1846, Brigadier General Stephen Watts Kearny and his Army of the West conquered New Mexico. Yet, Kearny announced to Mexicans, "We come amongst you as friends – not as enemies; as protectors – not as conquerors."[1] He made this claim to an enemy population he had just occupied. He did it while marching through the northern provinces that US political leaders intended to keep as US territory. Why, to Kearny, was this not a conquest?

In part, it was because US colonization had already begun. Ever since Mexico achieved independence in 1821, places like Santa Fe hosted ever greater numbers of Anglo-American merchants and traders. In addition to troops, merchants – some married to local women – accompanied Kearny. Men like James Magoffin, married to the Northern Mexican

---

[1] Emory, *Notes of a Military Reconnaissance*, 26–27, August 14, 1846. Kearny said this in Las Vegas, New Mexico, on August 14, 1846. Kearny's army career began in the War of 1812 (he was not a West Pointer), and he spent decades in service before Mexico. Lieutenant William Emory was an army topographical engineer and recent West Point graduate (Class of 1831) sent to map lands that would become part of the US. The language reflects words army commanders used with Native groups. Enlisted dragoon James Hildreth, writing of the southwestern Great Plains, recorded how Colonel Henry Dodge, leading an 1834 expedition, said to a Pawnee group, "we meet you as friends, not as enemies; to make peace with you." Previous experiences conquering Native groups shaped the army's approach to conquest in Mexico. Dodge sealed his words by exchanging a captive Pawnee girl for a white boy and restoring a Kiowa girl to her community, "one of the many acts of kindness" they promised to perform. He emphasized US sincerity to a Comanche leader: "your women and children were defenseless, we treated them kindly." Although officers like Colonel Dodge led this process, Hildreth, an enlisted man, felt part of a shared project of rescue. Hildreth, *Dragoon Campaigns to the Rocky Mountains*, Letter XVII, 161, 169, 171 Pawnee Village and Camp Comanche, July 13–23, 1834, Letter XVIII, 181, August 7, 1834, Fort Gibson.

María Gertrudis Valdes-Farías, and his brother Samuel Magoffin, had decades of experience in the region.[2] Merchants and officers alike sought to further US interests by imposing US political control.

It was a remarkably complex landscape that recent scholarship embraces. Brian Delay begins *War of a Thousand Deserts*, his study of how Indigenous raiding shaped the War on Mexico, by noting that the Treaty of Guadalupe Hidalgo's Article 11 obligated the US to "forcibly" restrain Indigenous attacks into Mexico, rescue any Mexicans held captive by such groups, and prevent the purchase of captured Mexicans. For Delay, this realization opened a "little door into a big story" of Indigenous power. The Comanches, Kiowas, Apaches, Navajos, and others regularly attacked Mexicans, capturing some, killing others, and seizing or destroying supplies. For many, the Comanches especially were a severe, even existential, threat.[3] By the time Taylor's Army of Occupation marched into Mexico, raiding had transformed Northern Mexico into an embittered and depopulated region.

Indigenous power unintentionally paved the way for US control by reducing and impoverishing much of the Northern Mexican population, creating an openness to US commerce and antipathy toward Mexico's federal government. Raiding allowed men like Kearny to "frame the dismemberment of Mexico as an act of salvation." The US would "defeat the savage Indians and redeem the Mexican north from what they saw as the Mexicans' neglect." Delay studies the interconnected political endeavors of US, Mexican, and Native groups to deal with the "savage Indians" and how these politics "came together in a forgotten nexus that reshaped North American boundaries for all of its people."[4] One piece of this process took place in 1846, where the US Army, in response to Indigenous raids, shed its Florida identity as captors of Native women and assumed a new one – rescuers of its national enemies, Mexican women.[5] In doing so, they rewrote the US laws of war.

---

[2] Magoffin was one of several married to influential local women. Emory wrote that "Mr. Liffendorfer, a trader, married to a Santa Fe lady, was sent in the direction of Taos, with two Pueblo Indians, to feel the pulse of the Pueblos and the Mexican people." Emory, *Notes of a Military Reconnaissance*, 18. August 5, 1846. See also: Magoffin, *Down the Santa Fe Trail and into Mexico*. US traders joined a long history of diverse groups using trade routes across the Great Basin. Blackhawk, *Violence over the Land*, 134.

[3] For more on Comanche power in the region, see: Hämäläinen, *The Comanche Empire*; Delay, *War of a Thousand Deserts*.

[4] Delay, *War of a Thousand Deserts*, xv, xvii–xix.

[5] For a close analysis of the numbers of Mexicans captured, with gender and age information when available, see Delay's "Appendix: Data on Comanche-Mexican Violence,

4 Rescuing the Enemy: Mexican Women and the US Army 149

The regulars emerged from their 1846 campaign in Northern Mexico with two distinct approaches for future conflicts that distinguished lawful enemies (uniformed male combatants) treated with consideration from unlawful enemies (other male enemies) treated as criminals. Army intellectual Henry Halleck later wrote an authoritative book on the laws of war informed by his experiences as a regular officer fighting in Mexico. He concluded that "all hostile collisions between nations" are divided into "two sorts of wars, *lawful* and *unlawful*."[6] Determinations of enemy conduct rooted in protecting women constructed the rhetorical space between the two and allowed the army to criminalize resistance.

In the best-known study of the laws of war that covers the conflict in Mexico, John Fabian Witt examines US relationships with the idea that "war can be constrained by law" from the Revolution through the Civil War. He argues that the decades leading up to the Civil War produced a tradition that ultimately caused Lincoln to label secessionists criminals, not soldiers. Witt asserts that in Mexico, the "councils of war" that General Scott created to try guerrillas (in Central Mexico) allowed the US Army to convict and execute members of an enemy military on criminal charges. In doing so, Scott had "given life to the idea of a war crime." He therefore established "a general principle of individual criminal liability for violations of the laws of war." Scott also applied this idea to guerrillas, whom officers branded criminal banditti, not civilized foes. Witt argues that Scott thus "criminalized an entire class of Mexican combatants."[7] Yet this criminalization process happened in all theaters of the Mexican War. And it happened first in Northern Mexico.

The US Army had to portray itself as legitimate to occupy the north successfully, and Secretary of War William Marcy gave commanders talking points to do so. Marcy provided Kearny with his proclamation, and gave similar instructions to others senior officers. He ordered Kearny to "act in such a manner as best to conciliate the inhabitants, and render them friendly to the United States." To Colonel Jonathan Stevenson, preparing to leave for California with his New York volunteers, Marcy

---

1831–48." Figure A.2 shows a significant increase in Mexicans killed or captured by the Comanche and Kiowa, from 70 Mexicans in 1843 to 652 in 1845, which decreased to 289 in 1846, and spiked again to 621 in 1847. Ibid., 319. Delay notes his figures are limited by a need for more research in northern provincial archives and that his data is most complete for Coahuila, Tamaulipas, Chihuahua, and Durango from 1842 to 1847. Ibid., 311–40.
[6] Halleck, *International Law*, 1878, 1:472.
[7] Witt, *Lincoln's Code*, 1, 7, 130, 138.

emphasized "it will be of the greatest importance that the good will of the people towards the United States should be cultivated. This is to be done by liberal and kind treatment. They should be made to feel that we come as deliverers." In like words, Secretary of the Navy George Bancroft wrote to Commodore John Sloat, the California-bound commander of the US Navy in its Pacific operations. Bancroft exhorted, "this country desires to find in California a friend, and not an enemy; to be connected with it by near ties; to hold possession of it, at least during the war, and to hold that possession, if possible, with the consent of its inhabitants."[8]

The version Zachary Taylor received bore the title "A Proclamation by the General Commanding the Army of the US of America." It announced to Mexicans that their "government is in the hands of tyrants and usurpers....Being disarmed, you are left defenseless, an easy prey to the savage Comanches, who not only destroy your lives and property but drive into a captivity, more horrible than death itself, your wives and children." In contrast, the US Army "come to make no war on the Mexican people."[9] Instead, Marcy put words of mutual benefit into his commanders' mouths. Mexicans would receive protection and give the US Army legitimacy in return.

By following the logic of protection, these men contributed to a lasting system of US conquest. What was popularly called Kearny's proclamation became the Kearny Code, which remains the basis for New Mexican law today. The battles of Central Mexico may dominate many US military histories of the War on Mexico, but the territories the US wanted to keep were a desert and a thousand miles away – in New Mexico, California, and Texas. In these places, the US Army deployed the logic of protection to claim Northern Mexican women, and thus Northern Mexico, as permanent recipients of US deliverance.[10]

---

[8] Thirtieth Congress, First Session, *House of Representatives Mexican War Correspondence*, 1848, 155, Marcy to Kearny; 161, September 11, 1846 Marcy to Stevenson at Governor's Island; 237, June 8, 1846 Bancroft to Sloat. Marcy's message continued, "Their rights of person, property, and religion, must be respected and sustained. The greatest care must be taken to restrain the troops from all acts of license or outrage." George Bancroft, a naval officer, was also a historian. As Secretary of the Navy, he established the US Naval Academy. As a historian, he authored numerous works, including a multivolume, romanticized history of the US. It is worth noting that the Romantic elements of army culture also existed within naval culture.

[9] Ibid., 166, Marcy to Taylor, No. 10, A Proclamation by the General Commanding the Army of the U.S. of America.

[10] For more on gender and Northern Mexico under colonization, see: Deutsch, *No Separate Refuge*; Gutiérrez, *When Jesus Came, the Corn Mothers Went Away*; Gonzalez, *Refusing the Favor*; Maciel and Gonzales-Berry, *The Contested Homeland*.

4 Rescuing the Enemy: Mexican Women and the US Army

Indeed, Marcy argued that US conquest would improve the lot of ordinary Mexicans. He wrote, "It is our wish to see you liberated from despots, to drive back the savage Comanches, to prevent the renewal of their assaults, and to compel them to restore to you from captivity your long-lost wives and children." The army claimed that its soldiers came not as enemies, but arrived "among the people of Mexico as friends and republican brethren, and all who receive us as such shall be protected, whilst all who are seduced into the army of your dictator shall be treated as enemies." Marcy concluded that the army "shall want from you nothing but food for our army, and for this, you shall always be paid, in cash, the full value."[11] Every part of this strategy, which began at the top of the army with the Secretary of War and reached down to each commander, assured Mexican women that the US would protect them. The proclamations claimed that the military would defend women and redeem them from raids, guard their persons from rape, and enable them to safely sell their market goods.

During the war, Mexican women became the perfect subjects for US military protection. The army won twice by redeeming Mexican women from Native captivity. First, rescue demonstrated US military superiority to Mexican men who failed to protect their women. These Indigenous groups would soon see, as one volunteer put it, that "they had men of a different character from Mexicans to deal with." US troops coopted *rescate*, previously performed by Mexican men to bring dependents home. As James Brooks notes, "Native and European men fought to protect their communities and preserve personal repute yet participated in conflicts and practices that made the objects of their honor, women and children, crucial products of violent economic exchange."[12] By claiming Northern Mexico for the US, soldiers replaced Mexican men as rescuers.

Second, rescue drew a line between "civilized" rescuers of female captives and the "savage" men who took them. To the army, redeeming captives increased the contrast between the categories of Indian and Mexican, whitening Mexican women and heightening the need for their rescue. This idea of the army as saviors and civilizers led to efforts to rescue Mexican women captured by raiders. At the same time, raiding encouraged the army to consider men who threatened them, and

---

[11] Thirtieth Congress, First Session, *House of Representatives Mexican War Correspondence*, 1848, 166–67, Marcy to Taylor, Proclamation No. 10, "A Proclamation by the General Commanding the Army of the U.S. of America."
[12] Edwards, *A Campaign in New Mexico with Colonel Doniphan*, 68.

therefore jeopardized US protection for innocents, as criminals. The US Army therefore increasingly punished rather than made war against the raiders, rebels, and guerrillas who threatened its control.

CAPTORS TO RESCUERS

In a glowing account of General John Wool's occupation of Parras, a city in Coahuila, author Frances Baylies insisted that Wool would "protect the people of Parras and the vicinity from massacre and plunder by the savages." To that end, Wool had already sent three groups to chastise the Comanche. A party from Colonel Doniphan's command rescued and returned "a number of women and children" to the Mexicans. The author concluded, "Was ever a war carried on, with as much humanity towards an enemy?" Baylies placed similar words into the mouth of a Mexican colonel who allegedly told Wool, "You are our greatest enemy, for you conquer us by your kindness and humanity. We cannot induce our people to take up arms against you."[13] By rescuing Mexican women – enemy women – the army legitimized conquest and cemented its self-styled identity as protectors.

The narrative derived its glory from protecting Mexican women from Indigenous captivity. The author wrote that Wool's "measures to protect the Mexicans, as well as Texans, living within the limits of Texas, now under the protection of the United States, were prompt and efficient. He compelled the Indians to surrender all whom they had seized and carried into captivity, including women and children." By protecting Mexicans, Wool legitimized US occupation so that "by this course, he reconciled the Mexicans to the American rule; and when they ascertained that the General was not only willing but able to protect them, their gratitude was unbounded."[14] With these tales of genteel conduct toward Mexicans and aggressiveness toward Native groups, Wool burnished his reputation as an officer who protected civilians.

The US Army's approach toward conquering Mexican women and land drew from a unique mythos of captivity and redemption. That narrative took shape out of both an older tradition of captivity narratives dating to the colonial era and recent stories of women taken by the Comanche. Accounts like Mary Rowlandson's, taken by Narragansetts in 1676 during King Philip's War, shaped the powerful cultural imaginary

---

[13] Baylies, *Major General Wool's Campaign in Mexico*, 65.
[14] Ibid., 10.

of a white woman seized by "savages" for centuries.[15] Rowlandson's *A True History of the Captivity and Restoration of Mrs. Mary Rowlandson*, published in 1682, helped launch the genre, which gave voice to a fear of helpless Euro-American women in the hands of Indigenous men. By 1800, captivity narratives were a "staple source" of entertainment. The "Indian" in these stories was "the consummate villain, the beast who hatcheted fathers, smashed the skulls of infants, and carried off mothers to make them into squaws." The evolving captivity narrative followed the army as it transitioned from forced removal in the 1830s to warfare and conquest in the 1840s.[16]

These stories emphasized white women's supposed innocence and need for protection, justifying extraordinary violence against Native peoples. In Northern Mexico, Comanche power added specificity to this generic fear of stolen white women. When the US invaded Mexico, the narrative of redemption specific to the nation's southwestern frontier – that of white women escaping Native, usually Comanche, captivity – was well known.

The genre of captivity narratives was an archetypal part of US culture. It comprised a set of "foundation texts," perhaps the "first American literary form dominated by women's experiences as captives, storytellers, writers, and readers." They had long shadows. Rowlandson's story served as the basis for the reigning "Indian play" of the 1830s, *Metamora* – over a century later. Close connections remained between the historical and the sensational, and Nancy Isenberg explains that "captivity narratives provided the foundation for romantic fiction." Fiction justified "white conquest" by reinforcing "Indians' ethical inferiority to the white race through vivid accounts of their acts of butchery and torture, and a primal lust for the scalps of white maidens."[17] This had obvious resonance for US soldiers in Mexico, who had more chances to rescue captives than US civilians.

The Second US–Seminole War spawned the latest, Mary Godfrey's *An Authentic Narrative of the Seminole War; and of the Miraculous Escape of Mrs. Mary Godfrey, and Her Four Female Children*, published in 1836 as a pamphlet novel. Unlike Mary Rowlandson, a real person whose account historians generally find accurate, Mary Godfrey may not

---

[15] Lisa Tanya Brooks, *Our Beloved Kin: A New History of King Philip's War* (New Haven: Yale University Press, 2018), 253.
[16] Pearce, *Savagism and Civilization*, 58.
[17] Derounian-Stodola, *Women's Indian Captivity Narratives*, xi.

have existed. The story came with a massacre-heavy abbreviated history of the Second US–Seminole War and describes Godfrey's flight into the wilderness with four young daughters. In an example of the protean quality of the genre, it is a captivity narrative without a capture. Godfrey and her children successfully flee the scene of the massacre and return to civilization with the help of a Black Seminole man who took pity on her and explained that he had two young children still enslaved by white people.[18]

The following year brought Dolly Webster's story. Webster wrote that capture forced her to live with "the Comanche Indians, a fierce and bloodthirsty race to be taken to the wilderness, far beyond the ken of civilization, without even a white companion to associate with." She emphasized the brutality of Comanche women especially, a stark contrast to the innocence that imbued white portrayals of Seminole women: the Comanches "appeared vicious and hostile; particularly the squaws, who were painted black" and who "claimed the privilege of inflicting blows on me."[19]

In contrast, captivity narratives like Webster's portrayed Mexican women as civilized and nearly white. Webster wrote that a sixteen-year-old "young Mexican lady" was one of her companions in captivity. She had fair skin, light hair, and spoke Spanish and Italian. Webster concluded that "She appeared to be a young lady of fine accomplishments, which she retained although she had been among the Indians so long; she was certainly as polite and agreeable a female as ever I saw. From all that I could learn, she must have been the daughter of some wealthy Mexican gentleman."[20] Webster referred to the Mexican women held as captives along with her as "ladies" but described Comanche women as "squaws" who were more "Indian" than woman.

Webster eventually escaped from captivity and made her way to San Antonio, where Mexican women helped her. "An old Mexican lady" cared for her, and the "ladies" of San Antonio gave her 190 dollars in silver to help her return home. In her narrative, Webster offered "grateful acknowledgments to the humane and hospitable people of San Antonio."[21] In Webster's estimation, her shared plight with female

---

[18] Ibid., 214–15, xii, 222–23. For a close reading of King Philip's War, and Mary Rowlandson, see Brooks, *Our Beloved Kin: A New History of King Philip's War*.
[19] Dolbeare, *The Captivity of Dolly Webster*, 8, 9. "Squaw" is derogatory and only used in quotation.
[20] Ibid., 10.
[21] Webster also received money "subscribed by the gentlemen" and clothes from for Webster and her young daughter, with whom she escaped. Ibid., 33–34. See also: Dysart, "Mexican Women in San Antonio."

4 Rescuing the Enemy: Mexican Women and the US Army

Mexican captives, and her kind treatment by Mexican women, whitened and elevated them.

Webster's gratitude echoed how Rachel Plummer (author of a similar captivity narrative) thanked a US woman who assisted her in Santa Fe after Plummer's 1839 capture by Comanches. She wrote, "I have no language to express my gratitude to Mrs. Donoho. I found in her a mother, to direct me in that strange land, a sister to condole with me in my misfortune, and offer new scenes of amusement to me, to revive my mind." These US women faced dangers well known to Mexicans, who witnessed the Comanche destruction of villages such as Salado and Las Animas even as the US Army marched across Northern Mexico.

The captivity narratives that preceded the US–Mexican War demarcated a sharpening line between civilized women with valid claims to protection and "savage" women who were beyond redemption. Sarah Ann Horn referenced this distinction in her 1839 captivity narrative when she recalled her Comanche mistress giving her "one of the [killed] Spanish lady's dresses, which I was glad to put on, though it was deeply crimsoned with blood." This interaction, and Horn donning both the Mexican woman's dress and her status as a captive, joined her with Mexican women's plight. Both were civilized captives defined in opposition to Indigenous captors. Another captivity narrative from the years soon after War on Mexico held the same distinction. Jane Adaline Wilson, captured in 1853, wrote she expected compassion from Comanche women as fellow females. Instead, they were "the cause of the new cruelties I now began to experience."[22] Such stories deepened US hatred of captive-taking Native societies and set in motion the regular army's shift from capturing (Seminole) women in Florida to rescuing Euro-American women in Mexico.

While narratives of Comanche captivity led soldiers to embrace the rescue of Euro-American women in general, a very different kind of captivity narrative shaped a specific image of kind and obliging Mexican women. In a break with the traditional reports of female captives, this was an all-male group – Texans and US men held prisoner by the Mexican government. The 1841 Texas-Santa Fe Expedition was a disorganized

---

[22] Parker and Plummer, *Parkers Narrative and History of Texas; to Which Is Appended Mrs. Plummer's Narrative*, 29; Balbontín, *La Invasión Norteamericana*, 21–22, August 30-31, 1847. Translation by the author; Wilson, *The Captivity and Sufferings of Mrs. Jane Adaline Wilson*, 13. See also: Meyer, *Mary Donoho*.

effort by the Republic of Texas to bring northern New Mexico under its control. It failed, and New Mexican governor Manuel Armijo, whom Kearny would force out of Santa Fe just a few years later, imprisoned its members and force marched them 2,000 miles to Mexico City.

The men eventually returned to US custody, leaving Mexico with a deep hatred of Mexican authorities and profound sense of gratitude to Mexican women. Journalist George Kendall noted the "universal kindness and hospitality of the *women* of New Mexico" who regularly fed and clothed them. Kendall, future founder of the New Orleans *Picayune*, published a popular account of the experience. Upon imprisonment, Kendall wrote, "that the women all pitied us was evident; for the commiserating exclamation of *pobrecitos!* as they gave us bread, cheese, and such food as they had at hand, fell from their tongues in softest and most feeling tones." Kendall coupled praise of Mexican women with condemnation of Mexican men, continuing, "They knew their husbands and brothers, and knowing them, felt that little of mercy or kindness could we expect at their hands." Captivity narratives filtered into the "Indian war romances" popularized before the war in Mexico. Richard Slotkin asserts that these romances made "the treatment of captives" into the "moral litmus test of class and racial character."[23] When men like Kendall applied this formula, Mexican women passed. Mexican men failed.

Kendall wrote, "Nothing can be more touchingly sweet than the pronunciation of [pobrecito] by a Spanish or Mexican woman. The tones come fresh and warm from the heart when an object worthy of compassion presents itself." The prisoners always considered themselves worthy. Kendall described how, on being marched past the town of San Miguel, "A tolerably well-dressed woman came running towards us from a small house, bringing a bottle of the country whiskey, and saying that it was for our use. This we drank on the spot, and as we thanked the good-hearted creature for her kindness, she appeared to feel deeply for us in our misfortunes." Kendall contrasted cruel male behavior with merciful women, writing that "even after we had been hurried off by our inhuman guard, the woman still remained to gaze upon us, looking her last at the *pobrecitos*, whom she really thought the sun would not set upon alive."[24]

---

[23] Kendall, *Narrative of the Texan Sante Fé Expedition*, 388–89; Slotkin, *The Fatal Environment*, 194.

[24] Kendall, *Narrative of the Texan Sante Fé Expedition*, 393. US troops made near identical remarks during the war. Volunteer Frank Edwards wrote that as he lay in a sick wagon, while his unit moved into Saltillo, he "beheld the prettiest girl I saw in all Mexico,

4 Rescuing the Enemy: Mexican Women and the US Army

Kendall's tale, a man's captivity narrative, did more than help create an archetypal kind Mexican woman who embraced US friendship. It began a merger, in US minds, of male archetypes. The "savage" Native captor and the brutal Mexican guerrilla blended into the composite image of a violent, brown-skinned criminal.[25]

Members of the Texas-Santa Fe Expedition, many of whom like Kendall participated in the US–Mexican War a few years later, left Mexico with the impression that "the almost universal brutality and cold-heartedness of the men of New Mexico are in strange contrast with the kind disposition and tender sympathies exhibited by all classes of the women." This dyad became a national one as Kendall's account – first published in 1844 and followed by the successful travelogue *Narrative of an Expedition across the Great Southwestern Prairies* in 1845 – grew in popularity.[26]

The army's experience as captors in Florida blended with Mexican frontier captivity narratives – George Kendall's as much as Sarah Horn's – and produced a different approach to protecting enemy women in Mexico. There, rescue allowed the army to draw a highly favorable contrast to raids by groups like the Comanche, a practice US troops reviled. With anger, soldiers noted the evidence. They helped a Mexican boy redeemed from "savages in the deserts of California" who killed his father and "carried off his mother." They camped at local haciendas and heard how their host "had recently lost a son to Navajo raids, and several peons had wives and children captured."[27] It is even more striking, then, that as late as 1842, the army had itself pursued a strategy of capturing women. Yet, by 1846, the army spent many resources (especially ink) on rescuing enemy women in Mexico.

---

standing at the door of a mean-looking dwelling in the main street. Her complexion, of marble whiteness, showed delicately a slight rosy color in the cheek, while her beautiful large dark swimming eyes, with their accompanying heavy lashes and eyebrows, rested with a pitying expression upon me." He concluded, "Oh the beauty of the exquisite Spanish word *pobrecito*, (poor fellow!) when heard from such lips – the sweetest of all sweet sounds." Edwards, *A Campaign in New Mexico with Colonel Doniphan*, 147.
[25] Halleck, *International Law*, 1878, 2:6–8, Chapter XVIII, Paragraphs 8–9. For more on longstanding and violent consequences of affixing criminality to Mexican men, see: Carrigan, *Forgotten Dead*; Martinez, *The Injustice Never Leaves You*.
[26] Kendall, *Narrative of the Texan Sante Fé Expedition*, 388–89, 393–94; Kendall, *Narrative of an Expedition across the Great Southwestern Prairies*.
[27] Thirtieth Congress, First Session, *House of Representatives Mexican War Correspondence*, 1848, April 5, 1847; Abert, *Examination of New Mexico in the Years 1846–'47*, 508, December 18, 1847.

Throughout Mexico, the US Army's occupation rested on claims that it protected Mexicans who accepted US rule. Soldiers understood women to be the group that most categorically posed no threat, reflecting Emerich de Vattel's famous conclusion that although women in an enemy country were indeed enemies, they were "enemies who make no resistance." Because occupation required that the army protect civilians, US units in the raiding country of Northern Mexico rescued enemy women. Officers frequently referenced Mexican requests demanding the army make good on its promise to protect. West Point graduate and regular army infantry officer Lieutenant Napoleon Dana wrote, "The people of Mier actually asked for a force there to guard them against the Comanches, and a hundred men were sent up to look after them."[28] But the rhetoric of rescue often flowed more readily than army assistance.

In many cases, efforts to redeem captives or prevent their seizure were decidedly limited in the context of comparatively grandiose claims that the army would correct Mexican failures to protect the north. Still, it did have meaningful successes. Zachary Taylor reported his successful redemption of a Mexican woman, two girls, and a boy from a group of "Lipans, Tonkaways, and Mescaleros" encamped near his army. He learned the group had Mexican captives, demanded them, and received them "to the number of four." Elsewhere, soldiers attempted and failed to rescue captives and punish captors. Army officer William Emory noted Mexican news of a Navajo attack on the town of Polvadera and how the army dispatched a company of dragoons. The dragoons arrived after the raiding party had, "besides horses, carried off fifteen or sixteen of the prettiest women" and decided they could not help.[29] Sometimes, officers merely reported such raids and the Mexican failure to stop them. Emory wrote, "Today we have a report, which appears well authenticated, that the Mexicans taking courage at the expectations of protection from the United States, had the temerity to resist a levy [from a Native group], and the consequence was, the loss of six men killed and two wounded."

At other times, officers prioritized balancing complex alliances with many Native power brokers over redeeming Mexican captives. Some gave instructions that were "very pointed – to exercise great caution in all matters relating to alleged Indian depredations." When the army had

---

[28] Vattel, *Law of Nations*, 351, Book III, Chapter VIII, Paragraph 145; Dana, *Monterrey Is Ours!*, 115, September 4, 1846.

[29] Emory, *Notes of a Military Reconnaissance*, 49–50, October 3 and 4, 1847; Thirtieth Congress, First Session, *House of Representatives Mexican War Correspondence*, 1848, 114, November 19, 1845.

4 Rescuing the Enemy: Mexican Women and the US Army 159

to cross inhospitable terrain, it needed Native allies and set aside the policy of protecting Mexicans. Many days into an arduous desert crossing, Emory wrote, the "mules were now fast failing, and the road before us unknown. These Indians, if willing, could supply us with mules and show us the road."[30] The logic of protection was most valuable in Mexican settlements and least helpful in the heartlands of Native power.

In contrast with the Comanche, Navajo, and Apache, Emory described the Pimas, favored by the army, as a "peaceful and industrious race" that was "in possession of a beautiful and fertile basin. Living remote from the civilized world, they are seldom visited by whites, and then only by those in distress, to whom they generously furnish horses and food." Of raiding tribes, Emory found their great power shameful. He marveled that "a savage and uncivilized tribe, armed with the bow and lance," held "as tributary powers three fertile and once flourishing states, Chihuahua, Sonora, and Durango, peopled by a Christian race, countrymen of the immortal Cortez." Emory claimed that "these states were at one time flourishing, but such has been the devastation and alarm spread by these children of the mountains, that they are now losing population, commerce and manufactures at a rate which, if not soon arrested, must leave them uninhabited."[31] Soldiers saw in the Pima their hopes for how US control could civilize the region (Figures 4.1 and 4.2).

Although army officers generally saw themselves as the primary actors in the story of Northern Mexico, when groups like the Pima encountered men like Emory, they probably found them minor, temporary figures. The region retained "native ground" characteristics where Indigenous people shaped relationships more than colonizers.[32] Yet, what Emory and his peers saw in the Pima world was not a successful Native culture but a little oasis of US-style civilization. Emory noted their "peaceful disposition is not the result of incapacity for war, for they are at all times enabled to meet and vanquish the Apaches in battle." He continued, "when we passed, they had just returned from an expedition in the Apache country

---

[30] Thirtieth Congress, First Session, *House of Representatives Mexican War Correspondence*, 1848, 114, November 19, 1845; Emory, *Notes of a Military Reconnaissance*, 70, October 31, 1847.
[31] Emory, *Notes of a Military Reconnaissance*, 76, November 5, 1847.
[32] The concept of a "native ground" comes from Kathleen Duval. Duval uses the concept to describe the Arkansas Valley from the sixteenth to the early nineteenth century. She argues that rather than accommodating or resisting Europeans, "Indians drew a successive series of European empires into local patterns of land and resource allocation, sustenance, goods exchange, gender relations, diplomacy, and warfare." DuVal, *The Native Ground*, 5.

FIGURE 4.1 "Pimo Village with a group of Indians," watercolor by Samuel Chamberlain, circa 1861. As in Captain Johnston's description below, regular army enlisted man and fellow dragoon Samuel Chamberlain's painting shows Pima women engaged in domestic pursuits, dressed in clean skirts of cloth and grass. Chamberlain inserted himself in the foreground, sketching. Of note, all Chamberlain illustrations used in this book come from the West Point Museum's original illustrated journal and use the corresponding page numbers for that handwritten version. For ease of reference, cited text is from the printed version of the journal. See also: Goetzmann, *Sam Chamberlain's Mexican War*. Courtesy of the West Point Museum Collection, United States Military Academy.

FIGURE 4.2 "Comanches on the War Path," watercolor by Samuel Chamberlain, circa 1861. Chamberlain's painting of Comanches "on the war path" evokes the sense of danger many felt when in the vicinity of Comanche raiding parties. Courtesy of the West Point Museum Collection, United States Military Academy.

4 Rescuing the Enemy: Mexican Women and the US Army

to revenge some thefts and other outrages, with eleven scalps and thirteen prisoners." With apparent approval, Emory wrote, "the prisoners are sold as slaves to the Mexicans." Officers seemed not to mind when Pima raided other Native groups. What mattered was they abstained from harming Mexican and US civilians. While raiding groups may "live principally by plundering the Mexicans," the Pimas, though "surrounded by the warlike Navajos and the thieving Apaches…nevertheless till their soil in peace and security."[33] Soldiers saw a reflection of Anglo-American ideals: men who were ready for war but loved peace.

Emory also wrote positively of the Maricopa, a group allied to the Pima. He found the women joyful and noted how they "made the air ring with their jokes and merry peals of laughter." He also appreciated their modesty:

Mr. Bestor's spectacles were a great source of merriment. Some of them formed the idea that with their aid, he could see through their cotton blankets. They would shrink and hide behind each other at his approach. At length, I placed the spectacles on the nose of an old woman, who became acquainted with their use and explained it to the others.

First Dragoon officer Captain Abraham Johnston wrote that

for want of an interpreter, an old woman with a fine countenance was taken; she had half a watermelon in her arms, and was naked, except a cloth from her waist to her knees – a state of nudity which would seem inconsistent with modesty, but here she proved that modesty is independent of refined taste, for she took upon herself the office of interpreter and performed it reluctantly, but with a very becoming modesty of manner.

This officer also emphasized the cleanliness and charm of Pima and Maricopa girls: "a parcel of young girls, with long hair streaming to their waists, and no other covering than a clean white cotton blanket folded around their middle and extending to their knees, were merry as any group of like age and sex to be met within our own country."[34]

Even better, the groups seemed to adhere to US standards of female chastity. Emory concluded from his stay that "they have a high regard for morality and punish transgressions more by public opinion than by fines

---

[33] Emory, *Notes of a Military Reconnaissance*, 86, November 8, 1847; 133, October 8, 1847.
[34] Ibid., 87, November 13–14, 1847; Johnston, *Journal of Captain A. R. Johnston*, 601, 612–13, November 13 and 29, 1846. Johnston (West Point Class of 1835) died days later at the battle of San Pasqual on December 6, 1846. Heitman, *Historical Register*, 374; Cullum, *Biographical Register*, 1:477.

or corporal punishments." By this, he meant that their marriage practices fit US ideas: "Polygamy is unknown amongst them, and the crime of adultery, punished with such fearful penalties amongst Indians nations generally, is here almost unknown and is punished by the contempt of the relatives and associates of the guilty parties." Emory's experiences led him to conclude that this was an ideal Indigenous group – peaceful agriculturalists who helped the US and respected marriage.[35]

Soldiers believed agriculturalists superior to raiders. Dr. John Griffin, who accompanied Kearny's expedition, reflected in his diary on "the honesty of my friends the Pimas Indians." Yet, binary distinctions between "savage" raiding and "civilized" cultivation limited US ability to interpret agriculture and pastoralism as evidence of civilization when practiced by Native groups who retained Mexican captives. Enlisted Missouri volunteer Jacob Robinson wrote of a Navajo leader called Sandeval, who guided Doniphan's expedition through part of New Mexico. Robinson described the beauty of the man's lands, full of his 5,000 sheep and 100 horses, and wrote that "a view of the green grass and fine trees, with his beautiful fields of corn and wheat, make one almost forget that it is the abode of an untutored Indian."[36] Although many US troops aspired to this sort of prosperity and economic independence, none of it made Sandeval more than a rude "savage" to Robinson.

Perhaps this was in part because, in the United States, men were meant to till the soil. In contrast, Apache and Navajo culture traditionally entrusted women with growing and gathering food. It was not only the evidence of agriculture that led Emory to favor the Pima over the "warlike Navajos and the thieving Apaches." He also assumed Pima organization of labor and sex reflected his ideas of gender. Pima men "till[ed] the soil," and Pima women behaved with "becoming modesty of manner," demonstrating sexual virtue through monogamous marriage.[37]

An account of the Doniphan Expedition offers an example of how the army – not only regulars but volunteers – explicitly used captivity narratives to highlight how pursuing the Comanche conferred legitimacy. With his First Missouri Regiment of Mounted Volunteers, Colonel Alexander Doniphan led the most famous volunteer campaign of the war. When one of his officers, Captain John Reid, arrived in Parras, a town in the

---

[35] Emory, *Notes of a Military Reconnaissance*, 133, October 8, 1847.
[36] Griffin, "A Doctor Comes to California," 52; Robinson, *A Journal of the Santa Fe Expedition under Colonel Doniphan*, 56, October 24, 1846.
[37] Emory, *Notes of a Military Reconnaissance*, 132–34. Washington, October 8, 1847.

northern province of Coahuila, locals told of a raid just made by the Comanche. They took nineteen "girls and boys into captivity" in addition to horses, mules, money, and property. Townspeople throughout Northern Mexico sought all the help they could get, and the people of Parras requested assistance from Reid. The army claimed that "although they were considered to be enemies to the Americans, it did not become the magnanimity of the American soldiers to see them robbed and murdered by a lawless band of savages, the avowed enemies both of the Mexicans and Americans." Officers justified their actions by insisting lawful warfare meant punishing unlawful captors: "Captain Reid undertook to recover the innocent captives and chastise the brutal savages." The soldiers said they fought the raiding party for two hours until the Comanche "made good their [re]treat" and Reid's party recovered the children and spoils. Missouri volunteer Jacob Robinson specified that they released eighteen "Spanish captives," twelve boys and six girls.[38]

The story of Reid's counter-raid was a short morality play. The author argued, "those whose moral scruples induce them to doubt the propriety of Captain Reid's brilliant sortie upon the Indians" should consider "that the Comanches have rarely failed to murder and torture in the most cruel manner, without discrimination, all Americans who have unfortunately fallen into their hands." He explicitly referenced captivity narratives: "The Comanches are our uncompromising enemies. Read the brutal treatment Mrs. Horn and others received from them, and you can but justify Capt. Reid's conduct."[39] The author's use of Sarah Horn as casus bello demonstrated how the army conflated captive US and Mexican women. Linking female captives across racial and national boundaries, the army whitened Mexican women into valid subjects of protection.

The author believed Colonel Doniphan deserved "the gratitude of both Mexicans and Americans, for the chastisement he visited upon the heads of these barbarous wretches," again othering the Native groups who took captives. To conclude this narrative, the author described how the people of Parras offered a letter of thanks for "rescuing Christian beings from the cruelty of the most inhuman savages."[40] Thus soldiers could receive the gratitude of their national enemies while invading that enemy's country and accept such words as nothing more than their just due.

[38] Hughes, *Doniphan's Expedition*, 131, May 18, 1847; Robinson, *A Journal of the Santa Fe Expedition under Colonel Doniphan*, 85, May 13, 1847.
[39] Hughes, *Doniphan's Expedition*, 131, May 18, 1847. Letter from Parras signed Don Ignacio Arrabe.
[40] Ibid.

The US occupation of Northern Mexico drew legitimacy from signs of – or claims to – Mexican gratitude. Army paternalism and its concern with redeeming captives grew alongside the oft-repeated dictum that the army was a benevolent occupying force and would protect the Mexican people in exchange for non-resistance to US military aims. Even if Mexicans were an enemy population, paternalistic officers displayed their gentility by redeeming captives. It was important for officers to act with mercy and forbearance when exercising power – a desirable public image for paternalists in any context, whether as husbands ruling over wives, as officers overseeing soldiers, masters controlling enslaved laborers, or leaders of an occupying army ruling an occupied population.

In August of 1846 as Kearny crossed New Mexico, a trail of pronouncements in his wake, Francis Lieber gave a commencement speech later published as *The Character of the Gentleman*. Lieber emphasized a chivalric ethic in war, and the importance of "a gentlemanly spirit" in "officers, and, indeed, in all the combatants toward their enemies, whenever an opportunity offers itself." The same month, Zachary Taylor noted a comparable obligation toward Mexicans in US-occupied Matamoros. Taylor wrote the Army Adjutant General that "I regret to report that the Comanche Indians have been committing extensive depredations upon the Mexican inhabitants near Mier." He deemed "it a paramount duty to protect the Mexican citizens from their ravages, and to apprehend and punish them if possible."[41]

Across time and space, Taylor and Lieber engaged with questions of what it meant to be chivalric in war. Lieber requested that gentlemanly protection and mercy be extended even to enemies; Taylor noted the practical use of attacking Comanches to redeem Mexican women. If he did not pursue the captors, "the cry would instantly be raised that the Indians are our allies" and disrupt a functioning occupation in which "the inhabitants are well disposed towards us." Thus, Taylor sent a company to Mier temporarily "to give security to the inhabitants, who have recently suffered from the depredations of the Indians."[42]

---

[41] Lieber, *The Character of the Gentleman*, 33, 72–74, 81, 84, 91; Thirtieth Congress, First Session, *House of Representatives Mexican War Correspondence*, 1848, 402, August 3, 1846, Taylor to Adjutant General.

[42] Thirtieth Congress, First Session, *House of Representatives Mexican War Correspondence*, 1848, 402, August 3, 1846, Taylor to Adjutant General, Matamoros; 408, August 10, 1846, Taylor to Adjutant General. Many Mexicans went further, comparing US volunteers to Comanche raiders who destroyed and pillaged. Guardino, *The Dead March: A History of the Mexican–American War*, 2017, 216.

4 Rescuing the Enemy: Mexican Women and the US Army 165

The presence of a supposedly uncivilized threat helped the US depict its occupation as necessary.

Therefore, Kearny's subordinate, Major Philip St. George Cooke, wrote to the Governor of Sonora that he "did not come as an enemy of the *people* whom you govern; they have received only kindness at my hands." Sonora did not contribute to Mexico's war on the US for "the excellent reasons that all her resources were necessary to her defense from the incessant attacks of savages; that the central government gave her no protection, and was therefore entitled to no support." The corollary was the US did provide protection and thus *was* entitled to local support. Protection prompted legitimacy.

Equally, protection delegitimized antagonists. Cooke continued, "To this might have been added that *Mexico supports a war upon Sonora*; for I have seen New Mexicans within her boundary, trading for the spoil of her people, taken by murderous, cowardly Indians." When officers like Cooke advocated for violence against Apaches, they took up a Mexican approach. The Spanish, and later the Mexican government in Sonora, had long sanctioned payments for Apache scalps. In addition to bounty payments for warriors, scalp hunters also received bounties for scalps of Apache boys and girls under fourteen.[43]

Native wives' status as enslavers of Euro-American captives made such women complicit in raiding, allowing soldiers to strip Indigenous women of female innocence. This consequence was clear in army language describing an Apache woman who formed part of a trading party from which the army hoped to buy seven mules. Her "garrulity and interference in every trade was the annoyance of Major Swords, who had charge of the trading, but the amusement of the bystanders." This woman's active participation in negotiations came accompanied with detailed descriptions: "She had on a gauze-like dress, trimmed with the richest and most costly Brussels lace, pillaged no doubt from some fandango-going belle of Sonora; she straddled a fine grey horse, and whenever her blanket dropped from her shoulders, her tawny form could be seen through the transparent gauze."

She cemented herself as a "savage" captor by wearing a captured dress and displaying an aggressive manner: "after she had sold her mule, she was anxious to sell her horse, and careened about to show

---

[43] Cooke, *Report of Lieut. Col. P. St. George Cooke of His March*, Appendix, December 18, 1846, "Report to Kearny" including quotes from a letter to the Governor of Sonora; Stevens, "The Apache Menace in Sonora, 1831–1849," 220.

his qualities – at one time she charged at full speed up a steep hill. In this, the fastenings of her dress broke, and her bare back was exposed to the crowd, who ungallantly raised a shout of laughter." Yet, she was "Nothing daunted" by this and instead "wheeled short round with surprising dexterity, and seeing the mischief done, coolly slipped the dress from her arms and tucked it between her seat and the saddle." Emory concluded, "In this state of nudity she rode through the camp, from fire to fire, until, at last, attaining the object of her ambition, a soldier's red flannel shirt, she made her adieu in that new costume."[44] When soldiers conflated Native men and women in anti-Indigenous logic, it pushed Native women farther outside the scope of protection, which narrowed to focus on Mexican women.

ROMANTICIZING RESCUE

This shift was most clear where war hastened changes in marriage patterns of US frontiersmen from a preference for US–Native alliances to an emerging norm of US–Mexican partnerships. Romance came before rescue. The cliché of the sexually attractive and available Spanish woman had long existed in army culture. During the Second US–Seminole War, army surgeon Jacob Motte described the Minorcan women of Spanish Florida with their "brilliant black eyes" and glibly defined marrying in the "Spanish mode" as taking a woman "on trial for six months" before the wedding. He appreciated the "dazzling beauty" around him, the "rich black tresses and olive complexions" of "Spanish descent," and the "lighter locks and whiter skins of America's daughters" in like measure, concluding he "was in Elysium." In a comment sometimes echoed by soldiers after Santa Fe's fandangos, Motte found that "the St. Augustine ladies certainly danced more gracefully... than any of my fair countrywomen" in the northern US.[45] But powerful US men, and powerful New Mexican women, did not marry one another to indulge in fantasies.

Kit Carson, who participated in Kearny's conquests of New Mexico and California, embodied changing US ideas of compatibility. In his life before the US–Mexican War, Carson married Native women. In 1835, he wed an Arapaho woman named Waanibe, or Singing Grass. She died several years later. They had two daughters, one of whom survived early

[44] Emory, *Notes of a Military Reconnaissance*, 73, November 3, 1847.
[45] Motte, *Journey into Wilderness*, 4, 62, 111–12.

childhood. Carson sent the girl, Adaline, to his sisters in Missouri and then to a Catholic seminary. He later married a Cheyenne woman called Making-Out-Road, who divorced him "after the fashion of her people, by putting his belongings outside their tipi near Bent's Fort."[46] Just a few years later, in 1843, Carson married a New Mexican woman.

Through his marriage to Maria Josefa Jaramillo – which required his conversion from Protestantism to Roman Catholicism – Carson transitioned from alliances with Native women to an enduring partnership with an old New Mexican family.[47] A few years earlier, in 1835, Josefa's sister Maria Ignacia married Charles Bent, another influential US man. Bent's family operated numerous trading posts in the region, including the important Bent's Fort, whose success relied on marriages between US traders and Native women. Yet, Charles Bent married Ignacia and became the civilian governor of New Mexico in 1846 when Stephen Watts Kearny left Santa Fe to conquer California.

On a frontier rapidly coming under US supervision, men like Bent and Carson who only years earlier sought partnerships with Native women now understood Mexicans as ideal wives. Like the Jaramillo sisters, some elite New Mexican women choose to embrace this dynamic and profit from US commerce. Others rejected it. Historian Deena Gonzalez notes that US men's accounts vastly overstated the willingness of Spanish-Mexican women to assimilate. She argues that colonization impoverished such women. Still, although fewer than ten percent of the female population married US men, that was enough for US powerbrokers to construct an identity. With those few critical marriages, US officers and officials could describe themselves as rescuers of beloved Mexican women.[48]

This tradition of elite US–Mexican marriages started decades earlier and increased as Anglo-Americans began to travel to New Mexico in increasing numbers. Thus, Stephen Kearny's assertion that his forces came "as protectors – not as conquerors."[49] One cannot conquer what

---

[46] Dunlay, *Kit Carson and the Indians*, 57. For more on Carson and these relationships, see Susan Lee Johnson's recent book: Johnson, *Writing Kit Carson*. Or, see Richard Slotkin's description of the Carson myth: Slotkin, *The Fatal Environment*, 198–207.

[47] Johnson, *Writing Kit Carson*, 16, 38.

[48] Gonzalez, *Refusing the Favor*, 5, 12. For marriage patterns between Mexican women and US men in California, see: Casas, *Married to a Daughter of the Land*. For mixed-descent Native families, to include at Bent's Fort, see: Hyde, *Born of Lakes and Plains: Mixed-Descent Peoples and the Making of the American West*.

[49] Emory, *Notes of a Military Reconnaissance*, 26–27, August 14, 1846. Kearny said this in Las Vegas, New Mexico, on August 14, 1846.

one already possesses. US presence in New Mexico, cemented by such marriages, generated a nexus of legitimacy in support of US territorial ambitions. The logic of protection, salient even in its generic form (the soldierly protection of women), gained force when applied to the special protection a husband owed his wife.

Dragoon officer A. R. Johnston emphasized Carson's commitment to his New Mexican wife and family. When offered a chance to return home to New Mexico, Carson wanted to take it but concluded that his duty lay with the army. Johnston reflected that "it requires a brave man to give up his private feelings thus for the public good, but Carson is one such! Honor to him for it!"[50] Whether soldiers rescued or married Mexican women, they bolstered army manhood at the cost of Mexican manhood. When US soldiers saved Mexican women from Native raids or maintained relationships with Mexican women, they defeated the Mexican army not simply as soldiers but as men. Army protection implied that Mexican men failed as protectors and Mexican women desired US partners. Although the army position relative to enemy *women* had changed from captor in Florida to savior and partner in Mexico, another relationship remained constant. In both Florida and Mexico, the logic of protection rendered enemy *men* impotent.

Emory, for instance, lamented Mexican men's treatment of a pregnant woman. He wrote, "We visited the camp of our Mexican friends, whom the general determined to release, and found there was a woman with the party in the agonies of childbirth. She was at once furnished from our stores with all the comforts we possessed. This poor creature had been dragged along, in her delicate situation, over a fearful desert."[51] While soldiers laughed at the skilled Apache woman who traded mules to them, they failed to see this Mexican woman as similarly capable. They considered her helpless: a vessel for protection.

US occupation and its norm of rescue spurred an explosion of wartime stories. Authors wrote into existence an array of beautiful Mexican heroines who accepted US lovers. Such works, written for large popular audiences, retained a vital element of the captivity narrative – rescue – while moving beyond that classic genre. The stories published just before the War on Mexico focused on Native raiders capturing white women, but the war produced a new literature. The latest stories asserted that

---

[50] Johnston, *Journal of Captain A. R. Johnston*, 572, October 6, 1846.
[51] Emory, *Notes of a Military Reconnaissance*, 97, November 24, 1847.

Mexican men were criminals and cowards, in contrast to noble and desirable Mexican women.[52]

Enabled by "twin revolutions" in transportation and communication that swept from the US into Mexico in the army's footsteps, military campaigns soon prompted cultural exchange. Soldiers' letters appeared in hometown newspapers, while books, wartime papers, and pamphlet novels found their way into soldiers' knapsacks. Soldiers, like US civilians, bought low-cost printed material made with improved printing presses and cheaply manufactured paper. New developments such as telegraph lines, steamboats, the national proliferation of penny presses, and networks of express riders enabled rapid transfers of information between the frontlines and the home front. The war proved a catalyst for further change when six New York newspapers banded together to transmit news from Mexico more speedily, creating in 1848 the Associated Press wire service. As prices fell, circulation boomed. The US overcame the "tyranny of distance," and troops in Mexico gained unprecedented access to popular media.[53]

Wartime papers, founded by soldiers who were also printers and by US civilians following the army, flourished. Soon, troops throughout Mexico had access to local war news and US national news. Soldiers in Northern Mexico might read the *American Flag* in Matamoros, the *Picket Guard* in Saltillo, the *American Pioneer* and *The Gazette* in Monterrey, or the *Anglo Saxon* in Chihuahua. *The New Mexican*, a Santa Fe newspaper that continues in circulation today, published its first edition just after the war in 1849 to serve a growing Anglo-American community.

Soldiers wrote directly to newspapers and to families who passed correspondence along to local publications. George Davis, who appears in the following chapter as the recorder in Isaac Kirk's trial, sent letters

---

[52] Jaime Javier Rodríguez posits a three-part process where the war's literature began with chivalric "stories in which Anglo and Mexican enemies are literally part of the same family," shifted to frontier stories, "an intermediate moment in which Anglos and Mexicans test each other's national loyalty," and then became western or bandit tales, "a final and more enduring zone that fixes and fixates on the features of the iconic Mexican bandit, a familiar mode of plotting and characterological structure strongly aligned with images of terrorists." Rodríguez's emphasis on the figure of the Mexican bandit as an increasingly "absolute villain" reflects the criminalization process this chapter charts. See also, Rodríguez's appendix of novelette titles. Rodríguez, *The Literatures of the U.S.–Mexican War*, 18, 82, 255–56.

[53] Howe, *What Hath God Wrought*, 4, 225, 627, 748, 854. For the communications revolution, see: John, *Spreading the News*; John, *Network Nation Inventing American Telecommunications*.

published by the *Alton Telegraph & Democratic Review* of Alton, Illinois.[54] Sometimes, soldiers captured imaginations and hearts across the nation, as with stories about the "Heroine of Monterrey," an archetypal Mexican heroine, merciful and brave. Her legend was born under fire during the Battle of Monterrey. The tale includes apocryphal elements, yet expresses an essential truth – Mexican women were present on battlefields, usually as soldaderas, camp followers who provided domestic services. Still, sentiment, not accuracy, was the aim of those who shaped the legend. To that end, the *Louisville Journal* printed a soldier's letter home, soon reprinted across the US.

The soldier described how in the heat of combat, he noticed a Mexican woman carrying bread and water to the wounded of both armies. He "saw the ministering angel raise the head of a wounded man, give him water and food, and then bind up his ghastly wound with a handkerchief she took from her own head." She went back for more supplies, and "As she was returning on her mission of mercy, to comfort other wounded persons, I heard the report of a gun, and saw the poor innocent creature fall dead." He pondered how a soldier could have done such a thing and concluded that it must have been "an accidental shot that struck her. I would not be willing to believe otherwise." Still, it made him "sick to my heart; and, turning from the scene, I involuntarily raised my eyes toward heaven and thought, Great God! And this is war?"[55] With the help of some comrades, he later found her body and buried her. Then he mailed the letter.

This small tale of a wartime tragedy became lodged in many hearts. The communications revolution enabled unprecedented kinds of "nationwide contest over public opinion," including vigorous debates over the war in Mexico.[56] The antiwar movement loudly proclaimed the injustice of US conquest and used soldiers' letters to highlight harm to innocents. The dead woman became the titular angel of John Greenleaf Whitter's "Angels of Buena Vista" in a poem that shifted the battle's location.

---

[54] George Davis, "From the Army," *Alton Telegaph & Democratic Review*, May 21, 1847, Vol. XII No. 21 edition.

[55] Conway, *The U.S.–Mexican War: A Binational Reader*, 173. These tales drew on American Revolutionary myths, especially that of Molly Pitcher, a similar type of battlefield angel figure. The decade before the Mexican War saw a proliferation of Revolutionary mythology, and it appears that popular motifs shaped gendered depictions of heroism in Mexico. For more on the US archetype of the battlefield angel, see: Cutter, *Domestic Devils, Battlefield Angels*.

[56] Howe, *What Hath God Wrought*, 230.

4 Rescuing the Enemy: Mexican Women and the US Army

She was the "The Heroine Martyr of Monterey" in sheet music written by Reverend J. G. Lyons. In a song to be played "andante con express" Lyons lingered on the burial scene and the lessons Christians should find in it. He described how US troops, "the foemen of her land and race," wept over her grave. Lyons moralized to his audience in the final verse:

> To sound her worth were guilt and shame
> In us, who love but gold and ease.
> They heed alike our praise or blame,
> Who live and die in works like these.
> Far greater than the wise or brave,
> Far happier than the fair and gay,
> Was she who found a martyr's grave
> On that red field of Monterey.[57]

Not battlefield courage nor accumulating wealth – increasingly dominant standards of US masculinity – but Christian submission and good works raised a soul to heaven. Lyons spoke to piano-owning middle-class families across the nation.

In Whittier's poem, the heroine accumulates another essential Christian value: forgiveness. The poet depicts Ximena, a Mexican woman who finds her husband as he dies, struck down by US fire. Like other women around her, she sets aside any thought of vengeance and helps a wounded US soldier and others on the battlefield.

> But the noble Mexic women still their holy task pursued,
> Through that long, dark night of sorrow, worn and faint and lacking food.
> Over weak and suffering brothers, with a tender care they hung,
> And the dying foeman blessed them in a strange and Northern tongue.

Whittier, like Lyons, concluded that the women's actions offered an example to Christians everywhere and hope for a moral future. He wrote, "not wholly lost, O Father! Is this evil world of ours."[58] Sentimental stories of Mexican women, often recorded by soldiers, meant something to the US Army and nation. To the military, stories of heroic Mexican women were a site of myth, which obligated the army to protect innocent and merciful (worthy) women. The same stories offered anti-war activists

---

[57] James G. Lyons (lyricist), "The Heroine of Monterey, Adapted and Arranged for the Piano Forte" (F. D. Benteen, Baltimore, 1847), 1–2. Industrial production enabled many middle-class households to buy a piano, which for many families "replaced the fireplace as the center of home life." Cheap printing presses, in turn, enabled such families to purchase sheet music. Howe, *What Hath God Wrought*, 642.

[58] Conway, *The U.S.–Mexican War: A Binational Reader*, 176–77.

opportunities to warn fellow citizens of greed's cost to souls. Depictions of dead women after a battle also sentimentalized the costs of war and fit them into an imperial context. To pro-war US readers, these Mexican heroines provided a moral framework for territorial expansion. In popular narratives, enemy women forgave killings and became colonized women, allies, and recipients of US protection and civilization.

Much as soldiers' letters shaped popular culture, popular writing shaped army culture. Many soldiers went to war accompanied by William Prescott's *History of the Conquest of Mexico*. Prescott's *Conquest* joined captivity narratives, "Indian plays" and sensationalist newspapers in preparing soldiers for war's great drama. Instead of merely hearing these stories, reading about exotic and beautiful women in a pamphlet novel, or imagining the exploits of Spanish conquistadors, war meant opportunities to bring fantasies to life. Soldiers would chastise Indigenous men, soundly defeat Mexican men, and come to the gallant rescue of beautiful Mexican women.

Prescott's "blockbuster bestseller" described the 1519 march of Hernán Cortés and his forces from Veracruz to Mexico City. Historian John Belohlavek argues that Prescott's book "not only foreshadowed the march of Winfield Scott in 1847 but also explored the racial and cultural dynamic of a Mexico forming an amalgam of Aztec and Spanish." Prescott, a Bostonian Whig, simultaneously romanticized the Spanish conquest of Mexico and warned of the consequences should the US do the same, writing in a letter to his sister that "The Spanish blood will not mix well with the Yankee."[59]

Ned Buntline, author and naval veteran of the Second US–Seminole War, was more sanguine. His take on the Heroine of Monterrey brought together a courageous Mexican woman and a noble US volunteer.[60] It ended happily. In his 1847 *The Volunteer, or the Maid of Monterey*, the titular maid returns to the young backwoodsman's home at the war's end, where they marry.[61] Their romance begins when hero George

---

[59] Belohlavek, *Patriots, Prostitutes, and Spies*, 197.
[60] Buntline later launched William "Buffalo Bill" Cody to fame by making him the hero of an 1869 dime novel and 1871 play. Slotkin, "Buffalo Bill's 'Wild West' and the Mythologization of the American Empire," 167.
[61] Buntline's maid may have begun as the Mexican composite figure of María Josefa Zozaya. According to folklore, Zozaya bravely participated in the Battle of Monterrey and inspired her countrymen. In some tellings, she fights and dies in battle. In others, she brings supplies to soldiers. For many Mexicans, Monterrey's heroines were fierce patriots, not gentle souls caring for enemy soldiers. Belohlavek, *Patriots, Prostitutes, and Spies*, 63. Another version came from regular officer Captain William Henry, who

4 Rescuing the Enemy: Mexican Women and the US Army   173

Blakey captures the heroine. She appears to be a male officer and Blakey demands his surrender. But then, "Blakey was astonished at the luxuriant and glossy curls which fell from beneath the young soldier's helmet as he raised it, and then a suspicion flashed across his mind that a female stood before him." Buntline continued, "A glance at the delicate foot and hand of the officer, one searching look at the long hair, and in the jet black eyes, so large, so dewy, and shaded by lashes of silken gloss, caused him to feel certain of it." He exclaimed, "By heavens, you are a lady! Speak, is it not so? Has it come to this that even the women of Mexico arm to repel their invaders?" Buntline, losing no chance to trumpet US courage and disparage Mexican men, had Edwina Canales reply, "It is time that they did so, señor, when the men prove so cowardly as those who have fled and left me to your mercy." Blakey, "in a tone of deep feeling" responded, "You are free, lady; Americans never war upon women." Blakey reflected a cultural touchstone – the separation of women from war.

Buttressed by popular literature, the US Army after Mexico preferred to remember the war as a glorious victory, fought by virtuous men like Buntline's hero, for the benefit of Mexican women like his heroine. Major General John Wool's hagiographer described the war much like Buntline did – a series of "marvelous events" that resembled "rather the fictions of romance and chivalry, than the precision and mathematical exactness of modern warfare."[62] Behind this persistent fiction lay an ongoing process of criminalizing purportedly illegitimate combatants.

CRIMINALIZING RESISTANCE

Despite army insistence on protecting Mexicans, who would be "respected and protected in their rights, both civil and religious," Kearny did not offer this protection to all. Justice came at a cost: "Those who remain quiet and peaceable, will be considered good citizens and receive

---

recorded that at Monterrey, it is "generally believed, that a company of Lancers was commanded by a woman. Her name was Dos Amades. Seized with a patriotic spirit, she unsexed herself, and dressed in the full suit of a captain of Lancers; she desired to be led against the foe" where "the thickest of the battle should rage." She was like "a second Joan d'Arc, but not, like her, successful." Afterward, she "retired to the walks of private life." Henry, *Campaign Sketches of the War with Mexico*, 233–34.

[62] Buntline, *The Volunteer*, 12; Baylies, *Major General Wool's Campaign in Mexico*, 5. Buntline published a second Mexican War story featuring a woman in uniform in 1847, titled *The Heroine of Tampico*.

protection – those who are found in arms, or instigating others against the United States, will be considered as traitors, and treated accordingly."[63] While establishing the army's mission to safeguard peaceful civilians, Kearny also established violent consequences for refusing protection. Army officers would apply those consequences to men who challenged occupation.

Kearny followed his promises and threats with a code of laws and a bill of rights. The documents reflected the army's interest in protecting women through provisions for punishing rape: "If any person shall unlawfully have carnal knowledge of any woman by force and against her will, he shall, on conviction thereof, be castrated, or imprisoned not exceeding ten years, or fined not exceeding one thousand dollars." The code also allowed the Attorney General and circuit attorney to collect fees for convictions, an incentive to prosecute: "For a conviction for homicide other than capital, for rape, arson, burglary, robbery, forgery, and counterfeiting, $10." It was a relatively high fee, second only to the twenty dollars for capital crimes.

Kearny wrote to the Army Adjutant General that his method bore fruit: "The inhabitants of the country [in the town of Tome] were found to be highly satisfied and contented with the change of government, and apparently vied with each other to see who could show to us the greatest hospitality and kindness." He assumed, "there can no longer be apprehended any organized resistance in this territory to our troops; and the commander of them, whoever he may be, will hereafter have nothing to attend to but to secure the inhabitants from further depredations from the Navajo and Eutaw Indians."[64] After persuading (or so he thought) Mexicans to accept army protection and US rule, Kearny believed this new union would be happy.

The Taos Revolt soon gave the lie to Kearny's famous phrase, that he had, "without firing a gun, or spilling a single drop of blood," conquered a peace in New Mexico.[65] In January 1847, thousands of Pueblo Indians and New Mexicans rose against US officeholders in a mass movement that shocked army leaders. US troops stationed in Santa Fe repressed the rebels with the help of New Mexican volunteers organized by a business partner of US officials. The army tried several dozen

---

[63] Thirtieth Congress, First Session, *House of Representatives Mexican War Correspondence*, 1848, 168. No. 12, "Proclamation of General Kearny, of 31st July."
[64] Ibid., 207, sections on "crimes and punishments" and "fees"; 174, September 16, 1846.
[65] Ibid., 170–71.

men the next day and eventually executed twenty-eight. Of the six men sentenced to death on the trial's first day, the court hanged five for murder and one for treason.

This decision struck eighteen-year-old wagon train traveler Lewis Garrard, who witnessed the hangings, as eminently unjust. He wrote, "it certainly did appear to be a great assumption on the part of the Americans to conquer a country, and then arraign the revolting inhabitants for treason." Of the man sentenced to die for betraying the US, Gerrard wrote, "Treason, indeed! What did the poor fellow know about his new allegiance?"[66] These hangings shifted US policy, criminalizing resistance and underscoring an intent to keep New Mexico.

Although Kearny and other officers claimed they immediately pacified locals by protecting them from Native raids, recent scholarship suggests army officers did less to protect New Mexicans from US soldiers. Chicano scholar Carlos Herrera argues, "the rebels agreed that a major cause of the Taos uprising involved the abusive behavior of US troops," especially the Missouri Volunteers.[67] Ironically, Captain John Reid and his men, described earlier (by fellow volunteer John Hughes) as the pursuers of Comanche raiders and rescuers of Mexican captives described earlier, were volunteers from Missouri. Moreover, army claims that New Mexicans were safe from Native raids were inaccurate. Raiding groups continued to take captives. After the war, the American Indian Agent at Santa Fe described how in 1850, the Apaches were "more impudent than ever" and noted his office's extensive and continued efforts to redeem captives.[68]

---

[66] Garrard, *Wah-to-Yah and the Taos Trail*, 177–78.
[67] Although the Taos uprising is the most famous act of New Mexican resistance in US accounts, resistance predated and followed it. The month before, an attempt to overthrow the local US government (the December Plot) failed when plans reached Governor Bent's Secretary, Donaciano Vigil. Days after the Taos Revolt, the January 24, 1847, Battle of La Cañada, and a subsequent battle at El Embudo Pass in February involved thousands of combatants. Carlos R. Herrera, "New Mexico Resistance to U.S. Occupation during the Mexican–American War of 1846–1848," in *The Contested Homeland: A Chicano History of New Mexico*, ed. David Maciel and Erlinda Gonzales-Berry (Albuquerque: University of New Mexico Press, 2000), 31–33.
[68] Calhoun, *The Official Correspondence of James S. Calhoun*, January 17, 1850, Calhoun to Brown. Captures of women and children continued to be regular news. *The New Mexican* reported on a US woman's death, Mrs. White, in captivity as a group led by Major Greer attempted a rescue: "Greer, to whom was confided the task of treating with the Utahs for her recovery, came within sight of their camp, when she was immediately shot down, almost in the presence of our troops." Greer "captured two young Indians, a number of animals, and all their camp equipment." *The New Mexican*, November 24, 1849, Volume I, Number 1.

The army claimed the status of protectors all the same, sometimes in perceived contrast to Spain's earlier conquest. To them, the US invasion was humane in opposition to Spanish exploitation. Where the Spanish used cruelty to seize New Mexico, the US claimed to conquer with kindness. Samuel Watson notes that army officers "envisioned the American union as the torchbearer for an empire of ordered liberty." Army leaders approached the wartime occupation of New Mexico with a sense of "genteel authoritarianism." The US Army claimed a bloodless conquest of New Mexico, but the period was exceptional for its violent resistance to US rule.[69]

Gendered ideas of how to treat enemy Mexican women powerfully shaped officers' claims of gentility, with significant consequences for the war. Officers told of Governor Charles Bent's death at the hands of Pueblo Indian participants in the Taos Revolt as a narrative based on US protection of Mexican women. According to topographical engineer Lieutenant James Abert, in a report the Secretary of War provided to Congress the following year, Bent's wife Ignacia Jaramillo Bent "brought him his arms, and told him to fight, to avenge himself; he could easily have killed some of the mob, who were entirely exposed to his aim, from the hold they were making." But "'no,' said he, 'I will not kill any one of them, for the sake of you, my wife, and of you, my children. At present, my death is all these people wish.' The murderers rush in, they kill him, they scalp him, and, horrible to relate, they parade the bloody scalp through the streets."[70]

This version declined to describe how rebels sought out those who administered the US occupation of New Mexico, whom the resistance movement considered legitimate targets. Abert's narrative also removed Ignacia. She had not stood by. She moved to a back room and worked with other women. They used spoons and household implements to dig through an adobe wall, pulling themselves and the children through, rebels in pursuit.[71] In Abert's story Bent's sacrifice, not Ignacia Jaramillo's actions, kept her and their children alive. Officers wrote about how Bent died protecting his Mexican wife, reflecting the army's logic of protection in New Mexico. The twenty-eight executed rebels showed how consequential that logic could be.

---

[69] Watson, *Peacekeepers and Conquerors*, 421, 438; Gómez, *Manifest Destinies*, 10–12.
[70] Abert, *Examination of New Mexico in the Years 1846–'47*, 441, February 17, 1847.
[71] Hyde, *Empires, Nations, and Families: A History of the North American West, 1800–1860*, 385–86.

4 Rescuing the Enemy: Mexican Women and the US Army

A volunteer, who heard of Bent's killing while marching toward Chihuahua with Doniphan's expedition, had another theory. He believed Bent's death was "not caused by the insurrection at Taos, but rather that this occurrence was used as a cloak to cover what was, undoubtedly, an act of private malice, instigated by his wife. She was a Spaniard, very beautiful, but had not lived with him for some years, and resided at Taos, where Bent had large properties." He "had been warned never to approach Taos," and when he did come, she had "taken part in the insurrection." The author plainly argues that she killed him, yet concludes, with the odd blinders of protection, that her part had been "so slight a one, that she could not be punished for it." The imperative to consider women harmless warred with his misgivings that Mexican women, with their ethnic, religious, and racial differences, were suspect.[72]

Where the army treated the Seminoles as a treaty-worthy Indigenous nation, its experiences with Native raiding societies in Mexico encouraged it to brand Indigenous enemies as criminals – captors, killers, and thieves. Increasingly, as with the mass executions of rebels following the Taos Revolt, it also affixed those labels to Mexican men who resisted the US outside of conventional battles. As the war continued and guerrilla attacks increased, the process sped along, criminalizing all resistance by men fighting out of uniform, Mexican or Indigenous. US rescues of Mexican women from Native captivity heightened the difference between Mexican and Native women in US eyes, but when it came to men, the opposite occurred. As the army clashed with raiders, rebels, and guerrillas, officers came to see Mexican and Native men as alike.

Henry Halleck, who served in the war, later wrote that those who resisted a military occupation ran "the hazard of being treated by the enemy as lawless banditti, not entitled to the mitigating rules of modern warfare." He published *International Law* years later in 1861, but drew on questions his peers posed to him in Mexico, his thoughts filtered by

---

[72] Edwards, *A Campaign in New Mexico with Colonel Doniphan*, 103. Richard Slotkin notes that US–Mexican War romances split on the question of whether Mexicans (at least those considered racially Spanish) should be assimilated into the US or expelled and destroyed as "savages." He writes, "the problem is posed in the characterization of Mexican men, particularly in the catchall figure of 'the ranchero'; but it is resolved only in the treatment of women," especially through determinations over whether Mexican women were fit to be wives of US men. Edwards's suspicion of Ignacia Bent reflects lingering uneasiness in army distinctions between "criminal" Mexican guerrillas (rancheros) and obliging Mexican women. Slotkin, *The Fatal Environment*, 1992.

the intervening years and improved by hindsight. As the army confronted continued Mexican resistance, it developed an ad hoc response that delegitimized Mexican guerrillas and Native warriors alike, reducing them to criminals requiring punishment. In Florida, the army fought Seminole warriors whenever it could find them. In Mexico it punished men who fought out of uniform as criminals.

Halleck, writing after the war, recorded how individual actions without state sanction "are not legitimate acts of war." Without state approval, seizing enemy property was merely robbery, and killing an enemy was murder: "Their acts are unlawful; and, when captured, they are not treated as prisoners of war, but as criminals, subject to the punishment due to their crimes." They were to be "regarded as outlaws, and, when captured, may be punished the same as freebooters and banditti," because acceding to a "lust of plunder" was crime, not war. An "informal and illegitimate war" was "more properly called depredation." Furthermore, "A nation attacked by such sort of enemies is not under any obligation to observe towards them the rules prescribed in formal warfare. She may treat them as robbers."[73]

In a similar vein, Emory recorded Kearny's words to Mexican inhabitants in the town of Las Vegas: "From the Mexican government, you have never received protection. The Apaches and Navajos come down from the mountains and carry off your sheep, and even your women, whenever they please. My government will correct all this." Kearny told them those "who remain peaceably at home" would get protection in property, persons, religion. Still, those who took up "arms against me, I will hang." Though some Mexicans might tell stories, "that we should ill-treat your women, and brand them on the check as you do your mules on the hip. It is all false."[74] Protection was legitimacy.

---

[73] Halleck, *International Law*, 1878, 2:7–8; Vattel, *Law of Nations*, 320. Halleck's *International Law* drew on Vattel, the most relevant author to the army's laws of war tradition, who wrote regular war was a "war in due form" because it followed "rules, prescribed by the law of nature, or adopted by custom." The critical requirements were that "Legitimate and formal warfare must be carefully distinguished from those illegitimate and informal wars, or rather predatory expeditions, undertaken either without lawful authority or without apparent cause, as likewise without the usual formalities, and solely with a view to plunder." Ibid., 319. Book III, Chapter IV "Of the Declaration of War," paragraph 67. For more on the violent consequences of such thinking, which made it easier for the US settlers and the army to consider Native groups to be criminals after the Mexican War, see: Cothran, *Remembering the Modoc War*; Madley, *An American Genocide*.

[74] Emory, *Notes of a Military Reconnaissance*, 26–27, August 14, 1846.

4 Rescuing the Enemy: Mexican Women and the US Army

Emory went further and raged against the criminality of the Mexican government itself. He wrote that in the hills, he saw Navajo hiding places where they "waited for night to descend upon the valley and carry off the fruit, sheep, women, and children of the Mexicans." The Navajos were "the lords of New Mexico" and, according to Emory, were in league with the Governor, Manuel Armijo, who "never permitted the inhabitants to war upon these thieves." Instead, those New Mexicans who declared themselves his opponents would soon "have a visit" from the Navajos. Emory echoed Kendall's earlier indictment of Armijo, in which Kendall claimed he could "relate many a thrilling story of [Armijo's] abuse of the rights of women, that would make Saxon hearts burn with indignant fire; for Saxon hearts enshrine the mothers of men as sacred and apart."[75] Both agreed that allegedly bringing Mexican women to harm condemned Armijo. Equally, US concern with reversing that process elevated the army's moral stature.

Army officers constructed the category of unlawful war as it existed in Northern Mexico by conflating violence between Mexicans and Native groups to tar all involved with the same brush of "savagery." Emory wrote of Apaches who "treacherous themselves" then "expect treachery in others. At everlasting war with the rest of mankind, they kill at sight all who fall in their power. The conduct of Mexicans to them is equally bad, for they decoy and kill the Apaches whenever they can." The army found that Apache men and women were unfit for civilization and that Mexican men were to blame. A dragoon officer wrote, the "boldness of the Navajos proceeds from their confidence in the cowardice of the Mexicans."[76] That the US was making war on Mexico and not the Navajos or Apaches mattered little. Protecting Mexican women did not hinder the army's war on the Mexican state. Instead, US rhetoric that it came "as protectors – not as conquerors" legitimized US military operations.

Army claims that Mexican men could not protect Mexican women fueled another engine of legitimization. Although masculinist thinking made it seem natural to soldiers for (strong) men to protect (weak) women, the occupiers wanted to extend that logic over the male population of Northern Mexico. They branded Mexican men as weak and

---

[75] Ibid., 47, September 30, 1847; Kendall, *Narrative of the Texan Sante Fé Expedition*, 485–86.
[76] Emory, *Notes of a Military Reconnaissance*, 71, November 3, 1847; Johnston, *Journal of Captain A. R. Johnston*, 570, October 4, 1846.

cowardly, unable to protect women from Indigenous men and so unfit to rule; or as unlawful guerrillas, criminals with no legitimate claims to power. In offering help to Mexican settlements plagued by raids, army leaders made clear that Mexican men would be junior partners in US administration of conquered lands. By punishing so-called criminals who challenged a purportedly benevolent occupation, the army gave teeth to the distinction between lawful and unlawful war.

Stories of Mexican women's captivity served the army in several ways. They legitimized occupation by grounding it in military obligations to protect civilians. They also clarified differences between civilization shared by the US, acquiescent Mexicans, and settled Native agriculturalists on the one hand and "savage Indians" on the other. Together, this allowed the army to use Mexican women's vulnerability to render New Mexico a valid addition to the United States. Moreover, captivity narratives created a gendered hierarchy that naturalized US claims to superiority because US men, rather than Mexican men, protected (via rescue) Mexican women.

When the army envisioned a future for the Seminoles during the war in Florida, its vision was forced migration. Army leadership sought to enact the federal policy they were duty-bound to follow. They would, as ordered, expel the Seminoles. While some soldiers advocated for a strategy of annihilation, and army strategy entailed the relentless destruction of Seminole resources, the army as an organization did not openly seek to extirpate the Seminoles, but to force them out of Florida and into Indian Territory. After 1846, the army's approach to war changed. Rhetoric on rescuing Mexican women from Native captivity reified a way to criminalize any resistance – from rebels, raiders, and guerrillas – that occurred outside of engagements with a uniformed enemy. Limiting the scope of what the army could do to lawful combatants loosened restraints on violence directed against other threats.

The army's perception of itself as an organization that rescued women from captivity sorted the men of Northern Mexico into a gendered hierarchy. At the bottom were Native groups who took captives, often brought into relief by unfavorable comparisons to agrarian groups such as the Pima and Maricopa. In the middle were Mexican men whose women had become captives and men who participated in supposedly criminal resistance to US occupation. At the top were white US troops – with officers at the pinnacle – who rescued captives and protected women.

4 Rescuing the Enemy: Mexican Women and the US Army

Based partly on the army's need to protect Mexican women, it developed an approach to unlawful war premised on the punishment of criminals and a lawful track for wars that regulated the actions of "legitimate" combatants. These dual approaches supported the US political vision of continental expansion across the US nation's desired space. By creating a broader set of options for army leaders when fighting against those they labeled criminals, the War on Mexico crafted tools the US Army would use in "Indian Wars" for the rest of the century.

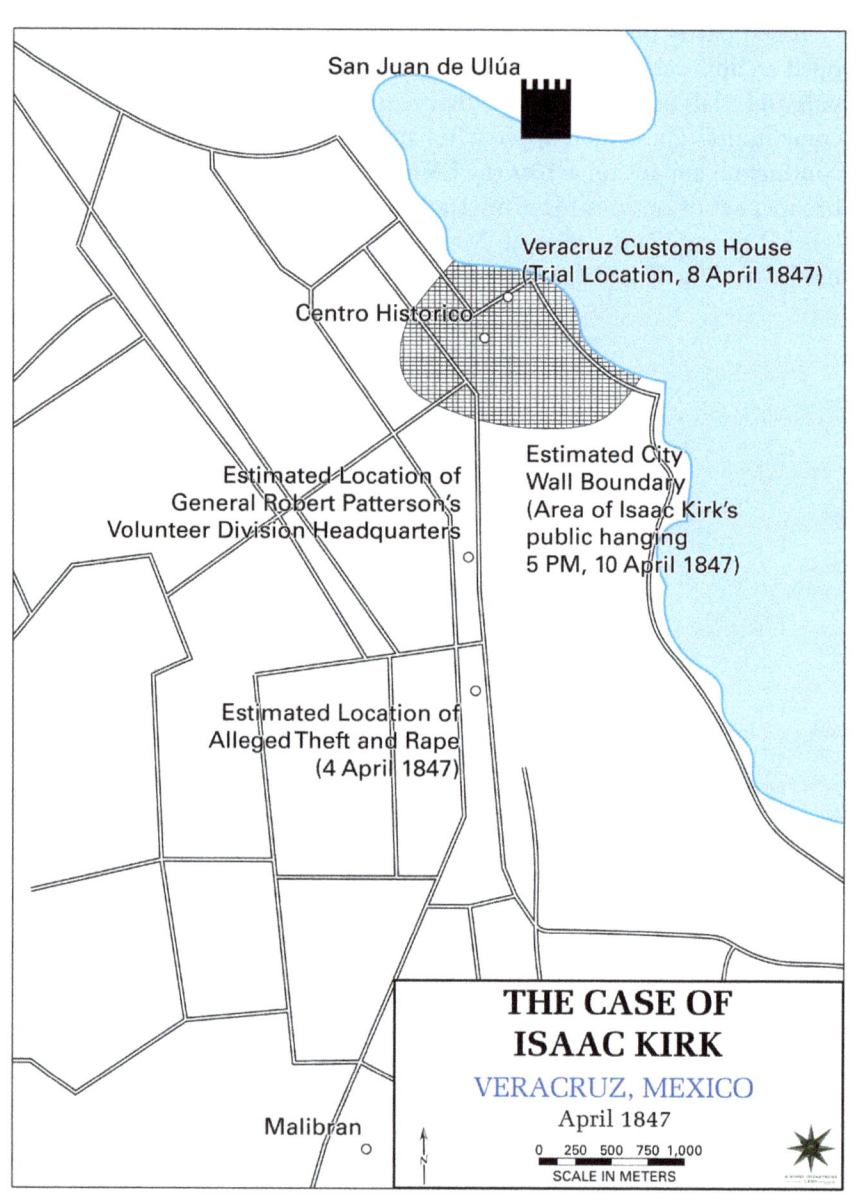

MAP 5 The Case of Isaac Kirk in Veracruz.
Map by Mr. Jeffrey Goldberg, Cartographer at the West Point
Department of History.

5

A Perfect Sacrifice

The Unexplored Rape Case That Radically Expanded Military Justice, 1847

On April 4, 1847, a man attacked and raped Maria Antonia Gallegas as she walked home from Veracruz. On April 10, at 5 pm, the US Army hanged Isaac Kirk for the crime. The officers involved said they did so for the benefit of the Mexican people. Before ordering Kirk to die, the military commission spent its week sentencing volunteer soldiers to reductions in rank, brief imprisonments, or fines. Kirk, an officer's servant rather than a soldier, had initially faced the same charge that the others faced: theft. Yet, the recorder carefully wrote over the word "Theft" in the original document to superimpose the word "Rape" (Figure 5.1).

When it came to Kirk, there was one especially obvious difference. While all the soldiers tried by the commission for theft were white, he was Black. More precisely, Kirk was a free Black man from Tennessee who stood accused of raping a "respectable Mexican woman." He faced a form of justice new to the US Army: a military commission. Volunteer officers composed it – citizen-soldiers that had signed up to fight in Mexico rather than career army officers – and a white southerner, Lieutenant Colonel Samuel Anderson of the First Tennessee Foot Regiment, led it.[1] It was the first US military commission to hand down capital punishment. It did so to sentence a Black man to death for allegedly raping a Mexican woman.

---

[1] Davis, *Autobiography of the Late Colonel George T. M. Davis*, 136. Military historian Thomas Spahr calculates that US forces in Mexico were forty-four percent regulars and fifty-six percent volunteers. Spahr, "Occupying for Peace," 80.

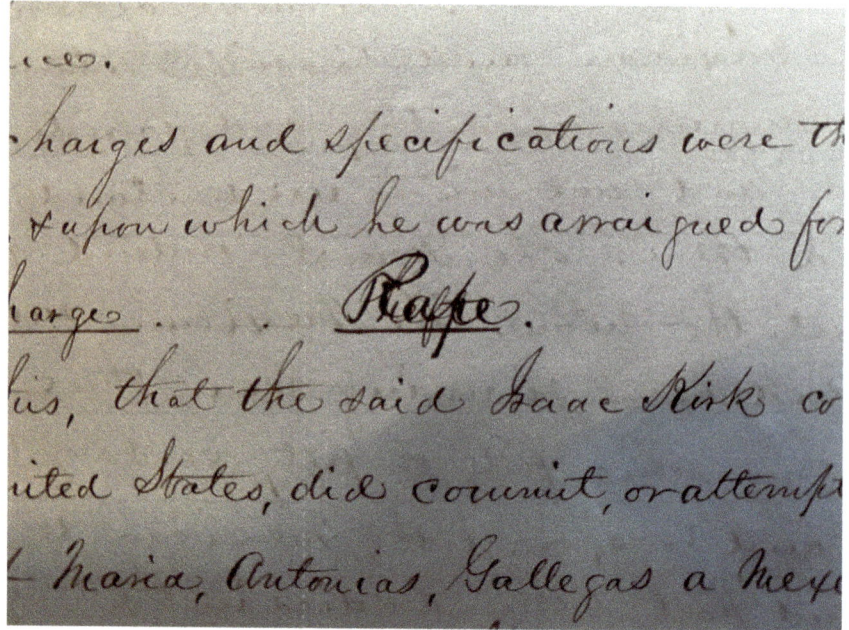

FIGURE 5.1 Photograph, detail from military commission, case number EE-363, 1847. This image shows where the court recorder transformed the charge of theft into rape. This change is visible only in the original document. Later transcriptions simply list rape as the first charge and theft as the second. Photograph by the author.

The case must have felt like a godsend to Commanding General Winfield Scott. His small army was about to fight its way across Mexico, from the port of Veracruz to Mexico City, intending to force the Mexican government to surrender and secure a favorable peace. Because Scott had only about 10,000 soldiers to conquer Central Mexico and its millions, he sought to convince the Mexican people to accept the US Army's authority. Yet, he knew that existing laws (Scott personally revised the 1825 *General Regulations*) and the US *Articles of War* (a relic from 1806) offered no way to try soldiers for crimes committed against enemy civilians or hold enemy civilians accountable for crimes against US troops.

With neither a firm legal basis to extend the system, nor the support of President James Polk, who distrusted his Whiggish general, Scott gambled. He put his military commissions into effect without foundation in US law, relying on his position as the commander on the ground and his

5 A Perfect Sacrifice: A Rape Case Expanded Military Justice

expectation that his innovation would succeed.[2] He needed to send a message that would win broad approval, and Kirk's death offered instant legitimacy. He hoped Mexicans would view a US death as evidence of the army's sincere commitment to protecting civilians, and he knew that US politicians would not object to hanging a Black man for rape.

Military commissions reflected court-martial procedures. Scott's predecessor, Major General Alexander Macomb, helpfully published these in his 1840 book *The Practice of Courts-Martial*. During the Second US–Seminole War of 1835 to 1842, Macomb sought to standardize officers' approaches to military justice. To a significant degree, he succeeded. In Mexico, Scott built on Macomb's accomplishments to radically expand the scope of military justice. Before Kirk, military law focused on upholding internal order – mostly by punishing soldiers for desertion, drunkenness, and disobedience. By taking the court-martial and magnifying those subjected to it through commissions, Scott gave military justice an external dimension it would never lose. After Kirk, officers would not only discipline fractious soldiers but occupied populations.

Military commissions were Scott's ad hoc solution to the problem of occupying Mexico. Scott's subordinate, Henry Halleck, leveraged this solution a few years later during the Civil War. Much like Scott he sought a way to hold enemy civilians (secessionists) accountable for guerrilla activity and found an answer in military commissions. Halleck worked with Francis Lieber to produce General Orders 100, which accomplished many things – among them, inscribing commissions into the laws of war – such that by century's end, General Orders 100 became the basis for the Hague Conventions. The US used military commissions many times after Mexico, not only during the Civil War, but in the Philippines, after World War II, and most recently to prosecute non-US citizens suspected of terrorism at Guantánamo Bay. The US also used military commissions to execute Native prisoners, as it did in 1862 Mankato, Minnesota, where a military commission ordered the mass hanging of Dakota men.[3]

---

[2] Military commissions were a new development in the US, but several early experiments preceded them. In 1780, a Board of General Officers decided to hang Major John André for espionage. In 1818 Florida, Andrew Jackson used a military tribunal of officers to hang British citizens Robert Ambrister and Alexander Arbuthnot. John Fabian Witt, *Lincoln's Code: The Laws of War in American History* (New York: Free Press, 2012), 25, 98–99.

[3] McCurry, *Women's War*, 32; Lieber, *Instructions for the Government of Armies of the United States, in the Field*, 6, Paragraph 13. Ní Aoláin and Gross, *Guantánamo and Beyond*, 1–2, 15. For the "determinative influence" of General Orders 100, also called Lieber's Code, on the laws of war, see: Kinsella, "Settler Empire and the United States," 1.

Military commissions shaped today's international order. They have an untold origin story.

The US declared war against Mexico less than a year before Kirk's death, in May 1846. By February 1847, several lines of advance through Texas, New Mexico, and California left the US in possession of Northern Mexico. Mexico continued to resist, so General Winfield Scott and his army left US-occupied Tampico for Veracruz. From there they would march inland toward Mexico City.[4] Scott gained Veracruz's surrender by bombarding the city, full of Mexican civilians as well as troops. His forces briefly occupied Jalapa and then Puebla before marching on Mexico City in September of 1847. The US Army occupied Mexico City until June 1848, when it received word that the US Congress had ratified the Treaty of Guadalupe-Hidalgo and ended the war.

As the army advanced, so did military commissions. They applied to all people living under occupation regardless of nationality in any situation where "an American might be a party."[5] The army claimed to occupy Mexico as a friend of the Mexican people. Scott, the architect and leader of the campaign, wrote this claim – that the US Army would protect Mexican women, and thus all civilians – in Kirk's blood.

RACIALIZING PROTECTION

The day after Kirk died, Winfield Scott issued a famous proclamation. He declared, "I have, from the first, done everything in my power to place [Mexican civilians] under the safeguard of martial law, against the few bad men in this army. My orders to that effect, known to all, are precise and rigorous." Scott continued, "under them, several Americans have already been punished, by fine, for the benefit of Mexicans, besides imprisonment; and one, for a rape, has been hung by the neck. Is this not a proof of good faith and energetic discipline?" His words won over many US observers then, and many historians since. Of the latter, one writes that "the strict discipline Scott imposed upon his army may have been the most important element of the successful occupation of Mexico City."[6]

---

[4] Conway, *The U.S.–Mexican War: A Binational Reader*. Conway includes the war's chronology on pages xxviii–xxix, and a map depicting the US lines of advance and major battles on page xxxi.

[5] Scott, *Memoirs*, 395.

[6] Thirtieth Congress, First Session, *House of Representatives Mexican War Correspondence*, 1848, 938, Scott, Proclamation to the Mexican People, April 11, 1847; Spahr, "Occupying for Peace," 255.

The Kirk case fit into US tropes about rape and race with extraordinary precision. By 1847, the US legal tradition reflected a longstanding practice of racializing rape. Since the US colonial era "the self-evident guilt of black men accused of raping white women" made cases involving Black assailants and white victims far more likely to lead to death sentences. By the time Scott's army landed at Veracruz, those legal patterns, amplified by the Jacksonian rise of universal white male suffrage, promoted the growth of stereotypes that associated an inclination to rape – and the ability of a victim to seek justice – to skin color.[7]

That hierarchy rendered Kirk the perfect sacrifice. The military commission referred to Kirk as a "colored man and a citizen of the United States." Given the legal (and other forms of) discrimination that free persons of color faced in 1847, that was something of a contradiction in terms. Nonetheless, it was a useful one. As a "colored man," Kirk probably faced a death sentence as soon as the court recorder's pen overwrote "Theft" with "Rape." As a "citizen of the United States," Scott could refer to Kirk simply as an American. Scott's deliberately vague phrasing – he soon declared that officers had tried "several Americans" who were "of the army" – was effective propaganda that produced the appearance of strict military justice applied to US soldiers. One historian claimed that Scott soon hanged "an American soldier for rape."[8] Minor errors of this sort may seem to be only a misplaced word or two away from the truth, but the word soldier removes much of the controversy embedded in Kirk's case. It was one thing for the army to hang a soldier and quite another for it to claim the right to execute anyone convicted of a serious offense.

These small mistakes obscure the case's vital, and before now unexplored, position in the development of US military justice. A key work on US military law praises Scott's policy for its success in limiting future violence against civilian populations. The new military commissions were, indeed, successful and influential. Such conclusions emphasize the genuine importance of Scott's innovation and the drastic widening of military justice that the commissions generated, yet imply Scott solved the problem of US crimes against Mexican civilians. Kirk's case, and its

---

[7] Sharon Block, *Rape & Sexual Power in Early America* (Chapel Hill: The University of North Carolina Press, 2006), 13.
[8] "Court-Martial Case Files, 1809–1894," Military Commission Proceedings for Isaac Kirk, Case EE363, Veracruz, April 8, 1847; Eisenhower, *So Far from God: The U.S. War with Mexico, 1846–1848*, 266.

legacy as a clear example of swift justice, haunts this interpretation and veils the harsher reality of persistent violence against civilians.[9]

The Kirk case also reflects a broader neglect of sexual violence in the conflict's military histories. For several works, a brief mention of it is the only reference to rape.[10] Others mention rape only to dismiss it. One quotes pro-war feminist Emma Willard to conclude that Mexico City "was spared the usual sack and rape by soldiers who, scorning to take advantage of the enemy's weakness, truly behaved like 'knights of old.'" Another cites a pro-war writer who believed that rape was one of several "treasonous" false accusations against US troops. One mentions the Kirk case to show how Scott communicated to "the Mexican people that his army would not abuse the population." Building upon this orthodoxy, one author finds that army officers ably enforced discipline. Others wrote histories of the war without reference to rape. This dismissal allows one to misinterpret Kirk's hanging as the end of a concise story of rape and punishment.[11]

When recent histories reference Kirk, they often reflect this assumption. Scott's biographer reached the same conclusion decades later, to argue that in contrast to General Zachary Taylor's Army of Occupation, where "unruly soldiers had literally gotten away with murder... Scott imposed martial law upon American soldiers and, to show he meant

---

[9] John Fabian Witt wrote that Scott developed an "innovative strategy" and quickly dealt with the problem of "indiscriminate retaliation by American volunteers." Witt claims Scott's military commissions were a "great success" and "a crucial piece of the widely praised campaign he waged from the sea to Mexico City." Witt, *Lincoln's Code*, 122–23.

[10] Peskin, *Winfield Scott and the Profession of Arms*, 160; Eisenhower, *So Far from God: The U.S. War with Mexico, 1846–1848*, 266.

[11] Johannsen, *To the Halls of Montezuma*, 32; Smith and Judah, *Chronicles of the Gringos: The US Army in the Mexican War, 1846–1848*, 448; Spahr, "Occupying for Peace," 3, 76; Winders, *Mr. Polk's Army*, 84. Spahr critiques David Clary's assertion that in Mexico City the "rapacity of the volunteers caused general outrages because of the widespread looting, the murder of civilians, hundreds of rapes, and nearly universal drunkenness." He mentions an "outrage" described by George Meade and cited Scott writing of Taylor's army: "Murder, robbery & rape on mothers & daughters, in the presence of the tied up males of the families, have been common all along the Rio Grande." Spahr, "Occupying for Peace," 115, 195, 208, 261, Note 54. Clary, *Eagles and Empire*, 379. Some works of Mexican history address wartime rapes. See: Peter Guardino, *The Dead March: A History of the Mexican–American War* (Cambridge, MA: Harvard University Press, 2017), 299–300; José María Roa Bárcena, *Recuerdos de La Invasión Norteamericana (1846–1848)*, ed. Antonio Castro Leal (México: Editorial Porrúa, 1947), 530–31; Laura Herrera Serna, ed., *México En Guerra, 1846–1848: Perspectivas Regionales* (México: Consejo Nacional para la Cultura y las Artes, 1997), 370–71.

5 A Perfect Sacrifice: A Rape Case Expanded Military Justice 189

business, flogged a thief and hanged a rapist for offenses against Mexican civilians."[12] By offering up Kirk's hanging as an example of meaningful military justice, this author again echoes Scott's performative claim that he successfully established order. This interpretation believes Scott's propaganda and contrasts it with the purportedly worse treatment of Mexican civilians by Zachary Taylor.

This kind of binary comparison between the two generals remains a typical device. One military historian offers a representative claim, writing, "Taylor came to symbolize the rugged West and Scott the sophisticated East" and describing how the men were "exact opposites" in many things: Taylor the democrat versus Scott the aristocrat.[13] Yet, overdrawn distinctions between Scott as the beau ideal of officership and Taylor as a classic frontiersman obscure many insights. They detract from Mexican civilians' everyday experiences under occupation, whether in Taylor's orbit or Scott's, and obviate challenges Mexicans faced when they found themselves in the US army's path.

The Kirk case shows how military ideas about race sharpened protection's importance to army culture. It remains relevant because scholars still contest the connection between race and the regular army. One finds that scientific theories of race "had little apparent impact on the antebellum officer corps," another that many scholars overemphasize the effects of racism. Certainly, US attitudes toward Mexicans were complex, and when the two groups interacted race was an ever-present but ever-changing concept. US troops approached Mexicans situationally, their views shaped by an individual's race, class, gender, ethnicity, behavior, and religion. Nonetheless, the logic of protection was, to apply Ann Stoler's language, a "logic of differentiation" committed to the "production of racialized knowledge."[14] The Kirk case demonstrates how ideas of race, in the context of a shifting landscape of other attributes, influenced the army and the war. Within a diverse Mexican population,

---

[12] Peskin, *Winfield Scott and the Profession of Arms*, 160. For more on Scott, see: Elliott, *Winfield Scott, the Soldier and the Man*; Eisenhower, *Agent of Destiny*.
[13] Winders, *Mr. Polk's Army*, 29–30.
[14] Skelton, *An American Profession of Arms*, 309–10; Spahr, "Occupying for Peace," 322; Stoler, *Haunted By Empire*, 50–51. This chapter predates existing studies of rape and the US Army by nearly a century. In her study of rape in US-occupied France during World War II, Mary Louise Roberts argues "that the army racialized the crime of rape" such that far more Black soldiers faced execution for it. These dynamics had deep roots, and were also present at Kirk's military commission. Roberts, *What Soldiers Do*, 196. For how racial difference shaped rape cases and victims' experiences, and the archival challenges of studying rape, see: Lawlor, "Contested Crimes."

protecting women helped the army stabilize racial categories. It shaped distinct approaches to Mexican men based on a racialized hierarchy that began with white male protectors and progressed downward to impotent, criminal Mexican men and sexually threatening Black men.

While the first military commissions tried US men for crimes against Mexicans, the army soon turned this legal tool against Mexican men accused of stealing from or attacking the army. In Veracruz, a commission found Antonio Gardino guilty of possessing stolen property, a trunk and an umbrella, and sentenced him to fifty lashes and six months' confinement to a chain gang. A commission found Juan Henriquez guilty of theft when he sold a horse placed in his care and sentenced him to the same. Commissions imposed punishments of fifty lashes on three US men convicted of similar thefts at about the same time in Veracruz, including one who stole military clothing stored at a charity hospital.[15]

Many works treat Scott's claim as plain fact – that hanging one (Black, civilian) rapist to protect a Mexican woman constituted legitimate proof that the US consistently protected civilians. Newer works that challenge exceptionalist interpretations have not considered the case, leaving the dominant narrative in place.[16] Scott's claim should be challenged. Doing so contextualizes a long process through which US military leaders depicted themselves as protectors. It shows Scott's declaration of US benevolence to be a strategic calculation – an end state that Scott hoped for, rather than a reality Mexicans experienced.

Asserting protection established a significant source of legitimacy for the US occupation of Mexico – one that echoes across centuries of scholarship. A classic military history of the war states that "the hanging of a camp follower...for the rape and robbery of a Mexican woman had a salutary effect on those in the army who might have been tempted to follow suit."[17] The "might have been" is important because it implies that

---

[15] "Court-Martial Case Files, 1809–1894," Case FF101, March 12, 1848, Vera Cruz.

[16] Books that unseat triumphal US narratives but whose scope does not extend to Kirk's case include: Guardino, *The Dead March: A History of the Mexican–American War*, 2017; Greenberg, *A Wicked War: Polk, Clay, Lincoln, and the 1846 U.S. Invasion of Mexico*; Delay, *War of a Thousand Deserts*. John Belohavek mentions Kirk when describing US fantasies of Mexican women, but misidentifies the crime as "insulting a Mexican woman," euphemistic and vague language from an abolitionist paper condemning Kirk's hanging. John Belohlavek, *Patriots, Prostitutes, and Spies: Women and the Mexican–American War* (Charlottesville: Virginia University Press, 2017), 191.

[17] K. Jack Bauer, *The Mexican War: 1846–1848* (Lincoln: University of Nebraska Press, 1974), 253. Scott's biographer reached the same conclusion decades later, to argue that in contrast to General Zachary Taylor's allegedly murderous Army of Occupation, Scott

5 A Perfect Sacrifice: A Rape Case Expanded Military Justice

Kirk's death actually prevented others from committing rape – that Scott solved the problem of crime before he began marching toward Mexico City. Yet, one doubts hanging a Black man deterred white soldiers. By reinforcing racial privilege, Kirk's death may just as easily have emboldened would-be assailants. Decades pass, and US military history remains mired in the world Scott made.

The records of these early cases remain little used. Scholarship mentioning Kirk relies on Scott's official description as published in general orders, resulting in a historiographical tradition that reifies Scott's pronouncement of the truth. Scott first issued his "Martial Law Order" on February 19, 1847 in Tampico, then reissued it soon after arriving in Veracruz, Puebla, and Mexico City.[18] It marked the first time US forces formally implemented martial law in US history – an important document. Still, closely reading the case challenges Scott's benevolent narrative. It also reveals voices that are mostly absent from archives, including Maria Antonia Gallegas's testimony and that of several enlisted men.

The Kirk case's distinctive tripartite racial dynamics enabled Scott to establish military commissions where Zachary Taylor had failed. When the war began, Taylor and Scott lobbied Washington to adopt regulations applicable to foreign wars. In October 1846, Taylor cited a case in Monterrey where one of his soldiers shot a Mexican lancer in cold blood during an armistice. He asked the Adjutant General how to deal with the murderer. In response, Secretary of War William Marcy wrote the government "seriously regrets that such a flagrant offender cannot be dealt with in the manner he deserved." Marcy concluded, "I see no other course for you to pursue than to release him from confinement and send him away from the army."[19]

---

safeguarded Mexicans. Peskin, *Winfield Scott and the Profession of Arms*, 160. See also: Charles Winslow Elliott, *Winfield Scott, the Soldier and the Man* (New York: The Macmillan Company, 1937); John S. D. Eisenhower, *Agent of Destiny: The Life and Times of General Winfield Scott* (New York: Free Press, 1997). Winders, *Mr. Polk's Army*, 29–30.

[18] Winfield Scott, *Memoirs* (New York: Sheldon & Company, 1864), 540, General Orders 287; "Registers of the Records of the Proceedings of the U.S. Army General Courts-Martial, 1809–1890," RG 153, NA, 1. This expanded scope may have encouraged the US to reinstitute the Judge Advocate General, an office discontinued in 1821 and reestablished in March 1849 following the war.

[19] Thirtieth Congress, First Session, *House of Representatives Mexican War Correspondence*, United States Serial Set 520 (Washington DC, 1848), 431, October 11, 1846, Taylor to Adjutant General, 431; November 25, 1846, Marcy to Taylor, 369–70. The witness for this case was from the Brazoria Company of Texas Volunteers. The alleged murderer was named Fitzsimmons.

Around the same time, Scott insisted they must expect troops to commit offenses beyond the limited scope of the 1806 articles of war that still governed the army of 1847. Those regulations mainly dealt with the army's internal functioning, such as how soldiers behaved toward superiors. Scott (and Taylor) needed more. When occupying a foreign country, US crimes against Mexicans and vice versa would surely occur. Scott argued there were many kinds of assault, including rape, that were "unprovided for by our written military code" and "of course, could not, in a foreign hostile country, often, if ever, be safely turned over to the courts of such country."

To close this legal gap, Scott suggested offenses not covered by military law should, when occupying a hostile country, "be duly brought before councils of war" that mirrored courts-martial.[20] Because "the good of the service, the honor of the United States and the interests of humanity, imperiously demand that every crime, enumerated above, should be severely punished," martial law would thenceforth cover the gap. Military commissions could stretch across the space between military regulations as written, and the military law Scott envisioned.

The occupying US Army needed a "supplemental code" and "that *unwritten* code is *Martial Law*, as an addition to the *written* military code, prescribed by Congress in the rules and articles of war, and which unwritten code, all armies, in hostile countries, are forced to adopt." This was "not only for their own safety, but for the protection of the unoffending inhabitants and their property, about the theaters of military operations, against injuries, on the part of the army, contrary to the laws of war." When Scott took command of the army at Tampico and prepared to launch his Mexico City campaign, he seized the opportunity to turn his plan into reality. In General Orders 20, he declared martial law and instituted military commissions to punish serious crimes, including "murder, poisoning, rape, or the attempt to commit either," and "malicious assault, battery, robbery, theft."[21] This system ensured the army could try cases involving Mexican and US nationals, whichever of the two were the aggressors.

---

[20] Callan, *The Military Laws of the United States*, 170, 172, 180–81, 184, 194; Thirtieth Congress, First Session, *House of Representatives Mexican War Correspondence*, 1848, 1264–65, Scott to War Department, October 15, 1846. This preference for extraterritoriality remains in place today.

[21] *General Orders, January to May 1847*, 23:25, General Orders 20, Headquarters of the Army, Tampico, February 19, 1847; Scott, *Memoirs*, 13–21, 541.

5 A Perfect Sacrifice: A Rape Case Expanded Military Justice

Just as in a court-martial, the judge advocate received the charges, summarized the case's circumstances, and created a list of witnesses. He informed the prisoner of his trial's time and place and the charges against him and requested from the prisoner the names of desired witnesses. The court then met, was sworn in, and listened while the judge advocate read the charges and the circumstances and examined the witnesses.[22] Then the judge advocate, who recorded proceedings, read them aloud to the court members before deliberations. The court required a minimum of five members present to proceed, the number on hand for Kirk's case. It decided guilt or innocence and the sentence. For a death sentence, two-thirds of the court had to concur, on guilt and the punishment.

Five of the seven appointed commission members were present for Kirk's trial: Lieutenant Colonel Samuel Anderson of the First Tennessee Foot Regiment, Captain Wright of the Fourth Illinois, Captain Charles Pearson of the Second New York Volunteer Regiment, Captain Michael Lawler of the Third Illinois, and Captain Shaw of the New York Volunteer Regiment. The other two volunteer officers appointed – Major Francis Bowman of the First Pennsylvania Regiment and Major Samuel Marshall of the Third Illinois – did not attend, leaving the commission with its minimum of five voting officers. Members of the court were "sworn by the Recorder in the presence of the accused, as was also the Recorder by the President of the Commission."[23]

Each court member had one vote and was "in the double capacity of jurors and judges; as jurors, they find the facts, and as judges, they award the punishment." The law recognized crimes might "be of different degrees of atrocity," and for rape, the court could sentence a guilty party to death or award *"such other punishment"* as they decided. Courts could also recommend mercy when mitigating circumstances made it appropriate. In Kirk's case, four of the five members present agreed on his guilt. None recommended mercy.[24]

The judge advocate's job was exceptionally difficult. While the articles of war were "silent on the subject of the Judge Advocate's assisting the Court with his counsels and advice as to any matters of form or

---

[22] Alexander Macomb, *The Practice of Courts Martial* (New York: Samuel Colman, 1840), 82–83.
[23] Military Commission Proceedings for Isaac Kirk.
[24] Macomb, *The Practice of Courts Martial*, 59–60, 67; "Court-Martial Case Files, 1809–1894," Case EE363.

law; it is nevertheless understood to be his duty" to hold the court to the prescribed manner of proceedings. Moreover, Congress abolished authorized positions for judge advocates in the army in 1821, so those appointed were typically ordinary line officers rather than trained lawyers.[25]

In an amalgamation of courtroom roles, the judge advocate was simultaneously adjudicator of courtroom issues, court recorder, prosecution, and defense. The appointed man was to "prosecute in the name of the United States, yet he is so far to consider himself as counsel for the prisoner." He should "object to any leading question," and prevent self-incrimination. He was to be especially vigilant during trials of enlisted soldiers "who, wanting all advantages of education or opportunities of mental improvement, must stand greatly in need of advice."[26] It was a type of paternalism that gravely disempowered the accused.

The court's dual role as judge and juror added to this disadvantage. While courts-martial involved many officers acting in various capacities, no court member was present solely to counsel or defend the accused. Courts-martial were a way to control soldiers more than a forum to seek justice, a tool for commanders to discipline subordinates so they would follow orders. They reflected the army's strict hierarchy, with little separation of powers. Military commissions magnified this effect by increasing the scope of military justice. Before Scott's Martial Law Order in 1847, the imbalanced powers of the court-martial mostly impacted soldiers, a majority-immigrant group whose treatment concerned few US civilians. After Scott's military commissions, martial law could dictate the fate of anyone under army authority – whether they came from the US or Mexico. The unique disadvantages to the accused inherent in courts-martial thus extended over all persons in an occupied area, resulting in an occupying army enabled by martial law to control the local population.[27]

THE CASE

On April 8, 1847, in a large room in the Veracruz customhouse, a military commission convened to hear Kirk's case. Kirk faced two charges.

---

[25] "Registers of the Records of the Proceedings of the U.S. Army General Courts-Martial," 1.
[26] Macomb, *The Practice of Courts Martial*, 80.
[27] Ibid., 57–59, 67, 80, Articles of War 87 and 69.

The first, rape, carried the specification that on April 4, "said Isaac Kirk colored man and a citizen of the United States, did commit, or attempt to commit a rape on the person of Maria Antonias Gallegas, a Mexican woman" on "the road between Malibran, and her residence called 'La Boticana' (Mexico)." The second, theft, specified that Kirk stole "from Maria Antonias Gallegas the sum of ten dollars and a comb." He pled not guilty.

Sergeant F. L. Nelson of the First Pennsylvania Regiment of Volunteers testified. While standing guard on April 3 in front of General Robert Patterson's headquarters, he noticed a Mexican man and his wife heading to the market. The next afternoon, he saw them returning. Gallegas testified that a man assaulted them on the walk home. He grabbed her by the throat, choked her, and ripped her clothes. Then, he pulled her by the hair into the chaparral and raped her. In Gallegas's words, she testified that the assailant "attacked me, catched me by the hair, threw me down and done what he choose to me." She recalled in court that "My husband ran after the Sergeant."

Fifteen minutes after Sergeant Nelson saw them pass by, he spotted Gallegas's husband running toward his guard post. Nelson said that the man "gave me to understand a negro man had assaulted them. The general ordered me to proceed at once and arrest the man." The two men ran down the road, the husband ahead of Nelson. After running three-quarters of a mile, Nelson was forty or fifty yards away and could see the assailant's "feet and legs, and the Mexican woman's also, with their heads and part of their bodies in the chaparral, apparently struggling. Not having my gun with me, I set the dogs belonging to the Mexican upon the prisoner when he jumped up and run off." Nelson continued, "I pursued him until he got in a thick chaparral, where he squatted down, and I lost sight of him."

Sergeant Nelson described the moment he found Gallegas: "Her hair was all down. Her neck and face covered with dust, her clothes was all torn, and was crying aloud." She had "the appearance of having had a violent struggle. And as soon as she got her eyes upon me, she came running towards me with her hands up, crying, ready to break her heart." Gallegas joined him, and they searched for the man. Nelson said, "The Mexican woman was close by me, when I found him sitting down. I asked her in his presence if the accused was the man, and she said yes. I told him, he must go with me" back to General Patterson's headquarters. Nelson went on to arrest the man and began returning at a brisk walk, with the assailant to his front, but the man's escape soon complicated his job. Nelson claimed that "as soon as he got where it was clear, he broke and run, and got away."[28]

Nelson reached the headquarters and reported it all to General Patterson, who told him to "take four men with our muskets, and shoot the prisoner down, if he did not surrender." Although the assailant escaped, Nelson seemed to know exactly where to find the man. He brought his newly armed party to the "place where the prisoner went" and "waited at the point on the road, where the prisoner soon came out." Nelson ordered the Black man he took to be the assailant "to stop, and he said he would not – he was going to his master. I replied, 'master or no master you must stop.' He said he would not." After this initial exchange, Nelson told the man he would shoot him if he did not comply, "at the same time presenting my gun. He then stopped, and I arrested him. He gave me some impudence, when I pricked him with the point of my bayonet, and that closed his tongue." This turn of events might have created some doubts had the commission been willing to entertain them. The prisoner's initial escape and the presence of Black populations among the army and in Mexico – officers brought free and enslaved Black servants on campaign and Veracruz had a significant Afro-Mexican population – call into question the possibility Nelson brought in the wrong man.[29]

Moreover, the timeline created uncertainty. Nelson's testimony established that the assault occurred in the afternoon. Gallegas estimated 3 or 4 p.m. William Ralston, a chaplain, testified that he ate lunch with Lieutenant Kirk – who employed Isaac and shared his surname – between noon and 1 p.m. and noted that Isaac attended "to the cooking arrangements." Lieutenant Kirk confirmed this, testifying that his general dining hour was one pm, and Isaac Kirk was present "for a good while

---

[28] "Court-Martial Case Files, 1809–1894," Case EE363, Veracruz, April 8, 1847. The case records Gallegas's testimony in English. General Patterson was unusual for a volunteer officer in that he was not native-born. He spent his early years in Ireland and emigrated to Philadelphia at a young age. Peterson, *The Military Heroes of the War with Mexico*, 239–40.

[29] "Court-Martial Case Files, 1809–1894," Case EE363, Veracruz, April 8, 1847. By the early 1800s, Mexico's Afro-descended population exceeded ten percent of the Mexican population. Gonzalo Aguirre Beltrán, *La Población Negra de México: Estudio Etnohistórico*, (México: Fonde de Cultura Económica, 1972), 232–33; Danielle Terrazas Williams, "Capitalizing Subjects: Free African-Descended Women of Means in Xalapa, Veracruz during the Long Seventeenth Century," (PhD diss, Duke University, 2013); Danielle Terrazas Williams, "'My Conscience Is Free and Clear': African-Descended Women, Status, and Slave Owning in Mid-Colonial Mexico," *The Americas* 75, no. 3 (July 2018): 352. See also: Carroll, *Blacks in Colonial Veracruz: Race, Ethnicity, and Regional Development*.

afterwards." As a Black servant in the lieutenant's army family, Isaac performed the labor a woman might if at home: he cooked and probably cleaned up afterward. Male subordinates, like women, could complete domestic tasks on army campaigns, and these duties probably filled Isaac's days.[30]

These times were rough estimates. Still, if accurate, the lieutenant noted that Isaac was asleep about an hour after the meal. Ralston established that the camp and Patterson's headquarters were at least a mile apart. Lieutenant Kirk also reported that he had lunch over a mile from Patterson's headquarters. If Lieutenant Kirk and Ralston began eating at 1 p.m. and finished an hour later, and Isaac cleaned up after the meal and then went to sleep, then Isaac might have been sleeping when the assault occurred that afternoon.

Isaac Kirk had at least a plausible alibi in place, and his jailers found no stolen goods on his person. Regarding the second charge of theft, Gallegas testified that "the negro also robbed me of ten dollars and of a comb." Kirk did not have a comb when searched. He had two dollars, eighty-seven and a half cents and witnesses explained why he had

---

[30] Johnson, *Roaring Camp*, 106, 111. The proceedings do not explain the shared surname between Isaac and Lieutenant Kirk. It may be a coincidence, or Lieutenant Kirk could have imposed his surname on Isaac upon hiring. The army may have adopted an employer's surname in court for convenience. Or, the lieutenant's family may have enslaved Isaac. Following this line of inquiry, the men could have been relatives. Lieutenant Kirk's testimony implied little prior knowledge of Isaac. It claimed another person, a "gentleman from Murray County, Tennessee," found Isaac for the lieutenant. Yet Lieutenant Kirk, called P. A. Kirk in his service records, enrolled and mustered into the regiment in June 1846 at Columbia, Tennessee – a city in Maury County – and the 1840 census includes a Peter A. Kirk. There is also a John Kirk in Maury County, who headed a twenty-one-person household of eight free whites and thirteen enslaved persons. There was likely a family connection between Peter and John, perhaps as brothers or cousins. The lieutenant, Peter, probably knew Isaac before the war and certainly knew the "gentleman" who sent Isaac to be a servant. It seems clear Peter dissembled in court, minimizing his knowledge of Isaac's past. The enslaver John Kirk was, like the lieutenant, in his thirties. He enslaved eight children under age ten, one young man aged 10–23, one man aged 24–35, and three women aged 24–35. It is unlikely that one enslaved adult man fathered eight children with the three women, though John could have purchased women with young children. Perhaps like many enslavers, John raped women under his control and enslaved their children. Based on these census records, Isaac Kirk may have been the young man of 10–23. If Isaac was the eldest of John's children by an enslaved woman, perhaps John freed him and the young Isaac chose to go to Mexico as a servant. Isaac might also have purchased or otherwise obtained his freedom. Or he may have still been enslaved when he died. "Sixth Census of the United States" (Bureau of the Census, 1840), Records of the Bureau of the Census, RG 29, NARA microfilm publication, M704, 580 rolls, NA.

this precise amount. Ralston paid Kirk a dollar the evening before his arrest. Lieutenant Kirk paid Isaac a dollar a few days earlier. Private Asahel Pipkin paid Kirk thirty-seven and a half cents the day before Kirk's arrest, and Private Matthew Cooper paid Kirk fifty cents the day of Kirk's arrest. This meticulous accounting failed to sway the commission, which found him guilty of theft and rape.[31]

The army may or may not have had the right man. The testimony also left an odd question unanswered, even unacknowledged. According to Nelson and Gallegas, her unnamed husband left his wife to be raped and then ran a mile and a half to bring an unarmed US savior. The husband had dogs with him capable of attacking the unarmed assailant, but he did not release them. It took Sergeant Nelson's arrival to unleash the dogs and drive away the rapist. Gallegas said that "When [Nelson] came, he got me away from the negro."[32] This detail emphasized how a narrative of army virility used Mexican men's alleged impotence as a foil. Nelson's testimony upheld the notion that Mexican women needed protection because Mexican men were cowardly and incapable – he who cannot defend his wife from rape is no man. The case exemplified protection's intermingled racial, ethnic, and gendered components. It located heroic white men above impotent Mexican men, and predatory Black men who made white protection necessary.

The commission did not attempt to find out more about Kirk's possible alibi, the potential for misidentification, the theft, or the husband's strange absence. These discrepancies may have been enough to acquit another defendant, but none questioned Kirk's guilt. The court had full faith in Gallegas's declaration that Kirk was "the same person who committed the rape upon" her. The court asked to confirm whether she resisted her attacker, and she testified that the "carnal connections" were "by violence and against [her] will." US legal tradition held with William Blackstone that to prove rape, a woman had to demonstrate that her assailant used violence and that she actively resisted throughout the attack.[33] By

---

[31] "Mexican War Compiled Military Service Records, 1st Tennessee Mounted Infantry," RG 94, Entry 516, NA, Washington DC. While Ralston is merely called a "Private" in the court martial file, his service record notes that he was paid as a private but was appointed Chaplain by James Thomas on July 8, 1846.

[32] "Court-Martial Case Files, 1809–1894," Case EE363.

[33] Blackstone, *Blackstone's Commentaries*, 210. Block, *Rape & Sexual Power in Early America*, 16. Winfield Scott had a disturbing personal experience with the notion that good women physically resisted assault. Scott's longtime aide, Erasmus Keyes, recorded

5 A Perfect Sacrifice: A Rape Case Expanded Military Justice 199

confirming her resistance, Gallegas verified that the commission had the information required to prosecute. Kirk's defense, two counsels specially provided for him who were likely army officers, declined to ask her any questions.

The commission sentenced Kirk to die. Scott approved the proceedings and sentence on the following day and published specific requirements to ensure the most public hanging possible. Scott's predecessor as general-in-chief had written that "one of the great ends of punishment is the prevention of crime by example." Accordingly, while a hanging involved far less ceremony than a firing squad, Macomb said officers should form their troops into a square around the gallows. A designated person would read the charge, sentence, and General Orders aloud, and then an executioner would hang the prisoner.[34]

Following this protocol, Scott's General Orders 101, published on April 9, specified that

> The General in Chief approves the proceedings and sentence in the case of Isaac Kirk. The sentence will be carried into execution at such hour tomorrow and such place within the city walls as may be designated by the governor of the city, who is requested to cause this man to be executed, and also to cause public notice to be given of the same in the Spanish language.[35]

The inclusion of a Spanish language notice was a special touch outside the normal process to amplify the salutary effect of Kirk's hanging.

On April 10, the US Army hanged Kirk as ordered, "on the plain outside the walls of the city," surrounded by US troops and Veracruzanos

---

an anecdote from Scott's youth to set up his punchline that Scott was "more scared by a broomstick in the hands of a woman than he could have been by a saber in the hands of a Turk." While on a long walk during vacation from college, Scott stopped at a farmhouse for a glass of milk. The woman of the house, alone in an isolated area, obliged and spoke with him. He returned this hospitality by, in his words, taking "manual liberties with her." Scott continued, "but at my first motion, she sprang away, seized a broom, and came at me with a fury such as only an earnest female can display." Related as a charming bit of color in Keyes's memoir, it must have been frightening for the woman. Keyes, *Fifty Years' Observations of Men and Events*, 23, 31, 34.

[34] Davis, *Autobiography of the Late Colonel George T. M. Davis*, 133; Macomb, *The Practice of Courts Martial*, 75–78. First names identified in: Robarts, *Mexican War Veterans*. There is no Captain Shaw listed under New York's regiments.

[35] *General Orders, Headquarters of the Army, in Mexico, January to May 1847*, vol. 23, 103. In contrast, for two other soldiers tried by the same military commission and convicted of theft, Scott's order merely designated the location of imprisonment as the Castle of San Juan de Ulúa.

alike, who bore witness to his passing.[36] Army officer Ethan Allen Hitchcock recorded the event, writing that he observed "A dreadful scene at 5 pm – the hanging of a man for rape."[37] On April 11, General Scott issued his famous "Proclamation to the Mexican People." He declared Kirk's death at the US Army's hands was proof "Americans are not your enemies," but rather "the friends of the peaceful inhabitants of the country we occupy." Mexicans would be "safe" under "martial law."[38]

Kirk's death helped Scott establish military commissions as legitimate and necessary components of the US laws of war. Equally, it showcased the ways military justice reflected both the army's hierarchical culture and US society's distinctions of gender, ethnicity, and race. It brought these ideas into alignment in a way that gave the army every incentive to prosecute. It featured a white enlisted hero, Sergeant Nelson, who obeyed his officer, General Patterson, to assist a woman who required white men's military protection. Nelson is like a character from wartime fictions, a noble young soldier who saves a Mexican woman from a villain's clutches.[39] The case readily assumed symbolic value, with Gallegas embodying Mexico and Nelson the US. Likewise, the commission endowed her Black assailant with symbolic brutality and her Mexican husband with archetypal cowardice.

Her husband's inability to defend her brought army courage into stark relief. Throughout the war, officers and enlisted men consistently

---

[36] Davis, "From the Army." Davis summarized various war news, including short descriptions of the others tried by his military commission, and a significantly longer one on Kirk. He noted that "The sentence was in accordance with the laws of the State of Tennessee," Kirk's state of residence, "for a similar offense," that is, rape committed by a Black man against a white woman.

[37] Major-General Ethan Allen Hitchcock, U.S.A, *Fifty Years in Camp and Field*, ed. W. A. Croffut (New York: G. P. Putnam's Sons, 1909), 250. Scott's General Orders 101, published on April 9, suggested Kirk would die on April 10 at 5 p.m. Most sources use April 10 as the date of Kirk's execution. Alabama volunteer officer Captain William Coleman recorded that on Saturday, April 10, they "hung a Negro who was from Tennessee for committing a rape on a Mexican woman." J. Hugh LeBaron and William G. Coleman, *Perry Volunteers in the Mexican War* (Westminster, MD: Heritage Books, 2008), 169–70. Hitchcock's first-person account records that the hanging took place on April 9, though he stipulates 5 p.m. I assume Hitchcock recorded the wrong date.

[38] Thirtieth Congress, First Session, *House of Representatives Mexican War Correspondence*, 1848, 938, Scott, Proclamation to the Mexican People, April 11, 1847.

[39] As Shelley Streeby notes, "a good deal of sensational literature was written by men, and much of it promotes competing ideologies of heroic masculinity and mobilizes representations of women's bodies as symbols of race and nation." Shelley Streeby, *American Sensations: Class, Empire, and the Production of Popular Culture* (Berkeley: University of California Press, 2002), 32.

viewed the women of Mexico as "superior in all classes to the men" and labeled Mexican men lazy and incapable.[40] Kirk's trial demonstrates this. Gallegas's husband is utterly absent from the record. The military commission assumed his irrelevance. Mexican men disappear in a story where a white man overpowers a Black man to save a Mexican woman.

The same commission tried others in addition to Kirk, all white volunteer soldiers facing charges of robbery or theft. Sergeant James Adams, Private Peter Murphy, and Private John Padfield of the Third Illinois Regiment of Volunteers faced charges of robbery and aiding and abetting in a robbery after they broke into the home of Rosalie Lopez and plundered it. Lopez provided a detailed list of jewelry, clothing, and household goods the men had stolen. Other women in her household were present during the break-in. The men offered "indecencies to the person of Rosalie Lopez...and the females of her family." Yet Lopez, a woman with sufficient wealth to produce a list of stolen valuables, did not elaborate on the "indecencies" she suffered.[41]

Gallegas was probably a woman of more modest means. She returned from the market at Veracruz on foot with her husband and had some money on her person. The combination of traveling as a pedestrian but carrying cash suggests she was of ordinary means, neither wealthy nor deeply impoverished. Unlike Lopez, who described her stolen items in detail but not the sexual aggression she alluded to, Gallegas described what happened to her property and her person.

Taken together, Lopez and Gallegas's testimonies could represent a class-based use of the justice system. Lopez's wealth may have made her reluctant to describe Adams's indecent acts for fear of reputational damage.[42] It may also be that Gallegas had a US ally in Sergeant

---

[40] Luther Giddings, *Sketches of the Campaign in Northern Mexico* (New York: G. P. Putnam & Co, 1853), 58. Reginald Horsman argues the collision of US and Mexican people in the Southwest – both during the Texas Revolution and during the Mexican War – was the "catalyst in the overt adoption of a racial Anglo-Saxonism." Horsman recognizes the gendered dimension at work, arguing that the stereotype of "receptive Mexican women and lazy, inept Mexican men was to sink deep into American racial mythology." Horsman, *Race and Manifest Destiny: The Origins of American Racial Anglo-Saxonism*, 234.

[41] Military Commission Proceedings, Veracruz, Cases EE337 (Adams, April 1, 1847), EE338 (Padfield, March 31, 1847) and EE365 (Murphy, April 8, 1847), RG 153, "Court-Martial Case Files, 1809–1894," NA.

[42] The commission found Adams and Murphy guilty of robbery and aiding and abetting a robbery. Adams received a two-month imprisonment, reduction to the ranks, and a fine of two months' pay. Murphy received a two-month imprisonment and a fine of three months' pay. Ibid.

Nelson whereas Lopez had only her word and that of other women. Or, because Nelson witnessed the rape and shortly after reported it to General Patterson, US involvement may have removed Gallegas's choice to stay silent.

Except for the Kirk case, the commissions avoided evidence of sexual impropriety, at least when white soldiers were perpetrators. Private Andrew Foster stood accused of robbing a Mexican woman, Maria Sylvester. Her testimony described how

> the prisoner and another man came to my house on the 20th of April about one or 2 leagues from Veracruz, the prisoner got off his horse, presented a pistol at the men (Mexicans) who were there. The prisoner took $5, a pair of earrings, two sashes, and a thimble besides took some improper liberties with me and the women that were there. They both went away afterwards.

The army did not punish Foster for taking "liberties" with the Mexican women he robbed – a catch-all euphemism for many kinds of sexual harassment and assault. And the commission found Foster not guilty.[43]

Similarly, Private John Williams stood accused of robbing Maria Manuela Castillo, "a Mexican of a quantity of property" in Veracruz. She testified that "about 15 days since, a league and a half from Veracruz, the prisoner came to my house about 4 o'clock A.M. and took, therefore, a skin, a pair of earrings, and a man's suit of clothes." With him, "there were two others. The prisoner is the only one I know as he presented his pistol at me and asked for money. I recognize him by the light of the candle." Williams was released.

Toward the end of testimony in Kirk's case, the Judge Advocate asked witness William Ralston what the punishment was for rape in Tennessee when committed by a Black man. He replied, "I have always understood it to be death. In the case of a slave, I know it to be so; I allude to the attempt when made upon a free white person, as I have witnessed both the trial and execution of a slave under such circumstances." For a rape "committed upon a free person of any other color," the punishment was probably "less than death."[44] Kirk's crime had effectively downgraded him to the level of an enslaved person and elevated Gallegas to the position of a white woman. US military justice followed a legal precedent established by slave states.

---

[43] "Court-Martial Case Files, 1809–1894," Case FF101, Veracruz, March 12, 1848.
[44] Military Commission Proceedings for Isaac Kirk.

Still, while Kirk's death echoed the punishment of an enslaved person for rape, Scott emphasized Kirk's freedom and purported status as a US citizen. The guilty verdict identified Kirk explicitly as a "citizen of the United States," and Scott's proclamation identified the rapist hanged as an American. The index for the compiled *General Orders of the Army in Mexico* also includes a brief entry. Rather than reflecting Scott's portrayal of Kirk as a US person, it focuses on the underlying issue of race, reading "Kirk, Isaac, (colored) tried and sentenced to death."[45] In the army's public-facing documents, Kirk was a citizen, a warning to other US men who dared harm Mexican women. In this internal document, the citizen was gone. Race remained.

Racial difference was not only a critical factor in the verdict; it must also have been an essential factor in Gallegas's decision to testify. Skin color was a vital element of social status in Mexico, and US observers often failed to grasp Mexican society's nuanced caste system. Patricia Seed writes that as colonial Mexico developed, "Spanish categories of status came to represent racial difference," and by the early 1800s racial disparity corresponded to social worth.[46] It may have been more permissible for Gallegas to report a Black man for rape. Criminality attached more easily to social inferiors, making convictions more probable. In contrast, it may have been challenging to obtain justice for a rape committed by a white man, thus perhaps less worth the risk of testifying.

When it came to US views of Mexican women, many emphasized differences in religion, race, language, and customs. That wide-ranging otherness allowed varied interpretations, from admiring descriptions of "Spanish" ladies, to detailed notes on pretty village girls, to disparaging accounts of "mighty ugly" creatures.[47] Men in the US Army drew conclusions about Mexican women based on much more than complexion – they did so through circumstantial calculations informed by behavior, dress, and perceived attractiveness.

For Gallegas, this meant that the circumstances of her rape would ultimately determine her social status in US eyes. As the alleged victim of a Black man for whom the army was responsible, the trial elevated her to "respectable woman" status, a worthy subject of military protection regardless of her position in Mexican society.[48] The racial difference

[45] *General Orders, Headquarters of the Army, in Mexico, January to May 1847*, 23: Index.
[46] Seed, *To Love, Honor, and Obey in Colonial Mexico*, 24, 205.
[47] Dana, *Monterrey Is Ours! The Mexican War Letters of Lieutenant Dana, 1845–1847*, 88, June 11, 1846.
[48] Davis, *Autobiography of the Late Colonel George T. M. Davis*, 136.

between Kirk and the military commission's members, and thus the racial difference between Gallegas and Kirk, raised her perceived class even as it raised Kirk's apparent criminality.

The commission also emphasized Gallegas's gender and need for soldiers to protect women. Although military hierarchy separated officers from enlisted men – a chasm less pronounced among volunteers than regulars though still present – a shared identity united Sergeant Nelson and General Patterson in safeguarding a Mexican woman and punishing her Black assailant. General Patterson ordered Sergeant Nelson to run to Gallegas' aid, and provided men and weapons to aid Nelson's pursuit. Nelson ran, fought, captured, arrested, and searched the suspect. Nelson and Patterson each remained in rank-based spheres of responsibility, with the officer directing and providing, and the noncommissioned officer carrying out orders and enforcing discipline. In a kind of complementarity, each worked toward the common goal of protecting Gallegas and providing justice. This shared protector-identity developed common ground.

The army's position as Gallegas's savior made the case a source of legitimacy not only for the US military but for those individuals who sealed Kirk's fate. In his autobiography, Lieutenant George Davis – the commission's Judge Advocate – depicted himself as a paragon of military justice. He assured readers he "religiously vowed that not one of the accused whose guilt was established beyond reasonable doubt should escape unwhipped of justice; nor, on the other hand, should an innocent man be brought under condemnation."[49] He underscored his benevolence in dealing with Isaac Kirk, a man from a "degraded and friendless race, with few...from whom he could expect either compassion or pity." This recognition imposed on Davis "a sleepless vigilance." He also claimed to ensure "able and competent persons to defend" Kirk, an interesting assertion given their failure to point out gaps in the case, and approved Kirk's death sentence.[50]

Like Davis, Scott used Kirk's death in his memoirs. He wrote that his "Martial Law Order" and Kirk's subsequent execution had "worked like

---

[49] Ibid., 132. Davis wrote his autobiography in old age, for his daughters and granddaughters, perhaps as a memento, or so sales would contribute to their support. His legal representatives published it posthumously in 1891.

[50] To inject a final note of Christian sympathy, Davis inserted the phrase "and may God have mercy upon your soul" into the sentencing portion of the official record. Davis reported that General Scott heaped praise on this choice, and after writing that there were "many flattering compliments to myself which I do not care to repeat," spent about a page repeating compliments. Ibid., 136–38.

a charm; that it had conciliated Mexicans; intimidated the vicious of the several races, and being executed with impartial rigor, gave the highest moral deportment and discipline ever known in an invading army."[51] Perhaps considering the events as distant memories made it easier for Scott to make these conclusions. But in 1847, he had not found it so simple.

Coercion and crime often bedeviled Scott's hopes for a model occupation. Still, army claims of benevolence proved enduring. Naturalized ideas of race and gender – especially white soldiers' responsibility to protect women – helped army officers justify the need for martial law and led to a remarkable expansion of military power. By emphasizing that army officers had to control those men who posed a potential threat to women, the Kirk case helped the US Army legitimize military commissions.

THE US ARMY AND CIVILIAN CASUALTIES IN VERACRUZ

The Kirk case was not only of great value to Scott as he sought to legitimize military commissions. It also established a protective framework for occupation that legitimized the civilian casualties recently incurred by the US bombardment of Veracruz. Just a few weeks before Kirk hanged, Scott's army bombarded the city, from 4:15 pm on March 22, 1847, to 8:30 am on March 26. The Mexican newspaper *El Republicano* reported a "horrible rain of projectiles" that "spilled death and fire on the city." Another article noted that Scott's strategy was clearly to target the city and hospitals so the bombing would destroy not the city walls but human lives. Lieutenant John Peck, a West Point officer, elaborated: "the town is crumbling to pieces under this iron rain. You can see the shot dash through the roofs and hear the explosions in the stories below. Buildings are fired often. The cries of the poor, of the women and children and wounded must be appalling. Lord have mercy on them." On March 25, Scott refused a request from the foreign consuls of Veracruz to evacuate persons from neutral nations along with all women and children.[52]

Scott's choice followed Taylor's actions in July 1846 while bombarding Monterrey. Taylor denied a Mexican request to evacuate "all the old and infirm men, all the women and children out of the city." Mexican sources described the misery that followed. US troops advanced directly through the houses, knocking down wall after adjoining wall, severely

---

[51] Scott, *Memoirs*, 396.
[52] Bauer, *The Mexican War: 1846–1848*, 249–51; "Toma de Veracruz," April 3, 1847, "Estado de Veracruz," 1; Reprinted in: "Toma de Veracruz," April 18, 1847; Peck, "The Sign of the Eagle," 75.

damaging the city and invariably killed noncombatants taking shelter. According to a local, Monterrey "was converted into a vast cemetery. The unburied bodies, the dead and putrid mules, the silence of the streets, all gave a fearful aspect to this city."[53]

Veracruz faced similar terror. One letter printed by a foreign neutral in Veracruz wrote bitterly afterward that "the bombardment has been so destructive that Veracruz, at present, is no more than a pile of ruins.... It would be futile to try to give you a description of the misfortunes of this unhappy population, its misery, and the barbarous manner in which the Americans have bombarded us, for which there isn't a single precedent in modern history." Of the bombardment, German-born artilleryman Frederick Zeh wrote, "we could hear from our trenches the plaintive cries of the people and the barking of dogs."[54] Both generals preferred to hasten victory rather than protect civilians.

Indeed, while military historians typically characterize Scott as the more chivalrous toward civilians, Taylor negotiated the more generous armistice and more quickly ended the US attack on the civilian-filled city of Monterrey. Doing so earned Taylor some of President Polk's bounteous ire. Polk preferred terms less favorable to the Mexicans and wanted more aggression from his general. In a letter to the Army Adjutant General, Taylor defended his decision, which guaranteed defeated Mexicans a retreat with battle honors and weapons. He wrote that his force of 6,000 men was not enough to guard the full Mexican garrison, who would have escaped "at the expense of valuable lives and much damage to the city." Taylor emphasized, "The consideration of humanity was present to my mind," which outweighed "the doubtful advantages to be gained by a resumption of the attack upon the town."

Taylor believed he was proven right after the battle. The army found the Mexicans' "principal magazine, containing an immense amount of powder, was in the cathedral, completely exposed to our shells from two directions." Taylor noted, "The explosion of this mass of powder, which must have ultimately resulted from a continuance of the bombardment, would have been infinitely disastrous, involving the destruction not only

---

[53] Streeby, *American Sensations*, 69. Quoted from Ramón Alcaraz, *The Other Side, or, Notes for the History of the War between Mexico and the United States*, trans. Albert C. Ramsey (New York: John Wiley, 1850).

[54] Conway, *The U.S.–Mexican War: A Binational Reader*, 85 From *El Monitor Republicano*, April 4, 1847," Carta particular de un appreciable estranjero que con imparcialidad describe detalladamente todos los desastrosos acontecimientos," translation by Gustavo Pellon. Also in: "Détail Sur Le Siege et La Capitulation de Veracruz;" Zeh, Orr, and Miller, *An Immigrant Soldier in the Mexican War*, 21.

5 A Perfect Sacrifice: A Rape Case Expanded Military Justice 207

of the Mexican troops but of noncombatants, and even our own people, had we pressed the attack."[55]

Yet Taylor in Monterrey and Scott in Veracruz made the same choice: bombard civilians for a rapid win. In his memoirs, Scott justified his refusal to evacuate noncombatants. He maintained, "this was better for the consuls, women, and children, as well as for the United States, than the temporary truce that [he] had rejected." In the chapter on Veracruz, Scott underscored low US casualties. He did not refer to women's deaths beyond claiming he successfully minimized risk to civilians.[56] Like the army paternalist he was, he believed swiftly bringing Veracruz under US protection was the best possible outcome for noncombatants.

Reports of civilian casualties soon spread in the US press. A correspondent from the *New Orleans Delta* noted of Veracruz that "the loss among the soldiery is comparatively small and the destruction among the women and children is very great," estimating a total of 6,700 shells shot during the siege for a weight of 463,600 pounds of ordnance hurled into the walled city. Veracruz "suffered a great deal during the siege." A cathedral "had its dome knocked off by a shell, which fell and killed a number of women and children." A US soldier described the plight of Mexicans, saying, "whole families had perished by a single shell… there was safety nowhere." A West Point graduate, Lieutenant Theodore Laidley, wrote to his father that he rode through the city soon after. It was "a sorry sight to see the desolation that the shells had made among the houses." Casualty estimates for the siege of Veracruz differ, but a moderate one is 350 Mexican soldiers killed, a comparable quantity wounded, 400 civilians killed, and 250 civilians injured.[57]

---

[55] Thirtieth Congress, First Session, *House of Representatives Mexican War Correspondence*, 1848, 359, Taylor to Adjutant General, November 8, 1846.
[56] Scott, *Memoirs of Lieut.-General Scott, LL.D Written by Himself*, 425, 428.
[57] Hughes, *Niles' National Register*, 1847, XXII:81, 100; Brackett, *General Lane's Brigade in Central Mexico*, 44; Laidley, *Surrounded by Dangers of All Kinds*, 56, April 2, 1847. The most conservative US estimates of Mexican casualties began in the 60s and 80s, with higher Mexican estimates including 1000 Mexicans killed. A British observer estimated 100 civilians killed and 80 soldiers. Estimates of property damage were 5–6 million dollars. Johnson, *A Gallant Little Army*, 49. One soldier wrote "the Mexicans informed us that the loss among the women and children was far greater than among the soldiers." Hughes, *Niles' National Register*, 1847, XXII: 51. The *New Orleans Delta* reported Mexican casualty estimations ranging from 500 to 1000, with all having in common high numbers of civilian deaths relative to soldiers. An exception is one Mexican estimate of 500 civilians and 600 soldiers killed. Smith and Judah, *Chronicles of the Gringos: The US Army in the Mexican War, 1846–1848*, 185. A Mexican narrative of Veracruz, printed first in Jalapa, called women and children followed by whole families the first victims of bombardment. Ibid., 92.

Nearly all reports included higher casualties among civilians. Pro-war newspaperman George Kendall, whose wrote about his imprisonment and forced march through Mexico in 1835 after the failed Texas-Santa Fe Expedition, described a similar scene. Kendall began a successful penny press soon after his release from Mexico, and in 1837 launched the New Orleans-based *Picayune*. Kendall accompanied Scott's campaign from Veracruz to Mexico City as one of the US Army's first war correspondents.[58] Even Kendall, a staunch supporter of aggressive action against Mexico, admitted, "it is certain that women, children and noncombatants have suffered the most." Kendall's separation of "noncombatant" from women and children suggests he views women and children as so far outside of war that noncombatants meant only adult men who were not soldiers.

Despite high civilian casualties, the army's supporters claimed a military *and* a humanitarian victory. Under the heading "Glorious Achievement," *The Washington Union* of April 10, 1847 wrote of Veracruz, "this great achievement has been effected with little loss of life on our part." The *Union* trumpeted minimal US losses while ignoring civilian deaths. Scott actually lamented that his triumph was *too* bloodless, worrying that the US public would not appreciate a victory that was "unaccompanied by a long butcher's bill." As Amy Greenberg asserts, "Scott clearly chose civilian deaths over US casualties."[59] He, and many others, approached the aftermath of Veracruz from a one-sided perspective.

Much as many historians have assumed that Scott's Proclamation on the Kirk case represented fact and thus have failed to reckon with it, an exclusive focus on US casualties obscures the war's full cost in lives. Thomas Spahr's discussion of "blood and treasure" of the conflict concludes, "the cost of the war with Mexico for the United States was great; the Americans sustained 12,876 deaths, 26,732 total casualties, and expended approximately $140 million."[60] Army reporting, too, described those 12,876 US deaths as the full measure of wartime deaths, and mentions of the

---

[58] Huntzicker, *The Popular Press, 1833–1865*, 98.
[59] Kendall, *Dispatches from the Mexican War*, 185, 107; Smith and Judah, *Chronicles of the Gringos: The US Army in the Mexican War, 1846–1848*, 186; Greenberg, *A Wicked War: Polk, Clay, Lincoln, and the 1846 U.S. Invasion of Mexico*, 171. The anti-war press condemned the bombing of Veracruz. Antiwar editor Jane Grey Swisshelm upon meeting a former soldier and friend in the street after the war, refused to take his hand saying there was blood on it. Samuel Black replied "I swear to you I never killed a woman or a child" and she replied "then you did not fight in Mexico" or participate in bombing Veracruz. Conway, *The U.S.–Mexican War: A Binational Reader*, 126.
[60] Spahr, "Occupying for Peace," 8.

5 A Perfect Sacrifice: A Rape Case Expanded Military Justice 209

war's civilian casualties remain rare in US scholarship. Because the army's casualty reports omitted civilians, only official deaths – narrowly defined as US soldiers – made it into US reports.

This successful narrative came from the same mindset that induced Scott to declare, in planning to bombard Veracruz, "I am strongly inclined – policy concurring with humanity – to…take the city with the least possible loss of life." He claimed bloodless success, but officers and soldiers who recorded what they found could not help but notice the blood. Lieutenant John Peck noted that "hundreds of poor women and children have been killed."[61] Even before they witnessed the aftermath, US artillerymen knew their bombs hit civilian targets. Artillery officer Francis Collins wrote on March 19, 1847 the Mexican garrison had "absolutely done their best to prevent us from constructing batteries, for the purpose of blowing down their houses about the ears of their wives and children." On March 22, he elaborated, US shells fell "through the roofs of buildings, bursting and scattering death and destruction" and the "screams and yells of the populace, whether in defiance or fear, could be distinctly heard, and now while I write I do hear them."

After Veracruz surrendered and Collins saw the place, he noted that "about one-half of the city was much damaged by the bombardment. Many of the higher classes of inhabitants left it before it was invested, and when they return and witness the ruin spread around their shattered dwellings, they will no doubt be thankful they were not at home." Describing the aftermath, he wrote, "The shells, falling on the tops of the houses, crashed through the roofs into the exterior and then exploding produced the most frightful and terrific effects." Collins reflected, "The thunder of these explosions was truly awful at the distance of a mile from the scene. There must have been the most horrible suffering and dismay among the women and children," probably a burden borne most acutely by poor families who lacked the resources to leave.[62]

---

[61] Bauer, *The Mexican War: 1846–1848*, 247; Peck, "The Sign of the Eagle," 78. Peck meant to insult Mexican soldiers. The full quote is "hundreds of poor women and children have been killed or injured for the maintenance of Mexican honor, while soldiers were safe in the bomb proofs." Mexican sources contradict Peck, noting that during the bombardment Mexican soldiers constantly patrolled the streets to maintain security. "Estado de Veracruz," 1.

[62] Francis Collins, *Journal of Francis Collins: An Artillery Officer in the Mexican War*, ed. Maria Clinton Collins, Vol. X, 1915, Nos. 2 & 3, April and July, *Quarterly Publication of the Historical and Philosophical Society of Ohio* (Cincinnati: Abingdon Press, 1915), 54–58.

Scott and his defenders argued that he followed the usual escalation of hostilities because he offered women the opportunity to leave before bombing began. Thus, those who remained must be "compelled to abide the consequences, and blame no person but themselves." Another soldier ridiculed the "virtuous indignation" of the British press after the bombing, noting the city was "duly warned," and the US could not do anything if Mexicans "chose to remain and be killed." A US soldiers' newspaper, *The Picket Guard*, reported, "Half the city is in ruins. The Mexican loss was 1500 to 2000, a heavy proportion of women and children. Gen. Scott admonished Morales in advance to send out the women and children, but he refused." The paper continued, "Afterward, on the 26th of March, Morales wanted permission to send them out, which was then not granted, and the city immediately proposed terms of capitulation." *The Picket Guard* believed Scott made the right choices.[63]

Yet as Colonel Ethan Allen Hitchcock, serving as Scott's inspector general, noticed, "few remained" in Veracruz "except the poorest people and the soldiers." Many poor Veracruzanos lacked the resources to leave the city. Artilleryman Frederick Zeh, himself a poor immigrant, reflected that "as usual, misfortune afflicts the poor most of all. During this siege, too, the wretched huts of the proletariat of Veracruz were dashed to pieces by our breach batteries." In contrast, he recorded that "The wealthy inhabitants had protected their buildings with sandbags and thus suffered only slight losses."[64] Better-off residents may have stayed because neither leaving property unguarded in the city nor taking it along and risking the roads were appealing.

Some US historians defend Scott's decision to deny foreign consuls' requests for neutral and noncombatant evacuations. One argues, the proposed single-day evacuation would have unacceptably delayed US operations, plus "a consideration for the safety of the civilians works both ways," and that the Mexican commander could have chosen to fight outside Veracruz instead of using the walled city for its intended purpose of defense. But during France's war on Mexico in 1838, called the Pastry War, French Admiral Charles Baudin worked with Mexican leaders to minimize civilian casualties as he prepared to bombard Veracruz.[65] Accepting civilian casualties was a solution, but not the only option.

[63] Moore, *Scott's Campaign in Mexico*, 13, 37; Osman.
[64] Hitchcock, U.S.A, *Fifty Years in Camp and Field*, 248; Zeh, Orr, and Miller, *An Immigrant Soldier in the Mexican War*, 22.
[65] Johnson, *A Gallant Little Army*, 45; Guardino, *The Dead March: A History of the Mexican–American War*, 2017, 438, Note 77.

5 A Perfect Sacrifice: A Rape Case Expanded Military Justice 211

Scott's perspective that his actions were logical, justified, and as humane as circumstances would allow is the view the US Army enshrined in its cultural memory. Writing a history of the Second Dragoons published in 1875, one officer encapsulated this simplified narrative of conventional military victory: the "investment" lasted several days, until "the garrison surrendered under terms agreed upon by a joint commission representing both armies." Then, "The garrison was permitted to march out of the city with the honors of war, to a field, where their arms were laid down." The US Army "entered and took possession of the city and castle." Gone were the civilians, the devastation, and the bombardment. Institutional memory supported Scott's focus on US losses as the sole relevant metric. Official casualty lists of Veracruz required an accurate listing of dead and wounded US troops but imposed no requirement to account for civilian deaths.[66] It was a pragmatic choice with significant consequences. Defining loss in US terms made the attack seem more humane and lessened military culpability for targeting civilians.[67] Far from protecting them, civilian status made Mexican women more vulnerable by making them invisible.

The army also enshrined Veracruz as a bona fide victory by describing it as a siege rather than a bombardment. Scott himself revised the Army *General Regulations* in 1825 to include specific procedures to be followed in a siege. The regulations stressed that bombardment was only one component of the more extensive operations that made up a siege, which should have more to do with digging trenches than firing ordnance. Both were accepted aspects of a siege, though Veracruz inverted this formula, having far more to do with artillery than engineers.[68] It is a testament to the situational character of regulations that in combat, even their author considered them guidelines, not rules.

Recognizing the attack for what it was – a bombardment of a city's civilian center designed to shock civilians and force a surrender – underscores rather than hides the human cost of conquest. A poem featured in *El Monitor Republicano*, "Veracruz y El General Scott," sought to capture this. The poet wrote, Scott did not point his mortars at the walls,

---

[66] Rodenbough, *From Everglade to Cañón with the Second Dragoons*, 136; Furber, *The Twelve Months Volunteer*, 556.
[67] Mexican papers also omitted individual women, noting devastation wrought on anonymous women and children. One article included a list of men deserving thanks for noble conduct but mentioned no women by name. "Estado de Veracruz," 1.
[68] Scott, *General Regulations for the Army*, 1825, 144–48.

where Mexican soldiers defended the city, but on its "defenseless and shocked" civilians:

> No apunta sus morteros el malvado
> donde el valor le desafía,
> dirige bombas mil noche y día,
> sobra el pueblo indefenso y consternado.

A more accurate claim, then, is Irving Levinson's conclusion. Scott "conducted the operation with scant consideration for civilian casualties." Although Scott, as John Fabian Witt argues, "brought the outlook of the *General Regulations* to the Mexican War in 1846," Scott did so selectively to enable rather than constrain his plans.[69]

Army officers had powerful incentives to obscure the civilian body counts that dominated early coverage of Veracruz. In a recent monograph on the war, Mexicanist Peter Guardino demonstrates that while the US Army sought to portray civilians' deaths during the bombardment of Veracruz as a military necessity producing minimal harm, Mexican observers and numerous foreigners roundly condemned civilian deaths. Veracruz was the "most widely reported battle of the war, and the most negatively reported."[70] Yet in military channels, condemnations of Veracruz gave way to the official story, as officers like Scott successfully changed the narrative to focus on generous terms of surrender at Veracruz and purported success in enforcing strict discipline.

Kirk's death was a tremendous boon to that narrative. Mexican civilians who watched Kirk die stood alongside US troops who had so recently launched a seemingly endless supply of artillery into their homes. Rather than watching while international attention focused on civilian deaths, Scott could shift some of that attention to Kirk's righteous execution. He could describe how the US Army struck down one of its own for Mexicans' benefit. Papers like *Niles' National Register* widely reprinted Scott's Proclamation and followed his progress in Mexico, where interested observers of great campaigns like the Duke of Wellington could track him from across the Atlantic.

Although the proclamation quickly made its way across Mexico, Mexican observers did not respond to Scott's efforts in the way he

---

[69] "Veracruz y El General Scott"; Levinson, *Wars within War*, 32; Witt, *Lincoln's Code*, 86.
[70] Guardino, *The Dead March: A History of the Mexican–American War*, 2017, 192; Greenberg, *A Wicked War: Polk, Clay, Lincoln, and the 1846 U.S. Invasion of Mexico*, 172.

5 A Perfect Sacrifice: A Rape Case Expanded Military Justice 213

hoped. *El Monitor Republicano* in Mexico City reprinted it in Spanish on April 17 – its editors translated Scott's words after seeing them in *The American Eagle* of April 13. They inveighed against Scott's offer of a "conditional and degrading" peace that threatened death to guerrillas who continued to resist, concluding, "¡Qué ridícula contradicción!" (what a ridiculous contradiction!).[71] A few days later, on April 24, another translation appeared accompanied by commentary on each paragraph. Regarding the section on a man hanged for raping a Mexican woman, the paper wrote that "one has been hanged: that is something. Most of the North American army is made up of evildoers: they have committed all kinds of crimes, some gruesome, as everyone knows, and only one has been punished." The only thing worse than this "something," Kirk's death, would be "nothing." Perhaps these journalists recalled the many reports of atrocities against Mexican civilians from northern Mexico the previous year, where US volunteers

---

[71] "Proclama," *El Monitor Republicano*, April 17, 1847, Número 782 Sabado. Translation from *The American Eagle* of April 13, 1847. Scott's original proclamation read: "I have, from the first, done everything in my power to place [Mexican civilians] under the safeguard of martial law, against the few bad men in this army. My orders to that effect, known to all, are precise and rigorous. Under them, several Americans have already been punished, by fine, for the benefit of Mexicans, besides imprisonment; and one, for a rape, has been hung by the neck. Is this not a proof of good faith and energetic discipline?" Thirtieth Congress, First Session, *House of Representatives Mexican War Correspondence*, 1848, 166–67, Marcy to Taylor, Proclamation No. 10, "A Proclamation by the General Commanding The Army of the U.S. of America." *El Monitor* translated the section referencing Kirk as follows: "Mis órdenes al efecto, sabidas de todos, son terminantes y rigorosas. En virtud de ellas han sido ya castigados algunos americanos, con multa impuesta a beneficios de los mexicanos, y con precisión, y ha sido ahorcado uno por rapto. ¿No es esta una prueba de buena fe y de severa disciplina?" A later edition also included a translated proclamation, and rendered the phrase dealing with the Kirk case as "y uno por haber violado a una Mexicana ha sido ahorcado." In Spanish, the paper's commentary on this phrase was: "ha sido ahorcado uno: ya es algo. La mayor parte del ejército norteamericano se compone de malhechores: estos han cometido toda clase de crímenes, algunos espantosos, como todos saben, y solo uno ha sido castigado. Peor es nada." "Proclama," *El Monitor Republicano*, April 24, 1847, Número 789 Sábado. Reprinted from Jalapa, April 18, 1847. A French language paper, *Le Courrier Français*, also translated the proclamation. In French, the Kirk section reads: "mes ordres à cet effet, tout le monde le sait, sont précis et rigoureux. Déjà, en vertu de mes dispositions, plusieurs américains ont été punis, soit par des amendes au profit des mexicains, soit par l'emprisonnement; un soldat a été exécuté pour crime de rapt." The paper explicitly renders the rapist a US soldier, an example of the obvious conclusion a reader would draw from Scott's vague language. See also: "Generales Scott y Taylor," *El Monitor Republicano*, April 21, 1847, Número 786 Miercoles. US papers also printed the proclamation. Winfield Scott, "Proclamation of General Scott to the Mexicans," *American Flag*, May 1, 1847, Vol. I, No. 94.

went mostly unpunished.[72] Scott said most in his army were good men who obeyed orders. *El Monitor* argued most were criminals and good men were the minority.

The power of Scott's proclamation was not only in its broad reach but in its official character as a General Order. Scholars who conclude that Scott's claim to be the protector of Mexican civilians was true (because he hanged a rapist) risk accepting army reports as complete representations of the truth. While such reports are widely used and useful resources, report writers sought to conform to the army's desired narratives. Reports and correspondence of senior officers emphasized bravery, battlefield successes, and paternalism. Brevet rank was made of such things. Officers categorically portrayed the US Army – or at least the portion of it they belonged to – as benevolent.

Yet, in other ways, reports of carnage, women struck dead in the streets, bombs leveling homes, and families killed helped the army. It showed Mexico the US meant business and would use "civilian casualties to achieve their aims" to persuade Mexicans that "this tactic might be used in the future on other cities."[73] Simultaneously, in army writing, proofs of civilian deaths faded into an official narrative of a humane act of military necessity.

As Scott's army moved out of Veracruz and marched toward Mexico City, it left behind immense devastation caused by US bombardment. Yet, it carried forward a narrative about how the US Army would conduct its campaign to win a peace and end the war: it came as friends of the Mexican people, to whom it offered protection. The army's gospel was it had killed one of its own, Kirk, for his sins against a Mexican woman and would thus bring justice and security wherever it went. Rather than the indiscriminate ruin wrought by US bombs on civilians in Veracruz, the army emphasized the extremely focused violence on Kirk's body. To achieve victory in the coming campaign, this was necessary.

Scott needed Mexicans to willingly supply his army rather than destroy their crops or give them to anti-US guerrillas. He had only about 10,000 effective soldiers to conquer a vast, populated region. His force was at once woefully undersized for the massive scope of its military objective and miserably oversized in the minds of his quartermasters, who needed to supply it for many months with minimal support.

---

[72] Guardino, "The Constant Recurrence of Such Atrocities: Guerrilla Warfare and Counterinsurgency during the Mexican–American War," 13.

[73] Guardino, *The Dead March: A History of the Mexican–American War*, 2017, 192.

5 A Perfect Sacrifice: A Rape Case Expanded Military Justice 215

Years later in his *Memoirs*, Scott included a widely known remark attributed to the Duke of Wellington that captured this dilemma. When Scott began his march from Veracruz to Mexico City, the Duke despaired that "Scott is lost.... He can't take [Mexico] City, and he can't fall back upon his base."[74] Scott urgently needed to secure Mexican supplies and avoid Mexican guerrilla attacks on his precious and vulnerable wagon trains. He needed to convince the Mexican people that the US offered protection. He needed them to believe that Mexicans should accept US military authority, allow the US Army to buy their crops, and refuse to support guerrilla warfare.

To accomplish this, Scott used a strategy premised on protection, beginning with Kirk's execution. Yet, just as rhetoric and reality were at odds after the bombardment of Veracruz, they would be at odds whenever US officers and soldiers encountered Mexican women throughout the country. Martial law incurred an obligation wherein the army demanded enemy civilians accept military authority. In return, it protected those civilians for the occupation's duration. An occupation marred by coercion and crime often proved official stories false. Reality would continue to be less heroic than Scott's proclamation. Still, army use of claims that it protected Mexican civilians – especially women like Maria Antonia Gallegas – became a cornerstone of Scott's campaign as he advanced toward Mexico City.

---

[74] Scott, *Memoirs of Lieut.-General Scott, LL.D Written by Himself*, 466.

MAP 6 The US Occupation of Mexico. Scott's force of approximately 10,000 marched through a densely populated region of 3.5 million. For detailed maps of the war's military history written from the US perspective, see www.westpoint.edu/academics/academic-departments/history/mexican-war. Map by Mr. Jeffrey Goldberg, Cartographer at the West Point Department of History.

6

Buying Benevolence

Contested Legitimacy during the US Occupation of Mexico, 1847

In the months before the Mexico City Campaign that would take General Winfield Scott and his army from Veracruz to the Mexican capital, General Zachary Taylor offered an insight that would, in retrospect, assume the tone of a prophecy. Taylor wrote to the US Army's Adjutant General to note that "the task of fighting and beating the enemy is among the least difficult that we encounter: the great question of supplies necessarily controls all the operations in a country like this."[1] At the beginning of 1847, US forces claimed control over Mexico's northern provinces. By the end of the year, the US Army had also brought the densely populated cities of Central Mexico under occupation. In large part, Scott's army made this so. It landed in Veracruz in March, and by September, entered Mexico City. During a rapid conquest, Scott sought to balance the "great question of supplies" against his equal need to legitimize control over Mexican civilians. For US officers in Mexico, the occupation rested on a premise of consent. The occupied were to submit to military rule, and the occupiers assumed, in return, an obligation to protect those under their control. Or so the theory went.[2]

---

[1] Thirtieth Congress, First Session, *House of Representatives Mexican War Correspondence*, 1848, 360. General Zachary Taylor to Army Adjutant General, November 8, 1846.
[2] Citing the earlier Hugo Grotius, Vattel noted how armies increasingly spared enemy peasantry, whose useful labors provided resources for the wise general. "If the inhabitants submit to him who is master of the country, pay the contributions imposed, and refrain from all hostilities, they live as safe as if they were friends; they even continue in possession of what belongs to them. The country people come freely to camp to sell their provisions, and care is taken that they shall feel the calamities of war as little as

The reality was far more complex, but Scott knew that the path to peace required this veneer of legitimacy. The support or least tacit non-resistance of the Mexican people was necessary to ensure the smooth movement of soldiers and supplies between coast and capital. More than a way to guarantee military victory, orderly occupation meant a political opportunity that isolated the Mexican government from the people, prompting negotiations. Thus, in the same message that trumpeted Isaac Kirk's death as a guarantee of justice, Scott proclaimed, "all good Mexicans" should "remain at home, or their peaceful occupations." He invited them to "bring in for sale, horses, mules, beef, cattle, corn, barley, wheat, flour for bread, and vegetables. Cash will be paid for everything this army may take or purchase, and protection will be given to all sellers." The army would get goods and services and give payment and protection. How would a small army conquer a large enemy population? It would buy Mexican consent.

Payment legitimized what the army took without permission and what it purchased from willing sellers. While Scott's martial law dictated payment for Mexican goods, he did not mean only consensual transactions. Mexican observers reported coercion. One Mexican newspaper noted that on arrival in Jalapa, the "perfidious" Scott called in the mayor to ask for food and supplies because "these barbarians, who devour, are hungry." The author feared these demands would become "a pretext" for worse "humiliations." Nearer to Mexico City, Scott advocated seizing cattle for cash, saying "our army is not going to starve."[3]

This strategy reached across theaters. Career regular General John Wool wrote to Vice Governor Gonzalez – a Mexican leader subordinated to an army major designated as the army governor – that if civilians in Santa Rosa, Monclova, Parras, and Saltillo "promptly" furnished the army with corn, flour, and barley, they would be "liberally paid." Military largesse came wrapped in threat: "any delay,

---

possible. A laudable custom, and truly worthy those nations who pretend to humanity, and advantageous to the enemy himself, who finds his account in this moderation; by protecting the peaceable inhabitants, keeping the soldiers in strict discipline, and preserving a country, the general procures an easy subsistence to his army, and saves him many losses and dangers." Elsewhere, Vattel argues that by allowing enemy civilians to hold property, and to buy and sell, one "has in this respect admitted them into the number of his subjects." Vattel, *Law of Nations*, 352, Book III, Chapter VIII, "Nations in War," paragraph 147, and 322 Book III, Chapter V, "Of the Enemy," paragraph 76; Grotius, *De Jure Belli Ac Pacis*.

[3] "Jalapa"; Johnson, *A Gallant Little Army*, 198. This occurred in Tacubaya.

6 Buying Benevolence: The US Occupation of Mexico 219

however, in furnishing the supplies required" would become evidence of "hostile intentions" and be met with "the punishment which such conduct justly merits." Historian Peter Guardino calls Scott's efforts to "intimidate Mexican civilians" into refusing to support guerrillas the "lesser-known second prong" of his "anti-guerrilla strategy." The better-known prong was his policy of protecting noncombatants.[4] Soldiers operating from within this strategy could veil seizures of Mexican assets with money, creating coercive norms that extended into relationships with civilians.

Mexican women were often the vendors of goods and services the army wanted. They sold produce at markets and made meals that sustained soldiers. According to Scott, these were elements of a reciprocal arrangement that generated legitimacy. Mexicans would *have* to admit the "barbarians of the north were their best customers."[5] In addition to food and drink, soldiers sought women for domestic help. Occasionally, women advertised to secure employment. In Mexico City, señora "Loreto Rios" offered "her services as housekeeper, laundress, seamstress, or cook, to any gentleman who may be in need of them" via a classified ad in a soldier's newspaper, the *Daily Mexican Star*. Men were to apply to Dolores Rios, perhaps her mother, for further information.[6] Soldiers' relationships with Mexican women ranged along a spectrum. On one end stood contractual and consensual agreements like the one the Rios women sought. On the other stood brutal seizures of women's bodies.

Sex is only part of the story, but is a topic one must grapple with to understand US conquest of Central Mexico. As Ann Stoler writes of colonization in North America, "sexual violence was fundamental to conquest, but so was colonizing the hearts and minds of women, children, and men." Scott attempted to win popular support when he hanged Isaac Kirk, then broadcast the news. Some soldiers used violence to conquer women's bodies. Others sought Mexican women as wartime companions, only to abandon them to retributive violence when their unit moved on.

---

[4] Baylies, *Major General Wool's Campaign in Mexico*, 48, March 18, 1847; Guardino, "The Constant Recurrence of Such Atrocities: Guerrilla Warfare and Counterinsurgency during the Mexican–American War," 14. The occupation required a few army officers to rule over a vast population. Where possible, they kept Mexican political leaders like alcaldes (mayors) and vice governors in place, subordinated to the US. Wool sought to hold Gonzalez responsible for people's behavior in Coahuila.
[5] Baylies, *Major General Wool's Campaign in Mexico*, 16, October 29, 1846.
[6] "Wants a Situation," *Daily American Star*, February 25, 1848, Vol. I, No. 125.

Soldiers' approaches to sex varied greatly. Some paid for sex, some formed longer-term relationships, others committed rape.[7] All participated in conquest.

The US Army's public commitment to a just occupation allowed renewed focus on discipline. To uphold national and military honor, officers claimed they had to rule regular enlisted men with iron fists. After all, officers could say, pointing to volunteers who killed civilians, look where indiscipline leads. Scott expressed this sentiment to Marcy, writing that as troops moved along the Rio Grande "respectable" volunteers on steamships had "committed atrocities" including "rape on mothers & daughters, in the presence of the tied up males of the family," that would "make Heaven weep."[8] Although the logic of protection encouraged all soldiers – officers and enlisted alike – to see themselves and their institutions as protectors of women, it also allowed officers to justify continued use of physical punishment against enlisted men who disobeyed.

Mexican primary sources and Mexico's historiography of the war centrally challenge US claims to a peaceful occupation. To those who experienced it, the war was patently an invasion – "la invasión norteamericana," or "la invasión de los angloamericanos," or "la ocupación yanqui," perpetrated by "los vandalos del Norte," (the North American invasion, the Anglo-American invasion, the Yankee occupation, the northern vandals).[9] Historians like the prolific Josefina Zoraida Vázquez speak of "los invasores" and "los invadidos" (the invaders and the invaded). Newspapers, as scholar Jaime Javier Rodríguez shows, seethed at "the basic, fundamental charge of U.S. American hypocrisy: the model republic reveals itself to be in fact just another tyrannical imperial power, not the great universal guide to liberty." But it was also "one grand violation that blurs into other invasions of Mexico," a "legacy of invasions," by Spain, the US, and the French. Because of this legacy, the

---

[7] Stoler, *Haunted by Empire*, 58. Reports of marriage are less frequent, but do exist. A US paper in occupied Puebla, the *Flag of Freedom*, reported that a US civilian in the quartermaster department, Mr. B. Tucker, married a Poblana woman, Maria de Luz Bravo, on February 26, 1848. The couple sent a notice of their wedding, along with slices of wedding cakes, sweet meats, and a bottle of alcohol to the paper's office. "Married," *Flag of Freedom*, January 29, 1848, Vol. I, No. XXIV.

[8] Scott to Marcy, quoted in: Guardino, *The Dead March: A History of the Mexican–American War*, 2017, 107.

[9] "Remitido"; Balbontín, *La Invasión Norteamericana*; Roa Bárcena, *Recuerdos de La Invasión Norteamericana*; Bustamante, *El Nuevo Bernal Díaz Del Castillo*; Córdova, *La Ocupación Yanqui de La Ciudad de México*.

6 Buying Benevolence: The US Occupation of Mexico 221

trauma of defeats, and loss of territory, "Mexican historical consciousness also often slides over the war." Still, it ultimately became a source of Mexican national identity, or *mexicanidad*, a journey from "a wrenching devastation toward national self-consciousness" that "catalyzed a sense of Mexican moral superiority in opposition to the hypocrisy of its northern neighbor."[10]

Occupied women's experiences give voice to the occupation's coercive elements and show how discourse about protecting women shaped army culture even as it framed wartime violence. Yet, in US military histories, where Mexican women appear at all, it is as US allies: Mexican women "warmed up to the Americans," accompanied them to balls, strolled with them, and sewed clothes for the army, to the dismay of Mexican men.[11] Simple depictions of Mexican women as friends of a benevolent occupation represent a selective reading of historical truth. The same is true of hagiographic portrayals of Mexican women who universally resisted the invaders. Individuals negotiated the dangers and opportunities of war as best they could.

Still, leaders like Scott believed (or hoped) Mexican women *would* think the US Army was benevolent. Military histories that embrace the idea that the army won over (an undifferentiated mass of) Mexican women have a particular lineage. They draw on officers' reports and proclamations that emphasize gentility, and popular works glorifying US actions in Mexico. In the 1846 poem "They Wait for Us," the US narrator described how Mexican – or rather, whitened and Europeanized "Spanish" – women waited longingly for the embrace of US soldiers:

> The Spanish maid, with eye of fire,
> At balmy evening turns her lyre
> And, looking to the western sky
> Awaits our Yankee chivalry
> Whose purer blood and valiant arms,
> Are fit to clasp her budding charms.[12]

---

[10] Vázquez, *México al Tiempo de Su Guerra Con Estados Unidos*, 12; Rodríguez, *The Literatures of the U.S.–Mexican War*, 162, 179, 155, 182; Guardino, *The Dead March: A History of the Mexican–American War*, 2017, 4. Resistance to the US was only one of several simultaneous conflicts in Mexico between 1846 and 1848. Uprisings occurred across Mexico before, during, and after the war with the US. Levinson, *Wars Within War*, xiv–xvi.

[11] Spahr, "Occupying for Peace," 212, 252, 263.

[12] McCarty, *National Songs, Ballads, and Other Patriotic Poetry*, 45. *The Boston Uncle Sam* originally printed "They Wait for Us" in June 20, 1846.

Mexican women who longed for US men were worthy subjects of national *and* romantic conquest. The poem claimed Mexican women innately recognized US troops as superior. Regulars were more specific. Captain William Henry noted, "women in crowds" watched his unit go past, "attracted as they *are* and *should be* by the button," a reference to the regulars. Lieutenant Daniel Harvey Hill, a West Point officer in the Fourth Artillery, wrote described how in camp near Matamoros, the Louisiana Volunteers "were emulating each other in making beasts of themselves," and although when the army first arrived, "the fair doncellas waved their handkerchiefs at the troops and manifested great joy," they had since "been intimidated by the brutal conduct of the volunteers."[13]

In contrast to Mexican women, "The *man*, her mate, is sunk in sloth, to love, his senseless heart is loth." US soldiers claimed that Mexican men, labeled cowards, could not win in a conventional battle against US forces. So, they pursued guerrilla actions to kill US troops in small numbers. Pure Mexican women were a perfect foil to criminalized Mexican men, at once lazy and violent, who were "accursed for deeds of yore, when Mexico once smoked with gore."[14] Believing Mexican women to be "Spanish maids" waiting for "Yankee chivalry" simultaneously boosted the occupation's claim to legitimacy and denigrated Mexican men who (tried and failed) to resist supposedly consensual romances between US soldiers and Mexican women.

The ideal of conquering (and then protecting) women served as ammunition for beleaguered regulars. Many US civilians vociferously supported volunteers, citizen-soldiers they considered America's brave sons, and looked down on the majority-immigrant regular soldiery as a rabble of foreigners. John Hughes, a volunteer soldier with the Missouri Cavalry, articulated his view of noble volunteers. In his quickly published 1847 book on the late 1846 Doniphan Expedition to Northern Mexico, he claimed their behavior was uniformly excellent and described how he had watched his "comrades in arms, after performing the severest toils…sometimes half faint with thirst and hunger…refuse to pluck the ears of corn that grew thickly around them." He noted with pride, "This exhibits a degree of moral firmness and

---

[13] Henry, *Campaign Sketches of the War with Mexico*, 264; Hill, *A Fighter from Way Back*, 2.
[14] McCarty, *National Songs, Ballads, and Other Patriotic Poetry*, 45.

a regard for the rights of property which is truly characteristic of the American people, is worthy of the highest praise, and is doubtless one of the happy results of our benign institutions." For Hughes, a shared "national feeling" in the army meant each man felt "he was a citizen of the MODEL REPUBLIC; and that he ought to look upon the disgrace of AMERICAN ARMS AS INDIVIDUAL DISHONOR." Those beliefs were patently the source for "their high moral sense and conscious superiority over the Mexican people.... This honorable feeling was never once forgotten or lost sight of by the CITIZEN SOLDIER."[15] For Hughes, the volunteers' unfailing refusal to take what they had not purchased encapsulated US morality.

Regulars bemoaned the volunteers' misbegotten popularity. Lieutenant Hill described "the prospect of the Regular Army" as "not very flattering. The enemy in front. Cowardly, lying and villainous Volunteers here to defame and misrepresent us and false-hearted Knaves in Congress to take away from us that reputation which is dearer to the soldier than his life."[16] Regular officers pointed to volunteer misconduct to ensure the regular army's future.

All of this added up to a set of expectations. The army would purchase goods and services from Mexicans, and in return, many soldiers expected affection – and sex. Soldiers claimed Mexican women willingly accepted US money and sexual partners. Simultaneously, army officers expected soldiers' obedience, including adherence to orders that insisted soldiers pay for what they took from Mexicans. In both the army's occupation of Mexico and soldiers' interactions with women, it faced questions of consent. Where Mexican women greeted the army – and where they accepted US payment for goods and services – US men claimed that such women, and by extension all worthy civilians, welcomed the occupation.

Cultivating an army identity as protectors of Mexican women began with depicting those women as consenting allies.[17] It radiated out to encompass a complex and critically important wartime strategy. To the

[15] Hughes, *Doniphan's Expedition*, 52.
[16] Hill, *A Fighter from Way Back*, 43.
[17] Shelley Streeby connects the appearance of consent with the reality of force by studying wartime story papers. She argues, they "presented models for relationships among different types of U.S. men, and developed the conventions of what I am calling international race romance – stories that try to 'reconcile the irreconcilable' and transform U.S. force into Mexican 'consent' by recasting violent inter-American conflicts as romantic melodramas." Streeby, *American Sensations*, 86.

extent that army protection of women was *real*, martial law and army money maintained sufficient order to allow it to secure foodstuffs and supplies to continue military operations. To the extent that army protection was *rhetorical*, the army used its claims to legitimacy to make levies on occupied areas (and women), fund army operations, and harshly punish those deemed threats. Officers' sphere of punishment included their immediate subordinates – the soldiers whose indiscipline jeopardized US claims to a generous occupation – and the guerrillas who came from a vast population controlled by martial law. The US Army found both strategies, the real and the rhetorical, critical to its invasion of Mexico.

PAYING FOR CONSENT

Scott framed conquest as a process that extended army protection. As he prepared to leave for Mexico City, he put his army on notice. Since they could "no longer expect to derive supplies from Veracruz," the military "must begin to look exclusively to the resources of the country." Yet, "these resources, far from being over-abundant near the lines of operations, would soon fail to support both the army and the population unless they be gathered in without waste and regularly issued by quartermaster and commissaries." To secure potentially scarce supplies, "they must be paid for, or the people will withhold, conceal, or destroy them." Therefore, "the people moreover must be conciliated, soothed, or well treated by every officer and man of this army, and by its followers." The stakes were high and clear. Military leaders understood that "no army can possibly drag after it to a considerable distance, no matter what the season of the year, the heavy articles of bread-stuffs, meat, and forage."[18]

The army feared the constant threat of guerrilla attacks on supply lines. In his study of Mexican guerrillas, Irving Levinson notes, "if the more than 3.5 million Mexicans living in proximity to Scott's intended line of march fully participated in an intense defense of the nation, literally hundreds of thousands of able-bodied and eager volunteers would be available to fight the invader." It was evident to all that "by contrast, if the great majority of Mexicans along Scott's route proved quiescent, the US Army's chance of success would be much greater." Scott

---

[18] *General Orders, January to May 1847.* 127, April 30, 1847, General Orders 128.

communicated this concern before his campaign began when he wrote to Secretary Marcy in December of 1846 that "I have no doubt that the Mexican policy is to carry on a guerrilla war, and avoid a regular battle whenever it can be done. Should they get some trifling success in this way, they will be mightily magnified and the Mexican people encouraged."[19]

Guerrilla disruptions often impacted supply lines. General Worth wrote to Scott that "many supplies bespoken on the route, of persons exceedingly well disposed, have been kept back by menaces and interposition of guerrilla bands." Worth saw guerrillas in opposition to friendly civilians, but some officers noticed how civilians supported guerrillas. One wrote to his commander that civilians allowed "their towns to be used as established depots and places of safety for goods systematically plundered by banditti who violate all the laws of war." Since the army "repeatedly proclaimed our determination not to regard as under the protection of those laws" civilians who supported guerrillas, such people must "be made to restore without compensation, like any other purchases of stolen goods." Accordingly, local commander Major General of Volunteers William Butler advocated for punishing civilians, as "any compromise in this matter would be unjust to the plundered merchants and would exempt the purchasers from a penalty which they have justly incurred by encouraging and abetting a system of lawless rapine."[20] This letter, written in early 1848, demonstrates how officers never rid themselves of guerrillas. But commanders like Scott hoped that rather than watch the problem develop into a more severe threat, they could conciliate most Mexicans by paying for what they took.

To this end, officers conjured a stream of assurances throughout the war. They insisted Mexicans "felt more secure in their persons and property than they did when they had the government in their own hands" and often sealed these claims with women's approval. When artillery officer Francis Collins recorded the last line in his journal of occupied Tampico, he wrote that while in the city, "The Mexican Senoritas condescended to bestow their smiles on the barbarous Yankees, who were present, and we

---

[19] Levinson, *Wars within War*, 22; Thirtieth Congress, First Session, *House of Representatives Mexican War Correspondence*, 1848, December 7, 1846, Scott to Marcy.

[20] Thirtieth Congress, First Session, *House of Representatives Mexican War Correspondence*, United States Serial Set 520 (Washington DC, 1848), 967, May 19, 1847, Worth to Scott; *Letters Sent, Commanding General, City of Mexico, February to July, 1848*, vols. 357, Butler to Bankhear [sic], Commander Orizaba, March 1848.

did not allow them to think their beauty passed unnoticed." In January of 1847, Collins was in Tampico with the rest of Scott's army, preparing to land in Veracruz. The poem "They Wait for Us," which began with Spanish maids longing for Yankee chivalry, ended in exchanges like the one Collins described, with "An army of reformers" who would conquer to "light the land anew, and shed rich blessings like the dew."[21] As told by US troops, the civilizing influence of the Anglo-American, delivered by a disciplined army, would benefit Mexico. Pretty young women, in turn, provided approbation.

The army made US occupation's "blessings" real through martial law. As soon as Scott occupied Veracruz, he issued general orders to "establish strict police regulations for securing good order and good morals" along with "a temporary and modest tariff of duties" to be used for "the benefit of the sick and wounded of the army, the squadron, and the indigent inhabitants of Veracruz." Rather than describing tariffs as the conqueror's right, Scott justified levies as support for the army's mission to care for the weak. Further orders magnified this concern with morality (and discipline), declaring pulperias – shops that sold pulque, a locally made alcoholic drink – must close, opening only under special license and until six pm.[22]

Both regular and volunteer officers congratulated themselves on establishing order and earning Mexicans' trust. Volunteer leadership in Veracruz wrote, Mexicans had "been conciliated by the exemplary conduct of the troops" and on leaving the town of Alvarado received thanks from "the alcalde, the cura, and the principal men, for the protection afforded to them and to their property," after negotiating for horses and beef cattle from the "fertile country." The officer concluded that he felt "perfectly assured that our march has made a favorable impression upon the inhabitants."[23]

In Northern Mexico, officers made similar claims about the army's success in protecting women. General Wool claimed in Monterrey, "Females and unarmed persons could traverse the streets at all hours of the night without danger of insult or violence." The army's rule there was so successful, "a timid girl of sixteen may walk alone in the dead

---

[21] Collins, *Journal of Francis Collins*, Vol. X, 1915, Nos. 2 & 3, April and July: 43–44, January 29, 1847; McCarty, *National Songs, Ballads, and Other Patriotic Poetry*, 45.

[22] Thirtieth Congress, First Session, *House of Representatives Mexican War Correspondence*, 1848, 930, March 28, 1847, General Orders 75, Scott; 932, March 30, 1847, Order No. 3, Worth.

[23] Ibid., 918, April 7, 1847, Quitman to Lieutenant H. L. Scott.

of night, from the bishop's palace to the queen's bridge, without fear of insult." On Wool's triumphant return to New York City, Wool's biographer quoted a newspaper editor's claim that Wool had "done his duty as a soldier, with consummate skill and indomitable valor, without any hankering after the flesh-pots of Egypt." He conquered Northern Mexico by avoiding supposedly bad local women and protecting the good, and did it "with a half-disciplined army, without losing a man or permitting an outrage; and, although an invader, was everywhere followed by the blessings of the Mexican people." He waged noble war that recalled, "in romantic minds, remembrance of the chivalry of Spain." Wool himself claimed in a speech soon after the war: "I am proud to say that in the course of that march of 900 miles, not a drop of human blood was shed, and no injury inflicted upon the inhabitants of the country."[24] Wool's supporters intended these propagandistic claims to cement his reputation. Like Wool, many soldiers equated US occupation with romanticized, chivalric protection of women.

Officers like Wool fit evidence of US crimes against Mexicans into this protective conquest framework. Such men described war and occupation as a series of victories over adversity: "great as was the triumph of the Americans on the battlefield, the moral triumph over obdurate, perverse, and remorseless natures was greater." Yet, they qualified their moral triumphs with partial acknowledgments that their soldiers, like other men, sinned. When shown evidence of crimes, platitudes like "the conquest of the human passions is beyond the power of man!" papered over criminal violence.[25] US leaders asserted that soldiers were only human, subject to passions like other men. Some level of crime was unavoidable.

It was "an established rule, in the army regulations, not to obstruct the passage of any person into camp, with provisions to sell." This rule applied to Mexican women, men, and children. Yet, soldiers came to understand Mexican women, rather than men or children, as their most natural allies. A private in the Tennessee volunteer cavalry, George Furber, wrote that while men viewed them with a "scowling appearance," women were happy because the soldiers "paid them promptly."[26] As regular officer Napoleon Dana wrote, the army forced Mexicans to get "all their corn ready for sale to us. They are obliged to do this whether they want to or not. We make them bring their produce and pay

---

[24] Baylies, *Major General Wool's Campaign in Mexico*, 62, 67, 68, 76.
[25] Ibid., 44.
[26] Furber, *The Twelve Months Volunteer*, 203.

them fair price for it." Dana straightforwardly acknowledged the coercion at play in this system, but officers highlighted the moral superiority of a conquering army that paid well. Stephen Watts Kearny's biographer described how Pueblo Indians "knew the difference between raiding Navahos, plundering Mexican soldiery, and these strange-tongued white men who paid cash for one's melons and grapes, eggs, and chickens."[27]

Purchasing power facilitated coercion. Soldiers offered cash, or army-controlled food supplies, in exchange for sex. To paraphrase Phillippa Levine, sex was part of the occupation's political economy.[28] More than that, Mexican women's willingness to sell goods and services, ranging from tortillas, to pulque, and sometimes sex, became a specific kind of proof. Where army leaders claimed paying for supplies secured Mexican consent and legitimized occupation of Mexican *territory*, individual soldiers claimed paying for sex similarly secured consent and legitimized occupation of Mexican *bodies*.

Some soldiers hoped prompt payment would secure easy access to sex. Before Private William Farrell raped Maria Dolores Hernandez, he used payment to force her husband, Manuel Antonio Telles, out of the house. In doing so, he intended to cover the rape with a veneer of consent. As Hernandez testified, Farrell and his accomplice William Alexander wrote an order for five pounds of beef. They made Telles leave immediately to fulfill it, threatening violence if he delayed. This ploy removed Telles from the property and compensated Telles because they promised him that he would get to keep the beef.[29]

The same system that obligated ordinary Mexicans to accept US cash gave Farrell about an hour at Hernandez's home, where she would be without her husband's protection. Once Farrell and Alexander got Telles out of the house, Hernandez's daughter Margarita testified, "Alexander told her mother they wished to f – k her." Hernandez ran to her front door, called for help, and her neighbor Juan Reyes responded. He came into the house and sat down, but this stalemate did not last. First Alexander, and then Farrell again used money to secure sex. Alexander asked Reyes for something to eat. When Reyes answered that he had no food to give, Alexander offered to send him to get five pounds of beef, that is, to the same errand as Hernandez's husband. Reyes said no, and so

[27] Dana, *Monterrey Is Ours!*, 120, September 17, 1846, near Marin; Clarke, *Stephen Watts Kearny*, 155.
[28] Levine, *Gender and Empire*, 134–35. Of the British Empire, Levine's original phrase was: "I see sex as part of the politics of Empire."
[29] "Court-Martial Case Files, 1809–1894," Case EE665, Jalapa, December 31, 1847.

6 Buying Benevolence: The US Occupation of Mexico

Farrell intervened. In Margarita's words, "the prisoner then told Reyes that if he, Reyes, would give him a <u>Lady</u>, he would give him $2. Reyes replied that he could not he did not belong to the house." Alexander rode away from the house in frustration, but Farrell repeated his offer of two dollars for a woman to Reyes, who again refused.

Farrell then resorted to physical force stripped of pretense. Reyes testified, "The prisoner then seized [Hernandez] round the waist and threw her in the bed, she then said to me 'Mr. Juan Mr. Juan see what he is doing to me.' I took the prisoner round the waist and told him it was not right, what he was doing." Farrell pushed Reyes away at the point of his pistol. Margarita later told the court what happened next: "The prisoner took his pistol in one hand, and threatened to shoot Reyes, he took hold of mother, and threw her on the <u>bed</u> tearing mother's chemise, he turned up her underclothes, and put the pistol to her breast, he then commenced fornication on her mother, and 'f – k – g' her." Margarita insisted that Reyes accompany her to their "master, Mr. Welsh" to relate what happened.

Perhaps the influence of the probably Euro-American Mr. Welsh, who may have taken offense at this assault on what was perhaps a peon family on his estate, forced the army to respond. The Commander of the US Army's Department of Jalapa, Colonel George W. Hughes, quickly sent a guard force to arrest Farrell, one of whom testified they found Farrell outside of Hernandez's home. Farrell fled. The guard chased and arrested him. Nine days later, a military commission and found Farrell guilty of rape. The army did not charge Alexander. The commission sentenced Farrell

> To forfeit all pay and allowances that are or may be due to him, to wear an <u>iron yoke</u> weighing eight pounds, with three prongs each one foot in length around his neck, to be confined to hard labor in charge of the guard the time [crossed out] the Army remains in Mexico and then to have his head shaved and to be drummed out of the service.[30]

It was no slap on the wrist, though it fell short of the capital punishment that doomed Isaac Kirk on far less evidence.

Farrell's crime hinted at a norm: offer to pay for sex with Mexican women, then use force if the woman or her male guardian declined. A case tried in Jalapa bears similarities. In it, a soldier offered payment before offering violence. Limited archival material on rape makes it impossible to confirm how frequently this occurred, but the two examples suggest a common theme of payment backed by violence. The army

---

[30] Ibid. Farrell raped Hernandez on December 22, 1847.

charged Corporal Theodore Smith with "assault with intent to kill," not rape, but Smith used violence much as Farrell did, as a last resort when his attempts to purchase sex failed.

Smith and a sergeant shouted outside the home of Francisco and Anna Maria, described as "Indians," saying that "both of us want women," to which Francisco answered, "there are none here." Anna Maria testified, "The sergeant said god damn and pointed the pistol at [Francisco's] head, and I told my husband that they were aiming at him. My husband seized the pistol and turned it on one side. My husband having hold of the pistol, was pulling or pushing the sergeant towards the door." The sergeant tried to hit Francisco, Francisco dodged the blow, and the other soldier, Smith, shot at Francisco in panic. The shot's charge set Francisco's shirt on fire, and the encounter left Francisco with a wound on his left side and another on his back.

The case reveals how white soldiers conceptualized their privileges over women. If a white man successfully fought off a man seeking to rape his wife, this was heroism. When a Mexican man did so, it was more like a crime. In the early days of the war, Captain William Coleman of the Alabama Volunteers recorded a Mexican man "taken prisoner for knocking down a white man who was insulting his wife." Francisco's physical defense of Anna Maria made him suspect and seems to have lessened the consequences for the two soldiers. The sergeant faced no charges. A military commission found Smith guilty of assault and sentenced him to forfeit thirty-five dollars paid to Francisco and eighteen months confinement, but recommended the prisoner to mercy. Smith may have faced lesser or no punishment.[31]

These cases represent exceptions to the relative silence on sexual violence in army reporting. Although private sources, like letters and memoirs, sometimes address rape, such crimes rarely entered army records. The anti-war press in the US used claims of mass rape to condemn the

---

[31] LeBaron and Coleman, *Perry Volunteers in the Mexican War*, 137, July 20, 1846 at Camp Belknap, near Matamoros; "Court-Martial Case Files, 1809–1894," n.d., FF180, Monterrey, February 8, 1848. The Farrell and Smith cases, and the Kirk case, comprise the sole references to sexual assault within case files EE331 to FF195 of Court-Martial Case Files held in RG 153 of the National Archives. Additional evidence of rape comes from letters, brief references in reports, and other archival material. Mexican newspapers occasionally mentioned rape (often in euphemistic and generic terms). One letter, reprinted in *Boletín de Noticias*, described troops' actions in Jalapa and noted that "one poor woman has already been the victim of their debauchery" – a sexual assault. The letter uses the word *disenfreno*. "Noticias de Jalapa," *Boletín de Noticias*, April 28, 1847, Número 5.

conflict but did so in generic terms, without referring to specific incidents. Boston's *Advocate of Peace* reprinted a typical example, a regular's letter condemning volunteers: "the women have been repeatedly violated (almost an every-day affair) houses broken open, and insults of every kind have been offered to those *whom we are bound by honor to protect.*"[32] US wartime newspapers, in contrast, did sometimes describe examples and strongly condemned harm to women when they received reports of violence. The *Flag of Freedom* in Puebla noted that three soldiers chased a Mexican man through the street (he claimed the soldiers sought to steal from him), and when the man went into his house, the soldiers fired into it. They struck a pregnant woman standing in the doorway, killing her and her child. The horrified editors of the *Flag* demanded the men face justice and insisted, "Americans come to this country to fight their country's enemies, but not to commit outrages upon the persons and property of the innocent."

The next column notes separate allusions to rapes: "*Outrages* of a most atrocious character have been committed lately in about this city; some of them have been detailed to us, but we refrain from giving them publicity."[33] That sense of decorum is another factor limiting historical knowledge of sexual violence. The paper called on "officers and soldiers of the United States Army who can feel for the honor of their country and their own reputation" to "strictly" punish the guilty. The *Flag* essentially mirrored Scott's conclusions following the Kirk case. Violence against Mexican women *was* a reprehensible violation of the army's responsibility to protect innocents, but perpetrators were exceptions whom the army's moral majority could punish.

Other men dismissed claims of rape with simple chauvinism. Lieutenant Napoleon Dana described how one woman's appearance, rather than the crime of rape, disgusted him: "there was an old hag of about sixty without a tooth brought up yesterday as a witness before our court-martial against an Irishman who was accused of committing violence on her person! The very idea was enough to make one throw up a breakfast which had been on the stomach for several hours."[34] Another reason for underreporting may have been that Mexican civilians understood a wartime truth – refusing an initial cash offer would only lead to violence. If so, perhaps some chose money to save their lives.

---

[32] "Outrages against Women in Mexico," 55.
[33] "Woman Killed," *Flag of Freedom*, December 15, 1847, Vol. I, No. XVI.
[34] Dana, *Monterrey Is Ours!*, 180–81. February 14, 1847.

In a letter to (then Senator) Lewis Cass, Wool conceded that US troops *did* commit numerous crimes, including rape. But he upheld his view of army morality by pinning crimes on deserters – a more politically salient target than volunteers when communicating with Congressmen. He wrote that US "deserters had been guilty of many enormities: on their way from Saltillo to the Rio Grande, they had not only plundered the inhabitants of horses, money, plate, jewelry, but ravished women, two of whom had died in consequence of their brutalities." It was these individuals who "make guerrillas, and cause us a great deal of trouble." Scott, in his various general orders intended to stop crimes against Mexicans, consistently described the handful of criminals lurking within his otherwise virtuous army. He noted, "many undoubted atrocities have been committed in this neighborhood, by a few worthless soldiers, both regulars and volunteers." Elsewhere, he urged "the great body of intelligent, gallant and honorable men who comprise this army" not to "tolerate the few miscreants, who perpetrate such crimes."[35] As commander of regulars and volunteers in Mexico, Scott could not afford to take sides and emphasized bad apples could come from either group. He sought to rid his army of what he claimed were dishonorable exceptions, but never could.

Scott's vision of justice invoked the logic of protection's growing importance in the 1840s, such that army leaders exhorted soldiers not merely to swear, as did the fictional knights of the round table, not to rape ladies, damsels, gentlewomen, and widows, but to actively protect *all* women. Early in the war, US Navy Commodore John Sloat – whose words echoed the sentiments of army regulars such as Scott, Taylor, Wool, and Kearny – issued an order before landing in California. Sloat declared, "I scarcely consider it necessary for me to caution American seamen and marines against the detestable crime of plundering and maltreating unoffending inhabitants." Still, he continued, "that no one may misunderstand his duty, the following regulations must be strictly adhered to, as no violation can hope to escape the severest punishment." These regulations included an absolute prohibition on entering civilian homes for enlisted seamen and marines "for any pretext whatever, without express orders from an officer." Having thus focused his remarks on

[35] Baylies, *Major General Wool's Campaign in Mexico*, 56, 62, 67, 68, 76, February 1847; Thirtieth Congress, First Session, *House of Representatives Mexican War Correspondence*, 1848, 914, 1 April 1847, Scott, General Orders 87; *General Orders, January to May 1847*, 23:30 April 1847, Scott, General Orders 128. Cass, a lifelong politician, had served as Andrew Jackson's Secretary of War, and knew many officers.

unruly enlisted men, Sloat added, "Let every man avoid insult or offense to any unoffending inhabitant, and especially avoid that eternal disgrace which would be attached to our names and our country's name by indignity offered to a single female, even let her standing be however low it may."[36] Sloat's vision of chivalry elevated it above the code's class-based origins and insisted on protecting all women.

Despite universalist rhetoric, the US military extended different levels of protection depending on women's class and race – ironically, a more historically accurate form of chivalry. When soldiers talked of chivalry, they used it as a freighted shorthand that meant some shifting combination of martial prowess and gentility that made them desirable to local women, hence "Spanish maids" longing for "Yankee chivalry."[37] Yet, the knights of old whom US troops in Mexico idealized had not limited violence against noncombatants, but perpetrated it: "as a code, chivalry had next to nothing to do with ordinary people at all." It existed to emphasize the "internal cohesion" of knighthood.[38] Chivalry in Mexico provided a similar function for the US Army, where discourse on protecting women promoted internal army cohesion.

Although men like Sloat intended for military protection to be universal, the reality often hewed closely to the social distinctions of race and class in US society. A clear sense of superiority led soldiers and journalists in Mexico to associate chivalric protection with "Spanish" women and sexual availability to "ordinary Mexicans," a system where soldiers maintained their honor by deferring to elite women while still raping Indigenous and mestiza women.[39] Thus, Scott directed a group of dragoons to serve "with a gallantry becoming the leader of an American army" as an escort to return Santa Anna's wife, Dolores Tosta de López de Santa Anna, to her husband's care. She was "in the habit of accompanying him in his campaigns." They ensured that this lady received courteous treatment.

Their first victory was to gain custody of her through military prowess. Their second was to prove moral superiority by ensuring she returned to

---

[36] Kaeuper, *Chivalry and Violence in Medieval Europe*, 228; Thirtieth Congress, First Session, *House of Representatives Mexican War Correspondence*, 1848, 246, John Sloat, General Orders, July 7, 1846, issued from the Flagship Savannah. Here, Kaeuper draws on Malory's *Mort D'Arthur*.
[37] McCarty, *National Songs, Ballads, and Other Patriotic Poetry*, 45.
[38] Kaeuper, *Chivalry and Violence in Medieval Europe*, 176, 185, 246. For the legal principle of distinction (between combatants and noncombatants) see: Kinsella, *The Image before the Weapon*.
[39] Robinson, *The View from Chapultepec*, 132.

her (defeated) husband in his enemies' safekeeping. Curiously, she had several such experiences. An enlisted volunteer described how a volunteer regiment captured Santa Anna's baggage train. Among the spoils were, famously, his prosthetic leg, but also her wardrobe. In a self-conscious display of chivalry, they ceremoniously returned it to her. They kept the leg.[40] Soldiers treated women like Dolores de Santa Anna according to perceived social status.

They also tended to judge female beauty based on a woman's proximity to Spanish-ness, which contained assumptions about status and lighter skin. Hence, soldiers recorded compliments such as "I scarcely believed she was a Mexican" or the same man's observation that "ladies of pure Spanish blood are eminently beautiful." Likewise, German artist Carl Nebel, who traveled throughout Mexico before the war, expressed a similar conflation of "woman" and "elite" when he observed that "all Mexican women use the mantilla," an expressly upper-class (and emblematically Spanish) garment.[41] Elite women received the privileged levels of protection encoded in a much older class-based chivalry. Still, developing race-based criteria qualified that privilege and established proximity to whiteness as evidence of women's worth.

Where Dolores de Santa Anna had a conspicuously polite set of experiences with the dragoons who escorted her home, dragoons – indeed, soldiers in general – could act quite differently with ordinary women. One group of dragoons attempted "to violate the women" and tear a young girl's clothes off in San Juan and Santa Rosa's ranches. Another patrol confiscated the contents of a local pulque shop, rode through a town with drawn sabers, fired pistols through the streets, and frightened women at a church service.[42]

Definitions of protection extending to all women, "even let her standing be however low it may," dominated army discourse.[43] The reality was that military chivalry left Mexican women who did not appear sufficiently Spanish exposed to violence. Because chivalric ideas, filtered through army paternalism, claimed to protect all Mexican women,

---

[40] Semmes, *The Campaign of General Scott in the Valley of Mexico*, 357. Kenly, *Memoirs of a Maryland Volunteer*, 397.

[41] Carpenter, *Travels and Adventures in Mexico*, 235, 270; Peck, "The Sign of the Eagle," 28; Nebel, *Voyage Pittoresque et Archéologique Dans La Partie La Plus Intéressante Du Mexique*.

[42] Curtis, *Mexico Under Fire*, 104–5; Chamberlain and Butterfield, *My Confession*, 74–75.

[43] Thirtieth Congress, First Session, *House of Representatives Mexican War Correspondence*, 1848, 246. John Sloat, General Orders, July 7, 1846, issued from the Flagship *Savannah*.

6 Buying Benevolence: The US Occupation of Mexico 235

violence against women became more hidden. By labeling violations of protection as exceptions, discourse about protecting women enabled violence rather than consistently limiting it.

Much as army writing on women's protection seemed more substantial on the page than in practice, such claims could radically alter (in print) the character of whole cities. Official army correspondence claimed, for example, that the mere emplacement of an occupation force fundamentally transformed Veracruz. Scott chose to bombard Veracruz purportedly because he feared the onset of yellow fever season on the coast and wanted to move his army to the lower-risk interior as quickly as possible. It is striking, then, that he wrote to the Secretary of War soon after bombarding Veracruz that the risk of disease had dissipated under the salutary regime of martial law. It took just seven days.

It was as though he had conquered not just the city but illness itself in the one week between the Mexican surrender on March 29, and his April 5 letter. Scott explained to Secretary Marcy that he planned to establish a depot and, "with proper care, I do not apprehend any great mortality in the garrisons" of Veracruz, "nor among the hired people of the quartermaster's and commissary departments, because we shall principally, if not only, occupy the waterfront of the city, separated from the inhabitants and open to the sea breezes." The US could avoid disease with rational design. In racially charged language, Scott told Marcy, "the greatest source of malignant fevers will be found in the want of ordinary cleanliness in doors, and in the streets, on the part of the inhabitants." He was doing everything possible "to correct their filthy habits."[44] For Scott, bringing Veracruzanos under army protection meant rendering them clean.

Officers wrote a transition from fetid backwater to prosperous garrison into being. They claimed under army rule Veracruz became not only healthy but happy. Scott continued, "the inhabitants of this city, under the excellent government of Brevet Major General Worth, are beginning to be assured of protection and to be cheerful." When the army left Veracruz at war's end, this belief that US occupation defeated crime *and* disease persisted. General Butler wrote to Marcy that the US departure from Mexico City "was accomplished in perfect order and tranquility" and noted Veracruz was now "remarkably healthy."[45]

---

[44] Ibid., 910, 5 April 1847, Scott to Marcy.
[45] Thirtieth Congress, First Session, *House of Representatives Mexican War Correspondence*, United States Serial Set 520 (Washington DC, 1848), 910, 5 April 1847, Scott to Marcy; *Letters Sent, Commanding General, City of Mexico, February to July*, 1848, vol. 3, 27 June 1848, Butler to Marcy.

According to Scott, the US Army brought no less than life, liberty, and happiness to Veracruzanos.

Still, while the army would pay for supplies, it made cities like Veracruz pay for the privilege of occupation. Scott imposed levies to fund progress. Just as the army would pay for what it took, officers expected payment for what it provided. The army extracted contributions in Veracruz, Puebla, and Mexico City, the Central Mexican cities occupied for extended periods. General orders published after Scott had completed his conquest enumerated targeted (but only partly collected) annual fees: $271,548 for Veracruz, $424,276 for Puebla, and $668,332 for the Mexico City area. Cities could substitute food, forage, or other supplies for money, and levies came with a reiteration of protection. Troops would "observe the strictest discipline and morals" and "treat the unoffending inhabitants with forbearance and kindness." They would maintain the "higher honor of our country, as well as the particular honor of this army" against "the few miscreants in our ranks." The army would strictly observe the laws of war toward "all Mexicans in arms" who respected US power but would relentlessly pursue "those atrocious bands of guerrillos and armed rancheros." The levy strategy combined a cost for protection with reminders that Mexican civilians and US troops alike must submit to officers' rule.[46]

During the war and the years following many described a magnanimous policy. One long-serving regular officer described how "our army in its early marches through the country, moved like a rich and powerful benefactor, scattering with a lavish hand, unheard of wealth among the rabble in its path." The occupation was "a blessing" because it shielded Mexicans from the "burdens and exactions of their authorities." They were better protected and given profitable markets for goods. A US colonel in Puebla wrote in a letter to Santa Anna that he "would willingly leave the question for the decision of the intelligent and impartial portion of the population of this city, by whom they have suffered most violence, from their own people or from troops of the army of the United States." Similarly, a volunteer officer from Ohio claimed his troops looked especially beneficent in contrast to the "worst excesses and crimes" of the Mexican army, who stole from their countrymen. The officer recounted

---

[46] Thirtieth Congress, First Session, *House of Representatives Mexican War Correspondence*, 1848, 1066, December 31, 1847, Scott, General Orders 395. Under the same rubric, Scott had also demanded a $150,000 levy on Mexico City on his arrival. In March of 1848, Secretary of War Marcy asked General Butler to enforce this request, which the Mexican government had not yet met. *Letters Sent, Commanding General, City of Mexico, February 21 to July 28, 1848*, 357: March 2, 1848, Butler to Marcy.

how "an intelligent Mexican" told him, "he preferred the presence of the American army to his own" because the it paid "a fair compensation." This officer could not understand how, given all of this, inhabitants instead of welcoming the army "frequently committed the most savage outrages upon our troops."[47]

For all the army's supposed success in conciliating Mexicans to US occupation, resistance remained an immutable fact. Artilleryman Francis Collins wrote of this dual phenomenon, where the army proclaimed both the Mexican people's gratitude and their continued opposition. Collins described how on hearing the military would move on, the people of Jalapa were "in a state of uneasiness and alarm. They say the surrounding country is infested with robbers and guerrilla bands and that as soon as we remove our protection from the town, they will rush in and rob, pillage, and murder the inhabitants." He continued, "This is a fine state of things truly, when these people must call on a foreign invading army to protect them against their own countrymen."[48]

He continued by disclosing a contradiction – the cooperation of many locals with the guerrillas: "It is a fact well known to us, however, that some of the citizens of Jalapa have been in the practice of furnishing these outlaws, and legal assassins with powder, and lead to assist them in carrying out their depredations against us." This led Collins to conclude, "they must now justly suffer themselves the murders and robberies, that they are no longer able to direct against those who have heretofore given them protection."[49] These guerrilla attacks happened wherever the army – especially its vulnerable wagons, trains, or small groups of soldiers – went.

When Collins and the army left Jalapa for Puebla, Scott noted severe threats posed during travel: "Puebla, it is known, does not hope to resist our progress, but stands ready to receive us amicably, or at least courteously." "Our difficulties lie in gathering in subsistence from a country covered with exasperated guerrillas and banditti." The road from Jalapa back to Veracruz's port, the army's primary connection back to the US, was equally fraught. Just a few weeks earlier, Scott wrote of attacks on wagon trains by "the exasperated rancheros." He had seen the "Mexican

---

[47] Giddings, *Sketches of the Campaign in Northern Mexico*, 90–91; Thirtieth Congress, First Session, *House of Representatives Mexican War Correspondence*, 1848, 1030, September 25, 1847, Childs to Santa Anna; Giddings, *Sketches of the Campaign in Northern Mexico*, 90–91.
[48] Collins, *Journal of Francis Collins: An Artillery Officer in the Mexican War*, Vol. X, 1915, Nos. 2 & 3, April and July: 67, June 10, 1847.
[49] Ibid.

papers of the 21st instant [April 1847] from the capital, which breathe any thing but peace." He knew Santa Anna was "engaged in organizing guerrilla parties, which policy the Mexicans have determined in future to adopt."[50] For Collins, US protection was temporary, a mere suspension of violence while one remained under the army's direct control.

Moreover, when US protection – patronage and martial law – left a place, it worsened retributive violence against the army's erstwhile allies. By foisting payments on Mexicans and taking supplies, the army legitimized its occupation and seizure of goods. In the eyes of guerrillas, those same payments transformed Mexicans who received army cash into collaborators. To those who fought against US rule, such persons rendered material aid to Mexico's national enemy. Protection bonded Mexicans to the US Army by exchanging currency for goods and services. Those bonds became ever tighter because US support isolated civilians who helped the US from Mexicans who did not, giving "collaborators" incentives to cooperate further.

Some civilians, like market women, benefitted from the guerrilla threat, using it to sell wares at higher prices for US cash. In turn, the threat of guerrilla attacks encouraged officers to amply compensate vendors. In Scott's words, if they treated civilians as enemies, "we may ruin and exasperate the inhabitants, and starve ourselves; for it is certain they would sooner remove or destroy the products of their farms than allow them to fall into our hands without compensation." Corn was an especially critical part of the quartermaster's plan to supply the army. One lieutenant wrote that "It is impossible with our means of transportation to move a very large force...until we get into a part of the country which can be made to subsist the army." He continued, "we have mills along for grinding corn, and when we begin to find corn in abundance for horses and men, we can begin to get along with less transportation." Soldiers came to understand that "wherever we can find plenty of corn, we can subsist our troops on cornbread and beef and will not have to transport the immense amount of bread, pork, and forage which we are now obliged to carry."[51] It was easier on the army's wagons and stomachs to buy food from locals than to cart hardtack and salt pork from ships docked in Veracruz.

---

[50] Thirtieth Congress, First Session, *House of Representatives Mexican War Correspondence*, 1848, May 6, 1847, Scott to Marcy, Jalapa, 946, 950–51, April 25, 1847, Scott to Cadwalader.
[51] Dana, *Monterrey Is Ours!*, 114, September 4, 1846, on the march to Cerralvo.

6 Buying Benevolence: The US Occupation of Mexico 239

Soldiers supplemented rations of corn and beef with local produce such as melons, grapes, apples, peaches, apricots, and pears that they "purchased liberally" from Mexican vendors. One officer wrote that when passing through settlements, "men, women, boys and girls, in great numbers would come out to the road, bringing with them vegetables, bread, milk, eggs, cheese, fruits, pepper, chickens, and other eatables, and with the utmost importunity, following along the lines, would seek a purchaser of their valuable stores." A soldier recorded that "whenever we encamped, in five minutes, women and children would roam through the tents to sell different articles, never meeting with insult or injury." Mexican vendors used the passing army as an economic opportunity, something apparent to the observer, who recorded, "In this manner, these traffickers drained most of the specie from the purses of the American soldiers."[52]

Women could also take advantage of the US fascination with sexualized "Spanish maids" to sell goods. Traveling through New Mexico, Lieutenant John Abert encountered extensive vineyards with "some pretty 'doncellas' plucking the fruit." Abert described the scene: "They had round flat-looking baskets placed on their heads, these were piled with thick-clustered bunches of the purple grape, from beneath which the bright black eyes of the 'doncellas' were sparkling. We could not pass by such a beautiful vineyard, so we stopped and asked for some fruit; some of the maidens, with merry faces, came towards us." But their intentions to exchange coins for sparkling eyes and conversations were frustrated when they were "suddenly stopped by the gruff voice of a man crying out, that he would himself bring the grapes."[53] As vendors, Mexican women were a critical component of the supply system, and they sold all kinds of food and drink. Although Mexican civilians cared little for US rhetoric, they seized opportunities to transform invasion into economic opportunity.

Women often had little choice but to interact with the army. Despite the army's claims to honor Mexican homes, the military routinely quartered officers and soldiers in private dwellings. A lieutenant described this low-level coercion as "the alcalde quartered us upon an old woman." A captain noted an incident where volunteers entered a house uninvited,

---

[52] Edwards, *A Campaign in New Mexico with Colonel Doniphan*, 143; Hughes, *Doniphan's Expedition*, 2, September 5, 1847. This quote refers to Hughes' travels through Albuquerque. Similar buying and selling unfolded along Scott's campaign route. Mexicans sold surplus produce to US troops throughout the country and the war.

[53] Abert, *Examination of New Mexico in the Years 1846–'47*, 464, October 13, 1847.

slept there, and stole a blanket on departure. US soldiers could also use force to overcome Mexican reluctance. On being told there were no quarters in a village inn, one lieutenant threatened the innkeeper to secure beds for the night. When told there was no food, they pressured residents into providing chicken and eggs.[54]

Just as US coercion could limit the options available to Mexican women, severe poverty conditioned women's choices, causing many women to sell to survive. In a stark example of need, after breaking camp in a small town, soldier Judge Moore described "crowds of half-clad women and children...hurrying to and fro through the quarters, picking up grains of corn and scraps of meat and bread, and tattered garments and worn-out shoes which the soldiers had thrown away."[55] Such conditions may have led to an experience related by war correspondent George Kendall. During the Battle of Monterrey, he watched as Mexican women near the US batteries busily made tortillas and sold them to US soldiers. Of this "singular scene," Kendall remarked on the "Mexican females cooking for the enemies of their country, while very likely their husbands or brothers were busy on the height above pouring death and destruction into their very midst." Other women in Monterrey "where the battle was raging" offered US soldiers oranges and other fruits, Kendall believing it an "attempt to propitiate our protection."[56] These women took advantage of gendered norms to be on a battlefield where Mexican men could not go without being named enemies. In the ever-changing calculus of civilians during war and occupation, Mexican women used femininity to improve their economic situations and guarantee protection – a contract sealed by sale and payment – as best they could.

PROTECTION AND PUNISHMENT'S LIMITS

While commanders such as Scott and Taylor wanted the power to stop crime, they only ever wielded moderate influence and struggled to punish volunteers. In contrast, regular officers were willing and able to punish regular enlisted men using various disciplinary practices. More than a logistical concern, army leaders explicitly connected supplies to affairs of honor. When soldiers committed crimes against Mexicans, they dealt

---

[54] Semmes, *The Campaign of General Scott in the Valley of Mexico*, 109, 181–82; Smith, *The Mexican War Journal of Captain Franklin Smith*, 120.
[55] Moore, *Scott's Campaign in Mexico*, 74.
[56] Kendall, *Dispatches from the Mexican War*, 128–29, 138.

double damage to their army, which "must suffer the consequences, in supplies and loss of character."[57] Payment mediated the difference between the honorable treatment of Mexican civilians and dishonorable marauding. To pay for goods was to contribute materially – and morally – to military success.

Nonetheless, wartime violence belied sweeping guarantees of protection. In March of 1847, Zachary Taylor reported to the army adjutant in Washington that the inhabitants of Saltillo were "generally returning to their homes, and in the country are engaged in planting their crops."[58] He described the strategy of protection's desired outcome. The army needed Mexicans at home growing crops, raising livestock, and producing supplies. It sought to portray occupied Mexico as safe. Officers worked to improve the army's reputation through a combination of personal example, exhortations to soldiers, emphasis on the good behavior of most, and the suppression of negative information. Regular enlisted man Frederick Zeh noted an ordinary soldier's frustration with all of this: "Why the high command made no requisitions from the inhabitants of San Agustín to meet the urgent requirements of this hospital, I still find incomprehensible. Over and over again, the enemy was treated with kid gloves at our soldiers' expense." No wonder, then, that Zeh and his comrades found that when the army did not provide them with food, "the musket proved an excellent key, for the doors then promptly sprang open and revealed to our yearning gazes a well-filled pantry."[59]

Regulars found themselves embittered not only by what they saw as unfair treatment given to an enemy but also by experiencing what they believed was arbitrary punishment. Apart from capital punishment, reserved for particular offenses, there were several authorized nonlethal corporal punishments for enlisted men. These included lashes (for desertion only), hard labor – with a ball and chain, iron collar, and manacles where needed to "control the refractory" – and "indelible" marking with a brand or tattoo.[60] Officers and sergeants supplemented these legal

---

[57] *General Orders, January to May 1847.* 127, April 30, 1847, General Orders 128. Other options that Scott eschewed in favor of cash payment might have been living off the land, or levying needed supplies directly from civilian communities. Scott chose payment in the hopes that it would be the least likely to foment organized resistance to the occupation.

[58] Thirtieth Congress, First Session, *House of Representatives Mexican War Correspondence*, 1848, 1125, March 28, 1847, Taylor to Army Adjutant General.

[59] Zeh, Orr, and Miller, *An Immigrant Soldier in the Mexican War*, 70, 76.

[60] Scott, *General Regulations for the Army*, 1825, 177, Paragraph 916.

punishments, resulting from courts-martial, with myriad illegal and informal ones. A popular soldier's song described a typical and hated example – bucking and gagging. One verse told how, often at an officer's behest, a sergeant would tie a soldier in a stress position, immobilizing the victim with a rod underneath his knees and his hands bound (the buck), then tie a gag in the soldier's mouth, and leave him exposed to the elements for extended periods:

> A poor soldier's tied up in the sun or the rain
> With a gag in his mouth till he's tortured with pain;
> Why I'm bless'd, if the eagle we wear on our flag,
> In its claws shouldn't carry a buck and a gag.[61]

George Ballentine, an English soldier in the regulars who recorded the "bucking and gagging" verses, noted other degrading punishments, like "standing on a barrel in the open street, exposed to the heat of the sun all day, and the derisive admiration of the street passengers." Another was riding the wooden horse, where a soldier had to sit atop a high wooden rail with his feet off the ground for long periods, perhaps even "a series of days and nights," according to Ballentine. These alternatives supplemented the "favourite punishment" of the buck and the gag, which reduced soldiers to a "helpless condition, unable to move hand, foot, or tongue" and required little more than a stick and a cloth – a field expedient method. Sometimes, there was an element of performance to this suffering. When officers ordered Frederick Zeh's friend bucked and gagged for an extended time, Zeh noted that "when no officer was nearby, however, Kessler got rid of the rope that bound him and passed the time drawing caricatures of his tormentor" (Figure 6.1).[62]

Though some officers disliked illegal punishments, many considered harsh measures necessary. Some military historians contrast a more professionalized officer corps, possessing traits like "specialized education, group consciousness, and social responsibility," with a degraded soldiery. This pairing allows such scholars to conclude that officers like Winfield Scott imposed strict discipline because it was necessary, as indiscipline and "desertion – primarily by immigrants in the regular army – continued to plague the occupation force," often "because these immigrant soldiers did not share the patriotic sentiment with their fellow soldiers." Scholars of the enlisted experience point out that "the number of foreigners who

---

[61] Ballentine, *Autobiography of an English Soldier*, 247.
[62] Ibid., 282; Zeh, Orr, and Miller, *An Immigrant Soldier in the Mexican War*, 41.

6 Buying Benevolence: The US Occupation of Mexico

FIGURE 6.1 "Major Sherman, trusses a Guard, and bastes a wounded patriot," watercolor by Samuel Chamberlain, circa 1861. Chamberlain's drawing shows an officer overseeing punishments. At regular artillery officer Major Thomas Sherman's orders, a row of men have been bucked and gagged while another suffers fifty lashes. Chamberlain identified the victim as Irish-born John Doughety, who had been medically discharged from a volunteer unit for combat-related injuries at Buena Vista and remained in Mexico to sell alcohol to soldiers. Courtesy of the West Point Museum Collection, United States Military Academy.

deserted from the American army and joined the Mexican forces was tiny compared to the number of immigrants who faithfully served during the war." Still, Nativists magnified instances of desertion to portray the immigrant enlisted man "as the unfaithful soldier who had no loyalty to his adopted country and no motivation to serve other than mercenary."[63] In reality, enlisted men, whether foreign or native-born, said they deserted because of how officers treated them.

In a letter of defense used in his court-martial for desertion, Private Edwin Davenport admitted that he had deserted but argued that he had good reasons. He described how he enlisted at sixteen, "full of hope and buoyancy, under the promises of good treatment and chances of promoting myself – and in the full expectation of having those promises fulfilled – how cruelly I have been deceived, those promises broken, and my prospects blighted, my present degraded situation is a proof."

---

[63] Spahr, "Occupying for Peace," 56, 62, 255; Steinhauer, Dale Richard, "Sogers," 109.

Davenport's story, in his telling, was a litany of abuse. Once, he was "tied up to the picket rope and beat over the head and back with a stick until it broke" by his first sergeant because he "had no straps to my pantaloons!" He had tried to get the straps but could not procure them. He complained to a Lieutenant Colonel, who recommended telling his Company Commander, who did nothing. He informed another Captain, who said it was Davenport's fault and the soldier "deserved it."

Davenport asked the court to consider what they would have done in his place. He queried, "Is not a private soldier a man? Is he not endowed with the same feelings as a commissioned or non-commissioned officer? Is he not entitled to clear treatment and protection against abuse?" Davenport insisted that he was driven to desertion "by the bad treatment of those from whom I had a right to look for kindness and protection."[64] The soldier's poem on "bucking and gagging" concurred:

> "Sergeant, buck him, and gag him," our officers cry,
> For each trifling offense which they happen to spy;
> Till with bucking and gagging of Dick, Tom, and Bill,
> Faith, the Mexican ranks they have helped to fill.[65]

Army officers broadcasted their commitment to the paternalistic treatment of soldiers, but those claims did not guarantee the fair treatment enlisted men like Davenport sought.

In contrast to civilian nativists, who rejected the notion of immigrant soldiers, army officers often embraced immigrant manpower, so crucial to US victory in Mexico, even as they benefitted from the ability to wield a heavy hand with immigrant soldiers. Winfield Scott, for instance, had (in a widely disregarded provision) barred foreign enlistments in the 1825 General Regulations. But as historian Dale Steinhauer argues, Scott praised immigrant soldiers' performance in Mexico by war's end. In the eyes of men like Scott, fighting Mexicans elevated immigrant soldiers – at least the Irish and German soldiers he singled out – into countrymen.[66]

---

[64] "Court-Martial Case Files, 1809–1894," EE485, Monterrey, September 17, 1847, Letter of defense in a court-martial for desertion by accused, Private Edwin Davenport, 2nd Dragoons. The court found Davenport guilty of desertion. They did not refer to his defense and presumably did not agree that ill treatment mitigated his desertion.

[65] Ballentine, *Autobiography of an English Soldier*, 247.

[66] This language relented somewhat by the army's updated regulations in 1841. Where the 1825 edition stated "no foreigner shall be enlisted in the army without special permission from general headquarters," the 1841 regulations stated recruits must be "'*effective, able-bodied citizens of the United States*,' native or *naturalized*" and had to "*speak and understand* the English language." Scott, *General Regulations for the*

Still, that acceptance was partial. Samuel Chamberlain, a native-born enlisted man whose disciplinary infractions tarnished a regular army career that ended in desertion, said it best. He wrote that the Irish were "the best material in the world to make infantry of, but requiring great efficiency on the part of the officers to enforce discipline."[67] Chamberlain encapsulated the post-Mexico consensus on the Irish, overwhelmingly the largest group of immigrants in the army, even as his own mixed military record in Mexico demonstrated the irony of nativist critiques that immigrant soldiers were the unreliable ones.

Chamberlain had seen the army's diverse soldiery. He described how, even in his prestigious and statistically more native-born dragoons, his squadron included "broken down lawyers, actors and men of the world, soldiers who had served under Napoleon, Polish Lancers, French Cuirassiers, Hungarian Hussars, Irishmen who had left the Queen's service to swear allegiance to Uncle Sam and wear the blue."[68] Chamberlain came to respect many of his peers, but ultimately, he also appreciated the importance of military discipline directed at foreign-born soldiers. Reflecting this ambivalence, Frederick Zeh had a complex relationship with the army and nativism. The German Zeh was a well-educated Protestant who spoke English. Before the regulars accepted his enlistment, a volunteer unit rejected it. Zeh wrote that at "the induction I was declared fit by the examining doctors, but the attending officer rejected me because of my foreign birth." Initially published in a local newspaper serving German-Americans, his writing emphasized the lingering discrimination directed at his community.

In a time well known for rampant discrimination against Irish immigrants, Zeh reminded his reader that Germans still faced unfair treatment. He recounted that "at that time nativism was flourishing in the United States, and immigrants, especially Germans, had to suffer many

---

Army, 1825, 354, Paragraph 1287; By Authority of the War Department, *General Regulations for the Army of the United States*, 121, Paragraph 687; Steinhauer, Dale Richard, "Sogers," 109.

[67] Chamberlain and Butterfield, *My Confession*, 179. Chamberlain always denied that he deserted, and claimed he had been properly discharged. Dale Steinhauer's work shows that Chamberlain's departure from service did amount to desertion, one of many such desertions in 1849 California, as news of the gold rush spread through the ranks. Steinhauer, Dale Richard, "Sogers," 195. Although that was the end of his time in the regulars, when the Civil War began, Chamberlain served in the volunteers as a Lieutenant Colonel in the 1st Massachusetts Cavalry Regiment. He was eventually awarded the brevet rank of brigadier general.

[68] Chamberlain and Butterfield, *My Confession*, 68.

indignities. When natives felt well disposed toward us Germans, they thought it flattering to call us 'sauerkraut.' Usually, they labeled us the 'G---d----- Dutch!'" In stark contrast, at the army recruiting office in Philadelphia, "My application was warmly received. This battery was, in fact, part of the regular army, where nativism had no say." Zeh estimated that about one-third of his hundred or so batterymates were US-born, and two-thirds were German, Irish, Scottish, Welsh, English, and Canadian.[69]

Zeh would experience privations and indignities alongside foreign and native-born peers. These included hunger, insufficient supplies, and humiliations by officers, though the good – camaraderie, battlefield success – invariably punctuated the bad. Of the bad, while Zeh's battery prepared to bombard Veracruz, he carefully chose a safe campsite to survive the expected counterbattery fire. As he bedded down, "the commanding officer, without further ado, stated that he wanted my place. Quietly I obeyed. I was now in a predicament, as there were no places left that could have afforded some degree of protection. Moreover, in the meantime it had become totally dark." Of the good, he described how once, after a hard-fought day, "Our sergeant, a Scotsman, had strong, heavily sweetened coffee waiting for us, which, after a twenty-four-hour diet of water, crackers, and pork, tasted exquisite and helped us promptly to forget all the perils we had endured."[70] Zeh experienced both nativism and acceptance, harsh discipline and paternal care, in an army that embraced the consequences of nativism – the ability to use (legal and illegal) physical punishments, and the absolute authority of native-born officers over enlisted men – if not the rhetoric.

An army culture that accepted immigrants *and* wielded harsh disciplinary measures ensured that as waves of immigration arrived from Ireland and other parts of the European world over the next decade, the army would readily assimilate increasing numbers of foreign-born soldiers into the ranks. It was a significant development, and the army relied heavily on immigrant recruits over the next decade. By 1860, soldiers were nearly seventy percent foreign-born, including over seventy-five percent of the infantry and over seventy-three percent of the artillery.[71]

---

[69] Zeh, Orr, and Miller, *An Immigrant Soldier in the Mexican War*, xii, 4–5, 7.
[70] Ibid., 17, 19–20.
[71] Steinhauer, Dale Richard, "Sogers," 111, Table 2.6. Steinhauer calculated, based on his 5% sample of enlisted men, the army of 1846–1848 (sample size 1,639) was 40.9% foreign-born, including 53% of infantry, 54.5% of artillery, 42.3% of mounted units, and 25% of new regiments called up for the war. Between 1849 and 1860 (sample size 2,502) the army became 69.6% foreign-born, including 75.3% of infantry, 73.3% of artillery, and 56.4% of mounted units.

6 *Buying Benevolence: The US Occupation of Mexico* 247

Regular officers increasingly made the regular army "one people while making them two," a single institution that combined two sharply differentiated groups – officers and enlisted men.[72] Immigrant soldiers' presence ultimately served officers' claims to professionalization by rendering physical punishment acceptable and even necessary.

As for the volunteers, Taylor found them vexedly hard to control yet remained unwilling to punish them. In May, Taylor wrote, "the commanding general is pained to find himself under the necessity of issuing orders on the subject of plundering private property" because of volunteers taking cattle. He insisted that all captured property "becomes from that moment the property of the United States." He vowed that "the army under his command shall not be disgraced by scenes of plunder," yet words did little to halt actions. Likewise, stationing guards "to preserve order in the town, especially among our own soldiers," and banning liquor had small effect. Taylor complained, while it had been his "constant aim to conciliate the people of the country.... The only obstacle I encounter in carrying out this desirable project arises from the employment of volunteer troops. Some excesses have been committed by them upon the people and their property, and more I fear are to be apprehended."[73]

Taylor was right to fear. Crimes continued despite orders to limit troop access to Mexican cities and civilians. In Monterrey, rather than facing punishment, soldiers merely heard from the chaplain. As described by West Point officer Lieutenant Napoleon Dana, the chaplain "gave it to the men hard today about drinking and excesses. There has not been as much drunkenness and rioting here as at Matamoros, but still, several murders have been committed on both sides, mostly by Texans." Orders noted the "many outrages that have been recently committed" in Monterrey, a euphemism that could refer to, among other crimes, rape, murder, assault, or theft.[74]

---

[72] Genovese, *Roll, Jordan, Roll*, xvii. Genovese meant US slavery, a far more coercive system than that of the army, but his depiction of how paternalism helped to create a single but completely stratified social system illuminates what regular officers sought to create.

[73] Thirtieth Congress, First Session, *House of Representatives Mexican War Correspondence*, United States Serial Set 520 (Washington, DC, 1848), 489, May 17, 1846, Taylor, Orders No. 62; 490, 497, Orders No. 65, May 23, 1846; Order No. 94, August 2, 1846; *Letters Sent, Headquarters of 1st Military Department and Army of Occupation*, vol. 1, 151, August 1, 1846, Taylor to President Polk.

[74] Dana, *Monterrey Is Ours!*, 145, October 18, 1846; Thirtieth Congress, First Session, *House of Representatives Mexican War Correspondence*, 1848, 512, November 27, 1846, Orders No. 146. 145, October 18, 1846.

Dana wrote more explicitly of numerous rapes: "The volunteers here have also been behaving shamefully. The fact is the army wants more active employment.... Many outrages have been committed on respectable females, some of the most hellish, devilish kind, and heart-rending in the extreme." He continued, "Some volunteers the other night, for instance, entered the house of a very respectable family, obliged the husband to leave the room. Some held him outside whilst two remained inside. One held a pistol to the lady's head whilst the other fiend incarnate violated her person."[75] There is no evidence these perpetrators faced military justice.

A few days later, Taylor's orders stated, "grave complaints" had reached him about "depredations." His response was to reiterate the importance of "respecting the rights of all Mexican citizens" because "the good faith of this country and of the army has been pledged to this course, and it is the interest of all to see that the reputation of neither be disgraced by scenes of plunder and marauding." Instead of punishing this violence, Taylor wrote to commanders that he would hold them "responsible for any excesses which may be committed upon your march" but "reposes such confidence in your good will and ability to prevent any thing of the kind that he trusts not to hear of any."[76] Taylor spoke the rhetoric of US protection but closed his ears to its failures as best he could. Sometimes, the reports were so loud that he had to hear, and thus, had to take some action, however limited, to discharge his responsibilities as a paternalistic officer.

Taylor had recently received precisely this kind of news. On December 25, 1846, Arkansas volunteers robbed and raped residents of Agua Nueva, and local Mexicans killed a volunteer soon after in retribution. The volunteers retaliated by murdering civilians near the village of Catana in February of 1847.[77] Of the plentiful examples of atrocities committed by US troops, a number included explicit acknowledgment, as in this case, that the army punished no one. Enlisted man Samuel Chamberlain later described the moment he arrived on scene. When he approached what he termed the "Massacre of the Cave," he followed the screams to a cavern full of armed volunteers and dead or wounded Mexican civilians (Figure 6.2).

---

[75] Dana, *Monterrey Is Ours!*, 142, November 29, 1846.
[76] Thirtieth Congress, First Session, *House of Representatives Mexican War Correspondence*, 1848, 512–13, December 2, 1846, Orders 149; *3rd Dragoons, Letters Sent*, 1: April 12, 1847. Taylor to 3rd Dragoons.
[77] Greenberg, *A Wicked War*, 156–57.

6 Buying Benevolence: The US Occupation of Mexico

FIGURE 6.2 "Massacre of the Cave," watercolor by Samuel Chamberlain, circa 1861. Chamberlain's depiction of US volunteers massacring civilian Mexican men at Catana in February 1847 while Mexican women pray, beg for mercy, and console the dying. Courtesy of the West Point Museum Collection, United States Military Academy.

Wailing women continued "clinging to the knees of the murderers and shrieking for mercy." But "no one was punished for this outrage; General Wool, in a general order, reprimanded the Arkansas Cavalry, but nothing more was done." *The Delta*, reporting from Taylor's occupation of Monterrey on April 4, 1847, described a massacre of twenty-four Mexicans, claiming "the officers in command – gentlemen and rigid disciplinarians – are using every method in their power to investigate the matter" and "Gen. Taylor has got his steam up on the subject" yet admitted that no US troops met punishment.[78]

When Mexican leader General Ignacio Mora y Villamil called upon Taylor to account for the massacre, Taylor claimed Mexican men's lawlessness and cowardice were the real problems. The real "outrage" was that US officers and soldiers had been "murdered" by Mexicans, and "an outrage of this kind preceded the melancholy affair of Catana." He continued, "I do not recall these facts for the purpose of justifying in

---

[78] Chamberlain and Butterfield, *My Confession*, 87–88; Hughes, *Niles' National Register*, 1847, XXII:184, 198–99. Estimates vary on Mexican casualties, ranging from four to twenty-four dead with more wounded.

any degree the practice of retaliation, for my government is at any rate civilized enough to draw the distinction between the lawless acts of individuals and the general policy which governs the operations of an army" but felt he must highlight that US warfare had been, generally speaking, conventional and civilized.[79]

Similarly, writing to the Army Adjutant General, Taylor emphasized that the massacre resulted from specific circumstances – the exception, not the rule. He wrote, men "from the regiment of Arkansas cavalry, exasperated by the murder of one of their regiment, left their camp at Agua Nueva, and attacked a number of unarmed Mexicans at Catana, two or three miles distant, killing and wounding several persons, without regard to age or sex." Interestingly, Taylor implied the volunteers attacked women and children, while in Chamberlain's drawing they exclusively slaughtered men.

Taylor wrote, the "most diligent means were employed, without effect, to discover the authors of this outrage." No soldiers were willing to testify. Mexicans also refused for fear of being killed. With none willing to name the murderers, Taylor concluded, it was "entirely impossible" to either prevent massacres or punish them.[80] At least, regulars thought it was impossible among the volunteers, whom Taylor, like other career officers, deemed rife with indiscipline. A longtime regular, Taylor used the massacre to highlight his institution's value.

Rather than face punishment, the Arkansas Cavalry simply mustered out of service as scheduled. In this, they followed other mounted volunteer units known for atrocities. Like most who committed crimes against Mexicans, Taylor's mounted Texas volunteers, known for criminal behavior, also left the service on time and without censure. He noted after they had been mustered out of the service, "with their departure we may look for a restoration of quiet and order in Monterrey, for I regret to report that some shameful atrocities have been perpetrated by them since the capitulation of the town." This was the same Monterrey that General Wool described as so safe that a beautiful young woman could walk alone at midnight without fear.[81]

---

[79] *Letters Sent, Headquarters of 1st Military Department and Army of Occupation*, 1847, 3:109, 118–19, May 19, 1847, additional letters to Army Adjutant General on May 26, 1847 and June 4, 1847.
[80] Thirtieth Congress, First Session, *House of Representatives Mexican War Correspondence*, 1848, 1138–39, May 23, 1847, Taylor to Army Adjutant General.
[81] Ibid., 430, October 6, 1846, Taylor to Army Adjutant General; Baylies, *Major General Wool's Campaign in Mexico*, 62.

6 Buying Benevolence: The US Occupation of Mexico 251

The Texans had been so bad that Taylor vented his frustrations to the Adjutant General, describing how they and other twelve-month volunteer units had committed such "extensive depredations and outrages upon the peaceful inhabitants" that there was "scarcely a form of crime that has not been reported to me as committed by them." Taylor understood how criminality damaged the occupation's legitimacy: "Were it possible to rouse the Mexican people to resistance, no more effectual plan could be devised" than this.[82] Taylor believed himself powerless to render army protection more meaningful for Mexican civilians and instead bore occasional witness to these miscarriages of military justice. He claimed, "the mounted men from Texas have scarcely made one expedition without unwarrantably killing a Mexican" and went as far as requesting the Adjutant General's Office "that no more troops may be sent to this column from the State of Texas." In this escalating cycle of violence, more volunteer cavalry meant more Mexican guerrilla activity in retaliation for volunteer depredations. And more guerrilla activity meant more volunteer cavalry along the roads to guard its supply lines, who would likely commit further crimes, and generate still more retribution. And so, Taylor wrote to one of his commanders in September 1847, citing a need for more cavalry along the army's main supply routes. He sent more Arkansas volunteer cavalry and elements of the regular army's Third Dragoons to meet that need.[83]

Scott did the same – he made his expectations clear in writing. In general orders, he harangued, cajoled, and appealed to his army to stop attacking Mexican civilians but took, like Taylor, limited action. Historian Peter Guardino finds Scott encouraged violence against Mexican guerrillas and their supporters – a category that could stretch to encompass any noncombatants – arguing that in Central Mexico army leaders "deliberately but unofficially used the behaviors they had earlier deplored" in northern Mexico to prosecute "a brutal counterinsurgency campaign," including authorization to execute guerrillas. Moreover, like Taylor, Scott claimed he would prosecute offenders and communicated to subordinate commanders that he did not want news of crime. In orders from Veracruz, he announced, "many undoubted

---

[82] Thirtieth Congress, First Session, *House of Representatives Mexican War Correspondence*, 1848, 1178, June 16, 1847, Taylor to Army Adjutant General.
[83] *Letters Sent, Headquarters of 1st Military Department and Army of Occupation*, 1847, 3:130, September 7, 1847, Taylor to Colonel Belknap.

atrocities have been committed in this neighborhood, by a few worthless soldiers, both regulars and volunteers, which, though stamping dishonor upon the whole army, remain unpunished." Yet a few months later, in a letter to Colonel Wilson, Governor of Veracruz, he wrote, "I have heard of many disorders and outrages said to have been committed by Major Lally's detachment, about Jalap[a]. I trust that the rumors greatly exaggerate the facts; or rather, that they are entirely false." He professed himself both entirely willing to visit justice on offenders and quite as eager to be told bad news was bogus. Scott concluded, "I will tolerate no disorders of any kind, but cause all to be rigorously punished. No officer or man, under my orders, shall be allowed to dishonor me, the army, and the United States, with impunity."[84] It was a coda to his dismissal of the alleged assaults, thefts, murders, and rapes. Rather than calling for investigations, Scott and Taylor were all too willing to label atrocities as rumors or isolated acts of retaliation.

Their continuous streams of general orders prohibiting crimes against civilians demonstrated not a commitment to justice but the reality that their demands had not produced change. Scott claimed such occurrences represented the actions of a "handful of scoundrels, who flout all religion, morals, law, and decency" who "dishonored" the rest of the army. The solution, in theory, was simple: "let every bad man be denounced in his act of guilt, seized, and reported for trial, and this army will march in triumph, and everywhere kindly received, and supplied with necessaries and comforts by the peaceful and unoffending inhabitants of the country."[85] It was easy to envision but difficult to manifest.

Scott used a tactic forged in the Kirk case to realize his goals. He hitched the newly ubiquitous newspaper, and his new military commissions, to the old horse of military propaganda. Scott published his orders alongside military commission and courts-martial proceedings in the many US-printed papers that cropped up in whatever cities the army occupied. Soldier-printers even self-consciously acted as Scott's instruments. The *Flag of Freedom*, produced in US-occupied Puebla, articulated this perspective in a piece describing their efforts as "a dose of

---

[84] Thirtieth Congress, First Session, *House of Representatives Mexican War Correspondence*, 1848, 914, April 1, 1847 General Orders 87, and 1029, October 13, 1847 Scott to Wilson; Guardino, "The Constant Recurrence of Such Atrocities: Guerrilla Warfare and Counterinsurgency during the Mexican-American War," 5, 15.

[85] Thirtieth Congress, First Session, *House of Representatives Mexican War Correspondence*, 1848, 914. April 1, 1847, Scott, General Orders 87.

6 Buying Benevolence: The US Occupation of Mexico 253

civilization." The editors wrote, after winning a battle, that US soldiers "pursue the retreating legions with the great civilizer of mankind – the Press."[86]

The military brought with it the US public's penchant for news. US journalists like George Kendall accompanied the army as war correspondents, and many printers enlisted. The *Flag* estimated that 1,000 to 1,500 men connected with the press fought in Mexico, who "fought and printed as they went along. At every stopping place and every town captured, they started a newspaper," and noted about a dozen US-printed papers operating. They concluded, "the press is altogether a new element in the prosecution of the war, and the troops of America have the honor of being the first to introduce it."[87] For Scott, this development was a substantive advantage. He "used these papers as a propaganda tool, and after occupying a new city, published court-martial proceedings on the front pages of the paper to demonstrate to the Mexicans the good order that he was determined to enforce." After the army occupied Puebla amid simmering discontent, "the first American paper published in the city contained the details of recent courts-martial displayed on the front two pages."[88]

This technique – printing messages in army-operated papers – was most likely to directly reach Mexican elites who had the access, literacy, and English language skills to interpret them. More indirectly, Mexican newspapers translated English language articles. Some army papers had a mix of works in both languages. Other pieces came with complete Spanish translations. Reprinting articles from other papers (US and Mexican) was a common practice that magnified army printers' impact. Moreover, US and Mexican publications engaged one another in their pages. In December 1847, two papers located in Mexico City, the *Daily American Star* and *El Monitor*, debated competing portrayals of a recent

---

[86] "American Newspapers in Mexico," *Flag of Freedom*, February 19, 1848, Vol. I, No. XXVII.
[87] Ibid.
[88] Spahr, "Occupying for Peace," 208. See the July 1, 1847 *American Star*, which published results of courts-martial dealing with desertion, absence without leave, drunkenness on duty, insubordinate conduct, highly unsoldierlike conduct, mutinous conduct, sleeping on post, conduct prejudicial to good order and military discipline, selling government property, and one of the more colorful charges known to military justice: "utter worthlessness." These charges dealt with internal matters of obedience and discipline, core concerns of regular army officers. Winfield Scott, "General Orders No. 192," *American Star*, July 1, 1847, Vol. 1, No. 6. Written by H. L. Scott, Acting Assistant Adjutant General, by command of Major General Scott.

speech, a typical example of conversations between presses.[89] Through this process of sharing, arguing, translating, and reprinting, US publications indeed magnified the effects of military justice throughout the US Army and across Mexico.

Paying high prices in cash for local supplies always came with a threat to take what the army needed by force should Mexicans prove unamenable to US terms. While the military made expansive claims to protecting innocent Mexican civilians, for Mexican women that protection often amounted to little more than a choice between selling goods and services willingly or unwillingly. Cash payments became a way of realizing both the army's vision of civilized war and understanding that vision's limitations.

The myth of affectionate Mexican women enabled a fiction of army unity that allowed officers to consolidate their authority and entrench officer paternalism as the dominant culture of the regular army. The implications of army paternalism reached far beyond its central tenet that the army protected women. Instead, it offered the officers who were its ablest practitioners a gentler exterior that rendered their violent exercise of authority over enlisted men invisible or acceptable. Army paternalism gained legitimacy through its rhetoric of protecting inferiors – soldiers dominated women, and officers dominated enlisted men. Paternalists thus heightened the differences of rank between officers and enlisted men. Beneath the soft glove of officers' claims to paternalism lay an iron fist of patriarchal authority used to discipline soldiers. The logic of protection helped officers fit the glove to the hand.

By the time the US Army finally marched into Mexico City in September of 1847, the broad potential of the logic of protection had narrowed into the right to demand payment for services given or taken. When Scott wrote that "protection will be given to all sellers," he meant that sellers would receive cash and that the army would punish those who disrupted

---

[89] "Principio Del Nuevo Orden de Los Negocios," *El Razonador*, December 22, 1847, Número 3, Vol. I. The paper reprinted several pieces from the *American Star* of December 18 and 19, 1847. It also included material from the December 19 *El Monitor Republicano*. For a paper with mixed English and Spanish articles, see *The American Flag* of March 29, 1847. "Ministerio de Guerra y Marina," *American Flag*, March 29, 1848, Vol. II, No. 186. For a US paper printed in English and Spanish, see *The Anglo Saxon (El Anglo Sajon)* of April 3, 1847. It included a long piece in both languages directed at Mexican citizens who were "men of a disposition to be honorable and just; who are fully aware of the degraded condition of their country" and so constituted a group the US might work with. "To the Mexican Public (Al Publico Mexicano)"; December 30, 1847.

6 Buying Benevolence: The US Occupation of Mexico 255

its supply chains. He also included explicit threats to guerrillas and to the communities, however large, that harbored them:

> On the other hand, injuries committed by individuals, or parties of Mexico, not belonging to the public forces, upon individuals, small parties, trains of wagons and teams, or pack mules, or any other person or property belonging to this army, contrary to the laws of war, shall be punished with rigor; or, if the particular offenders be not delivered up by the Mexican authorities, the punishment shall fall upon entire cities, towns, or neighborhoods.

Scott offered Mexicans a choice. They could be friends – and sell to the army what it demanded – or they could be enemies who frustrated army logistics.

If Mexicans "wisely" accepted, "then the Americans, having converted enemies into friends" (and sometimes into sexual partners) "will be happy to take leave of Mexico, and return to their own country."[90] Army strategy was pragmatic, intended to secure US supply lines and legitimize occupation. Sexualized portrayals of innocent Mexican women made such women appear to be "friends" and sellers to the US Army – appropriate subjects for payment, romantic conquest, and military protection. This strategy fueled regular army conceptions of their institution's superiority to volunteers and officers' desires to ensure strict discipline.

Regulars' convictions that they could, and did, better protect Mexican women than Mexican men or volunteer troops ultimately enhanced the regular army's distinct culture. Officers' sense of "genteel authoritarianism" reflected one aspect of the soldier-protector ideal.[91] Yet, officers' efforts to engineer a system of protective occupation through a process that equated payment with Mexican consent to occupation often generated the violence it had sought to eliminate against the very group they claimed to love and protect – Mexican women.

---

[90] Thirtieth Congress, First Session, *House of Representatives Mexican War Correspondence*, 1848, 937, Scott's Proclamation, 11 April 1847.
[91] Watson, *Peacekeepers and Conquerors*, 421.

7

"They Were Our Best Friends"

Army Misunderstandings of Mexican Women's Wartime Activities, 1847–1848

John Jacob Oswandel enlisted in the Pennsylvania Volunteers to fight in Mexico at age twenty-one and served with Scott's army throughout its Mexico City campaign. On his way home from the war, he passed through Puebla on June 3, 1848. The soldier knew it well. His unit defended the US-occupied town against a Mexican force led by Santa Anna in September and October 1847. Oswandel later wrote how Mexican women warmly welcomed the volunteers on their return, shaking hands and blessing the troops. As the army began marching east, one woman who had sold milk to the soldiers led many other vendors in giving "us three hearty cheers. We returned the compliment. Many of the women and men kept following us for over five miles, chatting, talking, and laughing of the times we had during the siege of Puebla." He reflected, "Our government is indebted to many of these Mexican women, and in particular to the huckster women, for saving the lives of many of our soldiers from the bloody assassins' hands." Oswandel concluded, "They were our best friends."[1]

When soldiers like Oswandel called Mexican women "our best friends," they echoed a sentiment commonly expressed by US troops (volunteers and regulars, officers and enlisted). Oswandel's characterization of women as allies – never as enemies – came from their services as cooks, vendors, and laundresses. That is, the archetypal friendly Mexican woman drew on a reality of women's labor and a persistent fiction of women's harmlessness. In part, the army understood its use of Mexican women's work through the laundress tradition. The US formalized this practice in 1802 when Congress established a 1:17 ratio of laundresses

[1] Oswandel, *Notes on the Mexican War*, 322, June 3, 1848.

to men, making these women – often wives of soldiers – a part of army life.[2] The laundress created a template for Mexican women who were both helpful because of services rendered and deserving of help as women who required protection.

In military minds, performing domestic labor made Mexican women like US laundresses. They were also women of an enemy country whose subordination to the military marked successful conquest. While conflating payment with consent legitimized seizures of Mexican goods and services, naming Mexican women affectionate friends of the US erased their military labor altogether. In many soldiers' eyes, women's wartime work was a labor of love.

The US Army's coopting of Mexican women's labor and affections reinforced its characterization of them as innocents. Moreover, the army's assumption that women were noncombatants meant army writing erased women's participation from US stories unless mentioning women enhanced the army's reputation. The war's US historiography largely inherited this blindness, and US military histories rarely consider Mexican women as complex or essential parts of the war effort. Those who do consider women's lives tend to offer descriptive – not analytic – accounts. These works tell us women were present, but not why women's actions mattered or how women's lives shaped the war or the army.[3] In short, such scholarship tells us how the war affected women, not how women influenced the war.

Reflecting this minimal engagement with women's wartime experiences, one scholar writes, "assuming that every relationship between a Mexican girl and an American soldier had a sexual dimension would be highly presumptive since engaging in questionable behavior with young Hispanic women would be taboo in both the northern and the southern society." Many nonsexual relationships indeed existed, but the question of racial or moral taboo did not significantly limit sex. This was also true in the United States, where interracial sex was not uncommon – including in slaveholding states where white enslavers routinely raped enslaved Black women.[4] Rather than US norms preventing sex between troops

---

[2] "Military Peace Establishment Act of 1802."
[3] Richard Winders ably describes US portrayals of US and Mexican women. Peggy Cashion's master's thesis describes how the war affected (primarily US) women. Exceptions come from nonmilitary historians, such as Amy Greenberg, an Americanist, and Peter Guardino, a Mexicanist. Winders, *Mr. Polk's Army: The American Military Experience in the Mexican War*; Peggy Mullarkey Cashion, "Women and the Mexican War, 1846–1848" (MA Thesis, The University of Texas at Arlington, 1990).
[4] Feinstein, *When Rape Was Legal: The Untold History of Sexual Violence during Slavery*, xiv.

and Mexican women, such norms probably motivated coercive sexual practices. Also, sex (willing or forced) with Mexican women sometimes occurred *because* US taboos gave rise to sexualized fantasies of Mexican women. Soldiers tended to believe Mexican women recognized US superiority and would submit to sexual advances.[5]

While conflating women and harmlessness was at least as old as the Euro-American laws of war tradition itself, it gained salience in the United States in conjunction with the US Army's rise as an institution. A particular approach to protecting noncombatants emerged from the Second US–Seminole War but blossomed during war with Mexico, when soldiers embraced Mexican women as the perfect subjects for army protection. When this process rendered women invisible, it also rendered women vulnerable, creating the harm it claimed to obviate.

When men across the army claimed Mexican women's affections, they demonstrated just how widespread and influential the logic of protection had become. That logic began with regular army officers seeking to assert the officer corps' gentility and control over an increasingly immigrant soldiery. It bolstered the regular army's worth as an institution while navigating rising democratic and nativist tides. The institution that departed Mexico in 1848 showed how widespread regular officers' ideas had become. Regular officers, regular enlisted men, and volunteers of all ranks expressed the belief that the army had made and kept its promise to protect women. The culture of army paternalism, developed by claims to a shared identity as conquerors and protectors of Mexico and Mexican women, had become a dominant army culture. That dominance manifested in their insistence that – sometimes despite evidence to the contrary – Mexican women were their best friends.

LAUNDRESSES, SOLDADERAS, AND THE OBLIGING MEXICAN WOMAN

The long tradition of army laundresses that dated in practice from the earliest days of the American Revolution and in law since 1802

---

[5] About sexual relationships between US men and willing Mexican women, John Belohlavek asks, "How do we define the image of these women? Are the terms *collaborator, camp follower,* and *victim* fair designations?" He finds US assaults on Mexican women "troubling and difficult to explain." This chapter explains by going beyond an indictment of the "base nature of many lower-class recruits, devoid of a firm moral center." Belohlavek, *Patriots, Prostitutes, and Spies,* 193, 54. 193. Political scientist Helen Kinsella offers a deep analysis of the "constitutive relationship of gender" and "military orientalism" during US counterinsurgency operations in Afghanistan. Kinsella, "Sex as the Secret," 1.

offered a convenient archetype for the combination of friendship, servitude, and sex that US soldiers expected from Mexican women.[6] In the male-dominated world of the army family, especially as it advanced into Mexico – the regulars brought fewer laundresses than usual, and the volunteers marched without official laundresses – soldiers sought out women to perform the domestic tasks of laundry, cleaning, and cooking. They found countless Mexican women ready to accept cash in exchange for these services, but just as often, they believed that women proffered love and friendship in addition to clean clothes or a meal. For many soldiers, to receive women's labor was to become the subject of feminine affection.

Dragoon Samuel Chamberlain, an enlisted man in the regular army, sketched many wartime scenes alongside journal entries. He later made some into paintings, basing several artworks on his experiences in Monterrey, where the army under General Zachary Taylor bombarded the civilian-filled city and then fought house to house, hand to hand, through the city's streets. This scene of horror must have included Mexican women. But when Chamberlain painted it, his brush passed over them. Only men populate his battle picture in downtown Monterrey.

The men who acknowledged women's presence did so to emphasize army gentility. Captain William Henry wrote that "bursting open another door, we came upon five rather genteel-looking women, with some children, and one or two men. They were on their knees, each with a crucifix, begging for mercy. As soon as they saw me, the cry was, 'Capitano! Capitano!'" He "reassured them" that "there was no danger," and they were "very grateful to find their throats were not to be cut." He concluded, "although we are fiercely fighting, and the blood of our officers and men has freely flowed, yet not one act of unkindness have I heard reported as being committed by either regular or volunteer."[7]

In contrast to his male-only war scene, Chamberlain's peace scene, set after the US victory, prominently features Mexican women strolling the plaza. Chamberlain, in effect, continued Captain Henry's narrative – the US Army's arrival had not, in these men's estimation, threatened women. It had guaranteed women's safety. Occupation made Mexican women safe (Figures 7.1 and 7.2).

Yet civilians, inevitably including women, were present in the city before, during, and after the battle. Moreover, women had always been

---

[6] "Military Peace Establishment Act of 1802"; US Army Military History Institute, "Army Laundresses: A Working Bibliography of MHI Sources."
[7] Henry, *Campaign Sketches of the War with Mexico*, 208.

FIGURE 7.1 "Street fighting in the 'Calle del Iturbide,' 'Capella Santa Maria,' Monterey," watercolor by Samuel Chamberlain, circa 1861. Chamberlain's painting of brutal street fighting during the US attack on Monterrey depicts an all-male sphere. It is a supposedly lawful battle between combatants that harmed few or no civilians. Rifle reports from upper windows imply Mexican soldiers' presence and thus legitimize forced entry into private homes, as depicted by the man with an ax in the lower left about to destroy a door and invade the house. Courtesy of the West Point Museum Collection, United States Military Academy.

part of army life, in peace and war. In the US tradition, such women were often army laundresses. In Mexico, they were soldaderas. The laundress tradition had deep roots in the Euro-American world. Laundresses even accompanied the chivalric armies of the Crusades that US troops so admired. One popular book with several editions published in the 1830s noted, as crusading armies prepared to depart "it was strictly enjoined that no woman should be permitted to accompany" the army "except washerwomen, and such as had accomplished fifty years." In British America, Kathleen Brown demonstrates the importance of laundresses'

7 They Were Our Best Friends

FIGURE 7.2 "Grande Plaza of Monterey as seen from the top of the Post Office," watercolor by Samuel Chamberlain, circa 1861. Chamberlain's scene of US-controlled Monterrey includes numerous Mexican women in the center of the plaza, often in their families' presence, strolling under the US Army's protection. Women's disappearance from images and records of war, yet presence in those of peace, suggests a strong need to preserve the fictive separation of women and war. Courtesy of the West Point Museum Collection, United States Military Academy.

work from Jamestown onward. She argues, "indeed, it is not simply the end product – the groomed, cared for body – but the organization of labor necessary to produce it that articulates a culture's deepest convictions about what it means to be civilized." Laundresses did intimate work intimately bound to the US civilizing project that the army claimed to advance in Mexico.

Mexican women regularly performed that essential work of US civilization. The task of cleaning dirty laundry connected Mexican women to the occupation in a way that rendered them less respectable than those who remained home. Brown explains, "The laundress's ability to be a mobile, independent, wage earner tarnished her reputation for chastity. If sexual virtue was embodied by the domestically contained matron...then her foil was the peripatetic laundress, whose labor gained her access to the intimate lives of her customers." Laundresses had literal knowledge of a man's dirty laundry and cleaned away evidence of illness, injury, and sex.[8] Mexican women's employment as laundresses functioned as proof of their capacity for civilization and suggested their sexual availability.

In the US Army, laundresses were often the wives of noncommissioned officers. They were essential parts of the enlisted community, especially given the isolation and arduous nature of frontier service. The 1841 General Regulations, the most recent pre-Mexico updates, continued the laundress tradition. Article XL included the provision, "four women will be allowed to each company as washer-women, and will receive one ration per day each."[9] Army leaders used the four women per company figure to allocate resources. Quartermasters determined requisitions for firewood and coal per person and counted laundresses alongside the soldiers. Allowances for straw bedding would be made "for washerwomen, in the proportion of one to every seventeen men." Based on this and knowledge that the regular army started the invasion of Mexico with 14 regiments of 10 companies each, there may have been about 560 laundresses when the war began.

The US Army also recognized matrons to supervise care for wounded and ill soldiers, at a ratio of one matron to twenty soldiers. Matrons would "receive 6 dollars per month, and one ration per day." Like laundresses, matrons were probably most often the wives of senior enlisted men. While the army did little to encourage married life, it enacted some specific privileges. When aboard ships, a necessity for many units as they journeyed to the theater of war in Mexico, the army mandated that companies reserve "a particular section for all the men having wives." In camp, laundresses had a place alongside other key elements of military labor: "The sergeant majors, quartermaster sergeants, trumpet, or drum majors, the sutlers and laundresses, will encamp on the same line, fifteen paces in the rear of the kitchens."[10]

Money due to laundresses was deducted out of a soldier's pay before soldiers received it. Even if a court-martial stopped a soldier's pay as punishment, the army ensured soldiers paid laundresses in full. A court-martial found Private Alexander Charles guilty of desertion in March 1847 while Scott's army in Tampico prepared to invade Veracruz. It sentenced him to be "marked indelibly" (branded or tattooed) on the right hip with a one-inch-long letter D, receive fifty lashes, be confined at hard labor with a

---

[8] James, *The History of Chivalry*, 245–46; Brown, *Foul Bodies*, 5, 31, 72.
[9] War Department, *General Regulations for the Army of the United States*, 37, Article XL.
[10] Scott, *General Regulations for the Army*, 1825, 262, 231, Form 26 on 264, 327, 151, 95, 49, 74. 262, 231, Form 26 on 264, 327, 151, 95.

twelve-pound ball and chain for the remainder of his enlistment, and then be dishonorably discharged. The court also stopped his pay "except [for] the just claims of the laundress and sutler."[11] It was a common phrase in courts-martial and reflected the established laundress tradition.

Still, the army institutionalized the presence of laundresses *and* barred them from full inclusion. The *General Regulations* required officers to report casualties (officers and enlisted men) and destroyed property (horses, equipment), but included no place for army women, who were not quite members of the army and not quite property.[12] At least, this was true for free women. Officers could claim the loss (death) of enslaved servants and seek renumeration. The reporting process erased laundresses from records of combat even though they were present on battlefields and in camps during the war.

Laundresses were with Zachary Taylor's Army of Occupation in its first battles and suffered through a "severe cannonade" in US fortifications opposite Matamoros. A regular officer noted, "all the camp women were left at Fort Brown; and they, poor creatures, underwent the horrors of the siege. I would rather have fought twenty battles than have passed through the bombardment of Fort Brown."[13] The little fort gained its name when bombardment cost its commander his life. Taylor dutifully wrote of his "profound regret at the loss of its heroic and indomitable commander Major <u>Brown</u>, died today from the effects of a shell." He listed his losses as one officer, one noncommissioned officer, and ten men wounded.[14] If a laundress fell in battle, no record marked it – officers

---

[11] "Court-Martial Case Files, 1809–1894," Case EE338, Tampico, March 23, 1847.
[12] Scott, *General Regulations for the Army, 1825*, 233–34.
[13] Henry, *Campaign Sketches of the War with Mexico*, 104. Henry offered a description of the women when the Third Infantry landed at San José Island near Corpus Christi, where they would begin the march toward Matamoros that began the war. When their boat could not cross the sandbar, "the men had to jump overboard into the roaring surf. They made a real frolic of it. Some old veteran camp-women took to the element as if they were born in it; while others, more delicately nerved, preferred a *man's back, and rode on shore.*" Ibid., 14–15. He describes the women sympathetically throughout his journal.
[14] *Letters Sent, Headquarters of 1st Military Department and Army of Occupation, 1846*, 2:16, 22, Taylor to Army Adjutant General, May 6 and 9, 1846. The presence of US laundresses offered subtle support to President Polk's justification for the war. Polk sent Taylor's forces – with their laundresses – to the Rio Grande, claiming it was US soil. When the two armies clashed, Polk claimed that Mexico had "spilled American blood on American soil." In contrast, when the army moved into (what was even by Polk's admission) Mexican territory, Taylor ordered the women to stay behind (many did not). As women, laundresses delineated Polk's border. When they were with the army, that army was within the US. When ordered to stay behind, it meant the soldiers were leaving the country for war in an enemy nation.

scrubbed women out of the narrative like stains on an otherwise pure garment, one meant to display male heroism and sacrifice.

As a result, the US Army's institutional history ignores women despite their official presence. The official Quartermaster Corps history includes no mention of women in any aspect of its US–Mexican War coverage.[15] It fails to address women's history as camp followers or laundresses and deletes female participation. This is perhaps a predictable oversight given its 1962 publication but highlights the opportunity to write a fuller history of army logistics.

Just as laundresses experienced the earliest fights of the war, many remained with the army throughout the conflict. When General Taylor advanced into Mexico, beyond the (baseless) US border claim of the Rio Grande, he ordered laundresses not to cross into Mexico. Given the 2,400-man size of Taylor's Army of Occupation and official 1:17 ratio of laundresses, the order applied to perhaps 140 women. It proclaimed, "The commanding general desires all the camp women and regimental baggage removed without further delay" and "directed one of the steamers to be employed in this service until the transfer is completed".[16]

Although some women must have been sent back to the US, evidence from personal correspondence and journals suggests many disregarded orders. The "Heroine of Fort Brown," laundress Sarah Bowman brought hot coffee and bean soup to artilleryman unable to leave their guns during the bombardment and traveled with the army for the war's duration. A shrewd businesswoman, Chamberlain encountered her running a successful "American House" where he spent the last few hours of a pass before he had to return to camp. The night after Buena Vista, a "well-known Laundress" called "Dutch Mary" brought coffee to the men on the battlefield. Describing preparations to march to Monterrey, a correspondent wrote of "camp women with children at the breast, and all sizes." Captain William Henry described four camp women who accompanied his brigade through Mexico. Upon making corporal in Mexico (he was later demoted), Samuel Chamberlain took his chevrons to Mrs. Charley McGerry to sew onto his uniform. Captain Franklin Smith notes the presence of two US camp women and their children "on

---

[15] Erna Risch, *Quartermaster Support of the Army: A History of the Corps, 1775–1939* (Washington: Quartermaster Historian's Office, Office of the Quartermaster General, 1962).

[16] *Letters Sent, Headquarters of 1st Military Department and Army of Occupation*, 1844, 1:228. Bliss to Major Ewing, 2nd Artillery, Camp near Matamoros, April 19, 1846.

FIGURE 7.3 "The Great Western as Landlady," watercolor by Samuel Chamberlain, circa 1861. Sarah Brown was better known as the "Great Western" for her tall and muscular physique (it was the name of a well-known and powerful steamship). Chamberlain painted her as a well-off proprietress in Mexico. Courtesy of the West Point Museum Collection, United States Military Academy.

the way to join their husbands at Tampico Veracruz or somewhere else" and notes elsewhere the existence of camp children in the army's daily life. Laundresses bore children while serving. Mrs. Roth gave birth on a ship traveling through the Gulf of Mexico, the journey's second birth. Captain E. Kirby Smith recorded that both mothers were well "and doing their regular washing for the men."[17] US laundresses remained with the regular army (Figure 7.3).

Officers sanctioned their presence, as the case of Mary O'Doherty, a laundress and a private's wife, demonstrates. A captain ordered her to

---

[17] Chamberlain and Butterfield, *My Confession*, 131, 192, 240; Allen, *Mexican Treacheries and Cruelties*; Hughes, *Niles' National Register*, 1847, XXI:130, March from Cerralvo to Monterrey, September 14, 1846; Henry, *Campaign Sketches of the War with Mexico*, 164; Smith, *The Mexican War Journal of Captain Franklin Smith*, 172, 183; Smith and Judah, *Chronicles of the Gringos: The US Army in the Mexican War, 1846–1848*, 43. 130.

leave the post while her husband was imprisoned for some unspecified transgression. A colonel's adjutant sent back a scathing admonition for Lieutenant Colonel Webb, the post commander, for the captain's callousness. The adjutant wrote that "the colonel sends her back to Cerralvo, with instructions to represent her case to you; as he recognizes the right of no officer under your control to expel from the post a member or follower of the army." His note continued: "the high opinion which he entertains of your justice and humanity forbids the idea that you would separate from her husband and turn upon the world, in a strange country, whatever might have been her offense, a helpless and unprotected female." Far from expelling army laundresses from Mexico, these officers expressly sanctioned women's presence. In the eyes of senior leaders, a woman could do no wrong sufficient to withdraw army protection. Regular officers also brought servants along on campaign. Hannah, a Black woman who operated an officer's mess for New Yorker Dr. Nathan Jarvis, a surgeon in the regular army, "had a large tent just outside the entrance to the fort" at Monterrey.[18]

Although only the regulars enjoyed the services of officially sanctioned laundresses, women sometimes accompanied volunteer units into Mexico. The wife of Private Cornelius Duffy of the First Massachusetts Volunteers served as a laundress for his company – records of her presence exist because he allegedly murdered her and faced a military commission. Brigida Mejia, a Mexican woman who lived next door, testified that Cornelius killed her. A Lieutenant found her body, surrounded by a pool of blood, and located Private Duffy in a nearby grog shop, with fresh blood on the soles of his shoes.[19] Army protection did nothing to safeguard laundresses from domestic violence.

Volunteer officer Lieutenant John Hollingsworth wrote that when he arrested a private, he soon had to deal with the soldier's wife:

---

[18] *3rd Dragoons, Letters Sent*, 1:55, March 11, 1848, Assistant Acting Adjutant General to Lieutenant Colonel Webb, 16th Infantry; Smith, *Chile Con Carne*, 175. Jarvis commissioned in 1833 and served in the Second US–Seminole War, where he witnessed the Jupiter River ambush described in the introduction. It is unclear whether Hannah was free or enslaved. Jarvis was a New Yorker who later fought for the Union, but officers from free states regularly used enslaved servants. Yoav Hamdani's sample, which includes a high proportion of records from New York, indicates that at the minimum and maximum range between 17.69% and 69.25% of military servants were enslaved. Among servants who officers took to war in Mexico, his dataset shows that between 27% and 81% were enslaved. Hamdani, "The Slaveholding Army," 130–31, 160–61.

[19] "Court-Martial Case Files, 1809–1894," Case EE649 San Angel, May 15, 1848.

"He has a wife here and she was furious on hearing of it. She had always done my washing."[20] Despite the continued presence of US women with regulars and volunteers throughout the war, the army's colossal appetite for women's labor meant demand outstripped US supply. Soldiers persistently sought Mexican women for domestic services to fill the labor shortage.

US troops believed soldaderas – the women who supported the Mexican army – were, like US laundresses, supposedly harmless, and characterized them as subordinates to husbands and fathers. To US troops, soldaderas were women who served enemies, not enemies themselves. Really, soldaderas were a "semiofficial quartermaster corps" for poor, enlisted Mexican men, responsible for feeding soldiers.[21] When done by male soldiers, such work would have been termed military labor and supported by army-purchased supplies.

Rather than consider soldaderas' work as enabling Mexico's forces, soldiers believed feminine emotion motivated such women. A correspondent for the *Veracruz Eagle* wrote, "I felt much interested in the numerous camp women – those devoted creatures who follow [Mexican men] through good and evil," characterizing the women as "slaves of the men," submitting to "the all-powerful influence of affection." The correspondent interpreted women as consecrating their actions to feminine virtue. Rather than toiling at military labor, their self-sacrifice and pure motives rendered their efforts women's work in US eyes. It was a pastoralization, not of housework, but of the work of war.[22]

The term soldadera comes from the Spanish conquest. Soldiers would give their pay, their *soldado*, to a woman. She, a paid servant, would buy and prepare provisions, making her a *soldadera*. Many soldaderas in the US–Mexican War were wives or relatives of soldiers, while others established temporary partnerships with soldiers for economic support. Few estimates exist to quantify the service of soldaderas in the war overall, but historian Peter Guardino notes that at least 5,000 soldaderas accompanied the approximately 20,000 soldiers of Santa Anna's army on the cold, hungry march to the Battle of Buena Vista (the Battle of La Angostura in Mexico) in February 1847. Also, a detailed record exists for the Mexican Revolution-era army interned at Fort Bliss in 1914.

---

[20] Hollingsworth, *The Journal of Lieutenant John McHenry Hollingsworth*, 4, 34–35.
[21] Salas, *Soldaderas in the Mexican Military*, 36.
[22] Hughes, *Niles' National Register*, 1847, XXI:164, Correspondent of the *Veracruz Eagle*, Jalapa, April 20, 1847; Boydston, *Home and Work*, 147.

It consisted of 3,557 officers and soldiers, 1,256 soldaderas, and 554 children, making women twenty-six percent of adults captured.[23]

US troops noticed soldaderas and used their presence to emphasize female suffering for unworthy men. The road of retreat from Buena Vista was lined with "dead men and women feasted on by coyotes." After Santa Anna's retreat following Cerro Gordo, a soldier wrote of a "wretched spectacle – several hundred Mexicans wounded, attended by gaunt, lean, hunger-stricken soldiers and women. On the road, we saw many dead and many women...many at the point of death from hunger, thirst, and cold." George Ballentine saw a "young and handsome though coarsely attired female" of no more than eighteen years among the dead, who he assumed followed her husband to war. Soldiers relied on the logic of protection to interpret soldaderas. They noted with disdain that the Mexican army was "accompanied by a great many women citizens," with "every camp-woman...loaded like a mule." They thought it "hard to see the poor women with their small children strapped upon their mother's back."[24] US troops saw soldaderas as wives, mothers, and daughters, and thus noncombatants regardless of their military labor. Their conclusion – love motivated Mexican women – transformed a complex reality of women's wartime activities into a straightforward narrative of female sentiment.

When his unit marched into the town of Santa Anna in California, regular officer William Emory wrote that Mexican leaders had made people "believe we would plunder their houses and violate their women." For men socialized in rising norms of domesticity, protecting homes *meant* protecting women. Amy Kaplan describes the importance of manifest domesticity – the inextricable and formative relationship between US domesticity and imperialism – in establishing "the domestic in intimate

[23] Guardino, *The Dead March: A History of the Mexican–American War*, 2017, 145; Salas, *Soldaderas in the Mexican Military*, xii, 36, 53, 82, 139. Manuel Balbontín, a Mexican artillery officer, wrote how in the days before the march, men and women died of cold. Despite "an order prohibiting fires, the soldier's women set the palms on fire around the camp, illuminating it, and the troops and even the officers quickly followed their 'bad example' and also lit fires, so the general had to permit it because of the cold, violent wind, and lack of coats for soldiers." Balbontín, *La Invasión Norteamericana*, 66, 70–71.

[24] Belohlavek, *Patriots, Prostitutes, and Spies*, 57; Hughes, *Niles' National Register*, 1847, XXI:184, "Incidents of the War," letter from a soldier in the Illinois regiment of volunteers, Camp Taylor, 5 March 1847; Ballentine, *Autobiography of an English Soldier*, 199–200; Coulter and Barclay, *Volunteers: The Mexican War Journals of Private Richard Coulter and Sergeant Thomas Barclay*, 558; Furber, *The Twelve Months Volunteer*, 558; Oswandel, *Notes on the Mexican War*, 51.

opposition to the foreign." Kaplan demonstrates that "the border between the domestic and foreign...deconstructs when we think of domesticity not as a static condition but as the process of domestication, which entails conquering and taming the wild, the natural, and the alien." She continues, "domestic in this sense is related to the imperial project of civilizing, and the conditions of domesticity often become markers that distinguish civilization from savagery."[25]

US leaders thus wrote of the war using the language of marriage, as when Secretary of War William Marcy wrote to General Winfield Scott that the army's goal must be to "induce the rulers and people of Mexico to desire and consent to" US terms of peace. The US Army would woo the Mexican people, imagining themselves as agents of a process where Mexican women fell in love with deserving US agents. This vision of consensual romance softened a reality of invasion. Army leaders shaped claims to success out of many such fictions, and the notion of willing Mexican women who longed for US partners provided a foundation for army claims to legitimacy. Laura Briggs notes, "in the symbolic economy of nationhood, woman has been the mother of the nation."[26] US occupiers courted the nation by courting its women.

This courtship, and reverence for home, permeated the army's logic of protection even as the military attacked Mexico's national home and the family homes of many Mexicans. After the war, Henry Halleck wrote in his *Elements of Military Art and Science* that men were "bound to protect our families against the attacks of others." Citizens would unite "in forcibly resisting" an enemy. But Halleck emphasized that in both cases, the soldier "must have no malice, no spirit of revenge" and "no desire to harm individuals." Soldiers had to fight the nation's enemy to preserve the national interest but were "prohibited from exercising any personal cruelty" and afterward obligated to treat enemies with kindness.[27] By recognizing that Mexican men had a natural right to protect their national and domestic homes, then noting their failure to do so when faced with the US military, the army replaced them as national protectors.

Furthermore, the army argued it provided far better protection than Mexicans, especially political leaders. General Winfield Scott compared US and Mexican manliness: "physically and morally, every two Americans

---

[25] Emory, *Notes of a Military Reconnaissance*, 118, January 6, 1847; Kaplan, "Manifest Domesticity," 581–82.
[26] Thirtieth Congress, First Session, *House of Representatives Mexican War Correspondence*, 1848, 1008, October 6, 1847, Marcy to Scott; Laura Briggs, *Reproducing Empire*, 6.
[27] Halleck, *Elements of Military Art and Science*, 11–12.

may be safely considered as, at least, equal to three Mexicans." Enlisted men also asserted superiority (including over their officers) by noting how in Mexico City, soldiers courteously yielded the sidewalk to ladies even when told to march in a straight line, at least when their leaders could not see them break ranks. The *Daily American Star* noted how a sergeant redirected his formation to avoid interfering with a lady's conversation and concluded that courtesy to women stood even higher than military discipline in soldiers' hearts – a small rebellion against officers in the name of enlisted gentility.[28]

Men like these took pains to show Mexican women (at least those they deemed ladies) deference and politeness. But many US troops considered Mexican women, even elites, to be lesser than US women. Amy Kaplan notes, "these visions of imperial expansion as marital union carried within them the specter of marriage as racial amalgamation." She continues, "while popular fiction about the Mexican War portrayed brave American men rescuing and marrying Mexican women of Spanish descent, the political debate over the annexation of Mexico hinged on what was agreed to be the impossibility of incorporating a foreign people marked by their racial intermixing into a domestic nation imagined as Anglo-Saxon." Soldiers sometimes expressed their ardent sexual interest in Mexican women by framing them as the exotic inferiors of white US women. One volunteer officer confirmed how Mexican women's "tresses may be like the raven's wing;" their eyes may "shame a night of starlight gleams;" but they lacked "That purity and modesty of mien" and the "blue eyes, fair locks, and snowy hands of our northern clime."[29] Poems like this shaped both soldiers' desire for Mexican women and such women's supposed inferiority.

Through various forms of literature, romantic notions of conquest colored US approaches to women in Mexico. *History of the Conquest of Mexico*, published in 1843 by William Prescott, was a companion to many US soldiers. This was especially true of men who participated in Scott's Mexico City campaign, which retraced Cortez's earlier invasion route from Veracruz to the capital. According to historian Nancy Isenberg, Prescott depicted "the Spanish conquest of the Aztec civilization as epic history and a romance of chivalry." Yet, he condemned

---

[28] Thirtieth Congress, First Session, *House of Representatives Mexican War Correspondence*, 1848, 1263, July 17, 1846, Scott to Secretary of War; "El Bello Sexo," *Daily American Star*, November 7, 1847, Vol. I.
[29] Kaplan, "Manifest Domesticity," 585; Giddings, *Sketches of the Campaign in Northern Mexico*, 58–59.

Cortez "as a cruel, deceptive, and immoral conqueror who treated Aztec women as concubines and spoils of war" and tarred Montezuma as a "pathetic figure" who became womanly in defeat. In contrast, Scott's army viewed itself as giving this history a civilized do-over. They would march into the Halls of the Montezumas not with Spanish cruelty and deception but as truly chivalric protectors who rejected Cortez's "selfish exploitation of women."[30]

Unlike the tales of Cortez and Montezuma, the legal underpinnings of conquest remained little known to officers and enlisted men. Indeed, because the laws of war remained a mystery to so many, Henry Halleck, already a noted expert on the subject as a young officer in Mexico, received so many queries that he collected his answers and later published *International Law*. Yet, even for Halleck, cultural notions of military and sexual conquest – not legal concepts – ordered his relationships with Mexican women.

In his diary, Halleck recounted how he and a group of men landed on the California coast and started on the road to Todos Santos to conduct reconnaissance. They headed through San Jose valley to the mountains and across a plateau. After a few days, they stopped for dinner at a ranch in Pescadero. Halleck's party bought chickens there and told the rancher's five daughters to cook them. Halleck lavished detail on a description of the encounter. The girls were "from 14 to 19 years of age" and "pretty" with "good Spanish features" and no "mixture of Indian blood," with figures "that queens might envy." They wore "dresses without sleeves & low in the bosom, like our belles at home when they wish to display their charms in the ballroom" because they were "too poor to afford *rebozas* with which Mexican ladies usually conceal their budding beauties." Every aspect of the girls' efforts to cook the men's dinner – including their poverty – became fodder for Halleck's sexualized narrative. Halleck continued, "these belles of Pescadero…presented us as lovely figures as the eye could ever wish to gaze upon…we waited in anticipation of a pleasant entertainment."[31]

The entertainment began when the girls carried out the meal in "an immense earthen dish," and a "difficulty" quickly arose. Each man in the party had only a meager, field-expedient cup and knife to enjoy the

---

[30] Winders, *Mr. Polk's Army*, 169; Isenberg, *Sex and Citizenship in Antebellum America*, 135; Halleck, *International Law*, 1861; Prescott, *History of the Conquest of Mexico*. Popular travel books also heightened US interest in the region. See: Calderón de la Barca, *Life in Mexico*; Sibley, *The Road to Santa Fe*; Dana, *Two Years before the Mast*.
[31] Halleck, *The Mexican War in Baja California*, 98–103.

food. While this worked well in camp, how would they serve dinner "up in proper style for the intended feast" now that there were "*ladies* to entertain?" Luckily, the men resolved this conundrum to their entire satisfaction. They rounded up a few plates, an old trunk for a table, and wood blocks for seats. Each of the men "selected a fair companion" who "seated herself by his side." Because wooden blocks were "rather short it became necessary for the gentlemen & lady to sit in rather close proximity, and, lest he might slip off the seat, it was equally necessary to press one arm rather tightly about her waist feeding both the entertained," ostensibly the girls, "and the entertainer[s]," the men. As "each gentleman had but a single cup, of course, the fair lady was obliged to drink from the same one with her cavalier."[32]

Just as insufficient seating and cups served as excuses for sexual advances, so did inadequate cutlery: "those who have never tried the experiment can hardly imagine what convenient things chicken legs are to hold up to the rosy lips of your sweetheart while she delicately nibbles off the fleshy encasement." Halleck glibly commented, "How true the remark that a well-bred gentleman of one country immediately falls into the forms and usages of fashionable society of another country!" He went even further and noted, their gentlemanly behavior reflected "the credit & reputation of the Model Republic."[33] Surely these actions were a sign of something, but one doubts it was good breeding.

After feeding the girls dinner "to their entire satisfaction," the men danced with the girls "till a late hour." Afterward, they ordered the girls to bed "in case of attack" while the men "retired to the exterior" to sleep "under the lea of the house." They remained in "close proximity to sleeping beauty (only an adobe wall between us), and the strong probability of a fight before morning." While no evidence indicated imminent attack, and the trip had thus far been uneventful, Halleck and his companions justified their behavior in the context of providing for and protecting Mexican girls. Although the girls prepared the meal, the men believed themselves the benefactors.

In their telling, they magnanimously hosted a feast. They chivalrously protected the women from an "anticipated attack" before withdrawing that protection early the following day when the party continued onward to Todos Santos.[34] Though Halleck predicated his dealings with these

---

[32] Ibid., 104–5.
[33] Ibid.
[34] Ibid.

girls on securing food for dinner, he presented the encounter not as a matter of logistics but as a romance. Halleck, known to his peers as an expert on the laws of war, nonetheless found that in his actual dealings with Mexican girls his cultural ideas about women and protection were the surer guide.

ARMY INCOMPREHENSION OF MEXICAN WOMEN'S COMBATANCY

US observers saw Mexican women who provided for the common defense as followers of their men. In Veracruz, a correspondent recorded, "the women and children were actively engaged in carrying away the sand" removed to dig out defensive positions. Regular officer George Meade described Mexican reports that there had been "a young women's procession" in Veracruz, "in which all the young and beautiful creatures of the place had turned out with shovels to work on the fortification." In Mexico City, men, women, and children constructed batteries and parapets. Volunteer soldier Judge Scott wrote of women's resistance in Mexico City: "even women, beautiful and innocent…fought like heroes beside their husbands, and fathers, and brothers."[35] How does one innocently fight a war?

In more quotidian examples, US troops similarly misinterpreted women's resistance to maintain their ideas of female noncombatancy, a necessary component for their identities as manly protectors. Maryland volunteer John Kenly wrote that he never "saw a Mexican woman show what we call temper, except upon one occasion" in Jalapa when a young Mexican "lad" working with US forces in a spy company drank from a woman's gourd on the sidewalk. After he returned it, she "threw it on the ground and crushed it under her foot."[36] Kenly interpreted her action as rooted in an (essentially harmless) fit of feminine emotion. He did not consider that a woman might protest her countryman working as an enemy spy.

---

[35] Hughes, *Niles' National Register*, 1847, XXII:36–37; Meade, *The Life and Letters of George Gordon Meade*, 1:188, Steam Transport "Alabama," Harbor of Anton Lizardo, March 8, 1847; Córdova, *La Ocupación Yanqui de La Ciudad de México*, 167, from the American Star; Moore, *Scott's Campaign in Mexico*, 195. Picayune editor, Tampico, February 20, 1847; Correspondence of the *Picayune*, United States Squadron, February 26, 1847. Meade read this in a Mexican newspaper, *El Locomotor*, published in Veracruz and distributed to his unit by a British ship.

[36] Kenly, *Memoirs of a Maryland Volunteer*, 370.

Like Kenly, when William Emory encountered Governor Manuel Armijo's sister and his wife in New Mexico, he seemed just as disinclined to record female resistance. Emory recorded how he called on "Madame Armijo" in Albuquerque to request her husband's map of New Mexico. He "found her ladyship sitting on an ottoman smoking, after the fashion of her countrywomen, within reach of a small silver vase filled with coal. She said she had searched for the map without success; if not in Santa Fe, her husband must have taken it with him to Chihuahua."[37] Emory accepted this answer – he did not press or consider that she could have lied or hidden the map to protect her family or resist the invasion. This acceptance may have contained several components – obliviousness to women's motivations, unwillingness to admit that Mexican women did not see him as an ally, or a habit of courtesy toward a lady that Emory believed more important than a map. Like most military men, Emory refused to consider a woman (especially an elite woman) an antagonist.

Soldiers refused many proofs of Mexican women's resistance. An article that appeared in the Mexico City newspaper *El Aguila Mexicana* signed "Varias Mexicanas" (several Mexican women), insisted that US men's attention insulted women's patriotism. Wartime papers like the *American Star* responded: "Why, bless your sweet souls we are no enemy of yours! Nor are we enemies even of your countrymen, unless we meet them on the field of battle! We admire you, ladies, and will continue to do so, despite all the effusions you can send us through the columns of the *Eagle*." Their embrace of Mexican women was complete. No woman could refuse it.

The *Star* was so loath to accept that Mexican women might not hold US men dear that it suggested a conspiracy: "But stop – may we not be too fast – is it not possible that the editor of the *Eagle*, jealous of the compliments we have bestowed upon his fair countrywomen, has resorted to this scheme to stave us off...?" Even a group of women doing no more than rejecting US flattery was an incomprehensible level of female resistance to these army newspapermen. It was a common sentiment, as enlisted man Frederick Zeh noted when he wrote that "Mexican women were always friendly to us; just their husbands, brothers, and fathers hated us."[38]

---

[37] Emory, *Notes of a Military Reconnaissance*, 42, 46. September 8 and 30, 1847.
[38] Conway, *The U.S.–Mexican War: A Binational Reader*, 103–4; Zeh, Orr, and Miller, *An Immigrant Soldier in the Mexican War*, 46.

7 They Were Our Best Friends

Cultural context shaped men's beliefs in women's friendliness. US troops carried a US understanding of women's separation from politics in a nation where rising universal white male suffrage came at a cost to women and people of color. For such men, the political invisibility of most US women rendered Mexican women's military invisibility more complete. Nancy Isenberg argues, "during times of war, masculine virtue and valor assumed a larger, national purpose of reaffirming the state's power to protect the strong over the weak." She argues, "military protection translated male valor into a rationale for the use of force" and notes that women, much like the "Varias Mexicanas" who refused US compliments, could not escape protection. Mexican women under US occupation were "conquered women" who were "crucial to the enforcement of martial law and military conquest." Indeed, "chivalry and military valor" became not only critical elements of army culture but also "a crucial part of antebellum political culture."[39]

Unlike the open letter, likely penned by educated elites, poor women in Mexico City sometimes took direct action against the US Army. Mexican historian Luis Fernando Granados notes the poverty of those involved in the Mexico City uprising of September 14 and 15, 1847 – when the US took possession of the city – and the vital class dynamics at work. Resistance was most intense in the poorest "lepero" neighborhoods. Mexico City's poor of both sexes expressed their discontent by "letting stones speak" from the balconies. They also threw sticks, bottles, and other items.

Similarly, on August 27, 1847, a US teamster caravan sought to resupply in Mexico City while protected by an armistice agreement. Over 30,000 Mexicans of both sexes filled the plaza.[40] They threw "a cloud of stones" at the drivers, cried out, "Let the Yankees die!" and called Mexican soldiers "cowards" for protecting the US wagons. A woman of the "low people threw a stone furiously," causing a US man to fall over "seriously wounded" and when seized by police, shouted, "I want to kill him, and to kill all of them: my poor son was killed by them, and now it is my turn for vengeance!" Mexican writer and wartime army officer Ramón Alcaraz explained that "it was requisite, in noticing her grief, to let her go at liberty."[41] In Alcaraz's telling, the police did not think

---

[39] Isenberg, *Sex and Citizenship in Antebellum America*, 103–6, 143.
[40] Córdova, *La Ocupación Yanqui de La Ciudad de México*, 119, Abraham Lopez.
[41] Alcaraz, *The Other Side*, 313–14. Alcaraz, a Mexican army officer, wrote several books on the Mexican War. He published this work in 1848 as *Apuntes para la historia de la Guerra entre México y los Estados Unidos*. An English language version followed in 1850.

a woman should face punishment, although she admitted to attempted murder and "seriously wounded" someone. Her aggrieved motherhood made punishment impossible. Even in the act of injuring an enemy, a woman could remain a noncombatant. Or perhaps the presumably Mexican police used the unassailable excuse of female harmlessness to avoid detaining a compatriot.

During all this, Mexican "ladies" looked on from their balconies as a mob attacked, "evidently enjoying the sport" and exemplifying the cautious approach upper-class women took when resisting. Regular officer Lieutenant Hill wrote that his landlady in Monterrey, "who is strongly Mexican in all her feelings," told him that "the ladies put on mourning for three days" when they heard the US won the city, her way of making her allegiance clear.[42] Among the people, stoning continued. After the US won the battle for Mexico City and settled into a military occupation, the Civil Governor General Quitman put Mexicans on notice – they were to remove all stones from balconies. Attacks sporadically continued, such as when a crowd of Mexicans threw stones at those administering lashes to a Mexican man convicted of attempting to murder a US soldier.[43]

Crimes committed by the poor against US soldiers in Mexico City were a form of low-intensity war, one in which women participated alongside men.[44] But soldiers tended to cast attacks on US troops as local men's acts of cowardice. Frederick Zeh, who believed Mexican women were "always friendly" and Mexican men "hated" US men, wrote that "hardly a night passed, after we first occupied Mexico's capital, without five or six drunken soldiers falling victim to the Mexicans' bloodthirsty treachery. They resorted to poison and dagger with equal success to thin the ranks of their hated foe."[45]

---

[42] Hill, *A Fighter from Way Back*, 29.

[43] Kendall, *Dispatches from the Mexican War*, 350; Córdova, *La Ocupación Yanqui de La Ciudad de México*, 299; Coulter and Barclay, *Volunteers: The Mexican War Journals of Private Richard Coulter and Sergeant Thomas Barclay*, 213.

[44] This open letter reflects the calls to arms and petitions women issued during the Mexican War of Independence. Elite women in Mexico City may have drawn on that revolutionary tradition. Arrom, *The Women of Mexico City, 1790–1857*, 32–38; Conway, "Sisters at War," 3–6; Di Tella, "The Dangerous Classes in Early Nineteenth Century Mexico," 96. Luis Fernando Granados, *Suenan Las Piedras: Alzamiento ocurrido en La Ciudad de Mexico, 14, 15 y 16 de Septiembre de 1847*, Colección Problemas de México (México: Ediciones Era, 2003), 14, 17, 19, 20, 43, 83, 90. Lepero was a derogatory term for the poorest people in Mexican society.

[45] Zeh went on to describe a cycle of violence: "Our soldiers, however, knew how to exact thorough revenge, inasmuch as they organized regular nightly raids on these

Although soldiers' perceptions of female noncombatancy held despite evidence of women's resistance, women's perceived attractiveness varied according to class and skin color. Lieutenant Napoleon Dana neatly demonstrated this divide. Of poorer and darker-skinned Mexican women, he penned a reprehensible and insulting description, saying of "the brown order of Mexican women as a race" that "they are without exception the most revolting, forbidding, disgusting creatures in the world, not even excepting our own Indians." Of more affluent and light-skinned women, he noted

> there were two very pretty women at church last Sunday, right fair and white. They were evidently not Mexicans but Castilian ladies. Everybody was looking at them, but I just gave them a passing glance. If there is anything I hate, it is this rudeness of staring at ladies, for I do think it excessively rude, and some do it most brazenly.[46]

There was an enormous space between these two sorts of women in his mind – creatures versus ladies.

It was a familiar binary, though few approached Dana's viciousness. Volunteer officer Luther Giddings expressed it in his description of the "fair senoritas of Matamoros." Giddings watched many women at their windows, smoking and talking, all alike "in having large dark eyes and black glossy hair," but it was hair infested with lice, such that "some of our young and adventurous soldiers, in whose minds romance and poetry had painted glowing pictures of Spanish beauty and grandeur, suffer a disagreeable disenchantment in the city of Matamoros." He continued with what to him was an obvious caveat: "Of course, the foregoing remarks will not be understood as referring to the *upper tendon* of Matamoros." Volunteer Frank Edwards wrote that women in Santa Fe "being mostly poor, are badly clothed, and are very dirty" with "ugly dark countenances." Because, he claimed, each woman was "almost the slave of the husband, who will sit day after day in the sun" and never help his "hard-working wife," women were "very fond of the attentions of strangers." In contrast, "those who have much white blood in them are pretty, but these are seldom found among the lower order."[47]

---

furtive bands of murderers and thus tried to render them harmless. The very strict order imposed by our local commandant soon reduced these excesses to a minimum." Zeh, Orr, and Miller, *An Immigrant Soldier in the Mexican War*, 48.

[46] Dana, *Monterrey Is Ours!*, 144, 180–81. October 12, 1846 and February 14, 1847.

[47] Giddings, *Sketches of the Campaign in Northern Mexico*, 58–59; Edwards, *A Campaign in New Mexico with Colonel Doniphan*, 50.

Agism also shaped perception. Soldiers valued young women as friends and potential sexual partners, but they described old women (except for elite matrons) as subhuman. West Point officer George Meade wrote that in Reynosa, he often stopped at local farmhouses to request a drink of water. Mexican girls always handed him a cup so charmingly that he described how their "ease of manner" was "even shown in the way they wear their clothes, always having them nicely made, clean, and gracefully worn," clad in the neat and "pretty patterned French calico or printed muslin" worn by the "lower orders." Despite their humble origins, these girls' youth, grace, and cleanliness elevated them above "the finely dressed ladies of the upper ten thousand" in the US. Frederick Zeh described young women in Jalapa as regular patrons of the city's beautiful baths. These women were "small but well built," with "dark and fiery" eyes, "black and shiny" hair, and "impeccably small" hands and feet. He found their faces "coarse" and that "women from the lower classes have Indian features," but concluded that "they wear very flattering clothing. A skirt with numerous folds, usually dark blue, reaches down to the middle of the lower calf, and a clean white blouse completes the outfit." In contrast, he wrote that women "by their fortieth year are already ugly, withered hags." On market women, who regularly fed US soldiers, Zeh cast naught but disparagement: "Without exception they are old, ugly women who never bathe. With their long, blackish gray, unkempt, disheveled hair, they often bend their heads over the kettle, stirring the picante and simultaneously running a free hand through their hair to fend off the vermin nesting there." Likewise, Edwards described market women in Santa Fe as "ugly old women."[48]

The army's heedless embrace of Mexican women as friends mattered because ignoring women's potential to be combatants shaped an inability to interpret many other actions Mexican women took. Major John Corey Henshaw demonstrated a common mistake – interpreting female mercy as romantic interest. While Henshaw lay sick in Puebla, two "very beautiful" and likely well-off women sent him food via a servant as he recovered. One scholar amplifies Henshaw's error by taking him at his word, agreeing the women loved and desired Henshaw, who tried to "chart a course of action that would avoid hurt feelings." In this telling,

---

[48] Meade, *The Life and Letters of George Gordon Meade*, 1:107, Matamoros, June 28, 1846; Zeh, Orr, and Miller, *An Immigrant Soldier in the Mexican War*, 42, 50, 52; Edwards, *A Campaign in New Mexico with Colonel Doniphan*, 58.

Henshaw needed to let the women down easily and communicate that he did not reciprocate their affection. Henshaw labeled it a "romantic adventure" and ultimately wrote "a letter of thanks for their generosity while regretting that his diet prohibited the ingestion of the sumptuous fare sent his way." The women would probably have disagreed. It is more likely that they acted out a long, profoundly important tradition in Mexican culture in which women fed the unfortunate, especially prisoners and the ill. Henshaw was no object of desire or admiration. He was one of pity.[49]

George Kendall, imprisoned in 1841 after the failed Texas-Santa Fe Expedition, attested to that tradition. In a scene repeated wherever they stopped, in San Miguel they "were visited by every girl in the town, and from the *ranchos* in the vicinity. Each time they brought us some little delicacy to eat; and if ever men came near being killed with kindness, we were the victims." Extensive female generosity toward the pitiable group meant the men "were often compelled to swallow a dozen meals a day." Only the food changed as they moved closer toward Mexico City. In Santo Domingo, the women "came running out of the mud houses in every direction, bringing tortillas, baked pumpkins, and dry ears of corn, and fairly shedding tears at our forlorn and miserable appearance." In Albuquerque Kendall observed a "poor village girl" coarsely dressed but perfectly beautiful, with dark eyes that "beamed upon us full of tenderness and pity," who shed "an unbidden tear of sorrow at our misfortunes" that fell on her "olive" cheek. She was "not more than fifteen" with a "bust of surpassing beauty" and "faultless" figure. He "could not but regret that the lot of one so kind-hearted and so fair had been cast

---

[49] Belohlavek, *Patriots, Prostitutes, and Spies.* 175. Henshaw originally wrote, in a letter to señorita Guadalupe García, Puebla, June 23, 1847:

> I cannot express to you in your own beautiful language how much I feel the many acts of kindness you and your lovely cousin Carmelita have shown me for some time past. But I regret to say that the state of my health is such that I am compelled to pursue a rigid course of diet which has prevented me from enjoying the things you have so often sent me as I could have wished. I feel that I would be doing wrong to permit either of you to take so much trouble for one who is unfortunately unable to appreciate them as they deserve. But allow me to assure you that I shall ever remain deeply sensible of your kindness and warmly cherish a recollection of them throughout my life. Accept for yourselves and family the sincere regard of your friend, J.C.H.

Henshaw, *Recollections of the War with Mexico,* 149. After Mexican independence, women's charitable organizations grew from this tradition of helping the needy. Arrom, *The Women of Mexico City, 1790–1857,* 43–46.

in such a place."⁵⁰ Kendall also sexualized Mexican women's generosity, but he came closer to understanding its purpose than Henshaw.

When US men mistook this tradition of female charity for love, they deliberately repurposed female heroism to condemn Mexican men. According to volunteer Frank Edwards, after the Battle of El Brazito near El Paso, "it was rumored that there were two Mexican women in the action serving at the cannon; and that a rifle ball striking one of them in the forehead, the other bore her off the field." Edwards continued, "I do not doubt it. The women have much more courage and even sense than the men." Elsewhere, the pro-US merchant Ann Chase talked to a soldadera from Puebla, who shared stories of her life's many hardships. Ann "could only listen, marvel at her fortitude, and ponder the lack of courage and leadership of the Mexican generals."⁵¹ These stories require context, not an uncritical use by scholars to depict angelic, heroic women and lazy, inept, cruel Mexican men.

When volunteer soldier Frank Edwards wrote that the women "have much more courage and even sense than the men" in Mexico, he intended to insult the men, not compliment the women.⁵² Nor did Edwards recognize the women in his story as military threats. He merely denigrated an enemy that he, like his fellows, saw as lesser than US troops. Female heroism and combatancy was not the point – it was the vocabulary of the insult.

Similarly, scholarly analysis of Ann Chase, the "Heroine of Tampico" fails to challenge army obliviousness toward women or confront the complexity of women's citizenship and Ann's choices. She married the US Consul in Tampico, Franklin Chase, but Franklin fled as the war began. He transferred all his property to Ann. She was Irish by birth though she emigrated to the US in 1824 at age fifteen and married a US citizen. She advanced a shaky claim to British citizenship to prevent property confiscation by Mexican authorities.⁵³ While married women under US law had no citizenship or legal identity as individuals, Mexican officials in Tampico generally respected Ann's assertions of her rights as a British citizen and a neutral party.

---

⁵⁰ Kendall, *Narrative of the Texan Sante Fé Expedition.* 433, 509, 521–23.
⁵¹ Belohlavek, *Patriots, Prostitutes, and Spies*; Edwards, *A Campaign in New Mexico with Colonel Doniphan*, 88. 66, 128.
⁵² Edwards, *A Campaign in New Mexico with Colonel Doniphan.* 88.
⁵³ "Franklin and Ann Chase Papers, 1824–1833: Finding Aid" (Dallas Historical Society), Collections of the Dallas Historical Society, Franklin and Ann Chase papers. Biographical Sketch.

She responded by actively spying for the US. Before the US Army landed in Tampico, Ann "climbed to the rooftop of her house and with the help of two friends raised the Stars and Stripes." If Mexican officials had caught a man passing intelligence to invaders and sowing misinformation, they might have deemed him a spy and hanged him. But to Mexican officials, Ann was only a nuisance, and to the US, she was just an ornament. The irony is that while it is reasonable to label her acts as espionage, neither the US nor Mexico *treated* Ann Chase as a spy. They treated her as a woman and, as such, refused to consider her a threat.[54]

While US observers allowed Ann a patriotic motive if a sentimental one, soldiers generally saw Mexican women not as nationalists but as members of the universal and stateless category of woman regardless of whether US or Mexican men commanded their labor. Mississippi volunteer Captain Franklin Smith noted, "the women like women everywhere else are always kind." Soldier John Kenly wrote, "they were Mexicans, yet they were women," and after spending two years among them, believed Mexican women were "as pure as those of any land, and that in the relations of wife and mother they are unsurpassed in the performance of domestic duties."[55] US troops considered women within a family-based tradition, rendering them private rather than public persons.

Women owed allegiance to families, first to fathers and after marriage to husbands. If women existed only as subordinates, they could not participate in war as combatants. Within the laws of war, fundamental similarities remained in the right to subjugate inferior peoples in war and men's right to dominate women based on female weakness. Under the rights of military occupation, Halleck gave voice to this relationship between submission and military conquest: "the duty of allegiance is reciprocal to the duty of protection." Women owed their allegiance to men and were entitled to protection, just as all inhabitants in occupied territory must give occupiers loyalty in exchange for peace.[56]

---

[54] Belohlavek, *Patriots, Prostitutes, and Spies*. 76. For female resistance and military justice in the Civil War, see: Curran, *Women Making War*.

[55] Smith, *The Mexican War Journal of Captain Franklin Smith*, 194; Kenly, *Memoirs of a Maryland Volunteer*, 239, 368.

[56] Halleck, *International Law*, 1878, 2:462, Chapter XXXII, Rights of Military Occupation; Kerber, *No Constitutional Right to Be Ladies*, 53. Kerber analyzes the relationship between promises of protection from men to women, and women's corresponding obligation to submit to men. She compares laws placing husbands over wives to masters over servants in a gendered hierarchy.

While Mexican women whose poverty preconditioned their choices often performed military labor for the US or Mexican armies, US observers categorized Mexican women's work as an extension of domesticity. They also misinterpreted Mexican women's interactions with US soldiers as proof of US superiority when many chose to support the US Army to secure economic advantage or protection through providing goods and services. In a remarkably straightforward example of the gap between women's practical motives for relationships with US troops and the latter's misperceptions of those relationships, enlisted man Samuel Chamberlain developed a relationship with two sisters in Parras whom he believed loved him. Then he found them with a Mexican man, at which point the sisters urged the man to, in Chamberlain's quaint Spanish, "matar el grande pendejo" (in polite translation, kill the big idiot).[57] There was a pragmatic quality in the sisters' efforts to befriend him, but little romantic motivation. Soldiers often expressed a belief that Mexican women found them irresistible, but Chamberlain's wounded pride serves as a corrective. While doubtlessly some relationships had a romantic element, others were premised on survival and rooted deeply in poverty, or existed to secure temporary protection from other US soldiers.

THE VIOLENCE OF PROTECTION

The logic of protection served the army well. Driven by the figure of the soldier as protector of women, it bolstered the US Army's sense of institutional superiority. It sprung from the cherished belief that the army waged war chivalrously, protected noncombatants, and conducted a just occupation of Mexico. One soldier thought, "the military occupation of the ports and the country by the United States is far more desirable to the Mexicans than their present anarchy." George Furber wrote, "the American soldiers...were found to be less oppressive than those of their own nation." Jacob Oswandel recorded a Mexican man telling him, "We deeply regret the Yankees' departure," as though it had been a war of liberation. Navy Lieutenant Raphael Semmes believed no country had "ever practiced more forbearance toward an enemy." Sergeant Thomas Barclay believed, "the United States in the present war has shown a forbearance and chivalrous spirit highly honorable." Yet, for Mexican women, noncombatant status was not benevolent. Instead, it reflected Linda Kerber's conclusion: "the wages of gender

---

[57] Chamberlain and Butterfield, *My Confession*, 71–72.

are not privilege."[58] Mexican women profited when they could from the occupiers but risked terrible consequences.

Roving guerrilla bands attacked women who engaged in sex with US troops. Chamberlain described how a woman invited his officer in the First Dragoons, Lieutenant Clarendon Wilson, into a hut. Later, guerrillas arrived. The officer escaped, but the woman turned up at a US camp with both ears cut off, reporting the guerrillas "lashed her down to a bed, where for hours she was subjected to the most hellish outrages," a reference to repeated rapes. Ear mutilation had a symbolic value soldiers may have recognized as a punishment for violating sexual mores, usually adultery, and here also applied to sex with an enemy.[59] US protection, always temporary and easily withdrawn, could invite shocking violence in its wake.

Samuel Chamberlain demonstrated this cycle of protection and retribution. In the first flush of their relationship, Chamberlain wrote the following poem about his lover, Carmelita Viejo, whom he claimed to have rescued from her abusive husband:

> She loved, and was beloved – she adored,
> And she was worship'd; after nature's fashion,
> Their intense souls into each other pour'd,
> If souls could die, had perished in that passion –
> But by degrees their senses were restored,
> Again to be o'ercome, again to dash on;
> And beating against my bosom Leita's heart
> Felt as if never more to beat apart.

He asked to have her "mustered in as a laundress," but his officers refused – presumably, officers confronted many requests like Chamberlain's from soldiers who sought positions for local women. After being forced out of US lines, Chamberlain claims Carmelita's husband and his band of guerrillas took her "to a lone ranch where she was outraged," a euphemism for rape, by the "whole gang of demons and then cut to pieces" (Figures 7.4, 7.5, and 7.6).[60]

---

[58] Semmes, *The Campaign of General Scott in the Valley of Mexico*, 194, 367; Coulter and Barclay, *Volunteers: The Mexican War Journals of Private Richard Coulter and Sergeant Thomas Barclay*, 183; Kerber, *No Constitutional Right to Be Ladies*, 304. Hughes, *Niles' National Register*, 1847.

[59] Chamberlain and Butterfield, *My Confession*, 213; Heitman, *Historical Register*, 702; Snyder, *Slavery in Indian Country*, 144.

[60] Chamberlain and Butterfield, *My Confession*, 206–8, 215–17. I render Chamberlain's eccentric spelling, "Carmeleita Veigho" into its common variant, "Carmelita Viejo." Chamberlain's unusual orthography likely reflects his limited grasp of the language, though his Spanish was probably much better than most of his contemporaries.

FIGURE 7.4 "A Close Shave," watercolor by Samuel Chamberlain, circa 1861. Chamberlain's cavalier depiction of this incident showed the officer's escape, but not the appalling violence soon inflicted on the woman by Mexicans. Courtesy of the West Point Museum Collection, United States Military Academy.

Later in life, Chamberlain named one of his daughters Carmelita, and before he died, he presented each daughter with a copy of his handwritten and illustrated journal. Carmelita remained a family name for generations. Chamberlain's great-granddaughter Maria Carmelita Pevear – married to the West Point Museum director, an institution that eventually acquired one of the journals – provided a brief oral history to her husband. He recorded it in a memorandum in 1956. She related a very different version of her name's significance: "The legend I heard was that Samuel had joined the Army as a drummer boy, [and] had been left for dead on the battlefields from which he was picked up by a kind-hearted Mexican rancher and nursed back to life by this man's three beautiful daughters. In gratitude, he named his three daughters after these girls." The museum director points out this story is easily disproven by reading the journal.[61] In the story handed down to his (female) descendants, Chamberlain's sexual relationship with Carmelita and her murder disappeared. Yet, the tale

---

[61] Todd, "The Samuel Chamberlain Journal and Paintings."

FIGURE 7.5 "El Tuerto and His Peon Wife," watercolor by Samuel Chamberlain, circa 1861. Chamberlain draws his rescue of Carmelita Viejo from her husband, who is whipping her. Chamberlain likely gave Carmelita white skin to emphasize her "Spanish" beauty, while using dark brown to paint her husband to underscore his "savagery." As always, he depicted himself as the hero. Courtesy of the West Point Museum Collection, United States Military Academy.

retained its essential belief that Mexican women were kind, speaking to the long half-life of ideas of women's innocence.

Chamberlain wrote a second poem, a companion to the first, to commemorate Carmelita after their relationship led to her murder. He used similar references to innocence, though he imagined her dying newly pregnant with their child:

> She died, but not alone; she held within
> A second principle of life, which might
> Have dawn'd a fair and sinless child of sin;
> But closed its little being without light,
> And went down to the grave unborn, wherein
> Blossom and bough lie wither'd with one blight.
> In vain the dews of Heaven descend above
> The bleeding flower and blasted fruit of love.[62]

[62] Chamberlain and Butterfield, *My Confession*, 217.

FIGURE 7.6 "La Belle Carmeleita," watercolor by Samuel Chamberlain, circa 1861. Here, Chamberlain shows himself riding with Carmelita Viejo. According to Chamberlain, when he could not secure her a position as an army laundress, she was forced to return to her husband, who Chamberlain tells us raped and murdered her. Courtesy of the West Point Museum Collection, United States Military Academy.

Then he moved on, suffering from grief, but not, it seems, from any sense of guilt, and with his perception of himself as a protector and lover of women absolutely intact. Like the many other US officers and soldiers who engaged in sex with Mexican women, Chamberlain knew such women risked retaliatory violence from Mexicans who interpreted their actions as a betrayal.

Despite the risk of violence, some Mexican women appear to have calculated that the economic and immediate protective benefits of an army relationship was worthwhile. Much as in other conflicts where a wealthy nation invaded a poorer one, some hoped the army would take them along. Josiah Gregg noted an army surgeon whose Mexican partner followed him from Chihuahua, dressed in men's clothing and shouldering a musket. Many soldiers sought out liaisons and agreed with Chamberlain that "Mexico is a country of romance." They pursued women through varied methods, including prostitution, concubinage, love affairs, and romantic friendships.[63]

Perhaps the relationship that most neatly embraced the army strategy of paying for what it took was when Mexican women engaged in prostitution. A Mexican observer characterized such women as "consisting chiefly of wicked, and sometimes allured girls, obliged by want to exchange their honor for a piece of bread for their families." These interactions ranged from single encounters to longer-term arrangements exchanging sex and domestic services for room, board, and money. Missouri volunteer soldier and future newspaperman Phillip Ferguson described women kept by many lieutenants in his units, including a thirteen-year-old Mexican girl later discarded by one officer and picked up by another. Ferguson remarked, "it seems to be a general thing among the officers to have mistresses," sometimes several at once. In Monterrey, Samuel Chamberlain reported, "all the Americans quartered in town, kept house with a good-looking senorita." The warnings of future violence came while US troops were still present, shown in the treatment some women received when with a soldier. The *Daily American Star* reported an incident in Mexico City. As a Mexican woman and a soldier walked along, "and as she leaned upon his arm a party of low Mexicans commenced throwing stones at them."[64] For Mexican women, like many women in wars of occupation, sex with enemies was a survival strategy, but a fraught one.

The US Army took its claims to protect women with it when it left. In a pattern seen in many other occupied countries following many other wars, local people scapegoated women alleged to have had sex with the enemy. The most famous of these, the post-World War II *tontes* – the ritual head shavings of about 20,000 women in liberated France from 1943 to 1946 – marked the "willingness of the general public to watch traitors being punished," and the use of violence against "collaborators" to affect a postwar purge. The ritual public and private punishments of such women reasserted a portion of national control. During the *tontes*, shaving "collaborator" women's heads allowed perpetrators to "move from a position of being the victim of violence to one where they inflicted it, and thereby reasserted their patriotic identity."[65]

---

[63] Smith and Judah, *Chronicles of the Gringos*, 304; Chamberlain and Butterfield, *My Confession*, 187.

[64] Alcaraz, *The Other Side*, 416; Edwards and Ferguson, *Marching with the Army of the West*, 342, 344, 349, Journal of Phillip Gooch Ferguson; Chamberlain and Butterfield, *My Confession*, 213; "Gallant."

[65] Virgili, *Shorn Women*, 1, 3–4.

In the wake of US occupation, some Mexican men imposed violent punishments on women labeled sexual partners of the invaders, and thus traitors. Chamberlain painted the scene. His depiction of Mexican peace celebrations in Saltillo featured murdered and dying women, some naked, loomed over by men with knives. According to Chamberlain, Mexican men raped twenty-three women during these celebrations, then cut off their ears and slit their throats. If true, then in committing this violence, Mexican men like Frenchmen in the 1940s helped recover their national virility, damaged during the war's rapid military defeats. As Mexican historian María Gayón Córdova has observed, Mexican men branded and shaved the heads of some Mexican partners of US troops, and some Mexican prostitutes who accepted US clients. Popular tradition named these prostitutes "Las Margaritas" and immortalized them in disparaging songs like "La Pasadita." As the army prepared to depart, women ran "around the wagon yards begging the teamsters to take them." In Mexico City, Mexicans stoned and beat some of these women. A local newspaper encouraged a halt to such actions, not because it believed the women to be guiltless but because the female sex of the "criminales" demanded compassion. The paper agreed these women merited punishment. Attacks continued (Figure 7.7).[66]

The army knew these women would face extreme violence. Even the infamous William Harney punished a man he thought to be Mexican (and turned out to be French) for harassing the Mexican wife of a US man in Mexico City. Harney's response marked recognition of a familiar pattern: Mexican men attacking Mexican women who developed sexual relationships with the enemy. Women followed the army by the hundreds on its departure from the Monterrey area to escape guerrillas who "resolved to kill all the 'Yankedos,'" another name for women who had sex with US men. When the army left Chihuahua, "at least one hundred and fifty women" attempted to follow, but army leaders sent them back per their orders. Phillip Ferguson associated women's attempts to follow the army as evidence of passionate attachment rather than a manifestation of women's credible fears of retributive violence. Regular

---

[66] Chamberlain and Butterfield, *My Confession*, 236–38; Virgili, *Shorn Women*, 219; Córdova, *La Ocupación Yanqui de La Ciudad de México*, 466, El Siglo XIX, 467–69; Conway, *The U.S.–Mexican War: A Binational Reader*, 168; Reilly, *War with Mexico! America's Reporters Cover the Battlefront*, 239–40. Accounts focus on Mexican men enacting violence on female "collaborators" so the role of "loyal" Mexican women in these rituals remains unknown, but "loyal" women may have participated in such punishments.

FIGURE 7.7 "Fiends and Fireworks, Saturnalian orgies in the Grand Plaza of Saltillo to Commemorate Peace," watercolor by Samuel Chamberlain, circa 1861. Chamberlain's painting of peace celebrations in Saltillo, Mexico, features the naked corpses of murdered or dying Mexican women flanked by murderous Mexican men in front of a fountain crowned with an image of the Virgin. Courtesy of the West Point Museum Collection, United States Military Academy.

artilleryman Frederick Zeh similarly trivialized women's distress. As he departed Toluca in May 1848, he wrote, "when we started marching back, only promises of a prompt return could dry the tears of our lovely girlfriends as we bade them farewell."[67] Still, the women and perhaps the soldiers knew violence would follow.

Mexican guerrillas used violence against Mexican women who had sex with US troops because many Mexicans saw sex with the enemy as a bodily betrayal of Mexican men and families and thus a particularly feminine manifestation of treason. These women became reprehensible to gender, family, and country, allowing extreme violence. Juliana Barr notes that Spanish male honor required the supervision of female sexuality. Peter Guardino observes that the concept of honor ordered Mexican society and justified social hierarchy, stating "for both the relatively humble and elites, behavior in sexual and family relationships was crucial to honor."[68]

Unlike Mexican women who had sex with US soldiers and were abandoned to punishment when the army left, the military did protect the men of its hired Mexican company. The unit, termed a "counter-guerrilla company" or a "Native Spy Company," was led by a Mexican man, Manuel Dominguez, and included 100 "men of the rank and file." According to US officers, it rendered faithful service, and so General Butler wrote to Secretary of War William Marcy to secure the company's future. In his letter, Butler noted that he agreed to provide twenty dollar bounties at the war's end, but Dominguez later agitated to be brought to US territory, fearing retribution.[69]

Butler knew he was right to be worried, for "painful if not serious consequences might grow out of their abandonment by us." He gave the order to transport the company's men to Corpus Christi, Texas, on the condition that they would receive nothing more from the US government. Then in July of 1848, Butler wrote Marcy with an update: "Dominguez with about 60 of his corps are here." Butler gave them rations and awaited

---

[67] Adams, *General William S. Harney: Prince of Dragoons*, 103; Edwards and Ferguson, *Marching with the Army of the West*, 361; Zeh, Orr, and Miller, *An Immigrant Soldier in the Mexican War*, 84.

[68] Barr, *Peace Came in the Form of a Woman*, 139; Guardino, "Gender, Soldiering, and Citizenship in the Mexican–American War of 1846–1848," 30–31.

[69] *Letters Sent, Commanding General, City of Mexico, February 21 to July 28, 1848*, 357: March 2, 1848, June 27, 1848, July 9, 1848, Butler to Marcy. Butler referred to Dominguez as a Captain. Ethan Allen Hitchcock, who recruited Dominguez and his men into US service, called him a "robber" and sardonically noted that the company "was commanded by 'Colonel' Dominguez." Hitchcock, *Fifty Years in Camp and Field*, 265, 313.

further orders. While the army abandoned Mexican women to retaliatory violence, it carefully evacuated, compensated, and cared for Mexican men who might face retaliation through coordination with top US officials.[70]

Why did the army knowingly return Mexican women, whom they claimed to protect, to such brutality while safeguarding Mexican men who served? Although Mexican men could serve in an official capacity, prompting official solutions like the spy company's relocation, Mexican women served in unofficial capacities based on individual agreements. US leaders felt no sense of institutional obligation to Mexican women who engaged in sex with or did cooking and laundry for US soldiers. Separating Mexican women from the official records of the war – a consequence of the logic of protection that subordinated (noncombatant) Mexican women to men who fought – did not generate protection. It made violence against women less visible and so more pernicious.

Because of women's unofficial status, army leadership did not consider violence against individual Mexican women to be a political issue. Where evacuating the Mexican spy company was a matter for international politics, women's murders were private acts. Feminist historian Antonia Castañeda describes how pervasive sexual violence committed by Spanish soldiers in Alta California against Amerindian women was not a result of soldiers' baseness, born of recruiting amoral, poor men, but rather a result of structural causes. It was "a political devaluation."[71] One can consider sexual violence in this form not as the result of aberrant or perverse soldiers, but of conquest that equated seizing territory with seizing women, and did not account for women once the conquerors departed.

Sexual violence in wartime Mexico, perpetrated by US and Mexican men, was not a peripheral phenomenon. It was central, linked inextricably to US racism, the conquest of Mexican land, and the aftermath of that conquest. As Antonia Castañeda argued of the region's earlier Spanish conquerors, "while rape and other acts of sexual brutality did not represent official policy on this or any other Spanish frontier, these acts were nevertheless firmly fixed in the history and politics of expansion, war, and conquest." More broadly, "in the history of Western civilization writ large, rape is an act of domination, an act of power.

---

[70] *Letters Sent, Commanding General, City of Mexico, February 21 to July 28, 1848*, 357: March 2, 1848, June 27, 1848, July 9, 1848, Butler to Marcy.
[71] Antonia I. Castañeda, "Sexual Violence in the Politics and Policies of Conquest: Amerindian Women and the Spanish Conquest of Alta California," in *Sexual Violence in Conflict Zones*, ed. Elizabeth D. Heineman (University of Pennsylvania Press, 2011), 52.

As such, it is a violent political act committed through sexual aggression against women."⁷² Just as US soldiers during the War on Mexico categorically refused to interpret women's activities as political and combatant actions, they failed to understand the political quality of violence against Mexican women.

The army's relationships with enemy women shaped military culture in meaningful ways. Army paternalism, well developed by 1848, embraced romanticized ideas of natural difference to reify the superiority of white men over others, regular soldiers over other white men, officers over enlisted men, and men over women. Each of these relationships could be, and was, measured by the army's supposed protection of Mexican women. Indeed, the core cultural belief that the army protected women was powerful enough by the war's end that soldiers were categorically unwilling to see what was in front of them: pervasive evidence of women's combatancy. Moreover, while seeing Mexican women as nonthreatening and sexualized allies caused soldiers to treat such women as subjects of protection, rhetorical protection created actual harm by excluding most evidence of violence against women from official records of the war. Invisibility produced vulnerability.

---

⁷² Ibid., 50.

MAP 7 Mexico and the Treaty of Guadalupe Hidalgo. Map by Mr. Jeffrey Goldberg, Cartographer at the West Point Department of History.

Conclusion

Beyond Men's Military History

In the 1830s, a new generation of army officers, the vast majority of whom shared a West Point education, graduated with deeply held beliefs regarding what it meant to be an officer in the army family – a stern father to enlisted men, the Native peoples whom the army considered its wards and the free and enslaved servants officers commanded, and a committed protector of helpless women and children. Paternalistic ideals encountered the complex and brutal reality of the Second US–Seminole War, where officers sought to assert their power, both to forcibly remove Seminole communities and condition enlisted men to their authority. War changed but ultimately strengthened the army's familial code.

The officer corps' Jacksonian dilemma was not to reconcile its practices with democratic norms but to demonstrate it could control the soldiers many US civilians regarded with suspicion. As the Second US–Seminole War unfolded, officers began to articulate an emergent logic of protection premised on the figure of the soldier-protector. By emphasizing the officer corps' duty to control enlisted men who posed a potential threat to women, this logic helped officers legitimize their authority. Simultaneously, it encouraged soldiers of all ranks to consider themselves protectors, elevating junior members of the US Army above other men and contributing to a shared regular army culture.

As the regular army fought in Mexico, a more widely shared culture emerged, animated by the imperative to protect women. At the same time, an officer's culture of patriarchy – concerned more explicitly with power and subordination – grew at its heart. This development lent army culture an internal coherence that radiated outward from a patriarchal core to guarantee officers' control over soldiers and an external

Conclusion: Beyond Men's Military History

coherence characterized by paternalism. That reputation helped the regular army, especially its officer corps, secure a respected position as a US institution.

One consequence of these developments was that soldiers viewed enemy women's wartime activities through a distorted lens. They were unable, or unwilling, to understand women as combatants. As a result, officers who wrote army reports scattered and buried the evidence that, when taken together, shows a wide array of actions that Seminole and Mexican women took to resist and survive. Such authors largely erased female combatancy from their records – a process typical of many wars. The key to uncovering women's contributions is a more critical look at official military documents. Although scholars often assume these materials represent dispassionate truths, one must consider how officers shaped the archive. Indeed, within the genre of army writing, one locates the gendered assumptions contained in the regular army's cultural foundations.

When military historians fail to see this erasure at work, they accept war as an all-male endeavor. Such scholars treat women as decorative additions, not essential parts of the story, valuable for a colorful anecdote or a personal highlight in the life of a significant man. Yet, if one pores over soldiers' letters, reports, diaries, journals, and newspapers, one finds evidence of women's impact. That this is possible for Seminole women who participated in one of America's least studied conflicts suggests historians might study women's combatancy more deeply in any number of wars. Women on a battlefield, so often viewed as exceptions or interlopers, were neither.[1]

In the Treaty of Guadalupe Hidalgo, Mexican negotiators (who insisted the laws of war must protect the Mexican people) and US peace commissioner Nicholas Trist wrote cultural imperatives that reflected the logic of protection into the fabric of peace.[2] The treaty narrowed

---

[1] Stephanie McCurry terms this a "process of erasure and trivialization" that begins when women's stories move beyond "suffering and sacrifice," and notes how "the pattern of denying or suppressing knowledge of women's participation in military conflicts forms a striking and persistent pattern across a range of postwar societies." McCurry, *Women's War*, 204. For silencing certain voices to preserve a dominant narrative, see: Trouillot, *Silencing the Past*.

[2] Scott and Trist, after an initial period of enmity, became close and lifelong friends. Trist, ashamed of the US invasion, ignored President Polk's recall message (it cost him his career) to end the war. The men worked with Mexican political and military leaders and the provisional Mexican president Manuel de la Peña y Peña sent commissioners to sign the treaty on February 2, 1848. Amy Greenberg shows how a fictional version of Trist

military protection to Euro-American women, excluded Native women from the purported privileges of female harmlessness, and committed Mexico and the United States to a set of shared rules in the event of future conflict.[3] This was unusual. Other US treaties during this era made few or no provisions regarding the treatment of civilians or prisoners, a trend that lasted until the 1864 First Geneva Convention.[4] Yet, the Treaty of Guadalupe Hidalgo referred expressly to "the established laws of war" and declared, "neither the pretense that war dissolves all treaties, nor any other whatever, shall be considered as annulling or suspending the solemn covenant contained in this article." Negotiators sought to ensure "civilized" conflict between conventional forces. During a war, "its stipulations are to be as sacredly observed as the most acknowledged obligations under the law of nature or nations."[5] Unsurprisingly, the imperative to protect women loomed large.

Focusing on what the treaty says about women reveals meaningful changes. Militaries could not imprison women, destroy their property, or seize their food without payment – all critical elements of army strategy a few years earlier in Florida. The treaty defined noncombatants, listing women as the first protected group:

upon the entrance of the armies of either nation into the territories of the other, women and children, ecclesiastics, scholars of every faculty, cultivators of the earth, merchants, artisans, manufacturers, and fishermen, unarmed and inhabiting unfortified towns, villages, or places, and in general all persons whose occupations are for the common subsistence and benefit of mankind, shall be allowed to continue their respective employments, unmolested in their persons.

---

appeared in a dime novel right after his departure from Washington on what President Polk intended to be a secret mission. Greenberg, *A Wicked War*, 211–18, 258–61. Of note, the treaty concluded the US–Mexico war, but conflicts within Mexico continued. Levinson, *Wars within War*, xiii; Spahr, "Occupying for Peace," 4.

[3] Nicholas Trist et al., "Transcript of Treaty of Guadalupe Hidalgo," *Our Documents* (1848). Scott supported and advised Trist, and Scott's rhetorical focus on protecting women is clear in Articles XI and XXII. This assessment of the Treaty owes a debt to Brian Delay and his deep analysis of another component of the treaty, the provisions committing the US to limiting Comanche raids. Delay, *War of a Thousand Deserts*.

[4] For example, the Treaty of Ghent between the US and Great Britain did not. At most, some treaties between the US and Indigenous nations said that the US would protect signatory groups from depredations by US settlers or neighboring Native peoples, including agreements concluded in the years 1795, 1804, 1808, 1818, 1828, 1833, 1834, 1835, 1838, 1842, 1851, 1853, 1854, 1855, 1856, 1857, 1858, 1861, and 1866. "Treaty of Ghent"; Kappler, *Indian Treaties, 1778–1883*, 42, 75, 95, 165, 389, 396, 418, 442, 446, 504, 521, 541, 589, 594, 601, 613, 710, 737, 762, 765, 772, 777, 809, 941, 1055.

[5] Trist et al., "Transcript of Treaty of Guadalupe Hidalgo," Article XXII.

Conclusion: Beyond Men's Military History

It was a return to a vision of restraint strongly reminiscent of Vattel and the European tradition – perhaps Mexican negotiators insisted on such language to refute how the US prosecuted its invasion.

The treaty also codified the army's transformation from Florida to Mexico by prohibiting the destruction of civilian settlements (the Florida policy) and insisting on paying a fair price for local goods (the Mexico policy). It continued,

> Nor shall their houses or goods be burnt or otherwise destroyed, nor their cattle taken, nor their fields wasted, by the armed force into whose power, by the events of war, they may happen to fall; but if the necessity arise to take anything from them for the use of such armed force, the same shall be paid for at an equitable price.[6]

The treaty's architects expanded the protections of noncombatancy beyond women to encompass US ideas of civilization. It protected non-fighting men who behaved according to Euro-American notions of land use – merchants, manufacturers, and farmers. It did not protect Native people who adhered to lifeways that the US and Mexico considered uncivilized. Although the treaty established a classically European laws of war framework for future conflict between the republics of the US and Mexico, it equally legitimized a less restrained approach to disputes with uncivilized enemies whom it deemed criminals. In the army's future "Indian Wars" the ideals of the Treaty of Guadalupe Hidalgo would not constrain military policy. The army could continue to burn Indigenous villages and crops.

Indeed, the document obligated the US to pursue Indigenous people. According to the treaty, if Mexicans were made captives by "savage tribes," the US government "engages and binds itself, in the most solemn manner, so soon as it shall know of such captives being within its territory, and shall be able so to do, through the faithful exercise of its influence and power, to rescue them and return them to their country." By legitimizing an army identity as rescuers of captives, the treaty improved cooperation and limited violence between the US and Mexico. It also allowed more violence against "savage" enemies that stole women.[7] Unlike in Florida, where the army sought to fight Seminole men who it considered to be legitimate combatants, by Mexico in 1848, the army came to label men who fought out of uniform – Mexican guerrillas and Comanche raiding

---

[6] Ibid.
[7] Ibid., Article XI.

parties alike – as criminals, in part because of how those men supposedly treated women.

It was as if winning the war in Mexico had allowed the army to detach itself from the long and miserable legacy of the Second US–Seminole War, even as the Treaty of Guadalupe Hidalgo helped it to retain what was useful from its Florida experiences. Richard Winders writes, "the Mexican War reshaped the image of the regular army, which emerged from the conflict with newfound confidence, born on the battlefield." This confidence came in part from the fact that, as Samuel Watson argues, "from the officer corps' perspective, the most important fact about the Mexicans was that they were not Indians."[8] The army appreciated how Mexico's army fought much like US forces, in large numbers, arrayed for a conventional fight. That Mexicans were ethnically more Native than Spanish did not change this conclusion. The US Army could wage a conventional war against the Mexican military and adorn itself with victories. Yet, the war presented an opportunity for more than military success. It proffered moral superiority.

Categories such as "noncombatant" and "prisoner of war" lost meaning in the Second US–Seminole War, where many officers believed it necessary to use any means available to secure the Seminoles' forced emigration from Florida. Rather than a chance to demonstrate gentility, conditions in Florida incentivized the army to bend the laws of war to meet the political mandate to force Seminoles into Indian Territory. However, officers never ceded their claims to righteousness. Instead, they used the logic of protection to recast practices like the widespread captures of Seminole women as a humanitarian policy, a way to bring dependent women under the benevolent control of army leaders.

Nonetheless, those assertions of virtue remained tenuous. In war against Mexico, a sister republic with uniformed soldiers, the US Army had a motive to emphasize adherence to the laws of war – US forces wanted to fight the Mexican military, not the Mexican population, Mexican guerrillas, or Indigenous groups. In Mexico, using the logic of protection served army interests by emphasizing Mexican women's affection for US men, lending urgency to the army's insistence on protecting noncombatants and its vociferous declarations that Mexican guerrilla activity and Indigenous raids were illegal.

Prisoners of war, now defined as uniformed male combatants, benefitted in theory from this change because the treaty provided for good

---

[8] Winders, *Mr. Polk's Army*, 64; Watson, *Peacekeepers and Conquerors*, 394.

conditions to alleviate their suffering: "They shall not be confined in dungeons, prison ships, or prisons; nor be put in irons, or bound or otherwise restrained in the use of their limbs." Simultaneously, the treaty limited the scope of who could become a prisoner of war. Women could not. Neither could men who fought out of uniform. Instead, such men would face punishment, perhaps execution, as criminals. As the "the exemplar of the noncombatant itself," women "embodied and thus solved the dilemma over the distinction between combatant and civilian."[9] The narrowed scope of prisoners of war reflected both the humanitarian impulse of protection and its corollary of violent punishment.

Likewise, the treaty clarified rank-based privileges: "The officers shall enjoy liberty on their paroles, within convenient districts, and have comfortable quarters; and the common soldiers shall be disposed in cantonments, open and extensive enough for air and exercise and lodged in barracks as roomy and good as are provided by the party in whose power they are for its own troops." It also limited which uniformed male opponents could be legally held as prisoners, reflecting reminders such as one from Zachary Taylor to General Wool that Mexican medical officers left to attend to wounded were not "in any sense prisoners of war, and therefore they cannot be detained longer than that duty may demand, nor can they be required to give their parole."[10]

Army paternalists believed the war's outcome would help them to better cement the regular army's place as a necessary, permanent, and benevolent institution. After the Second US–Seminole War, the army changed its regulations – Scott had revised the 1825 *General Regulations* and influenced the 1841 updates – to loosen restrictions on who could be held as a prisoner of war and deemed a combatant, to bring the policy in line with the practice of capturing Seminole women. After the US–Mexican War, the Treaty of Guadalupe Hidalgo restricted the population that could be made prisoners of war and expanded the definition of noncombatant, but only during an international conflict between the US and Mexico. Simultaneously, it promoted violence against Native peoples in wartime and peacetime by including provisions to redeem US and Mexican individuals from Indigenous captivity. As regulars came to see themselves as saviors of obliging Mexican women, the US Army

---

[9] Kinsella, "Sex as the Secret," 18.
[10] Trist et al., "Transcript of Treaty of Guadalupe Hidalgo," Article XXII; *Letters Sent, Headquarters of 1st Military Department and Army of Occupation*, 1847, 3:90, May 3, 1847, Taylor to Wool.

weaponized the logic of protection to wield legitimate violence in future wars on Native groups.

Still, the army never resolved the fundamental disconnect between the European-style wars it wanted and the "Indian Wars" it faced. In this, the treaty echoed a problem in West Point's curriculum. Both emphasized preparation for conventional conflicts even when faced with a reality that refused to conform. The treaty went further than West Point – it did not simply ignore the imperative to fight Native peoples. Instead, it promised protection from criminalized Indigenous groups and other non-uniformed enemies by reifying punitive violence.[11]

With its erasure of female combatancy, the genre of army writing set the stage for future clashes between comfortable beliefs that women were outside war and the inconvenient reality that they were not. In 1838, Thomas Jesup conjured a battle out of an ambush when he erased a Seminole woman who led a US detachment into harm from his report. A decade later, officers like Winfield Scott accomplished a similar feat on a grander scale when they severed the connection between Mexican women and records of the War on Mexico. They wrote women's labor out of army memory throughout the war and instead enshrined myths about Mexican women who loved the US Army and welcomed conquest. By war's end, the Treaty of Guadalupe Hidalgo followed. It not only erased women's stories from the war – it articulated a future where women's combatancy was a legal impossibility.

Henry Halleck had opportunities to grasp women's wartime activities during and after the US–Mexican War. Instead, he contributed to romanticized ideas of obliging Mexican women. As a result, he had to learn those lessons again during the Civil War – painfully. He inherited a status quo he helped to build, that "the obligation to protect women was written into the Union army's laws of war." But Confederate women's fierce resistance forced him to work with Frances Lieber to impose limits on those obligations.[12]

What then do we gain by restoring women to studies of war? US military history in the years before the Civil War remains a story populated

---

[11] US efforts fell short of the treaty's promises. In the negotiations preceding the 1853 Gadsden Purchase Treaty, US responsibility for Indigenous attacks on Mexicans, which continued after 1848, became a significant point of debate. Gadsden, "Gadsden Purchase Treaty."

[12] McCurry, *Confederate Reckoning*, 98. David S. Heidler and Jeanne T. Heidler, eds., "Henry Wagner Halleck," in *Encyclopedia of the American Civil War: A Political, Social, and Military History* (New York: W.W. Norton & Company, 2000).

almost entirely by men, primarily high-ranking ones. Yet, as military historian John Lynn argues, "bringing together military and women's history invites interpretative tensions."[13] From those tensions, much of value grows. Army paternalism emerged from a US context marked by expelling Indigenous groups to expand US territory and slavery. It shaped army culture from within, naturalizing officers' authority over army families that included enlisted men, wives, children, Native groups, and enslaved people. Considering discourse about women exposes changes to military law, policy, and strategy. Recognizing the logic of protection's enduring influence can illuminate studies of army culture.

Beyond men's military history lies a reckoning. Susan Lee Johnson describes how the California Gold Rush came to be "remembered as the historical property of Anglo Americans."[14] Likewise, war remains the historical property of men, aided by authors who only show weapons in male hands. But war has never been the property of men alone. Although militaries in nineteenth-century America and throughout history have mainly consisted of men, they are rarely all-male. That space between "mostly" and "always," between the reality of a majority male military, and an exclusively male collective memory, is an arena of great potential. And not only for military historians. This critique extends to feminist works that treat women as victims and peacemakers but struggle to comprehend them as warmakers. Efforts to frame women as essential to conflict prevention and resolution fall into this trap when considering women as war's natural opponents.[15] Attention to military records about women, the prototypical outsiders in histories of war, helps historians reenvision these discursive processes.

The army in Florida sorted all adult Seminoles into two categories: warrior and woman. This dualism, entrenched in bureaucratic reporting processes such as casualty reporting, shaped policy, army culture, and the war's history. When scholarship on war and conflict excludes women's combatancy, it ossifies this division. Our reality has long since moved beyond the pernicious separation of women's and military history. So must our thinking.

---

[13] Lynn, *Women, Armies, and Warfare in Early Modern Europe*, 7.
[14] Johnson, *Roaring Camp*, 11.
[15] A recent exception to this resilient trend is feminist political geographer Jennifer Greenburg's work analyzing US military women's work in Afghanistan. Greenburg, *At War with Women: Military Humanitarianism and Imperial Feminism in an Era of Permanent War*, 2.

Bibliography

PRIMARY SOURCES

Archival Collections

Dallas Historical Society
Franklin and Ann Chase Papers

Library of Congress, Washington DC
American Memory
A Century of Lawmaking for a New Nation
Journals of Congress
Debates of Congress
American State Papers
Indian Affairs
Military Affairs
Naval Affairs
Manuscript Division
John W. Phelps Letters
Nicholas Philip Trist Papers
Thomas Sidney Jesup Papers
Prints and Photographs Division
United States Statutes at Large
Military Peace Establishment Act of 1802

National Archives, Washington DC
Record Group 11
    Treaty of Ghent
Record Group 29
    Sixth Census of the United States

Record Group 46
  Annual Message to Congress
  Gadsden Purchase Treaty
Record Group 93
  Fort Brooke, Florida, General Orders
Record Group 94
  General and Special Orders, Mexican War, Volunteer Division
  General Orders, Headquarters of the Army in Mexico
  Letters Sent, 1st and 2nd Divisions
  Letters Sent, Commanding General, City of Mexico
  Letters Sent, Headquarters of 1st Military Department and Army of Occupation
  Mexican War Certificates of Merit
  Mexican War Compiled Military Service Records, 1st Tennessee Mounted Infantry
  Mexican War, Worth's and Scott's Command Orders Issued and Received
Record Group 108
  Headquarters of the Army, General Records
  Headquarters, Army, Endorsements on Communications Submitted
Record Group 153
  Court-Martial Case Files
  Office of the Judge Advocate General: Opinions of the Attorney General
  Registers of the Records of the Proceedings of the U.S. Army General Courts-Martial
Record Group 391
  3rd Dragoons, Letters Sent
  6th Infantry, Regimental Records, Letters Sent
  7th Infantry, Order Book
Record Group 393
  9th Military Department, Letters Sent
  Fort Brooke, Florida, General Orders

P.K. Yonge Library of Florida History, Special Collections
Colonel William Davenport Papers
General Duncan Lamont Clinch Family Papers
Joseph Van Swearingen Letters
Miscellaneous Manuscripts
Reynold Marvin Kirby Papers

United States Military Academy Special Collections
Adjutant Letter Book
Bugle Notes
Dialectic Society File
Library Records
Superintendent's Letter Book

Government and Military Documents

Cullum, George. *Biographical Register of the Officers and Graduates of the U.S. Military Academy, 1802–1867.* Vol. 1. New York: D. Van Nostrand, 1868.
Cullum, George. *The Early History of the United States Military Academy.* 3rd Edition. Vol. III. Boston, New York: Houghton Mifflin and Company, 1891.
Heitman, Francis B. *Historical Register of the United States Army, from Its Organization, September 29, 1789, to September 29, 1889.* Washington, DC: The National Tribune, 1890.
Lieber, Francis, ed. *Instructions for the Government of Armies of the United States, in the Field.* New York: D. Van Nostrand, 1863.
Scott, Major General Winfield, ed. *General Regulations for the Army.* Washington: Davis & Force, 1825.
The Centennial of the United States Military Academy at West Point, New York: 1802–1902. Vol. 1, Addresses and Histories. 2 vols. Washington: Government Printing Office, 1904.
The Rover (Anonymous Cadet Authors, Members of Dialectic Society). *The Empire of Reason, an Allegory, Addressed to the Dialectic Society, at the U.S. Military Academy, West Point, N.Y.* Newburgh, NY: Parmenter & Spalding, 1829.
Trist, Nicholas, Luis Cuevas, Bernardo Couto, and Miguel Atristain. "Transcript of Treaty of Guadalupe Hidalgo." OurDocuments.Gov, 1848.
War Department. *General Regulations for the Army of the United States.* Washington: J. and G.S. Gideon, Printers, 1841.

Newspapers and Magazines

Advocate of Peace
Alton Telegraph & Democratic Review
American Eagle
American Flag
American Star
Army and Navy Chronicle
Boletín de Noticias
Daily American Star
Daily National Intelligencer
Diario de la Guerra
El Monitor Republicano
El Noticioso Chiapaneco
El Razonador
El Republicano
El Universal
Espectador
Flag of Freedom
Frank Leslie's Illustrated Newspaper
Harper's Monthly

Le Courrier Français
Military and Naval Magazine
Niles National Register
The American Pioneer
The Anglo Saxon
The Daily Picket
The Gazette
The New Mexican
The Picket Guard

War Narratives

Enlisted Narratives

An American Soldier. *Recollections of the United States Army*. Boston: James Munroe and Company, 1845.

Ballentine, George. *Autobiography of an English Soldier in the United States Army*. New York: Stringer & Townsend, 1854.

Bemrose, John. *Reminiscences of the Second Seminole War*. Gainesville: University of Florida Press, 1966.

Bennett, James A. *Forts and Forays: A Dragoon in New Mexico, 1850–1856*. Edited by Clinton E. Brooks and Frank Driver Reeve. Albuquerque: University of New Mexico Press, 1948.

Carpenter, William W. *Travels and Adventures in Mexico*. New York: Harper & Brothers, Publishers, 1851.

Chamberlain, Samuel E. "My Confession." Illustrated Journal, c 1861. West Point Museum, Art Collection.

Chamberlain, Samuel E. *My Confession: Recollections of a Rogue*. Edited by William H. Goetzmann. Unexpurgated and Annotated edition. Austin: Texas State Historical Association, 1996.

Chamberlain, Samuel E., and Roger Butterfield. *My Confession: The Recollections of a Rogue*. New York: Harper & Brothers, Publishers, 1956.

Coulter, Richard, and Thomas Barclay. *Volunteers: The Mexican War Journals of Private Richard Coulter and Sergeant Thomas Barclay, Company E, Second Pennsylvania Infantry*. Edited by Allan Peskin. Kent, OH, and London, England: The Kent State University Press, 1991.

Edwards, Frank S. *A Campaign in New Mexico with Colonel Doniphan*. Philadelphia: Carey and Hart, 1847.

Edwards, Marcellus Ball, and Phillip Gooch Ferguson. *Marching with the Army of the West: 1846–1848*. Edited by Ralph P. Bieber. The Southwest Historical Series, IV. Glendale, CA: The Arthur H. Clark Company, 1936.

Elderkin, James D. *Biographical Sketches and Anecdotes of a Soldier of Three Wars as Written by Himself*. Detroit, MI, 1899.

Furber, George C. *The Twelve Months Volunteer; or, Journal of a Private, in the Tennessee Regiment of Cavalry, In the Campaign, In Mexico, 1846–7*. Cincinnati, OH, 1848.

George, Isaac. *Heroes and Incidents of the Mexican War*. Edited by J. D. Berry. Greensburg, PA: Review Pub. Co., 1903.

Goetzmann, William H. *Sam Chamberlain's Mexican War: The San Jacinto Museum of History Paintings*. Austin: Published for the San Jacinto Museum of History by the Texas State Historical Association, 1993.
Guild, Josephus C. *Old Times in Tennessee*. Nashville: Tavel, Eastman, and Howell, 1878.
Hildreth, James. *Dragoon Campaigns to the Rocky Mountains*. New York: Wiley & Long, 1836.
Hughes, John T. *Doniphan's Expedition*. Cincinnati, OH: U. P. James, 1847.
Kenly, John Reese. *Memoirs of a Maryland Volunteer: War with Mexico, in the Years 1846–8*. Philadelphia: J.B. Lippincott & Co., 1873.
McGaughy Jr., Felix P. "The Squaw Kissing War: Bartholomew M. Lynch's Journal of the Second Seminole War, 1836–1839." MS Thesis, Florida State University, 1965.
Moore, Judge H. *Scott's Campaign in Mexico*. Charleston, SC: J.B. Nixon, 1849.
Oswandel, J. Jacob. *Notes on the Mexican War, 1846–1848*. Edited by Timothy D. Johnson and Nathaniel Cheairs Hughes Jr. Knoxville: University of Tennessee Press, 2010.
Robinson, Jacob S. *A Journal of the Santa Fe Expedition under Colonel Doniphan*. Edited by Carl L. Cannon. Princeton: Princeton University Press, 1932.
Simmons, James W. "Recollections of the Late Campaign in East Florida." *Atkinson's Casket* (1831–1839), November 1836, No. 11 edition. American Periodicals.
Zeh, Frederick, William J. Orr, and Robert Ryal Miller. *An Immigrant Soldier in the Mexican War*. College Station: Texas A&M University Press, 1995.

Officer Narratives

Abert, James W. *Examination of New Mexico in the Years 1846–'47*. Washington, DC: The Secretary of War, 1848.
Alvord, Benjamin. *Address before the Dialectic Society of the Corps of Cadets*. New York: Wiley & Putnam, 1839.
Baylies, Francis. *Major General Wool's Campaign in Mexico, in the Years 1846, 1847 & 1848*. Albany, NY: Little & Company, 1851.
Beauregard, P. G. T. *With Beauregard in Mexico: The Mexican War Reminiscences of P.G.T. Beauregard*. Edited by T. Harry Williams. New York: Da Capo Press, 1969.
Brackett, Albert Gallatin. *General Lane's Brigade in Central Mexico*. Cincinnati, OH: H.W. Derby & Co., 1854.
Buchanan, Robert C. "A Journal of Lt. Robert C. Buchanan during the Seminole War." Edited by Frank F. White Jr. *The Florida Historical Quarterly* 29, no. 2 (1950): 132–51.
By a Lieutenant of the Left Wing. *Sketch of the Seminole War*. Charleston, SC: Dan J. Dowling, 1836.
By an Officer of the First Regiment of Ohio Volunteers. *Sketches of the Campaign in Northern Mexico in 1846 and 1847*. New York: George P. Putnam & Co, 1853.

Coker, Edward C. "A West Point Graduate in the Second Seminole War: William Warren Chapman and the View from Fort Foster." *Florida Historical Quarterly* 68, no. 4 (1989): Article 5.

Collins, Francis. Journal of Francis Collins: *An Artillery Officer in the Mexican War.* Edited by Maria Clinton Collins. Vol. X, 1915, Nos. 2 & 3 April and July. *Quarterly Publication of the Historical and Philosophical Society of Ohio.* Cincinnati: Abingdon Press, 1915.

Cooke, Philip St. George. *Scenes and Adventures in the Army, or, Romance of Military Life.* Philadelphia: Lindsay & Blakiston, 1857.

Dana, Napoleon Jackson Tecumseh. *Monterrey Is Ours! The Mexican War Letters of Lieutenant Dana, 1845–1847.* Edited by Robert H. Ferrell. Lexington: The University Press of Kentucky, 1990.

Davis, George. *Autobiography of the Late Colonel George T. M. Davis.* New York, 1891.

Denham, James M., and Keith L. Huneycutt. "Historic Notes and Documents: 'Everything Is Hubbub Here': Lt. James Willoughby Anderson's Second Seminole War, 1837–1842." *Florida Historical Quarterly* 82, no. 3 (2004): 313–59.

Doubleday, Abner. *My Life in the Old Army: The Reminiscences of Abner Doubleday.* Edited by Joseph E. Chance. Ft. Worth: Texas Christian University Press, 1998.

Du Pont, Samuel Francis. *Extracts from Private Journal-Letters of Captain S. F. DuPont, While in Command of the Cyane during the War with Mexico, 1846–1848.* Wilmington: Ferris Bros., Printers, 1885.

Elliott, Richard Smith. *The Mexican War Correspondence of Richard Smith Elliott.* Edited by Mark Lee Gardner and Marc Simmons. Norman: University of Oklahoma Press, 1997.

Emory, William H. *Notes of a Military Reconnaissance.* New York: H. Long & Brother, 1848.

Giddings, Luther. *Sketches of the Campaign in Northern Mexico.* New York: G. P. Putnam & Co, 1853.

Grant, Ulysses S. *The Personal Memoirs of U. S. Grant.* Vol. 1. 2 vols. New York: C. L. Webster & Company, 1885.

Griffin, John S. "A Doctor Comes to California: The Diary of John S. Griffin, Assistant Surgeon with Kearny's Dragoons, 1846–47 (Concluded)." Edited by George Walcott Ames, Jr. *California Historical Society Quarterly* 22, no. 1 (1943): 41–66.

Halleck, Henry W. *Elements of Military Art and Science.* New York: D. Appleton & Company, 1862.

Halleck, Henry W. *International Law.* New York: D. Van Nostrand, 1861.

Halleck, Henry W. *International Law.* Vol. 1. 2 vols. London: C. Kegan Paul & Co, 1878.

Halleck, Henry W. *International Law.* Vol. 2. 2 vols. London: C. Kegan Paul & Co, 1878.

Halleck, Henry W. *The Mexican War in Baja California: The Memorandum of Captain Henry W. Halleck Concerning His Expeditions in Lower California, 1846–1848.* Edited by Doyce B. Nunis, Jr. Los Angeles: Dawson's Book Shop, 1977.

Henry, William Seaton. *Campaign Sketches of the War with Mexico*. New York: Harper & Brothers, Publishers, 1847.
Henshaw, John Corey. *Recollections of the War with Mexico*. Edited by Gary F. Kurutz. Columbia and London: University of Missouri Press, 2008.
Heth, Henry. *The Memoirs of Henry Heth*. Edited by James L. Morrison. Contributions in Military History. Westport, CT: Greenwood Press, 1974.
Hill, D. H. *A Fighter from Way Back: The Mexican War Diary of Lt. Daniel Harvey Hill, 4th Artillery, USA*. Edited by Nathaniel Cheairs Hughes and Timothy D. Johnson. Kent: Kent State University Press, 2002.
Hitchcock, Ethan Allen. *Fifty Years in Camp and Field*. Edited by W. A. Croffut. New York and London: G. P. Putnam's Sons, 1909.
Hollingsworth, John McHenry. *The Journal of Lieutenant John McHenry Hollingsworth of the First New York Volunteers (Stevenson's Regiment), September 1846–August 1849*. San Francisco: California Historical Society, 1923.
Johnston, Abraham R. *Journal of Captain A. R. Johnston, First Dragoons*. Washington, DC: Wendell and Van Benthuysen, 1848.
Keyes, Erasmus D. *Fifty Years' Observations of Men and Events: Civil and Military*. New York: C. Scribner's Sons, 1884.
Laidley, Theodore. *Surrounded by Dangers of All Kinds*. Edited by James M. McCaffrey. Denton: University of North Texas Press, 1997.
LeBaron, J. Hugh, and William G. Coleman. *Perry Volunteers in the Mexican War: Perry County, Alabama, First Regiment of Alabama Volunteers, 1846–1847, and the Mexican War Diary of Captain William G. Coleman*. Westminster, MD: Heritage Books, 2008.
Macomb, Alexander. *Pontiac, or, the Siege of Detroit: A Drama, in Three Acts*. Boston: S. Colman, 1835.
Macomb, Alexander. *The Practice of Courts Martial*. New York: Samuel Colman, 1840.
Mahon, John K. "Letters from the Second Seminole War." *Florida Historical Quarterly* 36, no. 4 (1958): 331–52.
Mahon, John K. "The Journal of A. B. Meek and the Second Seminole War, 1836." *Florida Historical Quarterly* 38, no. 4 (1960): 302–18.
McCall, George Archibald. *Letters from the Frontiers: Written during a Period of Thirty Years' Service in the Army of the United States*. Philadelphia, 1868.
McClellan, George B. *The Mexican War Diary and Correspondence of George B. McClellan*. Edited by Thomas W. Cutrer. Baton Rouge: Louisiana State University Press, 2009.
Meade, George Gordon. *The Life and Letters of George Gordon Meade*. Vol. 1. 2 vols. New York: Charles Scribner's Sons, 1913.
Motte, Jacob Rhett. *Journey into Wilderness; An Army Surgeon's Account of Life in Camp and Field during the Creek and Seminole Wars, 1836–1838*. Edited by James F. Sunderman. Gainesville: University of Florida Press, 1953.
Peck, John James. *The Sign of the Eagle: A View of Mexico – 1830 to 1855*. Edited by Richard J. Pourade. San Diego: Union-Tribune Publishing Co., 1970.
Phelps, John W. "Letters of Lieutenant John W. Phelps, U. S. A., 1837–1838." *Florida Historical Society Quarterly* 6, no. 2 (1927): 67–84.

Preble, The Late Rear Admiral, U.S.N., Henry. "The Diary of a Canoe Expedition Into the Everglades and Interior of Southern Florida in 1842." *United Service; a Quarterly Review of Military and Naval Affairs (1879–1905)* 8, no. 1 (1905): 26–47.

Prince, Henry. *Amidst a Storm of Bullets: The Diary of Lt. Henry Prince in Florida, 1836–1842*. Edited by Frank Laumer. Tampa, FL: University of Tampa Press, 1998.

Rodenbough, Theophilus F. *From Everglade to Cañón with the Second Dragoons*. New York: D. Van Nostrand, 1875.

Schafer, Daniel L. *The Florida Historical Quarterly* 68, no. 4 (1990): 447–75.

Semmes, Raphael. *The Campaign of General Scott in the Valley of Mexico*. Cincinnati: Moore and Anderson Publishers, 1852.

Smith, Franklin. *The Mexican War Journal of Captain Franklin Smith*. Edited by Joseph E. Chance. Jackson and London: University Press of Mississippi, 1991.

Smith, Isaac. *Reminiscences of a Campaign in Mexico*. Indianapolis: Chapmans & Spann, 1848.

Smith, S. Compton. *Chile Con Carne, or, the Camp and the Field*. New York: Miller & Curtis, 1857.

Sprague, John T. *The Origin, Progress, and Conclusion of the Florida War*. New York: D. Appleton & Company, 1848.

White Jr., Frank L. "The Journals of Lieutenant John Pickell, 1836–1837." *Florida Historical Society* 38, no. 2 (1959): 142–71.

Mexican Narratives

Alcaraz, Ramón. *The Other Side, or, Notes for the History of the War between Mexico and the United States*. Translated by Albert C. Ramsey. New York: John Wiley, 1850.

Balbontín, Manuel. *La Invasión Norteamericana, 1846 a 1849. Apuntes Del Subteniente de Artillería*. México: Tip. de G.A. Esteva, 1883.

Bustamante, Carlos María de. *El Nuevo Bernal Díaz Del Castillo; o Sea, Historia de La Invasión de Los Anglo-Americanos En México*. Mexico City: Secretaría de Educación Pública, 1949.

García Cubas, Antonio. *El Libro de Mis Recuerdos*. México: Secretaría de Educación Pública, 1946.

Prieto, Guillermo. *Mi Guerra Del 47*. Mexico City: Universidad Nacional Autónoma de México, Coordinación de Humanidades, 1997.

Ramírez, José Fernando. *Mexico Durante Su Guerra Con Los Estados Unidos*. Mexico: Vda de C. Bouret, 1905.

Roa Bárcena, José María. *Recuerdos de La Invasión Norteamericana (1846–1848)*. Edited by Antonio Castro Leal. México: Editorial Porrúa, 1947.

Other Primary Sources

Allen, G. N. *Mexican Treacheries and Cruelties*. Boston and New York: Hall's, 1848.

Bassett, John Spencer, ed. *Correspondence of Andrew Jackson*. Vol. V, 1835–1838. Washington, DC: Carnegie Institution of Washington, 1931.

Beecher, Catherine E. *A Treatise on Domestic Economy: For the Use of Young Ladies at Home and at School*. 3rd Edition. New York: Harper & Brothers, Publishers, 1856.

Bettelyoun, Susan Bordeaux. *With My Own Eyes: A Lakota Woman Tells Her People's History*. Edited by Josephine Waggoner and Emily Levine. Lincoln: University of Nebraska Press, 1998.

Blackstone, William. *Blackstone's Commentaries*. 2nd ed., 1803.

Brougham, John. *Metamora; or, The Last of the Pollywogs, a Burlesque in Two Acts*. Boston: H. W. Swett, 1847.

Buntline, Ned. *The Volunteer: Or, The Maid of Monterey, a Story of the Mexican War*. Boston: F. Gleason, 1847.

Butler, Benjamin F. *The Military Profession in the United States, and the Means of Promoting Its Usefulness and Honour*. New York: Samuel Colman, 1839.

Calderón de la Barca, Frances. *Life in Mexico; The Letters of Fanny Calderón de La Barca*. Edited by Howard T. Fisher and Marion Hall Fisher. Garden City, NY: Doubleday, 1966.

Calhoun, James S. *The Official Correspondence of James S. Calhoun*. Edited by Annie Heloise Abel. Washington: Government Printing Office, 1915.

Callan, John F. *The Military Laws of the United States*. Philadelphia: George W. Childs, 1863.

Dana, Richard Henry. *Two Years before the Mast*. New York: D. Appleton, 1912.

Dolbeare, Benjamin. *The Captivity of Dolly Webster*. New Haven: Yale University Library, 1986.

Frost, John. *Pictorial History of Mexico and the Mexican War*. Edited by Charles Desilver. Philadelphia: Charles Desilver, 1862.

"Geneva Convention for the Amelioration of the Condition of the Wounded in Armies in the Field," 1864. International Committee of the Red Cross.

Garrard, Lewis Hector. *Wah-to-Yah and the Taos Trail*. Oklahoma City: Harlow Publishing Co., 1932.

Grotius, Hugo. *De Jure Belli Ac Pacis (On the Law of War and Peace)*. Translated by William Evats. Lawbook Exchange, Limited, 2013.

Horn, Sarah Ann, and E. House. "A Narrative of the Captivity of Mrs. Horn." In *Comanche Bondage*. St. Louis: C. Kremle, Printer, 1839.

Irving, Theodore. *The Conquest of Florida, by Hernando de Soto*. Philadelphia: Carey, Lea & Blanchard, 1835.

James, G. P. R. *The History of Chivalry*. New York: Harper & Brothers, 1830.

Jomini, Antoine Henri. *Life of Napoleon*. Translated by Henry W. Halleck. New York: D. Van Nostrand, 1864.

Kappler, Charles L., ed. *Indian Treaties, 1778–1883*. New York: Interland Publishing Inc., 1972.

Kendall, George Wilkins. *Dispatches from the Mexican War*. Edited by Lawrence Delbert Cress. Norman: University of Oklahoma Press, 1999.

Kendall, George Wilkins. *Narrative of an Expedition across the Great Southwestern Prairies*. London: D. Bogue, 1845.

Kendall, George Wilkins. *Narrative of the Texan Sante Fé Expedition*. Chicago: Lakeside Press, 1929.

Kent, James. *Commentaries on American Law*. Vol. 1. 3 vols. New York: O. Halstead, 1826.
Kent, James. *Commentaries on American Law*. Vol. 3. 3 vols. New York: O. Halsted, 1828.
Lieber, Francis. *Manual of Political Ethics*. Edited by Theodore D. Woolsey. 2nd Edition, Revised. Vol. 2. 2 vols. Philadelphia: J. B. Lippincott Company, 1893.
Lieber, Francis. *The Character of the Gentleman*. Columbia and Charleston, SC: Allen, McCarter & Co., 1847.
Locke, John. *An Essay Concerning the True Original Extent and End of Civil Government*. Edes and Gill, in Queen Street, 1773.
Locke, John. *Some Thoughts Concerning Education*. University Press, 1892.
Lyons, James G. "The Heroine of Monterey, Adapted and Arranged for the Piano Forte." F. D. Benteen, Baltimore, 1847.
Magoffin, Susan Shelby. *Down the Santa Fe Trail and Into Mexico: The Diary of Susan Shelby Magoffin, 1846–1847*. Edited by Stella M. Drumm. Lincoln and London: University of Nebraska Press, 1982.
McCarty, William. *National Songs, Ballads, and Other Patriotic Poetry, Chiefly Relating to the War of 1846*. Philadelphia: William S. Young, Printer, 1846.
Montgomery, Cora. *Eagle Pass; or Life on the Border*. Edited by Alex L. Mauldin. 2017 ed. Middletown, Delaware, 1852.
Nebel, Carl. *Voyage Pittoresque et Archéologique Dans La Partie La Plus Intéressante Du Mexique*. Paris, France: M. Moench, 1836.
Paley, William. *The Principles of Moral and Political Philosophy*. Vol. 1. 2 vols. New York: Collins, Keese, & Co., 1831.
Paley, William. *The Principles of Moral and Political Philosophy*. Vol. 2. 2 vols. New York: Collins, Keese, & Co., 1839.
Parker, James W., and Rachel Plummer. *Parker's Narrative and History of Texas; to Which Is Appended Mrs. Plummer's Narrative*. Louisville, KY: Morning Courier Office, 1844.
Peterson, Charles J. *The Military Heroes of the War with Mexico*. Philadelphia: W. A. Leary, 1848.
Poinsett, Joel Roberts. *Notes on Mexico, Made in the Autumn of 1822*. Reprint of the 1825 ed. New York: Praeger, 1969.
Prescott, William H. *History of the Conquest of Mexico*. New York: Maynard, Merrill & Co., 1843.
Robarts, William Hugh. *Mexican War Veterans*. Washington, DC: Brentano's, 1887.
Rees, James. *The Life of Edwin Forrest with Reminiscences and Personal Recollections*. Philadelphia: T.B. Peterson & Bros, 1874.
Sibley, George Champlin. *The Road to Santa Fe*. Edited by Kate L. Gregg. Albuquerque: University of New Mexico Press, 1952.
Simmons, William Hayne. *Notices of East Florida With an Account of the Seminole Nation of Indians*. Charleston, SC: A. E. Miller, 1822.
Stone, John Augustus. *Metamora: Or the Last of the Wampanoags; an Indian Tragedy in Five Acts as Played by Edwin Forrest*. Princeton, NJ: Princeton University Press, 1941.
Sully, Thomas. *Portrait of Alexander Macomb*. Oil on canvas, 1829. West Point Museum, Art Collection.

Thompson, Waddy. *Recollections of Mexico*. New York and London: Wiley & Putnam, 1846.
Todd, Frederick P. Memorandum. "The Samuel Chamberlain Journal and Paintings." Memorandum, March 5, 1956. West Point Museum, Art Collection.
US Army Military History Institute, Historical Services Division. "Army Laundresses: A Working Bibliography of MHI Sources," 2005.
Vattel, Emerich de. *Law of Nations*. Translated by Joseph Chitty, Esq. Cambridge: Cambridge University Press, 2011.
Weir, Robert. *Portrait of Winfield Scott*. Oil on canvas, 1856. West Point Museum, Art Collection.
Wheaton, Henry, and Coleman Phillipson. *Wheaton's Elements of International Law*. 5th English Edition, Revised Throughout. London: Stevens and Sons, 1916.
Wilson, Jane A. *The Captivity and Sufferings of Mrs. Jane Adaline Wilson*. Rochester: D. M. Dewey, 1853.

SECONDARY SOURCES

Adams, George Rollie. *General William S. Harney: Prince of Dragoons*. Lincoln and London: University of Nebraska Press, 2001.
Adelman, Jeremy, and Stephen Aron. "From Borderlands to Borders: Empires, Nation-States, and the Peoples in between in North American History." *The American Historical Review* 104, no. 3 (1999): 814–41.
Aguirre Beltrán, Gonzalo. *La Población Negra de México: Estudio Etnohistórico*. 2.d Edition. México: Fonde de Cultura Económica, 1972.
Anderson, Marilyn J. "The Image of the Indian in American Drama during the Jacksonian Era, 1829–1845." *Journal of American Culture* 1, no. 4 (1978): 800–810.
Arrom, Silvia Marina. *The Women of Mexico City, 1790–1857*. Stanford, CA: Stanford University Press, 1985.
Bachman, Walt. *Northern Slave, Black Dakota: The Life and Times of Joseph Godfrey*. Bloomington, MN: Pond Dakota Press, 2013.
Bank, Rosemarie K. "Staging the 'Native': Making History in American Theatre Culture, 1828–1838." *Theatre Journal* 45, no. 4 (1993): 461–86.
Baptist, Edward E. *The Half Has Never Been Told: Slavery and the Making of American Capitalism*. New York: Basic Books, 2014.
Barkawi, Tarak, and Ketih Stanski, eds. *Orientalism and War*. Oxford University Press, 2013.
Barr, Juliana. *Peace Came in the Form of a Woman: Indians and Spaniards in the Texas Borderlands*. Chapel Hill: The University of North Carolina Press, 2007.
Baud, Michiel, and Willem Van Schendel. "Toward a Comparative History of Borderlands." *Journal of World History* 8, no. 2 (1997): 211–42.
Bauer, K. Jack. *The Mexican War: 1846–1848*. Lincoln and London: University of Nebraska Press, 1974.
Bauer, K. Jack. *Zachary Taylor: Soldier, Planter, Statesman of the Old Southwest*. Baton Rouge and London: Louisiana State University Press, 1985.

Beard, Mary. *Women and Power: A Manifesto*. New York: Liveright Publishing, 2017.
Belohlavek, John M. *Patriots, Prostitutes, and Spies: Women and the Mexican-American War*. Charlottesville and London: University of Virginia Press, 2017.
Berkhofer, Robert F. *The White Man's Indian: Images of the American Indian from Columbus to the Present*. New York: Knopf: Distributed by Random House, 1978.
Best, Geoffrey. *Humanity in Warfare*. New York: Columbia University Press, 1980.
Betros, Lance, ed. *West Point: Two Centuries and Beyond*. Abilene, TX: McWhiney Foundation Press, 2004.
Blackhawk, Ned. *Violence over the Land: Indians and Empires in the Early American West*. Cambridge, MA: Harvard University Press, 2006.
Block, Sharon. *Rape & Sexual Power in Early America*. Chapel Hill: The University of North Carolina Press, 2006.
Boydston, Jeanne. *Home and Work: Housework, Wages, and Ideology of Labor in the Early Republic*. Oxford: Oxford University Press, 1990.
Brooks, James F. *Captives and Cousins: Slavery, Kinship, and Community in the Southwest Borderlands*. Chapel Hill and London: University of North Carolina Press, 2002.
Brooks, Lisa Tanya. *Our Beloved Kin: A New History of King Philip's War*. New Haven: Yale University Press, 2018.
Brown, Kathleen M. *Foul Bodies: Cleanliness in Early America*. New Haven: Yale University Press, 2009.
Brownmiller, Susan. *Against Our Will: Men, Women and Rape*. Toronto: Bantam Books, 1981.
Budd, Richard M. *Serving Two Masters: The Development of American Military Chaplaincy, 1860–1920*. Lincoln: University of Nebraska Press, 2002.
Butler, Judith. *Gender Trouble: Feminism and the Subversion of Identity*. New York and London: Routledge, 1990.
Carrigan, William D. *Forgotten Dead: Mob Violence against Mexicans in the United States, 1848–1928*. Oxford: Oxford University Press, 2013.
Carroll, Patrick James. *Blacks in Colonial Veracruz: Race, Ethnicity, and Regional Development*. Austin: University of Texas Press, 1991.
Casas, Maria Raquel. *Married to a Daughter of the Land: Spanish-Mexican Women and Interethnic Marriage in California, 1820–1880*. Reno, NV: University of Nevada Press, 2007.
Cashion, Peggy Mullarkey. "Women and the Mexican War, 1846–1848." M.A. Thesis, The University of Texas at Arlington, 1990.
Castañeda, Antonia I. "Sexual Violence in the Politics and Policies of Conquest: Amerindian Women and the Spanish Conquest of Alta California." In *Sexual Violence in Conflict Zones*, edited by Elizabeth D. Heineman, 39–55. University of Pennsylvania Press, 2011.
Chaudhuri, Jean, and Joyotpaul Chaudhuri. *A Sacred Path: The Way of the Muscogee Creeks*. Los Angeles: UCLA American Indian Studies Center, 2001.
Clarke, Dwight Lancelot. *Stephen Watts Kearny: Soldier of the West*. Norman: University of Oklahoma Press, 1961.

Clary, David A. *Eagles and Empire: The United States, Mexico, and the Struggle for a Continent*. New York: Bantam Dell, 2009.
Coffman, Edward M. *The Old Army: A Portrait of the American Army in Peacetime, 1784–1898*. New York, Oxford: Oxford University Press, 1986.
Conway, Christopher. "Sisters at War: Mexican Women's Poetry and the U.S.-Mexican War." *Latin American Research Review* 47, no. 1 (2012): 3–15.
Conway, Christopher, ed. *The U.S.-Mexican War: A Binational Reader*. Translated by Gustavo Pellon. Indianapolis/Cambridge: Hackett Publishing Company, Inc., 2010.
Córdova, María Gayón, ed. *La Ocupación Yanqui de La Ciudad de México, 1847–1848*. México: Consejo Nacional para la Cultura y las Artes, 1997.
Cothran, Boyd. *Remembering the Modoc War: Redemptive Violence and the Making of American Innocence*. First Peoples: New Directions in Indigenous Studies. Chapel Hill: The University of North Carolina Press, 2014.
Covington, James W. "Life at Fort Brooke 1824–1836." *The Florida Historical Quarterly* 36, no. 4 (1958): 319–30.
Cox, Paul Ronald. "The Characterization of the American Indian in American Indian Plays, 1800–1860: As a Reflection of the American Romantic Movement." ProQuest Dissertations and Theses. History Dissertation, New York University, 1970. ProQuest Dissertations & Theses Global.
Crackel, Theodore J. *West Point: A Bicentennial History*. Modern War Studies. Lawrence, KS: University Press of Kansas, 2002.
Curran, Thomas F. *Women Making War: Female Confederate Prisoners and Union Military Justice*. Carbondale: Southern Illinois University Press, 2020.
Curthoys, Ann. "Gender." In *New Keywords: A Revised Vocabulary of Culture and Society*, edited by Tony Bennett, Lawrence Grossberg, and Meaghan Morris, 140–42. Malden, MA: John Wiley & Sons, 2005.
Curtis, Samuel Ryan. *Mexico under Fire*. Edited by Joseph E. Chance. Fort Worth: Texas Christian University Press, 1994.
Cutter, Barbara. *Domestic Devils, Battlefield Angels: The Radicalism of American Womanhood, 1830–1865*. Dekalb: Northern Illinois University Press, 2003.
Danielle Terrazas Williams. "'My Conscience Is Free and Clear': African-Descended Women, Status, and Slave Owning in Mid-Colonial Mexico." *The Americas* 75, no. 3 (2018): 525–54.
Davis, Natalie Zemon. *The Return of Martin Guerre*. Cambridge, MA: Harvard University Press, 1983.
Delay, Brian. *War of a Thousand Deserts: Indian Raids and the U.S.-Mexican War*. The Lamar Series in Western History. New Haven: Yale University Press, 2008.
Denham, James M. "'Some Prefer the Seminoles': Violence and Disorder among Soldiers and Settlers in the Second Seminole War, 1835–1842." *The Florida Historical Quarterly* 70, no. 1 (1991): 38–54.
Denton III, Edgar. "The Formative Years of the United States Military Academy, 1775–1833." Dissertation. Syracuse University, 1964.
Derounian-Stodola, Kathryn Zabelle, ed. *Women's Indian Captivity Narratives*. New York: Penguin Books, 1998.

Deutsch, Sarah. *No Separate Refuge: Culture, Class, and Gender on an Anglo-Hispanic Frontier in the American Southwest, 1880–1940*. New York: Oxford University Press, 1987.

Di Tella, Torcuato S. "The Dangerous Classes in Early Nineteenth Century Mexico." *Journal of Latin American Studies* 5, no. 1 (1973): 79–105.

Drinnon, Richard. "Friend of the Indian: Colonel McKenney." In *Facing West: The Metaphysics of Indian-Hating and Empire Building*. Minneapolis: University of Minnesota Press, 1980.

Dunlap, William. *A History of the American Theatre*. New York: J. & J. Harper, 1832.

Dunlay, Thomas W. *Kit Carson and the Indians*. Lincoln: University of Nebraska Press, 2000.

DuVal, Kathleen. *The Native Ground: Indians and Colonists in the Heart of the Continent*. Philadelphia: University of Pennsylvania Press, 2006.

Dysart, Jane. "Mexican Women in San Antonio, 1830–1860: The Assimilation Process." *Western Historical Quarterly* 7, no. 4 (1976): 365–75.

Eisenhower, John S. D. *Agent of Destiny: The Life and Times of General Winfield Scott*. New York: Free Press, 1997.

Eisenhower, John S. D. *So Far from God: The U.S. War with Mexico, 1846–1848*. Oklahoma Paperbacks Edition, 2000. Norman: University of Oklahoma Press, 1989.

Elkins, Caroline, and Susan Pedersen. "Settler Colonialism: A Concept and Its Uses." In *Settler Colonialism in the Twentieth Century: Projects, Practices, Legacies*, edited by Caroline Elkins and Susan Pedersen. New York: Routledge, 2005.

Elliott, Charles Winslow. *Winfield Scott, the Soldier and the Man*. New York: The Macmillan Company, 1937.

Estes, Nick. *Our History Is the Future: Standing Rock Versus the Dakota Access Pipeline, and the Long Tradition of Indigenous Resistance*. London: Verso Books, 2019.

Faust, Drew Gilpin. *Mothers of Invention: Women of the Slaveholding South in the American Civil War*. Chapel Hill: University of North Carolina Press, 1996.

Feinstein, Rachel. *When Rape Was Legal: The Untold History of Sexual Violence During Slavery*. New York and London: Routledge, 2019.

Foos, Paul. *A Short, Offhand, Killing Affair: Soldiers and Social Conflict during the Mexican-American War*. Chapel Hill: The University of North Carolina Press, 2002.

Foote, Lorien. *The Gentlemen and the Roughs: Manhood, Honor, and Violence in the Union Army*. New York: New York University Press, 2010.

Ford, Lisa. *Settler Sovereignty: Jurisdiction and Indigenous People in America and Australia, 1788–1836*. Cambridge, MA: Harvard University Press, 2010.

Foucault, Michel. *Discipline and Punish: The Birth of the Prison*. Translated by Alan Sheridan. New York: Vintage Books, 1995.

Francaviglia, Richard V., and Douglas W. Richmond, eds. *Dueling Eagles: Reinterpreting the U.S.-Mexican War, 1846–1848*. Fort Worth: Texas Christian University Press, 2000.

Frank, Andrew, and A. Glenn Crothers, eds. *Borderland Narratives: Negotiation and Accommodation in North America's Contested Spaces, 1500–1850*. Gainesville: University Press of Florida, 2017.

Fuentes, Marisa J. *Dispossessed Lives: Enslaved Women, Violence, and the Archive*. University of Pennsylvania Press, 2016.

Garland, David. "What Is a 'History of the Present'? On Foucault's Genealogies and Their Critical Preconditions." *Punishment & Society* 16, no. 4 (2014): 365–84.

Genovese, Eugene D. *Roll, Jordan, Roll: The World the Slaves Made*. First Vintage Books Edition, 1976. New York: Vintage Books, 1972.

Goldstein, Jan. "Foucault Among the Sociologists: The 'Disciplines' and the History of the Professions." *History and Theory* 23, no. 2 (1984): 170–92.

Gómez, Laura E. *Manifest Destinies: The Making of the Mexican American Race*. Second edition. New York: New York University Press, 2018.

Gonzalez, Deena J. *Refusing the Favor: The Spanish-Mexican Women of Santa Fe 1820–1880*. Oxford University Press Paperback, 2001. Oxford: Oxford University Press, 1999.

Graf, Mercedes. "Standing Tall with Sarah Bowman: The Amazon of the Border." *Minerva Pasadena* 19, no. 3/4 (2001): 27.

Granados, Luis Fernando. *Suenan Las Piedras: Alzamiento Ocurrido En La Ciudad de México, 14, 15 y 16 de Septiembre de 1847*. Colección Problemas de México. México D.F.: Ediciones Era, 2003.

Greenberg, Amy S. *A Wicked War: Polk, Clay, Lincoln, and the 1846 U.S. Invasion of Mexico*. New York: Vintage Books, 2012.

Greenberg, Amy S. *Cause for Alarm: The Volunteer Fire Department in the Nineteenth-Century City*. Princeton, NJ: Princeton University Press, 1998.

Greenberg, Amy S. *Manifest Manhood and the Antebellum Empire*. Cambridge: Cambridge University Press, 2005.

Greenburg, Jennifer. *At War with Women: Military Humanitarianism and Imperial Feminism in an Era of Permanent War*. Ithaca and London: Cornell University Press, 2023.

Grenier, John. *The First Way of War: American War Making on the Frontier, 1607–1814*. Cambridge: Cambridge University Press, 2005.

Guardino, Peter. "Gender, Soldiering, and Citizenship in the Mexican-American War of 1846–1848." *The American Historical Review*, February 2014.

Guardino, Peter. "The Constant Recurrence of Such Atrocities: Guerrilla Warfare and Counterinsurgency during the Mexican-American War." *Journal of the Civil War Era* 12, no. 1 (2022): 3–27.

Guardino, Peter. *The Dead March: A History of the Mexican-American War*. Cambridge, MA: Harvard University Press, 2017.

Gutiérrez, Ramón A. *When Jesus Came, the Corn Mothers Went Away: Marriage, Sexuality, and Power in New Mexico, 1500–1846*. Stanford, CA: Stanford University Press, 1991.

Haber, Samuel. *The Quest for Authority and Honor in the American Professions, 1750–1900*. Chicago: University of Chicago Press, 1991.

Hagstrom, Jacob N. "Learning Asymmetric War: Army Officers in Florida, France, and Algeria, 1830–1845." ProQuest Dissertations and Theses. Dissertation in History, Indiana University, 2020. ProQuest Dissertations & Theses Global (2394419858).

Hämäläinen, Pekka. *The Comanche Empire*. The Lamar Series in Western History. New Haven: Yale University Press, 2008.
Hamdani, Yoav. "The Slaveholding Army: Enslaved Servitude in the United States Military, 1797–1861." Dissertation. New York, NY, 2022. Columbia Academic Commons. https://doi.org/10.7916/7b3r-y514.
Hartmann, Heidi. "The Unhappy Marriage of Marxism and Feminism: Towards a More Progressive Union." In *Women and Revolution: A Discussion of the Unhappy Marriage of Marxism and Feminism*, edited by Lydia Sargent. South End Press, 1981.
Henderson, Timothy J. *A Glorious Defeat: Mexico and Its War with the United States*. New York: Hill and Wang, 2007.
Herrera Serna, Laura, ed. *México En Guerra, 1846–1848: Perspectivas Regionales*. 1. ed. México: Consejo Nacional para la Cultura y las Artes, 1997.
Hoganson, Kristin L. *Fighting for American Manhood: How Gender Politics Provoked the Spanish-American and Philippine-American Wars*. New Haven & London: Yale University Press, 1998.
Honeywell, Roy John. *Chaplains of the United States Army*. Washington: Office of the Chief of Chaplains, Department of the Army, 1958.
Horsman, Reginald. *Race and Manifest Destiny: The Origins of American Racial Anglo-Saxonism*. Cambridge, MA: Harvard University Press, 1981.
Howe, Daniel Walker. *What Hath God Wrought: The Transformation of America, 1815–1848*. New York: Oxford University Press, 2007.
Hull, Isabel V. *Absolute Destruction: Military Culture and the Practices of War in Imperial Germany*. Ithaca and London: Cornell University Press, 2005.
Huntington, Samuel P. *The Soldier and the State: The Theory and Politics of Civil-Military Relations*. Cambridge, MA: Belknap Press of Harvard University Press, 1957.
Huntzicker, William. *The Popular Press, 1833–1865*. Westport, CT: Greenwood Press, 1999.
Hutton, Laurence. *Curiosities of the American Stage*. New York: Harper & Brothers, 1891.
Hyde, Anne F. *Born of Lakes and Plains: Mixed-Descent Peoples and the Making of the American West*. W. W. Norton & Company, 2022.
Hyde, Anne F. *Empires, Nations, and Families: A History of the North American West, 1800–1860*. Lincoln and London: University of Nebraska Press, 2011.
Isenberg, Nancy. *Sex and Citizenship in Antebellum America*. Chapel Hill and London: The University of North Carolina Press, 1998.
Johannsen, Robert W. *To the Halls of Montezuma: The Mexican War in the American Imagination*. Oxford University Press Paperback, 1987. Oxford: Oxford University Press, 1985.
John, Richard R. *Network Nation: Inventing American Telecommunications*. Cambridge, MA: Belknap Press of Harvard University Press, 2010.
John, Richard R. *Spreading the News: The American Postal System from Franklin to Morse*. Cambridge, MA: Harvard University Press, 1995.
Johnson, Susan Lee. *Roaring Camp: The Social World of the California Gold Rush*. New York: W.W. Norton, 2000.
Johnson, Susan Lee. *Writing Kit Carson: Fallen Heroes in Changing West*. Chapel Hill: University of North Carolina Press, 2020.

Johnson, Timothy D. *A Gallant Little Army: The Mexico City Campaign*. Modern War Studies. Lawrence: University Press of Kansas, 2007.
Kaeuper, Richard W. *Chivalry and Violence in Medieval Europe*. Oxford: Oxford University Press, 1999.
Kaplan, Amy. "Manifest Domesticity." *American Literature* 70, no. 3 (1998): 581–606.
Kaplan, Amy, and Donald E. Pease, eds. *Cultures of United States Imperialism*. Durham: Duke University Press, 1993.
Karsten, Peter. *The Naval Aristocracy: The Golden Age of Annapolis and the Emergence of Modern American Navalism*. New York: Free Press, 1972.
Keegan, John. *The Face of Battle*. Harmondsworth, Middlesex, England: Penguin Books, 1978.
Keen, Maurice. *Chivalry*. New Haven & London: Yale University Press, 1984.
Kerber, Linda K. *No Constitutional Right to Be Ladies: Women and the Obligations of Citizenship*. New York: Hill and Wang, 1998.
Keyssar, Alexander. *The Right to Vote: The Contested History of Democracy in the United States*. New York: Basic Books, 2000.
Khalili, Laleh. "Gendered Practices of Counterinsurgency." *Review of International Studies* 37, no. 4 (2011): 1471–91.
Kinsella, Helen M. "Sex as the Secret: Counterinsurgency in Afghanistan." *International Theory* 11 (2018): 26–47.
Kinsella, Helen M. *The Image before the Weapon: A Critical History of the Distinction between Combatant and Civilian*. Ithaca and London: Cornell University Press, 2011.
Knetsch, Joe. "The Hardships and Inconveniences: The Manatee River Forts during the Seminole Wars." *Sunland Tribune* 25 (1999): Article 7.
Knobel, Dale T. *Paddy and the Republic: Ethnicity and Nationality in Antebellum America*. Middletown, CT: Wesleyan University Press, 1986.
Krasnoborski, Edward J., Frank Martini, Raymond Hrinko, and Jeffrey Goldberg. *The Mexican War, 1846–1848*. West Point, NY: United States Military Academy Department of History.
Laura Briggs. *Reproducing Empire: Race, Sex, Science, and U.S. Imperialism in Puerto Rico*. American Crossroads. Berkeley: University of California Press, 2002.
Lawlor, Ruth. "Contested Crimes: Race, Gender, and Nation in Histories of GI Sexual Violence, World War II." *The Journal of Military History* 84 (2020): 541–69.
Leeman, William P. *The Long Road to Annapolis: The Founding of the Naval Academy and the Emerging American Republic*. Chapel Hill: University of North Carolina Press, 2010.
Lepore, Jill. *The Name of War: King Phillip's War and the Origins of American Identity*. New York: Vintage Books, 1998.
Levine, Philippa, ed. *Gender and Empire*. Oxford: Oxford University Press, 2004.
Levinson, Irving W. *Wars within War: Mexican Guerrillas, Domestic Elites, and the United States of America, 1846–1848*. Fort Worth: TCU Press, 2005.
Linhard, Tabea Alexa. *Fearless Women in the Mexican Revolution and the Spanish Civil War*. Columbia and London: University of Missouri Press, 2005.

Lowry, Thomas P. *Confederate Heroines: 120 Southern Women Convicted by Union Military Justice*. Baton Rouge: Louisiana State University Press, 2006.

Lynn, John A. *Women, Armies, and Warfare in Early Modern Europe*. Cambridge: Cambridge University Press, 2008.

Maciel, David R., and Erlinda Gonzales-Berry, eds. *The Contested Homeland: A Chicano History of New Mexico*. University of New Mexico Press, 2000.

Madley, Benjamin. *An American Genocide: The United States and the California Indian Catastrophe, 1846–1873*. The Lamar Series in Western History. New Haven & London: Yale University Press, 2016.

Mahon, John K. *History of the Second Seminole War, 1835–1842*. Gainesville: University of Florida Press, 1967.

Márquez, Jesús Velasco. *La Guerra del 47 y la opinión pública (1845–1848)*. México: Secretaría de Educación Pública, 1975.

Martin, Scott C. "Interpreting Metamora: Nationalism, Theater, and Jacksonian Indian Policy." *Journal of the Early Republic* 19, no. 1 (1999): 73–82.

Martinez, Monica Muñoz. *The Injustice Never Leaves You: Anti-Mexican Violence in Texas*. Cambridge, MA: Harvard University Press, 2018.

Mayer, Holly A. *Belonging to the Army: Camp Followers and Community During the American Revolution*. Columbia: University of South Carolina Press, 1996.

McBride, Keally, and Annick T. R. Wibben. "The Gendering of Counterinsurgency in Afghanistan." *Humanity: An International Journal of Human Rights, Humanitarianism, and Development* 3, no. 2 (2012): 199–215.

McCaffrey, James M. *Army of Manifest Destiny: The American Soldier in the Mexican War 1846–1848*. The American Social Experience Series 23. New York: New York University Press, 1992.

McCurry, Stephanie. *Confederate Reckoning: Power and Politics in the Civil War South*. Cambridge, MA: Harvard University Press, 2010.

McCurry, Stephanie. "Enemy Women and the Laws of War in the American Civil War." *Law and History Review* 35, no. 3 (2017): 667–710.

McCurry, Stephanie. *Masters of Small Worlds: Yeoman Households, Gender Relations, and the Antebellum South Carolina Low Country*. New York, Oxford: Oxford University Press, 1995.

McCurry, Stephanie. *Women's War: Fighting and Surviving the American Civil War*. Cambridge and London: The Belknap Press of Harvard University Press, 2019.

McGrath, Autumn Hope. "'An Army of Working-Men' Military Labor and the Construction of American Empire, 1865–1915." Dissertation. University of Pennsylvania, 2016.

Meberg, Justine. "Murder Most Fowl: A Centuries-Spanning True Story of Teaching, Vengeance, and Several Ducks, to Which Is Appended an Original Role-Playing Game of the Highest Historical Accuracy." *Teaching History: A Journal of Methods* 48, no. 1 (2023): 106–24.

Meyer, Marian. *Mary Donoho: New First Lady of the Santa Fe Trail*. Santa Fe, NM: Ancient City Press, 1991.

Missall, John. *The Seminole Wars: America's Longest Indian Conflict*. Edited by Mary Lou Missall. Gainesville: University Press of Florida, 2004.

Monaco, C. S. *The Second Seminole War and the Limits of American Aggression.* Baltimore: John Hopkins University Press, 2018.

Moody, Richard. *America Takes the Stage: Romanticism in American Drama and Theatre, 1750–1900.* Bloomington: Indiana University Press, 1955.

Morrison Jr., James L. *The Best School in the World" West Point, the Pre-Civil War Years, 1833–1866.* Kent, OH: The Kent State University Press, 1986.

Moss, Pamela, and Karen Falconer Al-Hindi, eds. *Feminisms in Geography: Rethinking Space, Place, and Knowledges.* Rowman & Littlefield Publishers, 2007.

Novak, William J. "The Myth of the 'Weak' State." *The American Historical Review* 113, no. 3 (2008): 752–72.

O'Brien, Jean M. *Firsting and Lasting: Writing Indians Out of Existence in New England.* Minneapolis: University of Minnesota Press, 2010.

Owens, Patricia. "Torture, Sex and Military Orientalism." *Third World Quarterly* 31, no. 7 (2010): 1041–56.

Pearce, Roy Harvey. *Savagism and Civilization: A Study of the Indian and the American Mind.* Edited by Arnold Krupat. Berkeley: University of California Press, 1988.

Peskin, Allan. *Winfield Scott and the Profession of Arms.* Kent, OH: Kent State University Press, 2003.

Peterson, Dawn. *Indians in the Family: Adoption and the Politics of Antebellum Expansion.* Cambridge, MA: Harvard University Press, 2017.

Porter, Kenneth Wiggins. *The Black Seminoles: History of a Freedom Seeking People.* Gainesville: University Press of Florida, 1996.

Porter, Patrick. *Military Orientalism: Eastern War through Western Eyes.* Critical War Studies Series. New York: Columbia University Press, 2009.

Prucha, Francis Paul. *American Indian Policy in the Formative Years: The Indian Trade and Intercourse Acts, 1790–1834.* Cambridge, MA: Harvard University Press, 1962.

Prucha, Francis Paul. *The Sword of the Republic: The United States Army on the Frontier, 1783–1846.* Lincoln: University of Nebraska Press, 1986.

Rabasa, José. *Writing Violence on the Northern Frontier: The Historiography of Sixteenth Century New Mexico and Florida and the Legacy of Conquest.* Durham: Duke University Press, 2000.

Rafuse, Ethan S. "'To Check the Very Worst and Meanest of Our Passions': Common Sense, 'Cobbon Sense', and the Socialization of Cadets at Antebellum West Point." *War in History* 16, no. 4 (2009): 406–24.

Reilly, Tom. *War with Mexico! America's Reporters Cover the Battlefront.* Edited by Manley Witten. Lawrence: University Press of Kansas, 2010.

Reséndez, Andrés. *Changing National Identities at the Frontier: Texas and New Mexico, 1800–1850.* Cambridge: Cambridge University Press, 2004.

Rivaya-Martínez, Joaquín. "Captivity and Adoption among the Comanche Indians, 1700–1875." Dissertation. University of California Los Angeles, 2006.

Roberts, Albert Hubbard. "The Dade Massacre." *Florida Historical Society Quarterly* 5, no. 3 (1927): 123–38.

Roberts, David. *Paternalism in Early Victorian England.* London: Croom Helm, 1979.

Roberts, Mary Louise. *What Soldiers Do: Sex and the American GI in World War II France*. Chicago & London: The University of Chicago Press, 2013.

Robinson, Cecil, ed. *The View from Chapultepec: Mexican Writers on the Mexican-American War*. Translated by Cecil Robinson. Tucson: The University of Arizona Press, 1989.

Rockman, Seth. *Scraping By: Wage Labor, Slavery, and Survival in Early Baltimore*. JHU Press, 2009.

Rodríguez, Jaime Javier. *The Literatures of the U.S.-Mexican War: Narrative, Time, and Identity*. University of Texas Press, 2010.

Roediger, David R. *The Wages of Whiteness: Race and the Making of the American Working Class*. London: Verso, 1991.

Rosen, Deborah A. *Border Law: The First Seminole War and American Nationhood*. Cambridge, MA: Harvard University Press, 2015.

Rotundo, E. Anthony. *American Manhood: Transformations in Masculinity from the Revolution to the Modern Era*. New York: Basic Books, 1993.

Rouleau, Brian. *With Sails Whitening Every Sea: Mariners and the Making of an American Maritime Empire*. Ithaca and London: Cornell University Press, 2014.

Ryan, Mary P. *Cradle of the Middle Class: The Family in Oneida County, New York, 1790–1865*. Cambridge: Cambridge University Press, 1981.

Salas, Elizabeth. *Soldaderas in the Mexican Military: Myth and History*. Austin: University of Texas Press, 1990.

Samuels, Shirley. *Romances of the Republic: Women, the Family, and Violence in the Literature of the Early American Nation*. New York: Oxford University Press, 1996.

Samuels, Shirley, ed. *The Culture of Sentiment: Race, Gender, and Sentimentality in Nineteenth-Century America*. New York: Oxford University Press, 1992.

Saunt, Claudio. *Unworthy Republic: The Dispossession of Native Americans and the Road to Indian Territory*. New York: W. W. Norton & Company, 2020.

Scallet, Daniel. "'This Inglorious War': The Second Seminole War, the Ad Hoc Origins of American Imperialism, and the Silence of Slavery." Dissertation in History, Washington University, 2011.

Schein, Edgar H. *Organizational Culture and Leadership*. John Wiley & Sons, 2016.

Schneider, Elena Andrea. *The Occupation of Havana: War, Trade, and Slavery in Eighteenth-Century Cuba*. Williamsburg, VA: Omohundro Institute and University of North Carolina Press, 2018.

Sedgwick, Eve Kosofsky. *Between Men: English Literature and Male Homosocial Desire*. Edited by Wayne Koestenbaum. Thirtieth Anniversary Edition. New York: Columbia University Press, 2016.

Seed, Patricia. *To Love, Honor, and Obey in Colonial Mexico: Conflicts over Marriage Choice, 1574–1821*. Stanford, CA: Stanford University Press, 1988.

Sellers, Charles. *The Market Revolution: Jacksonian America 1815–1846*. New York, Oxford: Oxford University Press, 1991.

Shank, Theodore Jr. "The Bowery Theatre, 1826–1836." ProQuest Dissertations and Theses. PhD Dissertation, Stanford University, 1956. ProQuest Dissertations & Theses Global (301992424).

Sharpe, Jenny. *Allegories of Empire: The Figure of Woman in the Colonial Text*. Minneapolis: University of Minnesota Press, 1993.

Shire, Laurel Clark. "Sentimental Racism and Sympathetic Paternalism." *Journal of the Early Republic* 39, no. 1 (2019): 111–22.
Shire, Laurel Clark. *The Threshold of Manifest Destiny: Gender and National Expansion in Florida*. Philadelphia: University of Pennsylvania Press, 2016.
Shire, Laurel Clark. "Turning Sufferers into Settlers: Gender, Welfare, and National Expansion in Frontier Florida." *Journal of the Early Republic* 33, no. 3 (2013): 489–521.
Skelton, William B. *An American Profession of Arms: The Army Officer Corps, 1784–1861*. Lawrence: University Press of Kansas, 1992.
Slotkin, Richard. *Regeneration through Violence: The Mythology of the Frontier, 1600–1860*. Middletown, CT: Wesleyan University Press, 1973.
Slotkin, Richard. *The Fatal Environment: The Myth of the Frontier in the Age of Industrialization, 1800–1890*. Norman: University of Oklahoma Press, 1998.
Smith, George Winston, and Charles Judah, eds. *Chronicles of the Gringos: The US Army in the Mexican War, 1846–1848*. Albuquerque: The University of New Mexico Press, 1968.
Snyder, Christina. *Slavery in Indian Country: The Changing Face of Captivity in Early America*. Cambridge, MA: Harvard University Press, 2010.
Spahr, Thomas W. "Occupying for Peace, The U.S. Army in Mexico, 1846–1848." PhD Dissertation. The Ohio State University, 2011.
Spierenburg, Pieter. "Introduction." In Edited by Pieter Spierenburg. *Men and Violence: Gender, Honor, and Rituals in Modern Europe and America*. Ohio State University Press, 1998.
Stansell, Christine. *City of Women: Sex and Class in New York, 1789–1860*. New York: Alfred A. Knopf, 1982.
Steinhauer, Dale Richard. "'Sogers': Enlisted Men in the U.S. Army, 1815–1860." Dissertation in History, The University of North Carolina at Chapel Hill, 1992.
Stevens, Robert C. "The Apache Menace in Sonora 1831–1849." *Arizona and the West* 6, no. 3 (1964): 211–22.
Stiehm, Judith Hicks. "The Protected, The Protector, The Defender." Special Issue *Women and Men's Wars* 5, no. 3 (1982): 367–76.
Stoler, Ann Laura. *Carnal Knowledge and Imperial Power: Race and the Intimate in Colonial Rule*. Berkeley: University of California Press, 2002.
Stoler, Ann Laura, ed. *Haunted by Empire: Geographies of Intimacy in North American History*. American Encounters/Global Interactions. Durham and London: Duke University Press, 2006.
Streeby, Shelley. *American Sensations: Class, Empire, and the Production of Popular Culture*. American Crossroads 9. Berkeley, Los Angeles, London: University of California Press, 2002.
Taylor, George Rogers. *The Transportation Revolution: 1815–1860*. Vol. IV. IX vols. The Economic History of the United States. New York and Toronto: Rinehart & Company, Inc., 1951.
Terrazas Williams, Danielle. "Capitalizing Subjects: Free African-Descended Women of Means in Xalapa, Veracruz during the Long Seventeenth Century." ProQuest Dissertations and Theses. PhD, Duke University, 2013. ProQuest Dissertations & Theses Global (1353105472).
The United States Army Chaplaincy. Vol. 2. 7 vols. Washington: Office of the Chief of Chaplains, Dept. of the Army, 1977.

Trexler, Richard C. *Sex and Conquest: Gendered Violence, Political Order, and the European Conquest of the Americas*. Ithaca, NY: Cornell University Press, 1995.
Trouillot, Michel-Rolph. *Silencing the Past: Power and the Production of History*. Boston: Beacon Press, 1995.
Ussishkin, Daniel. *Morale: A Modern British History*. Oxford: Oxford University Press, 2017.
Utley, Robert M. *Frontiersmen in Blue: The United States Army and the Indian, 1848–1865*. New York: Macmillan, 1967.
Van Kirk, Sylvia. *Many Tender Ties: Women in Fur-Trade Society, 1670–1870*. First American Edition, 1983. Norman: University of Oklahoma Press, 1980.
Varon, Elizabeth R. *Southern Lady, Yankee Spy: The True Story of Elizabeth Van Lew, a Union Agent in the Heart of the Confederacy*. New York: Oxford University Press, 2003.
Vázquez, Josefina Zoraida. *Dos Décadas de Desilusiones: En Busca de Una Fórmula Adecuada de Gobierno (1832–1854)*. México: El Colegio de México, 2009.
Vázquez, Josefina Zoraida, ed. *La guerra entre México y Estados Unidos, 1846–1848: Cuatro miradas*. San Luis Potosí, México: El Colegio de San Luis, 1998.
Vázquez, Josefina Zoraida. *La Intervención Norteamericana, 1846–1848*. México: Secretaria de Relaciones Exteriores, 1997.
Veracini, Lorenzo. *Settler Colonialism: A Theoretical Overview*. Houndmills, Basingstoke: Palgrave Macmillan, 2010.
Virgili, Fabrice. *Shorn Women: Gender and Punishment in Liberation France*. Translated by John Flower. Oxford: Berg, 2002.
Watson, Samuel. "Bicentennial History Pamphlet." United States Military Academy Public Affairs Office, 2002.
Watson, Samuel. "Flexible Gender Roles during the Market Revolution: Family, Friendship, Marriage, and Masculinity Among U.S. Army Officers, 1815–1846." *Journal of Social History* 29, no. 1 (1995): 81–106.
Watson, Samuel. "How the Army Became Accepted: West Point Socialization, Military Accountability, and the Nation-State during the Jacksonian Era." *American Nineteenth Century History* 7, no. 2 (2006): 219–51.
Watson, Samuel. *Jackson's Sword: The Army Officer Corps on the American Frontier, 1810–1821*. Modern War Studies. Lawrence: University Press of Kansas, 2012.
Watson, Samuel. *Peacekeepers and Conquerors: The Army Officer Corps on the American Frontier, 1821–1846*. Modern War Studies. Lawrence: University Press of Kansas, 2013.
Weigley, Russell F. *The American Way of War: A History of United States Military Strategy and Policy*. Bloomington and Indianapolis: Indiana University Press, 1973.
Weisman, Brent Richards. *Like Beads on a String: A Culture History of the Seminole Indians in Northern Peninsular Florida*. Tuscaloosa: University of Alabama Press, 1989.
Weisman, Brent Richards. *Unconquered People: Florida's Seminole and Miccosukee Indians*. Gainesville: University Press of Florida, 1999.

Welter, Barbara. "The Cult of True Womanhood: 1820–1860." *American Quarterly* 18, no. 2, Part 1 (1966): 151–74.
Wettemann, Robert P. "The Girl I Left behind Me? United States Army Laundresses and the Mexican War." *Army History* PB-20-99-1, no. 26 (Fall to Winter 1998 1999): 1–12.
Wickman, Patricia. *Osceola's Legacy*. Revised. Tuscaloosa: University of Alabama Press, 2006.
Wickman, Patricia. *The Tree That Bends: Discourse, Power, and the Survival of Maskoki People*. Tuscaloosa: University of Alabama Press, 1999.
Wik, Reynold M. "Captain Nathaniel Wyche Hunter and the Florida Indian Campaigns, 1837–1841." *Florida Historical Quarterly* 39, no. 1 (1960): 62–75.
Wilentz, Sean. *Chants Democratic: New York City and the Rise of the American Working Class, 1788–1850*. Oxford: Oxford University Press, 2004.
Williams, William Appleman. *The Tragedy of American Diplomacy*. New York and London: W.W. Norton & Co., 1962.
Winders, Richard Bruce. *Mr. Polk's Army: The American Military Experience in the Mexican War*. College Station: Texas A&M University Press, 1997.
Witgen, Michael. *An Infinity of Nations: How the Native New World Shaped Early North America*. Early American Studies. Philadelphia: University of Pennsylvania Press, 2012.
Witt, John Fabian. *Lincoln's Code: The Laws of War in American History*. New York: Free Press, 2012.
Wright, J. Leitch. *Creeks & Seminoles: The Destruction and Regeneration of the Muscogulge People*. Indians of the Southeast. Lincoln: University of Nebraska Press, 1986.
Young, Iris Marion. "The Logic of Masculinist Protection: Reflections on the Current Security State." *Signs* 29, no. 1 (2003): 1–25.

Index

Page numbers in *italics* refer to figures. Those followed by "n" refer to footnotes.

abolition, 99, 190n16
Agua Nueva (Catana) Massacre, 248–51, *249*
Albany, 36, 46
Albuquerque, 274, 279
Alcaraz, Ramón, 275
Alvarado, 226
ambush, Jupiter River (Powell's Battle), 1–4
Apache, 148, 159–66, 175, 178–79
Arapaho, 166
army regulations
  casualty reports, excluding women from, 120–23
  enlisting only single men, 102
  flags of truce, 134–37
  prisoners of war, 133–34
  separate rank-based messes, 47
  standardized reports, 102

Ballentine, George, 54–56, 56n50, 241–44, 268
battle for Mexico City, 275–76
Battle of Buena Vista (Battle of La Angostura), 264–68
Battle of El Brazito, 280
Battle of Monterrey, 94, 169–70, 172n61, 206, 240, 259
Battle of the Withlacoochee, 100
Battles of Palo Alto and Resaca de la Palma, 143

Belohlavek, John, 14, 172, 190n16, 258n5, 279, 281
Bemrose, John, 99–101, 104
Bent, Charles, 167
Bent's Fort, 167
Black experiences, 48n35, 58, 197n30, 257
  Afro-Mexicans, 196
  as (free or enslaved) servants to army officers, 7, 62, 95, 131n56, 183, 196–98, 263, 266
  Black Seminoles, 2, 39, 66n71, 87, 99n74, 111, 118n26, 119, 123, 127, 140, 154
  criminalization of Black men, 186–87, 190–91, 202–3
  prohibited from enlisting, 17, 36
Blackstone, William, 79, 198
Bowman, Sarah, 263–64, *265*
Buffalo, 36
Buntline, Ned, 172–73, 172n60

California, 149, 157, 232, 268, 271
captivity narratives
  Godfrey, Mary, 153
  Horn, Sarah Ann, 155
  Kendall, George, 155–57
  Plummer, Rachel, 155
  Rowlandson, Mary, 152–53
  Webster, Dolly, 154–55
  Wilson, Jane Adaline, 155

327

Carson, Kit, 166
Castillo, Maria Manuela, 202
Cedar Keys, 118
Cerralvo, 266
Chakaika's camp, 96
Chamberlain, Samuel, 95, 160, 243, 244–50, 245n67, 259, 264–65, 281–88, 289
Chase, Ann, 280–81
Chihuahua, 169, 274, 286, 288
chivalry, 63–64, 140, 233
Civil War, 14, 23, 40
Clinch, Duncan, 85, 100, 129
Coahuila, 219n4
Collins, Francis, 209, 225, 237–38
Comanche, 148–58, 160, 162–65, 297
communications revolution, 29, 169–72, 252–54
courts-martial, 193–94
 in Florida, 50–51
 in Mexico, 243–44, 262–63
Creek (Muscogee), 28n63, 74–75, 94, 139–40
criminalization
 of guerrillas, 149, 177–78
 of Indigenous groups, 152, 178–80

Dade's Massacre, 75–77, 81–82
Dana, Napoleon, 158, 227, 231, 247–48, 276–77
Davis, George, 169, 204
Delay, Brian, 148

Edwards, Frank, 156n24, 177n72, 277–78, 280
El Paso, 280
Elderkin, James, 94, 96
Emory, William, 147n1, 158–68, 178–79, 268, 273–74

Farrell, William, 228–30
First US–Seminole War, 5, 80
Fort Bliss, 267
Fort Brown, bombardment of, 263–64
Fort Cummings, 110
Fort Dade, 140
Fort King, 83, 112–14
Fort Mellon (Fort Fanning), 110, 118
Fort Russell, 83

Gallegas, Maria Antonia, 195–99
Genovese, Eugene, 247

genre of army writing, 1–4, 10–11, 25, 28–29, 111, 295, 300
Greenberg, Amy, 26–27, 39, 208
Grotius, Hugo, 78–79, 217
Guardino, Peter, 212, 219, 251, 267–68, 290
guerrillas, 214–15, 219, 224–25, 237–38, 251–55, 283, 288–92

Halleck, Henry
 and the Civil War, 185, 300
 and the laws of war, 6n11, 108, 149, 177–78, 281
 in Mexico, 269–73
 and West Point, 76–78
Hamdani, Yoav, 7–8
Harney, William, 95–98, 288
Henry, William, 222, 259, 263n13, 264
Henshaw, John, 278–79
Hernandez, Maria Dolores, 228–30
Hitchcock, Ethan Allen, 41, 86–87, 97, 139–40, 199–200, 210
Hull, Isabel, 11–12
Hunter, Nathaniel, 99

immigrant soldiers
 economic motivations of, 52
 limited promotion opportunities, 58–59
 lower desertion rates, 54
 nativism, 37, 93, 242–47
 racial benefit to, 56–58
 recruitment of, 35–37
imperialism, 48
 and gender, 13–14, 85, 107, 140–42, 268–71, 301
 and postcolonial studies, 10
 and slavery, forced removal, 31, 48
 within the army, 6, 72–73
Indian plays
 Forrest, Edwin, 66–67
 Metamora, 64–66
 Pontiac, 67–68
Indian Territory, 31, 72, 94
Indigenous power in Mexico
 army efforts to redeem captives, 163–65
 negative depictions of Indigenous women, 165–66
 Pima and Maricopa encounters with the US Army, 159–62
 positive depictions of Indigenous women, 161–62
internal civilizing mission, 53–54, 65, 78, 93
Isenberg, Nancy, 153, 270–71, 275

Jackson, Andrew, 106
Jacksonian era, 8, 23–24, 43, 62–70, 107, 187, 294
Jaramillo sisters, Maria Ignacia and Maria Josefa, 167–68
Jesup, Thomas, 1–3, 31–32, 87–88, 113, 122–39
Johnson, Richard Mentor, 47–48
Johnson, Susan Lee, 15, 42, 301
Johnston, Abraham, 161, 168

Kaplan, Amy, 10–13, 268–70
Kearny, Stephen Watts, 147–50
Kendall, George, 179, 207–8, 240, 253, 279–80. *See also* captivity narratives
Kent, James, 78–80
Kerber, Linda, 281–83
Kinsella, Helen, 120
Kirk, Isaac, 197n30, *184*
  absence of scholarship on case of, 190–91
  case of, 195–99
  death of, 183, 187, 199–200
Kirk, Peter, 196–98, 197n30
Kissimmee, 135

Las Vegas, 178
laundresses, 59–61, 101, 256–67
laws of war, 192
  Civil War, 5–6, 134, 148–49, 185, 295–300
  fighting Indigenous peoples, 81, 123–28
  and gender, 5–7, 64, 84, 107–10, 133–41, 271, 281
Lieber, Francis, 6, 109, 136, 164–65, 185
Lopez, Rosalie, 201
Lynch, Bartholomew, 87–95, 99–101, 103

Macomb, Alexander, 17–23, *18*, 67–71, 121, 143, 185, 199
Mahon, John K., 2, 4, 39
manhood, variants of, 26–27
Marcy, William, 149–51, 191
Maricopa, 161–62
martial law
  called for in Mexico by Scott, 191–92
  under Kearny in Northern Mexico, 173–77
Matamoros, 164, 169, 222, 247, 263, 277
McCall, George, 94, 107, 116–18
McCurry, Stephanie, 8, 14–15, 26, 108

Mejia, Brigida, 266
Mescalero (Apache), 158
Mexican War of Independence, 276n44
Mexican women at war
  attacking US forces, launching projectiles, 275–76
  constructing defensive positions, 273
  protesting collaboration with US forces, 273
  providing military labor, 267–68
  publishing open letters, 274–75
  seizing economic opportunities, 219, 228, 238–40, 256
  soldaderas, 267–68
  targeted assassinations, 276
  upper-class women's symbolic resistance, 276
Mexico City, 186, 188, 213, 217, 219, 236, 254, 270, 273–74, 287
  popular resistance in, 275–76
Mier, 158, 164–65
military commissions
  mechanics of, 193–94
  used against Mexican men, 190
  used to try white volunteers, 201–2
military justice. *See* courts-martial; military commissions; punishment
Monclova, 218
Monterrey, 169, 191, 227, 247–51, 264–66, 276, 287–88
Montgomery, Mrs., death of, 83–85
Motte, Jacob, 86–87, 104–7, 116–17, 132, 138–39, 166

Narragansett, 153
Native Spy Company, 290–91
nativism. *See* immigrant soldiers
Navajo, 158, 157–62, 174, 178–79, 228
Nelson, F. L., 195–99
New Mexico, 150, 155–68, 174–80, 239, 274
New York City, 35–37, 46, 52, 60–61, 64–66, 89, 227
noncommissioned officers, 22, 51, 54–61, 103–4, 230, 246, 270
  administering punishments, 8, 241–44
  in the Isaac Kirk case, 195–200, 204
  native-born requests for officer's commissions, 92–93

Oswandel, J. Jacob, 256, 282–83

Parras, 152, 162–63, 218, 282
paternalism
    and army officers' internal civilizing mission, 49–50
    and the army family, 41, 51, 54–56, 265–66
    claiming women's affections, 257–58, 281–82
    dying for the army family, 75–77, 83–85
    English and European variants, 8–10
    as gendered domination, 6–7
    misinterpreting women's pity, 278–80
    officer demands on enlisted men, 70–72
    regular army critiques of Seminole men, 85–88, 104
    in slaveholding US, 7, 100, 111, 247
    working-class, 39
Patterson, Robert, 196
Pescadero, 271
Phelps, John, 50, 99, 111
Philadelphia, 246
Pima, 159–62, 160
Polvadera, 158
popular literature
    set in Florida, 115–16
    set in Mexico, 172–73
postcolonial studies, 10–13
Prince, Henry, 37, 85–88, 102, 110–13, 124, 130, 135–36
professionalization, claims to, 23–25
Puebla, 186, 220, 231, 235–37, 252–53, 256, 278, 280
Pueblo Indians, 144, 174, 176, 228
Punishment, 243
    illegal practices, 241–42
    inflicted on regulars in Florida, 51
    inflicted on regulars in Mexico, 241–44, 243
    legal options, 241
    violence inflicted on soldiers and enslaved people, 8, 51

race, 5, 17, 143, 187, 189–90, 203. *See also* Black experiences; immigrant soldiers, racial benefit to; Kirk, Isaac; paternalism in slaveholding US; sexual relationships; sexual violence
    and the army family, 8, 41–43
    class-based views of Mexican women's race, 234–35, 276–78
    differences in US and Mexican views of, 203–4

rape. *See* sexual violence
religion
    army chaplains, 52–54, 78n18
    Catholicism, 23–24, 52–53, 57, 167
    to enforce officers' authority, 55–64
    Protestantism, 23–24, 42, 53–54, 64, 245
    Second Great Awakening, 52–53
    temperance, 53–55
Reynosa, 278
Roberts, Mary Louise, 189n14
Rochester, 52
Romanticism, 17
Rosen, Deborah, 5, 79, 108n3
Saltillo, 169, 218, 232, 241, 288
San Antonio, 154
San Juan, 234
San Miguel, 156, 279
Santa Fe, 147, 155–57, 169, 174–75, 277–78
Santa Rosa, 218, 234
Santo Domingo, 279
Scott, Winfield
    author of army regulations, 5, 9, 134
    bombardment of Veracruz, 205–12
    challenges of military occupation, 214–20, 251–52
    Martial Law Order, 191, 194
    military commissions, 183–86, 191–92, 199–200, 199n33
    Proclamation to the Mexican People, 186, 212–14, 218
    at war in Florida, 106, 118, 126
    at war in Mexico, 143, 149, 186
    and West Point, 19, 35
Second US–Seminole War
    institutional importance of to US Army, 39–40
    officer's wives in Florida during, 83
    overview of, 31–32
Seminole women at war
    army burning of crops and settlements, 129–32
    brokering peace, 113
    brokering surrender, 113–14
    deaths of, 73–74
    escaping from custody, 110–11
    forced to be guides, 117–18
    hunted and captured, 137–39
    spiritual power, 114–17
    spreading misinformation, 112

supplying the war effort, 31–32
under interrogation, 118–19
violent resistance, 112
sexual relationships
army officers and Indigenous
women, 94
army officers and Spanish-descended
women in Florida, 95, 166
changes in ideal partners from
Indigenous to Mexican women,
166–67
prostitution, 93, 139, 287–88
US men and Mexican women, 223, 255,
258, 272, 282–88
sexual violence
absence of in archives, military histories,
188, 230n31, 230–33
perpetrated in Mexico, 217–20, 222
retributive violence inflicted on Mexican
women, 283–90
Shire, Laurel Clark, 48, 72–73, 90
Skelton, William, 23, 38, 42, 79
slavery, 257. *See also* abolition; Black
experiences, Black Seminoles; Black
experiences, as (free or enslaved)
servants to army officers; Kirk, Isaac;
paternalism, in slaveholding US;
punishment, violence inflicted on
soldiers and enslaved people
in Florida, 40, 98, 100, 111, 127
and imperialism, 48
within the army, 7, 202
Smith, Theodore, 230
soldaderas. *See* Mexican women at war
Sonora, 165
Sprague, John, 86n41, 84–87, 110
St. Augustine, 83, 98, 100, 119, 137
Steinhauer, Dale, 21–22, 54, 58–59, 103, 244
Stoler, Ann, 13–14, 72–73, 189–90, 219
Streeby, Shelley, 12–13, 29, 200n38, 223n17
Sylvester, Maria, 202

Tampa (Fort Brooke), 55, 75, 83, 90, 93, 102, 110, 123
Taos (Taos Revolt), 174–77
Taylor, Zachary
bombarding Monterrey, 205–7, 260–61
in Florida, 123–28, 135

in Mexico, 158, 164, 189, 217, 263–64, 299
and military justice, 191, 248–51
Todos Santos, 271–73
Toluca, 290
Tome, 174
Treaty of Guadalupe Hidalgo, 295–300
Trist, Nicholas, 295

US occupation of Mexico
crimes against civilians, 247–52
levies imposed on Mexican cities, 235–36
Mexican challenges to US claims of
peaceful occupation, 220–21
paying for and seizing supplies, 217–19, 224, 254–55
US claims of benevolent occupation,
221–22, 226–27, 235–37, 241, 259, 282–83
use of the press, 252–54
US–Mexico War, overview of, 144

Vattel, Emerich de, 5, 78–79, 133, 158, 178, 217, 297
Veracruz, 205, 235–36
US bombardment of, 207–12
volunteer army units, 140n84, 164n42
regular army critiques of, 73, 88–89, 104, 121, 220–23, 247–52
self-professed heroism of, 172–73, 223, 226

War of 1812, 34, 39, 48, 104
Watson, Samuel, 23, 41, 51, 176, 298
West Point
curriculum, 77–81
Dialectic Society, 44–46, 62–63
history of early military academy, 41–44
and the Market Revolution, 47
Wheaton, Henry, 79–80
Witt, John Fabian, 108n3, 149, 212
Worth, William, 34

Xalapa (Jalapa), 186, 218, 229–30, 237–38, 273, 278

Zeh, Frederick, 206, 210, 241–46, 274–78, 290

For EU product safety concerns, contact us at Calle de José Abascal, 56–1°, 28003 Madrid, Spain or eugpsr@cambridge.org.

www.ingramcontent.com/pod-product-compliance
Ingram Content Group UK Ltd.
Pitfield, Milton Keynes, MK11 3LW, UK
UKHW020949091225
465811UK00010B/1336